PRENTICE HALL

FINANCE
AND
ACCOUNTING
INTERNET
GUIDE

A Guided Tour of the Information Superhighway

PRENTICE HALL

BRENDA J. MIZGORSKI, CPA

Library of Congress Cataloging-in-Publication Data

Mizgorski, Brenda J.
    Prentice Hall finance and accounting Internet guide : a guided tour
of the information superhighway / Brenda J. Mizgorski.
      p. cm.
    Includes index.
    ISBN 0-13-095285-0
    1. Accounting—Computer network resources.   2. Finance—Computer
network resources.   3. Internet (Computer Network).   4. World Wide Web
(Information retrieval system).   I. Title.
HF5625.7.M59   1999
025.06' 657—dc21   99-10588
                                                        CIP

Acquisitions Editor: *Luis Gonzalez*
Production Editor: *Sharon L. Gonzalez*
Formatting/Interior Design: *Robyn Beckerman*

Printed in the United States of America

10 9 8 7 6 5 4 3 2 1

ISBN 0-13-095285-0

Permission granted to reprint excerpts from *The Net: User Guidelines and Netiquette*
by Arlene Rinaldi.

PRENTICE HALL
Paramus, NJ 07652

On the World Wide Web at http://www.phdirect.com

To Marc,
for his love, support, friendship, and patience

CONTENTS

Chapter 3

Internet Demystified 13

Chapter 4

Enhancing Your Internet Power 26

Chapter 5

The Year 2000 and Beyond 37

Section 2

GETTING CONNECTED AND USING THE WEB
45

Chapter 9

Back Office Productivity 67

Section 3

THE 1999 DIRECTORY OF ACCOUNTING AND FINANCE RESOURCES
73

Chapter 10

Internet Resources Directory by Discipline. 75

Chapter 11

Business and Finance Resources 149

Section 4

CREATING A PRESENCE ON THE INTERNET
293

Section 5

MARKETING YOUR SERVICES ON THE INTERNET
323

Chapter 18

Chapter 19

Section 6

CREATING MAXIMUM PRODUCTIVITY AND INTERCONNECTIVITY
345

Chapter 20

Chapter 21

Ideas to Help You Work Faster and Smarter 353

Appendix: Netiquette Guide 359

Glossary of Internet Terms 366

Web Site Index—By Chapter 383

Index 421

INTRODUCTION

Welcome to my book. I am writing this book to provide you with useful information to fully maximize your Internet experience. You may be looking for accounting-related resources. Or maybe you are trying to stay on top of the industries that your clients operate in. Maybe you would like to build your own Web site or learn how to effectively market yourself on the Internet. If any of these benefits sound useful to you or your employees, please read on.

This book is broken down into six sections. Below I have outlined each section to give you an indication to the exciting topics that lie ahead:

Section 1—Internet Crash Course for Accountants

At a minimum all accountants should at least know how to carry on a conversation about the Internet and its capabilities with a potential or current client. If they fall behind and do not embrace this new technology, they will become obsolete. The first section is designed to make sure this does not happen. It helps the user gain an educational awareness of the Internet's origin, capabilities, and future impact. It is designed to prevent accountants from embarrassing themselves due to a lack of "cyber" knowledge. This is where the acronyms will be explained and Internet jargon will be demystified. In addition, the section will include some "future thinking" revelations and recent developments to tantalize the interest of some accountants who may already know most of the history and jargon.

Section 2—Getting Connected and Using the Web

This section takes you on a journey from "Reading about the Internet" to "Surfing the Internet." There is a good amount of "hand holding," checklists, and comparisons in order to help you make the right Internet connection and browser choices. Speaking to other accountants, I find they have a hard time transitioning to the active role of connecting to the Internet and using it in their business practices. Many of them cannot find the time to get connected to the Internet. This section is designed to get you up and running.

Section 3—The 1999 Directory of Accounting and Finance Resources

Once you are "plugged in" to the Internet, Section Three provides you with a myriad of accounting-related resources. The Directory will solve your frustration of not finding useful Web sites to use in your everyday job. Hundreds of accounting-related Web sites are featured and are indexed by category for ease of use. Further, each Web site includes a brief narrative that highlights the Web site's features.

Section 4—Creating a Presence on the Internet

The remaining sections discuss the many possibilities open to you if you choose to be a part of the Internet or create an Intranet. The first step is addressed in Section Four, Web page and site creation. As the Webmaster of CPAnet (www.cpanet.com), I receive much E-mail from accountants who want to start a Web site. This section shows users how to do it on their own or how to hire an appropriate Web host. Tips, checklists and primers are available to guide you through this process.

Section 5—Marketing Your Services on the Internet

Section Five discusses various ways to market yourself on the Internet. Since traditional marketing and publicity methods may not be appropriate, this section teaches the user to "think out the box" to create dynamic Internet marketing ideas. The most recent Internet statistics and demographics are presented and discussed. Further, this section addresses ways to increase the number of Web site visitors.

Section 6—Creating Maximum Productivity and Interconnectivity

The last section will go over the basics for building an Intranet as well as using the Web to its full potential. Finally, the section will end with various ideas as to how an Intranet or a combined Internet/Intranet can improve your employees' productivity and boost client service.

Updates and Feedback

Due to the timeliness of the information contained in this book, it may be necessary from time-to-time to make Web site address changes and to provide clarifications. You can receive information about these updates by visiting the updates page at http://www.cpanet.com/book/updates/. Also, if you have any feedback to provide, please e-mail me at mizgorski@cpanet.com. All comments and questions are welcomed and greatly appreciated.

SECTION I

INTERNET
CRASH COURSE
FOR
ACCOUNTANTS

(a.k.a. "Everything you ever wanted to know
about the Information Superhighway")

Chapter 1

IN THE BEGINNING . . .

Introduction

Virtually every subject matter is documented on the Internet. Although some resources are more trustworthy and accurate than others, the Internet is an amazing resource to learn and edify yourself. There is even a wealth of information about the inception of the Internet itself. It is not imperative you understand the very intricacies of the Internet's inception, however, it wouldn't be a bad idea to take a read of this chapter to gain insight and a knowledge base of Internet information. You can tap into this resource of knowledge when clients inquire of you for information, or you could just wow them at a social function.

In this section I am going to walk you through a brief history of the Internet by highlighting historical resources on the Internet. If you choose to delve into the history further, I have included the sources of this historical perspective.

Before we jump into Internet history, here is a side note. Not only is the history of the Internet documented, but also the inception of accounting as a vocation. Check out *Accounting: A Virtual History* at http://www.acaus.org/history/ which documents accounting back to 3500 B.C.!

What Is the Internet?

The Internet consists of a worldwide system of free-standing computer networks and servers. Each of these computers "serve up" its Web pages when a request is made by a client's browser. For public (non-password) sites, the typing of the Uniform Resource Locator (URL), the formal name of a Web site address (for example, http://www.yahoo.com), from the client's browser constitutes a request to the server to display a particular Web page.

History of the Internet—Who Invented It?

The Internet was created to establish a decentralized network among U.S. government defense agencies and strategic command posts. The purpose of the Internet was to create a network infrastructure that would survive even if a large portion of the network were destroyed, specifically in the event of a nuclear war. It was conceived by the Advanced Research Projects Agency (ARPA) of the U.S. government in 1969 and was originally referred to as the ARPAnet. Over the years the ARPAnet expanded to include those affiliated with defense work such as academicians, researchers, and major defense contractors.

> **➡ Quick Note: Internet History Books**
>
> If you are interested in reading more about how the Internet was formed, take a look at these books: *Where Wizards Stay Up Late: The Origins of the Internet* by Katie Hafner & Matthew Lyon, *Architects of the Web: 1,000 Days That Built the Future of Business* by Robert H. Reid, *Netizens: On the History and Impact of Usenet and the Internet* by Michael Hauben et al., and *Exploring the Internet: A Technical Travelogue* by Carl Malamud.

Between 1982 and 1987, Bob Kahn and Vint Cerf became key members of a team that created TCP/IP (Transmission Control Protocol/Internet Protocol), the common language of all Internet computers. After the TCP/IP formation, the loose collection of networks which made up the ARPAnet is seen as an "Internet" (an inter-connected system linked together in a network), and the Internet, as we know it today, was conceived.

By 1990, the organization of the Internet's success, the ARPAnet, was decommissioned, leaving a legacy of over 300,000 hosts which constituted the vast network-of-networks called the Internet.

Internet History Resources

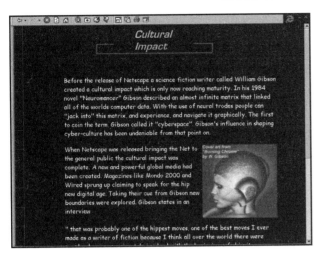

Net Hype's History of the Internet

http://jrowse.mtx.net/net/hype.html

Would you like to be all knowing on the history of the Internet? For starters, check out the History of the Internet slideshow. The documented history at this Web site reads like a novelette in addition to a very cool presentation of the facts, stories, and figures.

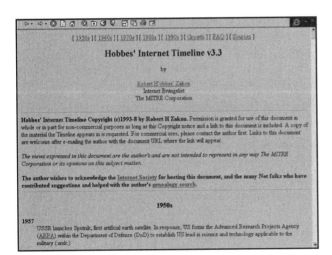

Hobbes' Internet History

http://info.isoc.org/guest/zakon/Internet/History/HIT.html

Robert H. Zakon, Internet evangelist for the MITRE Corporation, maintains an authoritative history of the major technical and personal milestones in the Internet's development. The site has detailed information by decade for easy browsing.

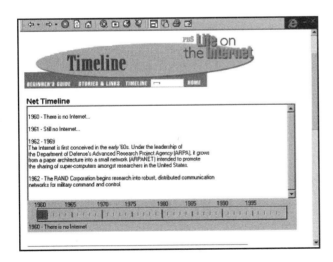

Internet Timeline

http://www.pbs.org/internet/timeline/

PBS has created a nifty interactive timeline. Just click on the year you are interested in and receive information about the Internet's history at that point in time. The site also includes links to its popular documentary "Triumph of the Nerds."

> ➡ **Quick Note: Internet Quotes**
>
> "Technology serves to institute a new, more effective, and more pleasant form of social control and social cohesion."
> —Herbert Marcuse, 1964
>
> "Societies have always been shaped more by the media by which men communicate than by the content of the communication."
> —Marshall McLuhan

Who Owns and Runs the Internet?

The Internet is available for public use, however, many of its resources are privately owned by organizations and companies that have developed the infrastructure or backbone of the Internet.

No one organization is in charge of the Internet. Each site is responsible for its own maintenance, including its hardware, software, and network connections. In addition, at present the Internet is mostly self-regulated and all Internet sites agree to abide by the rules of the popular consensus of Internet inhabitants. The Internet Society (http://www.isoc.org/), an international nonprofit organization, has been very active as the guide and conscience for the workings of the Internet.

> ➡ **Quick Note: Where Did the Term "Cyberspace" Come From?**
>
> The phrase was actually coined by science fiction writer William Gibson in his 1984 novel, *Neuromancer*. Long before Netscape appeared, Gibson spun a tale of an infinite matrix that linked together all of the world's computer data. Life imitating art . . .

Although the Internet is not owned by any one company or organization, there are a few corporate behemoths who have a considerable financial stake in the Internet. IBM, AT&T, MCI, and Sprint have all made substantial long-term investments in building the Internet's communication infrastructure. As expected, these companies are very involved in the future direction of the Internet by exercising their power of infrastructure control.

How the Internet Works—Just the Basics

The Internet Infrastructure

The current infrastructure of the Internet is a Web page that gets you from point A to B. When you request to see a Web page on your computer, the data travels through a maze (or web—hence the term *World Wide Web*) of connections. This section explores each of the "pit-stops" a Web page travels through to complete your requested task.

The Pit-Stops of an Internet Web Page

Stop #1—Your Internet Service Provider Server   Your Internet Service Provider, or ISP, is the company that provides you with access to the Internet. The majority of ISPs lease equipment to have access to Points of Presence (POP) on the Internet. These POPs are geographically based and, depending on your ISP's size, the number of POPs it possesses will vary.

Each POP has its own IP (Internet Protocol) address. The actual POP may reside at rented space owned by telecommunications carriers. The larger ISPs, such as UUNet (http://www.uunet.net/), PSINet (http://www.psinet.com/), and Netcom (http://www.netcom.com/), have their own lines and aren't as dependent on telecom carriers.

Stop #2—The ISP's Regional Network   Some of the major ISPs skip this stop since they have direct access to one of the four network access points (NAPs—addressed in Stop #3). However, for the majority of the five thousand ISPs worldwide, they are required to band together with other geographically central ISPs. Some of the major U.S. regional networks are CERFnet (Western U.S.), BARRNet (Northern California), NEARRNET (Northeastern U.S.), and SURAnet (Southeast U.S.).

Stop #3—Network Access Points   Originally there were four NAPs: New York, Washington, D.C., Chicago, and San Francisco. They were established by the National Science Foundation to transition ARPAnet into the commercially operated Internet. Several new NAPs have been established, such as WorldCom's MAE West and ICS Network Systems' Big East.

Stop #4—U.S. Commercial Backbone   Based on the formal definition of a backbone as it relates to the Internet, the U.S. Commercial Backbone is "a set of paths that local or regional networks connect to for long-distance interconnection. The connection points are known as network nodes or telecommunication data switching exchanges (DSEs)" (source: whatis.com). The backbone carries your Web page request across the U.S. or internationally until it is ultimately received by the computer that houses the requested data.

Stop #5—Process on Other End   Once your Web page request is received by the appropriate server, data is processed and the page is served up and sent back to your computer through the same process: through the NAPs, regional networks, your ISP, and to your computer.

The Internet Protocol

The Internet Protocol is the protocol used to transport data (Web pages, E-mail messages, etc.) over the Internet. When data is transported, either sent or received, it travels in a series of packets. Each packet may take an entirely different physical route. The protocol has no desire to connect the packets of information, it is merely transporting a single packet. It's up to the TCP protocol to put the packets back in the right order which together create the entire TCP/IP language process among computers.

Internet Operational Understanding Resources

Atlas of Cyberspaces

http://www.cybergeography.org/

To view the Internet Infrastructure visit Martin Dodge's Atlas of Cyberspaces, which contains an extensive collection of maps for graphical depictions such as ISP and Internet backbone networks, three-dimensional information spaces, and information landscapes.

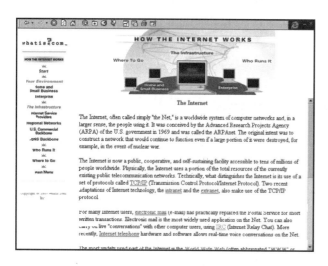

How the Internet Works

http://www.whatis.com/tour.htm

This is a great detailed guide about how the Internet works, complete with illustrations. This guide has many hyperlinks within its text to take you to term definitions of other sections within the Web site. Many whatis.com definitions are featured in this book's glossary.

Chapter 2

WHY INVEST IN THE INTERNET?

Introduction

This chapter addresses the reasons why you and your business should invest in the Internet. If you are already convinced, consider this chapter as a self-affirming voice telling that you are doing the right thing. It may help you gauge how much to further invest in the Internet. For others who aren't as sure, read on for the many benefits of Internet involvement.

Wealth of Information Online

By using the Internet as a knowledge base, you can instantaneously retrieve information that you used to wait for days or weeks to retrieve. It is true that some Web sites on the Internet are trivial and useless, however, if you know which sites to visit, the majority of the resources on the Internet are rich and available for nothing. Where else can you pull up a company's 10-K report within seconds? The SEC EDGAR Web site can do just that (www.sec.gov). Looking for the latest updates to your software programs or information library service (such as RIA, Lexis-Nexis, or CCH)? Current updates are found on the Internet. The Directory in Section 3 will give you hundreds of Web sites to visit for helpful information.

Inexpensive to Communicate

Most people connect to the Internet to use E-mail. E-mail communications are only a minute fraction of the cost of sending snail-mail publications and information. If you have international contacts, the cost savings can be substantial.

Not only do you have the cost component, but you should also consider the timeliness in which you are communicating. For snail-mail that can take days for delivery, you can send a quick message within seconds. Processes, such as audits and tax return preparation, can be sped up through the sharing of files and E-mails, which in turn will free up staff time to generate additional revenue. Additionally, files can be uploaded through File Transfer Protocol (FTP) for quick access.

You must remember, just because you aren't using the features of the Internet does not mean your competition is not. Firms will use this as a competitive advantage until everyone is online.

Your Clients Are Online!

By now you should have seen an increasing number of clients jumping on the Internet, either with E-mail, only a Web site, or both. E-mail is rapidly becoming the preferred way to conduct quick and efficient communications between client and firm. If your clients have asked to be contacted by E-mail, that's a big signal to get online. If you don't, you may be perceived as an Internet laggard.

There are many ways you can improve client service once your clients are online. Offer them tips via E-mail, send them to your online newsletter, or publish your latest checklists or surveys. In addition, you can create a private directory which is password-protected to provide a way to share more sensitive information between you and your client. Keep in mind you should be cognizant of the types of information that is best shared in this type of environment.

Traditional Business Models Are Changing

Many of the traditional ways of doing business are changing due to the Internet. If you are an auditor, there have been many new issues to consider such as the online reporting of financial statements, gaining an understanding of internal controls as it relates to electronic commerce and other electronic data interchange (EDI) issues. Furthermore, the future issue of sales tax and general taxation of Internet transactions may not fully kick in for a couple years, however, it will be an important issue to consider in conducting business.

The landscape of business communications has drastically changed with the emergence of E-mail. Even fax technology is changing with the emergence of Internet faxing. Where individuals conduct business has changed, too. The commercialization of the Internet has given rise to increases in home-based business, remote offices, virtual offices, and telecommuting.

Advising Your Clients About E-commerce Issues

How can you possibly advise your clients about critical electronic-commerce issues when you are not investing in the Internet yourself? How will you be able to answer questions such as "Should I sell my products online?" and if so, "What is involved and how do I maintain my site?" and "What legal and tax issues are involved?"

Even if your client has adequate resources in-house or via outsourcing to answer these questions without your help, you have missed an excellent opportunity to become more involved in your client's business. Furthermore, if you are retained to perform an audit, review or prepare tax returns and your client conducts online business, it is essential you have a firm understanding of your clients' internal control systems and information workflow involved to accurately perform your job.

Make Your Business Available

You already have business information and resources of interest already prepared to market your firm. Why not put it on the Internet? You can open up potential markets, bring an awareness about your existing products and services, and obtain new clients. By establishing a presence on the Internet, you have made an active sign to others of your commitment and benefits of the Internet.

Part of establishing an Internet presence is not knowing exactly what opportunities may come your way. If you have some unique characteristics to your firm, other firms and organizations may choose to network with you or provide you with resources of which you were not aware. Additionally, if you have an interesting Web site, you may be the lucky recipient of free press in trade journals and magazines.

Release Time-Sensitive Information

Inform your clients that time-sensitive information such as your press releases will be available at your Web site. If there is pending tax legislation that may affect your clients, provide the latest updates online. If you have important information to report to your tax clients and it's too close to a deadline to communicate via snail-mail, the Internet and/or E-mail methods of communication will prove extremely beneficial. Nineteen ninety-nine will be a big year for the need of quick reporting of Year 2000 issues, especially as the new millennium draws near. Your clients will thank you for being on top of things.

Create New Revenue Streams

With any new technology, there are always new opportunities for revenue. The Internet is no exception. As the Internet industry matures, additional opportunities will evolve. Currently new assurance services are sprouting up such as eTrust and WebTrust to aid with Internet reliability and trust issues. Future revenue streams for those involved in accounting and finance includes providing E-commerce consulting services, online tax return preparation and information knowledge base services.

Research Resources

By jumping online, you can tap into the wealth of research resources. Many accounting and finance organizations have provided either full-text or abstracts of their publications online. You can check out the various news updates to gather the latest news affecting your practice.

Another excellent resource on the Internet is the mere fact you have information about your client's and potential clients' industries at your fingertips. Similar to the wealth of resources available to the accounting profession, you can find the same for various industries such as healthcare, telecommunications, and insurance. Remember if you aren't checking out these resources, someone else is.

Networking Opportunities

The Internet creates new networking opportunities. Since the Internet cuts through geographical boundaries, you have the potential to network with anyone in the world. Individuals can be easily accessed with a simple click to their Web site and an E-mail. Many special interest forums and virtual communities such as my site CPAnet.com provide additional networking potential.

Stay Up on the Technological Revolution

If you don't stay current on the latest in Internet technological developments, you will certainly be left behind. This is not a fear tactic—it's a fact. Think about all the changes that have taken place in computing, from hardware and software to the Internet. Did you stay on top of those developments? What if you hadn't? Wouldn't you agree that firms still using MS-DOS have some catching up to do? If you keep your learning curve at a steady clip, you most likely will be able to digest enormous amounts of information. The Internet can help you make this a doable goal.

Chapter 3

INTERNET DEMYSTIFIED

Introduction

Many aspects of the Internet are very confusing. At one time, cookies and Spam were considered food items, and now they bring on a whole new meaning when addressed in Internet-speak. This chapter is designed to help demystify some of the more popular and nebulous components of the Internet. Internet acronyms and buzzwords are given meaning to what they are and in some cases what they are not. In addition, this chapter explores the pieces that make up the Internet puzzle.

Pieces of the Internet Puzzle

This section will help you decipher the components collectively referred to as "the Internet." Although you can learn to drive a car without knowing what's under the hood, I don't consider these components to be engine parts. These components are more like buttons and dials on a dashboard—you need to know what each button does before you can effectively use them. With that said, the Internet provides four common services, which are:

Common Internet Services

- Multimedia Information Services—World Wide Web
- Communication Services—E-mail, Telnet, USENET, IRC
- Information Retrieval Services—FTP and Gopher
- Information Search Services—WAIS, Archie, Veronica

Multimedia Information Services

WWW

The World Wide Web (WWW) is founded on the concept of developing a standard format for all documents in order for the easy display on any type of computer. In addition, the standard was to facilitate the linking of documents. Ultimately, the viewing and linking would be performed using a Web browser interface application.

The WWW was developed in the late 1980's by CERN (the European Lab for Particle Physics) for its researchers to easily transfer and view documents. Once the service was made public, the WWW has never been the same.

Web Resources

Even though there are over 153 million Internet users, a very large number of financial professionals are still not connected to the Internet. This section is to provide you with some resources for learning how to use the Internet.

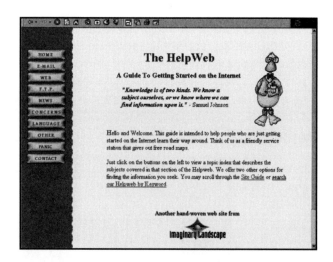

A Guide to Getting Started on the Internet

http://www.imagescape.com/helpweb/

This easy-to-read Internet primer holds your hand through those difficult first days of an Internet newbie. It even has a panic button if you get too stressed!

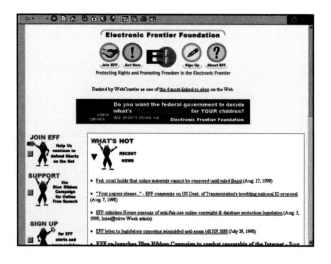

Guide to the Internet—Electronic Frontier Foundation

http://www.eff.org/papers/eegtti/eeg_toc.html

Don't let the update date (1994) bother you, many of the basic concepts covered here have not changed. The guide covers the Internet origins and using the Web.

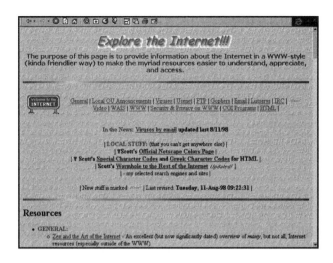

Internet Help Desk

http://w3.one.net/~alward/

The Internet Help Desk contains links to help you explore the various aspects of the Internet and the Web. The site has troubleshooting resources, guides, and FAQs.

Online Discussion Forums

Online discussion groups, whether they are E-mail discussion, web-based, or via newsgroups, are excellent ways to interact with the financial community. Not only are you provided with a wealth of reading resources, but you also have the ability to voice your own opinions or pose your own questions. Once you find the right online discussion groups for your needs, you will definitely find ways to make your business and your life run more smoothly.

> ➡ **Quick Note: Facts About Threaded Discussion Groups**
> - Also referred to as forums.
> - All messages of the group are posted to a Web site.
> - Some include a username and password because they provide profile customization features (i.e., subscribe to thread).
> - Some are moderated which generally provides better information.
> - As with anything you read, be aware of the information source and check out any sources you use.

Discussion Group Examples

- Financial Manager—http://www.electronicaccountant.com
- General—http://www.accountingnet.com
- Budgeting & Payroll—http://www.ppccontroller.com/html/message_board.html

Multimedia Applications and Browser Plug-Ins

Browser plug-ins give your browser even greater enhanced functionality and add a whole new dimension to what you can do on the Web. Chapter 4 is devoted to exploring browser plug-ins for maximum functionality.

Communication Services

Communication services on the Internet include E-mail, Telnet, USENET, and IRC. Below, each service is profiled with its primary features.

E-mail

Although voicemail messages are generally answered first, E-mail has become the standard in general business correspondence. When it comes to low cost and information volume, even voicemail can't beat E-mail. There is no other medium that will allow you to send a message (long or short) to a colleague in Australia virtually for free. Furthermore, I haven't received a voicemail yet that included a spreadsheet attachment! As you can tell, I'm an E-mail aficionado. Unfortunately for those who are not keen on communicating via E-mail, you will have to use it eventually. This communication mode will be with us for quite a while.

E-mail Etiquette

In order to conduct E-mail business on the Internet, etiquette and common E-mail courtesy is needed. When sending E-mail messages, be courteous to your online clients, business affiliates, and colleagues by following these guidelines:

- Use a concise and descriptive subject line in your mail header. Leaving the subject line blank does NOT constitute a concise or courteous action.

- For emphasis of a word use an asterisk (*). This would be in lieu of using bold or underline formatting. Some E-mail programs do not even recognize formatting, while others do not interpret the information correctly.

- Use common acronyms to help your recipient read your E-mail quickly. Common acronyms include BTW (by the way), OTOH (on the other hand), WYSIWYG (what you see is what you get) and IMHO (in my humble opinion).

- Do NOT type in capitals—it is deemed as shouting in the Internet world and is considered extremely rude.

- Use emoticon symbols to express emotions. Remember, sarcasm does not translate well without facial expressions and/or verbal inflections. Make sure people understand how you feel about a situation by displaying emotion. I would recommend using them sparingly. You don't want your E-mails to look like a "smiley-fest." Here are some common emoticons (look sideways now) :) smiley face—use for humor, laughter, and friendliness; : (frown—use for upset, anger, and sadness. For additional acronyms as well as emoticons see: http://www.netpath.net/~gwicker/email.htm.

- Always include a complete signature, including your name, position, affiliation and other pertinent information (i.e., address, phone, E-mail, Web site address, etc.). Most E-mail packages have the capability to save your signature so you can automatically paste it into each E-mail you compose.

Usenet

After the World Wide Web and E-mail, Usenet newsgroups are probably the most popular feature of the Internet. When I recently downloaded the current list of newsgroups provided through my Internet Service Provider's (ISP) news server, I had over thirty-three thousand to choose from!

Usenet Resources

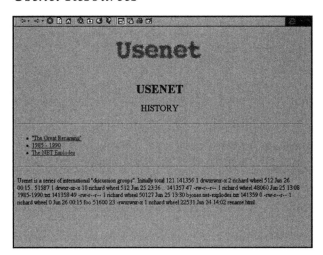

Usenet History

http://www.vrx.net/usenet/history/

Interested in the history of the Usenet? If so, check out this detailed documentation of the life of Usenet.

Usenet Newsgroups   If you want to subscribe to accounting-related Usenet newsgroups, here's a list to start with:

ACCOUNTING NEWSGROUPS
news:alt.accounting
news:misc.business.consulting
news:alt.business.internal-audit

TAX NEWSGROUPS
znews:misc.taxes.moderated
news:misc.taxes

COMPUTING NEWSGROUPS
news:biz.comp.accounting
news:microsoft.public.industry.accounting

SECURITY NEWSGROUPS
news:comp.os.ms-windows
news:comp.security.misc
news:comp.security.unix
news:comp.admin.policy
news:comp.society.privacy

OTHER NEWSGROUPS
news:soc.org.nonprofit

List Servers, Mailing Lists, and Newsletters

E-mail continues to be the most popular application on the Internet. Why is E-mail so important to the financial and accounting community? Aside from general business correspondence, E-mail allows us to receive a wealth of timely information via mailing lists and newsletters. We have total control over what we subscribe to and therefore we can tailor the information we receive to our needs.

➤ Quick Note: Facts About List Servers

- Easy to get on—just send message to list administrator.
- Steady stream of information, targeted topics.
- Many provide messages in digest form, batched and sent daily (cuts down on E-mail clutter).

➤ Quick Note: Tips For Success

- Scan subject lines to save time and read only things you are interested in.
- Use proper netiquette—see Appendix.
- When replying, include only relevant parts of the original post.
- Don't send administrative messages and requests to the list. Send them to the administrator's address.

List Server Resources

List Server Discussions of Interest   List server subscriptions usually include an E-mail to the list server administrator. However, online forms have recently popped up on the Internet to help ease the pain of subscribing.

ACCOUNTING AND AUDITING STANDARDS
E-mail listserve@tapnet.com. In the body include the text:
subscribe tax-aa-stds-app.

ACCOUNTING AND TAX LIST
E-mail listproc@scu.edu.au. In the body include the text: atax-1@scu.edu.au

ACCOUNTING TECHNOLOGY DISCUSSION GROUP
E-mail owner-can-acctech@hookup.net.

BANKRUPTCY AND INSOLVENCY LIST
E-mail tci@bankrupt.com.

CONTROL SELF ASSESSMENT
E-mail majordomo@teleport.com. In the body include the text
SUBSCRIBE CSA-L or SUBSCRIBE CSA-L-digest (for digest version).

INTERNAL REVENUE SERVICE MAILING LIST
E-mail majordomo@pen-west.irs.gov.

MANAGEMENT ACCOUNTING LIST

E-mail listserve@tapnet.com. In the body include the text:
subscribe cpa-inet-use.

TAX ANALYSTS

Visit http://www.tax.org/notes/default.htm

TAX PRACTICE ISSUES LIST

E-mail listserve@tapnet.com. In the body include the text:
subscribe tax-prct-issues.

LIST OF MAILING LISTS

http://www.kentis.com/alllist.html

➡ Quick Note: The Natural Life Cycle of Mailing Lists

Kat Nagel originally documented the social development of mailing lists. Here's a synopsis of her findings.

- Initial Enthusiasm—introductions and happiness about finding subject in common.
- Evangelism—moaning about lack of posts, recruitment strategies begin.
- Growth—more people join, length of threads increases, occasional off-topic remark.
- Community—many threads, information and advice exchanged in dynamic setting, old and new members alike enjoy the environment.
- Discomfort with Diversity—exponential increase in messages, complaining takes place, off-topic threads increase.
- Stagnation—flaming occurs, newbies are rebuffed, traffic drops and any discussion of interest takes place via private E-mail.
- Maturity—some have quit the list; however, most hover in the Community stage with Discomfort arising every so often.

List Serve Page Examples

INFOBEAT

http://www.infobeat.com

Financial News—Sign-up for E-mail based messages, such as market updates and financial news articles.

FINANCENET

http://www.financenet.gov/financenet/start/news.htm

Offers extensive mailing lists for governmental accounting, etc.

Telnet

Telnet is a user command function that gives remote access to another computer. Access is only given if permission is granted and the host computer has authority over granting what privileges the remote computer has over specific applications. Telnet is most likely used by individuals who need to use specific applications or data located on a particular computer.

IRC

What Is IRC?   IRC stands for Internet Relay Chat and is generally used interchangeably with other terms used to describe online chat, such as BBS (Bulletin Board Systems). The IRC system involves client/server software and the online chat is conducted via text-base transmissions. IRC systems can support multiple users and are by design to provide close to real-time interactivity.

To learn more about IRC, visit the IRC Help Page at http://www.irchelp.org/. For more information about the most popular IRC client available, ICQ ("I Seek You"), and to learn how ICQ can enhance your Internet Power, see Chapter 4.

➡ Quick Note: Electronic Communications

For more information on electronic communications see *The Net: User Guidelines and Netiquette* by Arlene Rinaldi (http://www.fau.edu/rinaldi/net/elec.html). Also, net etiquette is addressed in the Appendix.

Information Retrieval Services

Current information retrieval services consist of File Transfer Protocol (FTP) and Gopher. A brief introduction of each of these services is addressed in this section. Additional information about FTP as well as an FTP primer is included in Chapter 15.

FTP

FTP is the standard way to send files over the Internet. You are required to have an FTP software program installed on your computer to be able to "FTP." These FTP programs have a user command interface where the program connects with the server you specify, logs in, verifies authorization, and then permits you to send (upload), receive (download), and perform other file maintenance procedures.

When you sign up with an ISP, it will most likely provide you with its preferred FTP software application along with instructions. Popular FTP programs are WS_FTP (http://www.ipswitch.com), CuteFTP (http://www.cuteftp.com), and FTP Explorer (http://www.winsite.com).

Gopher

Gopher is a menu-based system of indexing and categorizing computer files. These files are stored on computers called Gopher servers and are reached through your browser using the gopher:// protocol (instead of http://). To visit a Gopher and learn more about it, visit: gopher://gopher.tc.umn.edu.

Information Search Services

Information search services such as WAIS, Archie, and Veronica were extremely popular until the web browser interface and protocol arrived. Their functions have diminished somewhat, not due to their obsolescence, but mainly due to the fact there are so many other resources on the Internet.

WAIS

WAIS stands for Wide Area Information Servers (or Service). WAIS is a system that creates a directory of servers in which each contains specialized subject databases. With the advent of the Web, and the volume of search capabilities it provides, WAIS lost much of its appeal. However, if a Web search does not supply the information you are looking for in your research efforts, you may want to try WAIS for your highly specialized searches. Visit http://town.hall.org/util/wais_help.html to learn how to conduct a WAIS search. A public access WAIS client is available at telnet://wais@quake.think.com/.

Archie

Archie is the search engine for FTP server files. Archie visits anonymous FTP sites, reads the directory contents, and indexes the FTP files. Use the ArchiePlex Web-based forms interface for easy Archie searching (http://cuiwww.unige.ch/archieplexform.html). In conducting your online research, if you already know your topic is likely found at an FTP server, perform an Archie search.

Veronica

Veronica is similar to Archie, but where Archie searches and indexes FTP server files, Veronica indexes and provides a search interface to help find Gopher sites. You can search all of Gopherspace using Veronica at gopher://gopher.cc.utah.edu/.

Internet Acronyms and Buzzwords

Cookies

What Is a Cookie? A cookie is a small file that is placed on your computer in order to preserve specific information about your visit to the Web site that gave you the cookie. There are various uses for cookies. Cookies can be used to later identify the browser type and version you are using, can identify a user and save Web site customization preferences, and can keep track of what has been ordered.

Some believe cookies are an invasion of privacy. If you feel this to be the case, you can either delete your cookies or have your web browser notify you before cookies are added to gain your approval.

What a Cookie Is Not   A cookie cannot be used to steal data off your computer. That includes data from your hard drive such as files and E-mail addresses. However, if you do complete questionnaires or online registration forms at a Web site that creates a cookie, this information may stay resident in the cookie until the cookie expires.

Cookies are not as bad as they sound: they are just notes left on your computer. Those who feel strongly about the evilness of cookies from a privacy standpoint may want to check out some of the cookie-tweaking software utilities, such as CookieCrusher (http://www.thelimitsoft.com/cookie.html) and Cookie Pal at the ZDNet Software Download (http://www.hotfiles.com/).

Cookie Facts

- For Netscape Navigator, cookies are included in a text file called cookies.txt.
- For Internet Explorer, a file is created for each cookie and the information is resident in a directory called cookies.
- You can specify in your browser preferences to warn you when cookies are added.
- Any cookie you do not want, you can delete it with no harm to your computer.
- Cookies do eventually expire. In your browser set-up options, you should have some control regarding expiration dates.
- A potentially better recipe for cookies is Open Profiling Standard (OPS). OPS is intended to "provide guidelines for collecting user information, so that users can retain some control over information in their profiles."

Cookie Resources

COOKIE CENTRAL

http://www.cookiecentral.com/

Cookie Central is a one-stop clearinghouse for cookie information and resources. A site dedicated to the use and abuse of cookies.

COOKIES GUIDE

http://shrike.depaul.edu/~ngreely/cookie.htm

This site is devoted to all things cookie. It tells you who is watching you and why. It goes through positive and potentially negative aspects of cookies.

ANDY'S COOKIE NOTES

http://www.illuminatus.com/cookie.fcgi

Here you will find a good cookie description and how to use cookies on your own site. The site also has links to additional resources.

E-commerce

What Is E-commerce?   E-commerce, or electronic commerce, is more than online shopping. Under this category falls the online transaction activities such as online stock and bond transactions, the online buying and downloading of software, and business-to-business transactions. In addition, many people hope the evolution of micro-transactions, which can be likened to pay-per-view content will soon fall under the E-commerce umbrella. In any case, electronic commerce involves the exchange of money over the Internet.

E-commerce Technology Standards   Due to the financial significance at stake with E-commerce transactions, there has been much attention devoted to the setting of E-commerce standards. The E-commerce community (as well as the government) has not settled on any one standard. E-commerce is one of the newest features to the Internet and the standards evolve daily. Below is a laundry list of the latest standards for E-commerce as well as the organizations and Web page addresses where you can obtain additional information:

EDI—ELECTRONIC DATA INTERCHANGE

http://www.eia.org/eig/eidx/

http://www.disa.org/

Created by government in early 1970's. Allows large organizations to transmit information over private networks.

OBI—OPEN BUYING ON THE INTERNET

http://www.openbuy.org/

Originated to create a standard where different E-commerce systems can talk to one another.

OTP—OPEN TRADING PROTOCOL

http://www.otp.org/

Intends to standardize several payment-related activities such as purchase agreements, receipts for purchases, and payments.

OPS—OPEN PROFILING STANDARD

http://developer.netscape.com/ops/proposal.html

The idea behind this standard is to give consumers the ability to control the profile and preferences they choose to share with merchants.

SSL—SECURE SOCKETS LAYER

http://www.w3.org/Security/

This protocol was created to provide a secure connection to the server. SSL uses public key encryption, currently one of the strongest encryption methods.

SET—SECURE ELECTRONIC TRANSACTIONS

http://www.visa.com/cgi-bin/vee/nt/ecomm/main.html?2+0

SET encodes the credit card numbers stored on merchant's servers.

TRUSTE

http://www.etrust.org/

Seeking to build public trust in E-commerce.

Spam

What Is Spam?   The word *spam* as it relates to the despised E-mail has been blessed as a word in the latest edition of the New Oxford Dictionary of English. The new dictionary defines spam as "irrelevant Internet messages sent to a large number of people." It generally is referred to when E-mail that advertises a product or service is sent to a mailing list or newsgroup. Spam is considered a breach of netiquette, uses large quantities of bandwidth, and has driven people to form organizations to fight spam's existence. You'll find some spam help in Chapter 9.

What Spam Is Not   Spam as it relates to the Internet has no direct affiliation with the pink and processed meat product in a blue can. If you really must know (which I did!), the widely accepted version is that the term was adopted from a Monty Python's Flying Circus bit. The skit was about a group of Vikings that sang a useless song about SPAM, the food product, and sang it so loud and repetitively that it drowned out all other conversation, which is likened to junk E-mail's effect. The exact chorus to the song? "SPAM, SPAM, SPAM, lovely SPAM, wonderful SPAM." Sing loud and repeat.

Virtual Communities

A virtual community is a service that usually by definition is provided to its membership for free and includes a myriad of resources to help spark interaction and a sense of belonging. Virtual communities usually involve bringing together individuals with common interests and the focus of the Web site is to help learn more about this interest.

Online communities provide its membership several ways to interact including discussion forums, mailing lists, and chat. Some communities such as Tripod (http://www.tripod.com) and GeoCities (http://www.geocities.com) also provide free Home Pages.

Java and Active X

What Is Java and Active X?   Both Java and Active X are programming technologies used to create animated and interactive Web pages. Sun's Java language can be likened to the C++ language. However, Java-based applications have the unique difference of its ability to run on any operating platform. Although Java's easy transferability is present, it's not a programming language you can just pick up.

The Active X set of technologies from Microsoft provides tools to link other programs to the Web (i.e., Word and Excel).

What Java Is Not—It Is Not JavaScript!

Java should not be confused with JavaScript. These technologies are merely loosely affiliated with each other. JavaScript started as a scripting language from Netscape, originally termed "LiveScript." JavaScript is an interpreted scripting language, whereas Java is a programming language. Nearly anyone with a little time and technical intrigue can learn JavaScript.

JavaScript Resource

JAVASCRIPT FOR BEGINNERS GUIDE

http://builder.cnet.com/Programming/Javacript/

Another excellent tutorial from C\net, the JavaScript guide will walk you through the basics and then will take you through an interactive example, complete with code. The guide also provides additional JavaScript resources.

Other Terms Explored

We will be exploring other terms in the following section as well as in other spots of the book. The list below provides you a quick cross-reference where additional Internet terms are explored in detail. In addition, take a look at the Glossary section for more term definitions.

To learn more about:

- VPN—Virtual Private Networks, visit Chapter 20.
- ISDN—Integrated Services Digital Network, visit Chapter 6.
- DHTML—Dynamic HTML, visit Chapter 15.
- Webcasting—visit Chapter 4.

ENHANCING YOUR INTERNET POWER

Introduction

To capture the power of the Internet you might need a little "push." Push technology rang in 1998 with a lot of hype and has proved to be one of the biggest flops of the Internet. Push technology in its early form hasn't gone over well at all. Too much information was pushed to desktops, making critics upset about draining the resources of the Internet by clogging up its bandwidth arteries.

Rightly so, this is a fact of push technology: once you set up the preferences, the information is pushed to you to read or not read, which can be construed as wasteful. This chapter is designed to touch on the highlights and lowlights of push technology. Used wisely, there is a place and purpose for having information pushed to your desktop.

Another way you can enhance your Internet experience is to select a few plug-ins for download. Most plug-ins give you the ability to hear audio, see video, or both. This chapter explores the most popular plug-ins.

What Is Push Technology?

Push technology or Webcasting (a relatively new term to describe push) is a subscription based and prearranged updating of information. The fact that it is subscription based denotes the fact the user has to sign-up or request the information be "pushed" to his/her computer at times available from the provider and prescribed by the user. Webcasting subscriptions are generally free, however, there are some pay-per-view Webcasts which fall under the E-commerce category of microtransactions.

The push transmission takes place over the Web and the information is primarily viewed in a browser interface. The more comprehensive push services, such as PointCast, provide software and its own browser environment (or a direct connection to your preferred browser via its interface). The following section will address some of the more popular push programs.

Traditional Push Technology Resources

If you are considering push technology applications, here are a couple of pointers. Most push programs are available for download on the Internet. Check a few out before you decide on one. Also, you should start out slow. Don't go crazy and download every possible push application you can find all at once. If you do, choose to download a few of the resources, and make sure to push a low level of content to your site. You have to remember information will be pushed to you on a constant basis. Albeit, the information will trickle in throughout the day, it can really add up.

PointCast

http://www.pointcast.com/

The PointCast Network is a free Internet service that delivers personalized news and information to your desktop. PointCast has news that may otherwise be unavailable from sources such as the *Wall Street Journal*, the *New York Times*, and CNN.

In order to use PointCast, you need to download the program. The program is a very large file, which can be a deterrent to using the PointCast program. Also, PointCast can drain your system resources and can sometimes take on a life of its own with its automatic updates. I found the drain on my resources to be prohibitive. When I installed the program, I loaded up my preferences with every possible download option. However, you can control some of these options. I recommend starting out with limited requests for information (maybe the *Wall Street Journal* and a couple of industry news selections, for example).

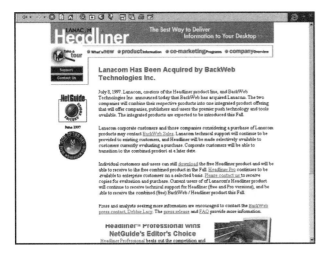

BackWeb Headliner

http://www.headliner.com/

Just like the title says, BackWeb Headliner only pushes the headlines to your desktop, minimizing the impact on corporate networks and computer resources. The program gives you access to hundreds of channels from *USA Today* and MSNBC to fluffy stuff such as David Letterman's "Top Ten List." For the interface you have the choice of either a scrolling ticker, screensaver, or news title interface.

Intermind Communicator

http://www.intermind.com/

Intermind does not have as many channels as PointCast and Backweb Headliner, but if you are interested in product support updates and other technical updates, check out Intermind's resource. The updates are not revised all that frequently, so you may want to liken it to a weekly magazine than a daily newspaper.

Downtown

http://www.incommon.com/

Downtown is for ticker fans. It has over two dozen channels from reputable sources such as the *Los Angeles Times*, and each channel you select shows up in the Downtown taskbar. InCommon was recently purchased by Tibco (www.tibco.com) and Downtown is now EventConsole and ContentBroker.

WebSprite

http://www.dvorak.com/

Similar to Downtown with its ticker interface, WebSprite leans more heavily toward business and financial headlines. WebSprite's interface is real simple, with no fancy buttons or gadgets.

IBM News Ticker

http://www.software.ibm.com/java/news-ticker.html

The IBM News Ticker allows you to build a news ticker for your own site.

A Push Technology Comparison

The following table compares the major push technology programs currently available. As Webcasting fully evolves, the utilities and programs of preferences will become more self-evident. However, in the meantime, choosing the right program generally involves some major trade-offs in program functionality and characteristics.

Product	What It Downloads	Pros/Cons	Suitable If You . . .
BackWeb Headliner	Headlines with summaries	Small profile, not intrusive; have to go online to read stories.	Seek hard-core news and other information.
Intermind	Headlines and summaries or full stories, depending on the channel	Efficient delivery, good for technical support information; news content is minimal.	Need technical support information and prefer channel updates in browser format.
PointCast	Headlines, summaries, and full stories	Provides quality information, manageable number of channels; ads can be distracting.	Want filtered Internet content from only the best news channels.

Source: *PC World* Online (http://www.pcworld.com/).

Other Push Resources

This section highlights some of the resources you can download and/or subscribe to in order to create a self-made push environment. Depending on how much information you need to have pushed to you, the traditional push technology applications may be more of a burden than a gift. Therefore, this section will give you a little more flexibility to pick and choose what is right for you.

MSNBC News Alert

http://www.msnbc.com/

I really like the MSNBC News Alert. For better or worse it has pushed the top stories to my desktop, usually before anyone else has found out (except those using the News Alert!). The MSNBC News Alert is part of the Cool Tools features.

To get the News Alert all you have to do is download a small program and install it on your desktop. A little bull's-eye will be placed in your system tray and it will blink red when you have updates. Although the news services that will be pushed to your desktop are more restricted than PointCast, the MSNBC News Alert is a tiny program that packs just enough punch to be effective. You will receive news primarily from MSNBC and ZDNet from Ziff Davis.

Infobeat—E-mail Newsletters

http://www.infobeat.com/

Subscribe to a few E-mail newsletters and you will have created your own little push network. Currently, there are few resources where you can subscribe to more than one mainstream newsletter at a time, so for now you may have to visit several Web sites to sign up for your favorites. Or you can perform a search at one of the mailing list search engines, such as Reference.com (http://www.reference.com/). You can sign up for multiple E-mail updates at Infobeat and Hotmail (when you sign up for a free E-mail account at http://www.hotmail.com).

After Dark Online

http://www.afterdark.com/

Do you want your news on the wings of toasters? For the lighter side of push technology, visit After Dark, and check into their After Dark 4.0 screensaver program. The program includes news updates from six channels, including *USA Today*. Animations accompany the news in screensaver style.

Push Technology Tips and Tricks

A Push Trick

Here's a little push trick I like. The goal is to help minimize the inflow of pushed E-mail and HTML newsletters into your primary in-box. Recently, I set up a free E-mail account through Microsoft's Hotmail (http://www.hotmail.com) and changed my subscriptions to various updates to this account. Now I can easily see my urgent E-mail and then spend time at my leisure reading the latest news when I visit my Hotmail account.

This is an especially nice feature to include in your daily Internet practices if you work remotely. Sometimes I find myself in front of an Internet browser, but nowhere near an application that I can use to check my E-mail. Well, now with Hotmail I can check all my E-mail accounts or just spend a little time online reading my news. Excite (http://www.excite.com) also offers free Web-based E-mail accounts.

PushUser

http://www.zdnet.com/products/pushuser.html

For a push technology guide, complete with tips, tricks and reviews, visit ZDNet's guide.

Webcasting—A Broader Term

As I mentioned at the beginning of this section, the term Webcasting is relatively new. I believe it may be an attempt to reposition and replace the term "push technology" since the concept of push technology has had mixed reviews among the Internet community (such as taking up too much bandwidth and diminishing system resources to a trickle).

Webcasting encompasses more than push technology. It is also referred to an online event that utilizes streaming audio and video, such as a press conference to make an earnings announcement. I have also seen this term to describe a live or pre-recorded feed of conferences and social events. If you would like to take a look at some of the latest Webcasts visit Broadcast.com (formerly AudioNet) at http://www.broadcast.com.

In addition to streaming audio and video, Webcasters have been busy evolving into new areas. For instance, BackWeb Headliner is working with companies such as McAfee (Network Associates) to send software updates to your PC, and most Webcasters are aggressively tackling the intranet market to push company news to employee desktops.

Using Plug-ins for Maximum Internet Functionality

Grant it, Web browsers alone are still amazing and awesome resources. But why not make the Internet experiences even better? If you have access to a computer and connection that can handle streaming audio and video, I strongly recommend Real Network's RealPlayer (formerly named RealAudio and RealVideo). Once you have the program installed visit the directory resources listed in Chapter 12 and you will get a feeling for what Internet plug-ins can do for you. Plug-ins are browser add-ons that are downloaded and installed onto your computer. Basically, plug-ins give your browser greater functionality.

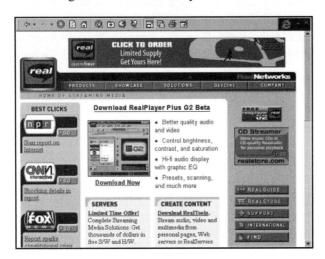

RealNetworks RealPlayer

http://www.real.com/

RealNetworks (formerly Progressive Networks) is the company that created the RealPlayer streaming audio and video application. It is free to download at the site. The RealPlayer is a combination of the RealAudio application with added streaming video technology. The latest RealNetworks news is at the home page, as well as a drop down menu to help you navigate the site. The company is also responsible for the Daily Briefing http://www.dailybriefing.com/ and Timecast http://www.timecast.com/ sites to get the most from your RealPlayer.

RealPlayer is only one plug-in example. There are also plug-ins that let you chat online (i.e., ICQ), view archived voluminous documents (i.e., Acrobat Reader), and conduct online videoconferences (i.e., Cu-SeeMe). This section will introduce you to the best plug-ins online (and they are free!).

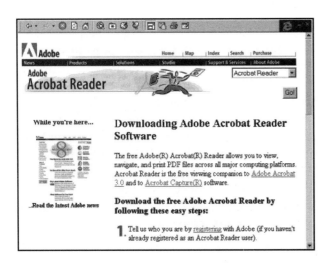

Adobe Acrobat Reader

http://www.adobe.com/prodindex/acrobat/readstep.html

If you want to read any files that are presented in the Portable Document Format (PDF), then you will need to install the Adobe Acrobat Reader. At the bottom of the page, click on the Adobe PDF link for more information about the format, how the format is changing the publishing industry and links to sites using PDF in a substantial way.

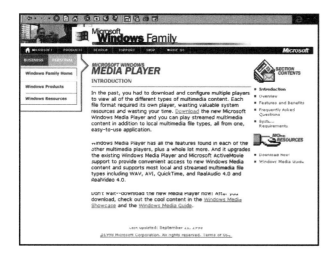

Windows Media Player

http://www.microsoft.com/windows/mediaplayer/

With the Microsoft Windows Media Player, you can play streamed multimedia content in addition to local multimedia files. Windows Media Player supports most multimedia file types including WAV, AVI, QuickTime, and RealAudio 4.0 and RealVideo 4.0. You shouldn't see the Microsoft Net Show program anymore as it has fully integrated the Net Show functionality into its Media Player.

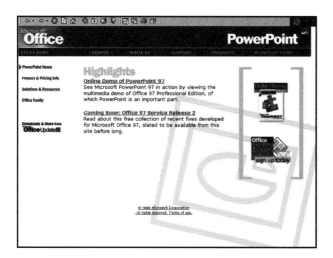

Power Point—Animation Player

http://officeupdate.microsoft.com/welcome/powerpoint.htm

The Animation Publisher provides interactivity to your Power Point presentations as they can be converted to slide show Web pages. Viewers use the Animation Player to guide them through the presentation. Publisher is a free Power Point add-in and the Player is a free Internet extension. Other interactivity features to the Publisher include incorporating RealAudio and animation files.

Cornell Video Conference (Cu-SeeMe)

ftp://gated.cornell.edu/pub/video/html/Welcome.html

Cu-SeeMe is a free videoconferencing program under copyright of Cornell University and its collaborators. With Cu-SeeMe, as the Web site states, "you can videoconference with another site located anywhere in the world. By using reflector software, multiple parties at different locations can participate in a Cu-SeeMe conference, each from his or her own desktop computer."

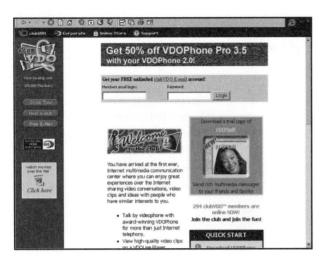

VDOLive Player

http://www.vdo.net/

The VDOLive Player is a free viewer that allows you to see all VDO content. The content can be accessed either live or on-demand. VDO also provides other plug-in products such as VDOPhone which is compatible with Microsoft's Net Meeting and VDO Mail, a program that allows you to send audio and/or video E-mail.

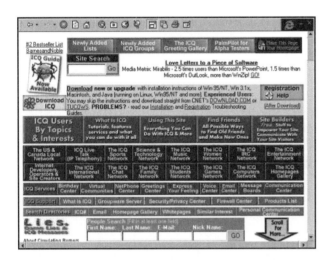

Mirabilis—I Seek You (ICQ)

http://www.icq.com/

ICQ is one of the most, if not the most, popular online chat program on the Internet. You can download it for free. The Web site has tons of resources about learning how to fully utilize ICQ. You can build an online chat community for your Web site if you like!

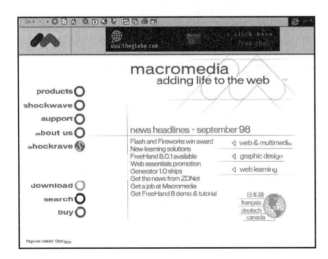

Macromedia Shockwave

http://www.macromedia.com/

Shockwave is a highly versatile program and many techno-savvy programmers have been playing around with it to display the latest animation effects at their Web sites. You will need to have this plug-in installed to visit sites using the Shockwave technology. Installing it in the first place is somewhat of a drag, since you don't want to be bothered with software installations when you just plan to visit a site. However, not to worry, once the Shockwave program is installed, the rendering of "Shockwaved" pages is simple.

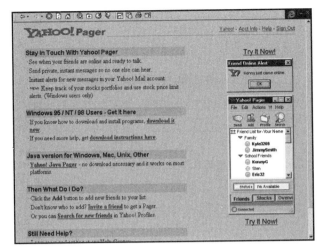

Yahoo! Buddy Pager

http://pager.yahoo.com/

Along the same premise of ICQ, the Yahoo! Buddy Pager will alert you when your colleagues are online and available to chat. Although ICQ has better functionality and more display status options (i.e., with ICQ you can display, available, away, chat later, etc.), the Yahoo! Buddy Pager may be better for newbies.

An ICQ Primer

What Is ICQ and Why Is Everyone Talking About It?

ICQ ("I Seek You") is a program that lets you find and chat with your clients and colleagues online in real time. You can create a contact list containing only people you want to hear from. You can send them messages, chat with them, send files, and more. In the advanced setting, you can designate whether you are available or not available to chat, among other chat "statuses."

How Do You Use ICQ?   According to ICQ's provider, Mirabilis, LTD (purchased by AOL not too long ago), they have a method to get you rolling with ICQ in twenty-six seconds:

- Download and install the ICQ Installation file.
- Register yourself using the registration wizard.
- Add your friends and associates using the Add Contacts Wizard. These are the people you want to be notified about.
- Right-click on a user's name in the Contact List in order to initiate (send) events (like Chat, File transfer, etc.).
- When an event arrives, a flashing icon appears near the user who has sent it. Double click on it to accept.
- General functions (like adding a new friend, preferences, etc.) can be done from the ICQ menu, by clicking the ICQ button.

When I downloaded the program, it took me a little longer than twenty-six seconds to set up my ICQ program. It's a very slick program and a nice addition for those who need to economically communicate long distance.

ICQ Resources

ICQ SITE GUIDE

http://www.icq.com/webguide.html

The ICQ Site Guide is a comprehensive look at what features ICQ has to offer, a detailed tutorial, FAQs, and launching points to other ICQ resources. This is a great place to start and to get your feet wet.

PEOPLESPACE DIRECTORY

http://www.icq.com/people/

The ICQ PeopleSpace directory is a search engine of the 11 million plus ICQ members. Some user profiles are more detailed than others. Use this directory to track down long-lost colleagues and acquaintances. The site includes a connection interface so you contact them via ICQ directly from the site.

THE YEAR 2000 AND BEYOND

Introduction

The Internet evolves extremely fast. The hot trends of today could be the trends that take effect and shape the future of the Internet, or they could be the latest fad. Nevertheless, a general awareness of the latest Internet trends should be of interest to you. This chapter addresses how certain issues such as demographic shifts, domain registration implications, and privacy issues are forming the Internet today, for the year 2000 and beyond.

The Shift of Web Demographics

In a recent survey, some 77 million Americans, or 30 percent of the population, are now online. Not only has the number of people increased substantially over the last couple years, but also the online population is nearing the identical statistical makeup of the United States (54 percent men and 46 percent women—*source:* Nua Internet Surveys). Since the inception of the Internet, men have dominated cyberspace; however, women are flocking to the Internet in droves, nearly constituting half of online users.

What does the gender shift indicate? Studies have shown that women use the Internet differently from men, and women are shifting and changing the way the Web works. For instance, women are considered more task-oriented when using the Internet. Women integrate the Internet into their lifestyles to accomplish goals such as online shopping. Currently, women make 70 percent of online purchases.

However, demographic studies of Internet users have not been around that long. Expect more to be revealed about the Internet's user composition, habits, and preferences. To learn more about current Internet demographic trends, it would be wise to point you to a few survey sites instead of rattling off obsolete statistics. You will find these resources in Chapter 18.

The Future and Fate of the Domain Name

You may have heard the buzz about the handing over of the domain naming authority to multiple entities. Currently, Network Solutions, Inc. (a.k.a. InterNIC at http://www.internic.net) is responsible for the registration of the most popular domain names (TLDs), .com, .org, and .net. Many are interested in Network Solutions's future role and the fate of its current monopoly power.

Here is the latest update. On October 6, 1998, officials from the Department of Commerce's National Telecommunications and Information Administration (NTIA) and Network Solutions, Inc., have agreed to a two-year extension agreement for coordination of some domain name system functions. The current plan for the transition to a shared registration system in a phased approach begins March 31, 1999 with full implementation by June 1, 1999.

The government plans to hand over control to a U.S.-based nonprofit company. The exact details have not been fleshed out yet. However, according to the U.S. plan for reforming the Internet's name and address system, the U.S. government has asked the private sector to set up the new entity which will "represent the interests of industry and consumers across the world." Interactive discussions have taken place between the government and the Internet community as to how this new organization should be operated.

Another change on the domain name front is the formation of Geneva-based Council of Registrants (CORE), a group of eighty-seven registrars in twenty-three countries established to register new TLDs. The organization had planned to register seven TLDs of .firm, .shop, .web, .arts, .rec, .info, and .nom. However, CORE put its new TLD launch on hold when the U.S. government issued its plan in February 1998. It is expected that additional TLDs will be available in the future, however, there are not firm dates when the new names will be available for registration.

ISP Consolidation

Over the last three years the number of Internet Service Providers (ISPs) has exploded. This List (http://www.thelist.com), which is the definitive count of the number of ISPs online, has the current count at 6,400. So far the Internet boom has been able to sustain this type of growth, though competition increases and ISPs look for ways to differentiate themselves.

Once a very disorganized business model, the ISP business has given way to more structure, and businesses are adequately demanding more service and performance from their providers. The ISP market is quickly becoming a commodity service, and price is becoming one of the few factors the ISPs can compete on. Another way ISPs can differentiate themselves is through stronger customer support, better user interfaces, and faster connections.

Faced with these challenges, ISPs are starting to look at consolidation as a way to quickly gain these competitive advantages. In addition, ISPs are looking for ways to obtain greater efficiencies which traditionally lead to economies of scale-type consolidations. Market watchers believe the number of ISPs will continue to increase in the niche, rural and specialized provider arenas. However, as a whole, market consolidation is inevitable. No one carrier appears to have a dominant stronghold on the ISP market.

So how do you determine if your ISP will survive consolidation or if you are headed toward possibly a transition to a new ISP? Here are some things to look out for:

- High reliability and low disappointment level for connection speed and technical "glitches."
- Value-added services, such as personal push, Virtual Private Networks, and the potential to reserve network space on an as-needed basis.
- High customer support for not only 24/7, but has responsive good track record for fixing your problems.

Barriers to Entry—Portal Combat

ISPs aren't the only business battling over your attention. Web portals are working to capture your eyes and pocketbooks. First of all, what is a Web portal? If you are new to this term, do not fear—you aren't too far behind. The term was coined to describe a heavily trafficked Web site which is used as a starting point to find information on the Internet.

Most of the popular search engines such as Yahoo!, Excite, and AltaVista are considered all-purpose Web portals. In addition, AOL, GeoCities, and other virtual communities fit the bill as well. Web portal sites are free and generally have banner advertising and commission-based transaction revenue streams.

In addition to the all-purpose Web portals, trends are indicating the emergence of what is being called as Category Portals. These are niche-based directories that Internet users visit first when conducting research or finding information on a given subject matter. The audience of a Category Portal is more targeted than mega-portals such as Yahoo! Although a single category does not command as much traffic, niche markets can get more for advertising due to its targeted and focused market segment. In months to come, look for increasingly intense competition from all portals as they each try to carve out a share of the portal market.

E-commerce Issues

WebTrust

WebTrust was conceived in an effort to provide Internet consumers with an electronic version of the "Good Housekeeping Seal of Approval" to tell consumers a Web site is legitimate and conducts honest business. WebTrust, like the Internet, involved international participation. It is a joint effort between the AICPA and the Canadian Institute of Chartered Accountants (CICA). Both organizations have entered into an agreement with VeriSign to provide the secure seal component of the program. The WebTrust program is designed to adhere to President Clinton's objectives outlined in "A Framework for Global Electronic Commerce." You can find this report at http://www.iitf.nist.gov/eleccomm/ecomm.htm.

WebTrust engagements fall under the AICPA statement on attestation standards. If the Web site passes inspection, an "independent accountants' report" is issued and a tamper-proof seal is added to the Web site. Furthermore, as part of the audit process, the site is required to include its online business practices on the site.

The WebTrust examination focuses around three broad areas: business practice disclosures, transaction integrity, and information protection. For a complete explanation of WebTrust, visit the AICPA's WebTrust site (http://www.aicpa.org/WebTrust/index.htm) and download the 35-page document entitled, "WebTrust Principles and Criteria for Business-to-Consumer Commerce." In the document you will find detailed criteria lists, practitioner's report examples and a self-assessment questionnaire.

Taxation on the Internet

The House and Senate have recently approved their own versions of the Internet Freedom Act (S. 442 and H.R. 4105). The Internet Freedom Act places a moratorium on new Internet taxes, which is viewed as essential to help spur the growth of electronic commerce. The act also directs the President to pursue international trade agreements to help stave off the arbitrary taxation of E-commerce. Although the two acts differ in the length of the moratorium as well as a few other aspects, both the House and the Senate are in agreement over the need to give the Internet some time to develop innovative approaches to E-commerce.

However, whether it is 2001 or later, eventually there will be some forms of taxation mechanisms placed on Internet transactions. Many argue existing taxing authorities can handle the same types of transactions in the virtual world than in the physical world. It appears the biggest challenge on the horizon is how to harness a system for how international Internet transactions should be treated. The bill calls for the creation of a commission to help study issues such as these and will report its findings to Congress.

If you would like more information about the Internet Tax Freedom bill, visit the site that provides information on the proposed legislation by Rep. Christopher Cox (R.—Calif.) and Sen. Ron Wyden (D.—Ore.) at http://www.house.gov/chriscox/.

Privacy Issues

Users Fear the Net

A survey conducted in April 1998 by Louis Harris & Associates found that 61 percent said they "have never seen a privacy policy posted on a Web site" and a whopping 81 percent said they were "concerned about their privacy when surfing the web." Although I believe these survey findings would show some improvements in some respects, many are still very uneasy.

Take myself for example. I use the Internet constantly, divulge personal information, and make online purchases. Just because I do all these things doesn't mean I'm not concerned. I'm quite aware of the data miners trying to turn a profit off my personal information. Just think of all the people that won't even get online for fear of having their identities stolen and their information sold.

It is a fact the Internet industry is in a nascent stage and the infrastructure of Internet-related policies and self-regulation are still taking form. Having the opportunity to influence this process and set the ground rules in which privacy policies on the Internet should be adhered to can be a powerful position. In the next section I will discuss some of the players working in this area, jockeying into position to be "the one" to qualm the fears of Internet consumers.

The Privacy Players

- Online Privacy Alliance (http://www.privacyalliance.org/) is a 50-member alliance created to self-regulate and rehabilitate the online commerce image and to head off the possibility of Internet legislation and government intervention.

- Center for Democracy and Technology (http://www.cdt.org/) recently advised consumers on protecting Web privacy and has provided recommendations in its *Guide to Online Privacy*.

- Federal Trade Commission (http://www.ftc.gov/) recently issued a very threatening report on consumer online privacy.

- U.S. Department of Commerce (http://www.doc.gov/) recently sponsored a privacy conference to address the Internet privacy crisis.

- Better Business Bureau (http://www.bbb.org/) has an online privacy initiative, which has recently been endorsed by several companies behind the Online Privacy Alliance.

- TRUSTe (http://www.truste.org/) focuses on privacy issues surrounding data collection on the Internet. Its branded logo, or trustmark, alerts users to what will happen to their personal information from a privacy standpoint.

- WebTrust (http://www.aicpa.org/) is a joint venture between AICPA and the Canadian Institute of Chartered Accountants and is working on a "Good Housekeeping" seal of Web site approval to build consumer's confidence in Web-based purchases. See the E-commerce issues section of this chapter for further WebTrust information.

➡ **Quick Note: Additional Resources**

For more information, check out the book *CPA's Guide to Web Commerce* by John Graves, published by Kent Information (http://www.kentis.com/).

The Next Generation of Fax Technology

Internet Faxing—What Is It?

Internet faxing is an alternative to both fax machines and fax modems. It is comprised of a network of fax servers and Internet faxing software. Together, these components create an E-mail-to-fax conversion. Internet faxing uses TCP/IP to transmit the information (the Internet's communication protocol). To Internet fax you would send a file by E-mail. This E-mail file attachment would be received by a nearby fax server (computer set up to process faxes) and in turn routed to a fax server near the recipient. Once the E-mail is routed to the receiving fax server, it is converted into analog form and is sent to your intended recipient via a local phone call. Whew—that was a mouthful!

What Does This Mean for Future Business?

What this mainly means for business is that the bottom line looks better. Companies will be able to avoid paying long-distance faxing charges. However, for most faxing, the overall savings may be down the road a year or two. Currently, the Internet fax companies are charging more per minute than traditional long-distance telephone carriers. However, just like the traditional fax machine, as this becomes the accepted method of faxing, prices will drop dramatically. Check out below the companies that are currently paving the way with their E-mail-to-fax software and get ready to jump when business buys into this new technology.

Other cost savings will be seen by the disappearance of the fax machine, fax paper, and routine maintenance. Furthermore, the overall resolution of the Internet fax is much better than the traditional fax machine's crude dpi (translation = resolution) and conversion mechanisms.

> ➡ **Quick Note: Companies in the Internet Faxing Business**
>
> Faxaway—http://www.faxaway.com
> NetCentric—http://www.netcentric.com
> The Phone Company—http://www.tpc.int

The Year 2000 Issue

Discussion, spin, and buzz abound about the year 2000 and the upcoming problems that this special year will ring in. Time is drawing near, and the more you know about 2000, the better off you and your clients will be. Accountants are one of the largest groups that will be impacted by the new millenium. So take a look at these resources, make sure your "Year 2000" house is clean, and then visit some of the lighter resources I've highlighted for planning your New Year's Eve party.

Are You Millennium Ready?

According to many of the Year 2000 (Y2K) Web sites that have sprouted up in the last year or so, the clock is ticking and there isn't much time left to make your computer system millennium ready. The following sections are designed to guide you through the basics of determining if your system can handle the date changeover. If you use these simple guidelines and some publicly available software, a quick assessment can be performed. If your computer system is fine, you are home free. If your computer system isn't ready for Y2K, you will need to access the additional ammunition resources listed at the end of this section to address specific issues.

Determine Your Y2K Readiness

The Millennium Bug could be in any of three areas of your computer: software applications, operating system or BIOS, the initial instruction set of computers operation. When the computer is first turned on, it uses its BIOS (Basic Input/Output System) to check the system's real-time clock (RTC). If the RTC is on the fritz (à la Y2K), you are in trouble, since the operating system also uses the RTC information.

- Hardware compliance: some Pentiums, 486s and their predecessors are at risk for Y2K non-compliance. To determine your status, download the YMARK2000 program from the National Software Testing Laboratories (http://www.nstl.com/). YMARK2000 temporarily simulates the Year 2000 and then reports how your computer was able to handle the date changeover. Apple Macintosh users are able to rejoice as Macs have been Y2K ready since the Mac's inception. Sarcastic sidebar: "Be careful, the Mac will encounter its date problem in the year 29940!"

- Operating system compliance: if you are using Windows 3.x or early versions of Windows 95, you may need to upgrade your operating system.

- Software compliance: start contacting your various software vendors. A good starting point is the program manufacturer's Web site, as most have Y2K information online. The Y2K compatibility success or failure will vary from program to program and you may have to consider replacing some of your software programs to keep your dates in order.

Make sure your clients have conducted an assessment of all systems including systems that feed into the accounting system. Especially important are custom programs which may have not considered Year 2000 issues.

Users with software that isn't Year 2000 compliant have three choices: repair, replace, or outsource. These Y2K Web sites will give you some information you can pass on to your clients as well as potentially provide you with consulting service opportunities.

Other Year 2000 Issues

Y2K Job Bank Open for Business Recently the government announced the opening of a Year 2000 Job Bank that is supported by the U.S. Department of Labor (http://it.jobsearch.org/). America's Job Bank draws together IT/Y2K jobs and resumés. Employers are using the bank to find talent to meet the year 2000 challenge.

The Check Run   Make sure you and your clients order your new checks early. It has been noted there will be a huge rush on ordering of new checks since all checks that show "20" instead of "19" printed on the date line will need to be replaced.

Good Samaritan Legislation   President Clinton has proposed laws calling for companies to share their Y2K plans. Namely, the legislation is referred to as the Good Samaritan legislation, where companies would be protected from overall liability for Y2K issues if they revealed and shared their solutions with others.

On the Lighter Side   Visit Möet & Chandon's site at http://www.champagne.com/ to help prepare for the impending shortage of bubbly. Here you will also find ideas and resolutions for your Millennium celebration. Everything2000.com is another must-visit site.

Will There Be an Internet 2?

You may have heard some buzz in the media about the next Internet, specifically, Internet2. To shed some light on the subject, Internet2 is an actual project, however, it initially plans to benefit the university community. Academia heavily depended on NSFnet, administered by the National Science Foundation, to conduct its research. However, when the system was privatized and commercialized, frequent congestion resulted in ineffective research.

Enter Internet2. The Internet2 project is designed to develop the next generation of applications and resources for the university community. Furthermore, the government is getting involved in Internet2 through its adoption of Internet2 goals as part of the White House's Next Generation Internet (NGI) Initiative. Just as the Internet has evolved to all users, the plans are eventually for all Internet users to benefit from both Internet2 and the NGI. With goals to communicate at speeds one thousand times faster than today, once this technology is incorporated into the commercial Internet environment, the functionality of the Internet will drastically change again.

SECTION 2

GETTING CONNECTED AND USING THE WEB

Chapter 6

CONNECTING TO THE INTERNET

Introduction

How do you know you are making the right connection decision? Are you spending the right amount of money? Choosing the right online companies? Planning for future expansion? Although no decision is foolproof, there are steps you can take to help minimize Internet connection issues. This chapter will go over basic Internet connections, hardware considerations, and how to choose the right Internet provider.

Finding the Right Internet Connection for You

This section covers some of the more popular ways to connect to the Internet. Specifically, you can connect via an Online Service Provider (OSP), Internet Service Provider (ISP), or a dial-in connection from your telephone provider. Alternatively, if you decide to have a substantial presence on the Internet, maybe you will start out with an ISP and move to a Web host environment or on to your server. This section will give you some general insights to the various ways you can connect to the Internet and help you decide which one is right for you.

Online Service Provider

When you choose an Online Service Provider (OSP), you decide to hitch up with subscription-based companies such as AOL, Microsoft's MSN, and CompuServe. Both AOL and CompuServe were around before the advent of the Web, and have nicely integrated their online services with resources available on the Internet.

An OSP is a great way to start out if you are new to the Internet. I signed up for AOL in January 1994 and was amazed with the amount of information available within the AOL network. It has truly become a virtual community. However, as the Web became available, I became more Internet savvy and decided I didn't need as much hand-holding, so I switched to an Internet Service Provider (ISP).

Internet Service Provider

An Internet Service Provider (ISP) provides a dial-up connection to the Internet. For the monthly fee, an ISP also includes other services and features such as space on its server, E-mail accounts, special software, and domain name registration services. ISPs can have either regional or national access to the Internet. If you travel a lot, you may want to consider a connection with an ISP with multiple dial-up connections.

For me, leaving AOL and signing up with an ISP was a good move. Just about the time I cancelled my AOL account, I started checking into the possibilities of getting my own domain name and making my Web presence official. Although AOL had software programs and Web site assistance, I was unable to have my own domain name.

ISPs usually give you more flexibility on pricing than OSPs. ISP pricing menus are generally broken down based on the services and features you would like, so you have the option to design the right package for you and not overpay for features you are not interested in. Although the "AOL comparable" plan is generally priced the same as AOL, some of the ISP benefits you may find are personalized customer service, no flashing ads upon sign-in and less busy signals.

Web Host with Separate Dial-up Connection

If you decide to or are thinking about adding more features and interactivity to your new or existing Web site, you may want to consider a Web host. Generally a Web host does not provide you with a dial-up connection so you will have to get a separate account for the actual dial-up. If your telephone carrier does not provide reasonable dial-up rates, check out your local ISPs. Since you will not need server space at the ISP (your site will be on your Web host's server), you may be able to negotiate a price break.

So you may ask: What is the benefit of using a Web host when I'll need a separate dial-up? The primary service a Web host provides is hosting other Web sites. An ISP is primarily concerned about providing an Internet connection; providing guidance and resources to your Web site efforts come secondary. Additionally, if you plan to have discussion forums or online chat, Web hosts are best prepared to serve you.

Own Server with Dial-up Connection

This option is by far the most costly, time consuming, and potentially risky. If you are considering the purchase of your own Web server, you need to perform your research thoroughly before making the various necessary decisions. I don't plan to take you through the intricacies involved in purchasing and setting up your own Web server; the subject matter warrants its own book.

However, I will provide a few resources for you to check out to help you with your research. You will find these resources in Chapter 20, Hit the Efficient Frontier with an Intranet. Even though the chapter primarily addresses intranets, you will also find information about suggested Internet server configurations and additional resources.

Before I send you off to Chapter 20, I would like to mention one Internet server you may want to check out Microsoft's Internet Information Server 4.0, or IIS 4.0. IIS is bundled with the Windows NT 4.0 Options Pack that is free and available via download. IIS is a suite of applications (FTP server, mail and news servers, among others) plus features for building and administrating your Web site. In addition to its own features, IIS 4.0 offers a layering build-upon approach which allows you to easily integrate other Microsoft servers such as SiteServer and Commerce Server.

Hardware Connections—New Choices for Access

There are a few new hardware choices when connecting to the Internet. In order to keep this book as current and forward thinking as possible, I have included only the potential mass-market new technology alternatives. To get details on the latest access technologies visit "The Speed of . . ." resource guide at Whatis.com.

56 Kbps Modem

What It Delivers
- 52 Kbps downstream
- 33 Kbps upstream

What It Costs
- Modem hardware: $49 to $89
- Standard ISP rates, no additional charges

Worth Noting
- All ISPs are upgrading to 56 Kbps technology.
- K56flex and x2 standards merge in 1998.
- 2.5 million users beginning of 1998.
- The 56 Kbps modem is not the fastest way to access the Internet, however, it will be a standard for a little while longer. Dedicated or POTS (Plain Old Telephone Service) service.

ADSL

What It Delivers
- 1.5 Mbps downstream
- 128 Kbps upstream

What It Costs
- Modem hardware: $199 to $299
- $40 plus ISP rates, installation $200 (approx.)

Worth Noting

- Technology is launching end of 1998 by RBOCs and GTE.
- Access is limited by distance from telco central office.
- There are five thousand users as of January 1998.

Cable Modem

What It Delivers

- 1 to 2 Mbps upstream and downstream

What It Costs

- Modem hardware: either included in service or $199 to $249
- $35 to $50, installation $50 (often waived)

Worth Noting

- Launched in late 1996, current players are @Home, MediaOne, Express/Road Runner.
- 66 percent of all cable systems will be ready for cable modem technology by 2000.
- There are 110,000 users as of January 1998.

How to Connect to the Internet Now!

If you aren't connected now, you very well can't go to any of the Web sites I have listed at the end of this chapter. Therefore, I am including the contact information for some of the main OSPs and ISPs. I have limited this list to companies that have reputations for getting you online really quickly and have been reviewed positively in computer magazines. This list is not an endorsement.

In order to make the right decision, you need to know what *you* need from your online provider. If you need some help, take a look at the next section for suggested interview questions. Also, for hometown service and patronage, don't forget to interview regional ISPs. Although service varies widely among regional ISPs, some are excellent and many are working on a national presence.

America Online

- http://www.aol.com/
- 1-800-827-6364
- $21.95/month for unlimited access
- Five hundred POPs across the country
- 10MB of Web space
- Fifty free hours for new users

AT&T WorldNet

- http://www.att.net/
- 1-800-967-5363
- $19.95/month for 150 hours
- Access numbers in all fifty states
- 5MB of Web space
- Free month for new users

Concentric Network

- http://www.concentric.com/
- 1-800-939-4262
- $19.95/month for unlimited access
- Access to over three thousand U.S. cities
- 5MB of Web space
- thirty-day free trial

Earthlink Network

- http://www.earthlink.net/
- 1-800-395-8425
- $19.95/month for unlimited access
- More than 1,200 local dial-up numbers
- 6MB of Web space
- Refer a friend to this service and get a free month

MindSpring Enterprises

- http://www.mindspring.com/
- 1-800-719-4600
- Range of dial-up accounts from $6.95 to $26.95
- More than 250 POPs
- 5MB of Web space

Netcom

- http://www.netcom.com/
- 1-800-638-2661
- $19.95/month for unlimited hours
- More than three hundred POPs nationwide
- 1MB of Web space

How to Choose an ISP

Support, Support, and Support

If you pick an ISP that is lacking in technical support, you are in for a very frustrating experience. It's true that it is hard to identify if a potential ISP will have good technical support until you actually have your account set up. However, look for the following to help pinpoint a good tech-support operation:

- Support available 24/7.
- Provides a local or 800 number available to take calls.
- Actively pursues E-mail requests.
- Assigns a technical support representative to your account.
- Provides references of satisfied customers.
- Has a very informative and well-designed support area at ISP site, including FAQs and discussion forum.

Web Hosting Features

Allocated Server Space   Many ISPs give you between 2MB and 5MB of space for a Web site, which is usually plenty. However, check to see what the additional charge is for more space if you plan to make significant Web site expansions.

Download Volume Charge   Some ISPs include a charge when a certain level of Web download activity is reached (i.e., 1GB). It is important to check out what the limit is and what the additional fee would be especially if you plan to have a significant amount of traffic at your Web site. Usually the ISP will give you some guidelines regarding what size of a Web site would exceed its established limit.

Pay close attention to this potential charge if you plan to host any large files. Significant files that could give you trouble in this area are application files distributed via FTP, large PDF documents or streaming audio/video. Some ISPs offer RealAudio for an extra fee, however, they may not include the download activity limits as part of the RealAudio charge. The files are very large and you could easily approach your limit.

Front Page Support   If you use Microsoft's Web publishing program, Front Page, you need to make sure the ISP supports Front Page Extensions. When I was considering a switch last, many ISPs did not support Front Page and I decided to go with a Web host instead to ensure I had the best Front Page support.

E-mail   Most ISPs include at least one POP E-mail account. If you need more than one, ask about additional charges and find out if you will be able to add additional accounts later. In addition, inquire about its policy on spam and find out if they use spam filters to minimize junk E-mail.

➡ **Quick Note: The ISP Interview Checklist**

Ten Key Questions for Picking an ISP

1. Does the ISP offer a variety of line types and speeds that fit your current needs, and can its service evolve to meet your future needs?
2. Where are your offices in respect to an ISP's peering point location? How close you are to a peering point will affect the performance of your Internet access.
3. Will the ISP register your domain name with InterNIC and coordinate the setup of telco lines?
4. Do they provide service contracts with guaranteed up time?
5. Does the ISP provide redundancy in its Network Operations Centers?
6. Do you require an ISP that can provide connectivity services in foreign countries?
7. What type of security expertise does the ISP offer you? For instance, will they assist with the configuration of firewalls and offer VPN (Virtual Private Network) services?
8. Do you want your ISP to install and maintain the communication equipment?
9. Do you require E-commerce support or Web, FTP, and database hosting services?
10. Is the ISP you're considering in the midst of an acquisition? This could affect its future service.

Source: *ZD Internet Magazine,* December 1997.

National ISPs/OSPs Web Sites

This section includes a more comprehensive listing of the major national ISPs and OSPs than the few sites suggested earlier in this chapter. If you are looking to pick an ISP that specializes in business connection and Web host accounts (for example, IBM and GTE), this listing is probably more comprehensive than the list mentioned earlier whose sites were to help you get online in a jiffy.

AGIS—APEX GLOBAL INTERNET SERVICES
http://www.agis.net/

ANS COMMUNICATIONS
http://www.ans.net/

AMERICA ONLINE
http://www.aol.com/

AT&T WORLDNET
http://www.att.com

COMPUSERVE NETWORK SERVICES
http://www.compuserve.com/

CONCENTRIC NETWORK
http://www.concentric.net/

DIGEX
http://www.digex.net/

EARTHLINK NETWORK
http://www.earthlink.net/

EPOCH INTERNET
http://www.eni.net/

GENUITY
http://www.genuity.net/

GRIDNET INTERNATIONAL
http://www.gridnet.com/

GTE INTELLIGENT NETWORKS/BBN
http://www.bbn.com/

IBM INTERNET CONNECTION
http://www.ibm.com/

MCI INTERNET
http://www.mci.com/

MINDSPRING ENTERPRISES
http://www.mindspring.com/

MSN PREMIER
http://www.msn.com/

NETCOM
http://www.netcom.com/

PSINET
http://www.psi.com/

SAVVIS COMMUNICATIONS
http://www.savvis.com

SPRINT BUSINESS
http://www.sprintbiz.com

TCG CERFNET
http://www.cerfnet.com

UUNET TECHNOLOGIES
http://www.uu.net/

Free E-mail Resources

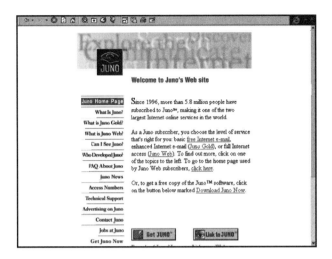

Juno

http://www.juno.com/

Juno includes a free E-mail account as well as a free connection to get your E-mail. If you don't have any type of connection to the Internet and would like to have at least access to E-mail, check these guys out. It's true that nothing is free, but in this case the price you pay is viewing only a few flickering ads when you use Juno's E-mail interface to retrieve your messages.

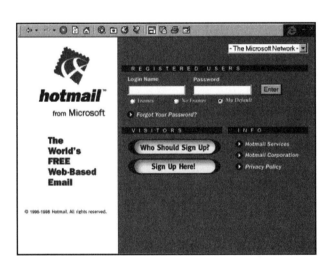

Hotmail, Yahoo! and Excite

http://www.hotmail.com/
http://www.yahoo.com/
http://www.excite.com/

I will not profile these resources separately since they are virtually the same. If you have a connection to the Internet and either did not receive an E-mail account with that connection or would like another E-mail address, visit any or all of these sites. Each site offers Web-based E-mail accounts for free. In addition, if you would like to view all your E-mail addresses in one spot on a Web page, the sites support this feature by quickly adding your other E-mail addresses to the preferences.

Chapter 7

THE INTERNET TREASURE HUNT

Introduction

Some estimates tally the number of home pages up to a whopping fifty million. That's a lot of information (as well as junk) to wade through. Since there is so much useful information on the Internet, and there is probably even more useless information (due to Web sites devoted to Mentos the Freshmaker, Play-Doh, and Pamela Anderson), it is imperative we get right down to business and find what we want in an efficient manner. This chapter will help you decide which search Web sites to use and when, show you search techniques to make research more smooth, as well as point out a few search engines you may not know about.

Different Types of Search Sites

Although most of the sites that fall under these three categories are collectively referred to as search engines, it is helpful to gain a little insight on how these sites differ. This section describes primarily how some search sites collect their information differently from others.

Search Engines

A search engine is also referred to as spiders and robots. They canvas the information superhighway, indexing what they find along the way. These search engines troll around and periodically revisit to re-index Web sites that are already their databases. AltaVista is an example of a popular search engine.

Directory

A directory is different from search engines in that people actually visit sites and decide to include or exclude the site from its directory. These sites are generally organized by topic as well as by search. You can find the ubiquitous directory format at the Yahoo! Web site.

Hybrid

These are the sites that have elements of a search engine and a directory. Substantially all of the major search sites have a hybrid mechanism of some sort. Search engines have started to add browsable directories while directories have co-branded with search engines to provide more results for visitors after they view all directory entries.

Metacrawlers Engines

Metacrawlers are also referred to as metasearch engines. Metacrawlers do not house search engine or directory services database information at their sites. Instead, these crawlers provide a quick interface and programming to be able to perform simultaneous and multiple searches of various search engines. Popular metacrawlers are MetaCrawler (http://www.metacrawler.com) and Inference Find (http://www.inference.com/infind/).

Specialty

These sites focus on a particular niche of the Web. Popular specialty or category directories range from newsgroups, mailing lists, shopping, news, financial and travel. For an example of category search engines, check out Exes at http://www.exes.com/ for travel and FinanceWise at http://www.financewise.com/ for finance.

General Search Engine Tips

Use one of the major search engines as your primary search engine. These engines are best suited for daily use and have millions of pages indexed in their databases. The top search engines are profiled in Chapter 13.

1. Read the help pages of any search engines you use. This will save you a lot of time in the long run.

2. Use nouns and objects as search keywords. Verbs and conjunctions are thrown out by most search engines.

3. Use around six to eight keywords in query. The more keywords you use, the more focused your search will be.

4. Truncate words to ensure singular and plural results. Many search engines accept the wild card symbol asterisk (*), and a search on "tax*" would provide results such as taxes, taxation, etc.

5. To include possible synonyms, use "OR" in search. Use this term if there are multiple ways your concept can be described. Otherwise try to avoid since it broadens your search results.

6. Use quotes (" ") to define phrases or concepts. Phrases restrict results to exact matches.

7. Link concepts with "AND" in the search. Both conditions must be met to produce search return.

How the Majors Stack Up

Search engines are starting to provide more than just search information. Many search engines are now being called "Web Portals" (See Chapter 5). If you want to utilize your search engine as your starting page, consider the following comparison of features offered. It is up to you to decide how important these features are to you. Excite had the best overall Web portal ranking.

	Directory Search	News/ Finance	Creating Community	Customization
AltaVista	Good	Poor	Poor	n/a
Excite	Excellent	Excellent	Excellent	Excellent
Infoseek	Good	Good	Poor	Fair
Lycos	Good	Fair	Excellent	Good
MSN Start	Fair	Good	Poor	Good
Netcenter	Good	Good	Good	Poor
Snap!	Fair	Good	Fair	Fair
Yahoo!	Excellent	Excellent	Good	Excellent

Source: *PC Magazine* (September 1998).

Obscure Search Alternatives

This section mentions a few of the more obscure search engines. Although they are somewhat hard-to-find resources, primarily since they haven't been around all that long, they are gaining speed and acceptance.

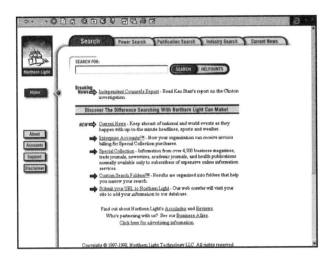

Northern Light Technology

http://www.northernlight.com/

Unlike popular search engines like Yahoo! and Excite, Northern Light gives users the option to search both the Web and the Special Collection, a custom database of 1,800 premium content sources that include Business Wire, UPI, Newsbytes, and A&G.

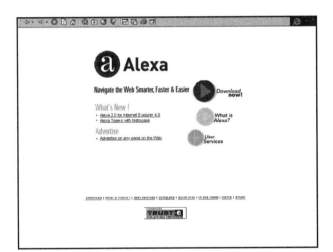

Alexa

http://www.alexa.com/

Alexa is a free Web navigation application service. It works with your browser and accompanies you as you surf, providing information along the way and suggests related sites. Alexa application interface is easy to use since it appears as a toolbar at the bottom of your browser. In addition, you can use Alexa to reach unavailable and 404-not-found pages.

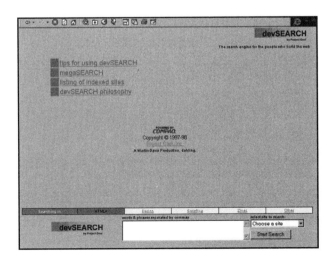

Developer's Search Engine

http://www.devsearch.com/

This is the search engine for those who built the Web. It indexes only sites that are relevant to making Web pages.

Choose the Best Search Engine for Your Purpose

You may think that every Web site looks the same. Well, think again. Depending on what you need, you may want to use different search engines. For me, it's hard to switch from my preferred search engine (which is Yahoo!, by the way), but after an unsuccessful first search, I will usually venture off to another search engine based on my needs. This section will help you determine what search engine to use based on your purpose. I opted to not include the Web site addresses here, but most are well-known addresses and they are all profiled in detail at Chapter 13.

To Browse and Search by Topic, Use:
- Yahoo!
- Lycos
- Infoseek

To Find What Is Available on the Internet, Use:
- AltaVista
- MetaCrawler
- Inference Find

To Find Images, Sounds, and File Extensions, Use:
- Yahoo!
- Lycos

To Find Web Site Summaries, Reviews, or Rankings, Use:
- Lycos
- Excite
- WebCrawler

To Find Similar Web Site Suggestions, Use:
- Excite
- Alexa

To Find Information by Industry:
- Infoseek

To Define and Highly Limit Your Search, Use:
- HotBot

Search Resources

Search Engine Watch

http://www.searchenginewatch.com/

Search Engine Watch is a great resource. I highly recommend a visit to this site to learn more about search engines and read about all the latest rankings in an aggregated format. The site also publishes a newsletter and provides premium information on a subscription basis. There is plenty here and if you are looking for a search engine lesson, you'll be at this site for a few hours. In addition, if you have been looking for the content of the Search Insider Web site (http://www.searchinsider.com/), it has been incorporated into Search Engine Watch.

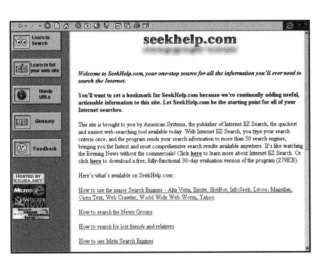

Seek Help

http://www.seekhelp.com/

Seek Help provides a tutorial guide on how to search the Internet, how to get listed on search engine sites, and a full directory of search engines. The directory is indexed by search engine type and by function, such as how to search for special category search engines.

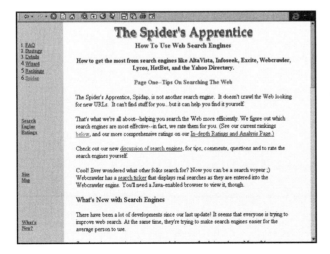

The Spider's Apprentice

http://www.monash.com/spidap.html

The Spider's Apprentice includes tips, FAQs, and how search engines work. The site also includes an in-depth look at six of the top search engines.

Chapter 8

THE WEB BROWSER FACE-OFF

Introduction

Over the past several years, the players within the Web browser market have virtually dwindled down to two winning applications, Microsoft's Internet Explorer and Netscape's Navigator. If you aren't using one of these two browsers, you won't have the functionality or power to tap into the best of the Web.

In this chapter, I will highlight some of the differences between the current browser versions in the market as well as the Beta versions that are close on the horizon. A couple of Web site resources are provided to help you stay up on the browser competition as well as help you decide which browser best fits you and your organization. At the end of the chapter, I will briefly mention a few alternatives to the "Top 2."

A Side-by-Side Browser Comparison

This section profiles the current browser technology on the market today. Over the past two years Microsoft and Netscape have slowed down in version releases. However, both appear to be on the fast track to new releases and further advancements of browser technology (see the next section on the current Betas). The latest browsers compared here are Netscape Communicator 4.0 and Internet Explorer 4.0.

In many ways, both browsers contain the same features. Therefore, in order to provide a point of comparison, instead of comparing features where both browsers possess the same characteristic (i.e., subscriptions, cascading style sheets, and dynamic HTML). Instead, I have opted to listing features in which the two browsers differ. Take a look at the table on the following page.

Next Generation Browsers—The Betas

Both Microsoft and Netscape have betas for Internet Explorer (5.0 in Beta) and Navigator (4.5 in Beta), respectively. While Internet Explorer 5.0 appears to be more incremental, Netscape is taking a more innovative approach by pioneering some new features.

Feature	Communicator 4.x	Internet Explorer 4.x
Configurable toolbars	Some	Yes
Offline browsable cache	No	Yes
Application Sharing	No	Windows 95/NT 4.0 only
Push desktop applets	No	Yes
Performance test *	637	773
Large GIF download	22 seconds	16.5 seconds
Load HTML	35.4 seconds	26.8 seconds
Remote desktop	No	Windows 95/NT 4.0 only
Ratings systems	No	RSACi, PICS
MPEG video	No	Yes
Source code available	Yes	No
Solaris, HP, Linux, OS/2, and other Unix platforms	Yes	No

Source: Clnet Browser Comparison Chart (http://www.browsers.com/)
*—performance test by CaffeineMark 3.0, higher number is better.

Microsoft Internet Explorer

Microsoft's IE 5.0   The current consensus on the release of IE 5.0 is that IE 5.0 is yet another version of incremental improvements. Most of the enhancements are considered back office improvements, revisions to make the creation of IE-based programs easier for developers.

One major change to IE 5.0 is that Microsoft has decided to ditch its Active Channels bar. Although this is only one gateway to its Active Channels, its "in your face" interface increased the chances viewers would visit the various Active Channel sites. Microsoft stated the Active Channels bar hasn't been as popular as they had hoped.

However, to date Microsoft has been fairly tight-lipped about exactly what the next version of IE will contain. Microsoft said it is not abandoning push content and are committed to its Active Channel content.

Netscape Navigator

Netscape Takes on New Territory   Netscape's latest browser, Netscape Communicator version 4.5, has some heads turning in the Internet industry. Like its earlier browser versions, this generation of the Netscape Communicator has some interesting innovations build into it. In addition, many of the new features are designed to closely integrate the Communicator with Netscape's new Internet hub, Netcenter (http://www.netcenter.com/). The Communicator feature that is getting the most attention is called Smart Browsing.

What Is Smart Browsing?   Smart Browsing features include the following:

- Keywords replace need for entire URL. Insert a simple key word, such as "travel" and you will automatically be transported to a site of interest.
- Visit a Web site and use the "What's Related" drop-down list for additional recommended Web sites.
- Integrated filtering. The NetWatch function automatically screens sites based on content ratings.

Other Features:

- Ability to store information. In tandem with the Netscape Netcenter portal, Netcenter lets you enter and store E-mail addresses and bookmarks at the Web site. The feature allows you to synchronize this information with Communicator and gives you remote access (i.e., hotel, client site) to your addresses and bookmarks across different computers.
- Smart Update is another Netcenter tie-in. Netcenter contains a database on the latest software and plug-in patches that can be accessed automatically.

Browser Resources

Stay up on the latest browser releases and features by checking in with the following browser resources:

Browsers.com

http:// www.browsers.com/

Clnet has done it again by producing another great Internet resource. Browsers.com has the latest IE and Navigator downloads at the top of its page, along with the latest reviews, news, and patches. The site also includes in-depth Survival Guides for both browsers. If you are looking for different browsers, Browsers.com covers them as well.

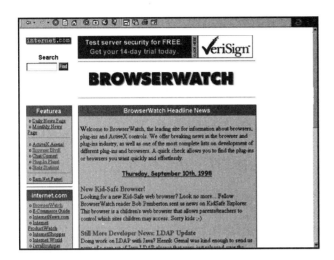

BrowserWatch

http://www.browserwatch.com/

BrowserWatch is a service of Mecklermedia Corporation's internet.com Web site. You will find many resources here including daily and monthly news, browser downloads, and plug-in information. The site even produces statistics on which browsers are visiting the BrowserWatch Web site. To access the statistics, visit Stat Station.

Alternatives to the Big 2

Why would you even consider an alternative browser to Internet Explorer and Navigator? Well, the reasons can vary. Maybe it's your pure antipathy for the Microsoft-Netscape duopoly and you are looking for a way to vent (I wouldn't mind venting once in a while). Or maybe it's more from necessity. Some wanna-be Internet users have hardware that is too old to use either of the big two browser suites. Maybe you want your full-featured browser to fit on a floppy. Whatever your reason may be, this section provides you with alternatives. None are as good as the mainstream Big 2, but that may not matter to you.

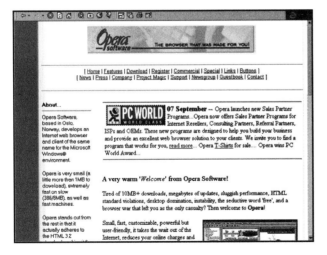

Opera

http://www.operasoftware.com/

Opera is fast, small and does just about everything it's supposed to do. Opera is faster than any browser around, including IE 4.01. The big downside is Opera has no Java support. It fits in an extremely small footprint which allows you to run it on a 386SX with only 4MB of RAM. The installation program fits on a single floppy. If you are short on resources, you may want to check out Opera.

Arachne

http://www.naf.cz/arachne/xch/

If you are really short on resources, i.e., you need a DOS-based Internet suite. Who would have thought you don't even need Windows to surf the Web? This program packs everything in, mail, FTP and a graphical-file browser all in a super fast suite. You should at least be curious by now.

Softerm Plus+

http://www.softronics.com/

This alternative browser has a strong following. The positive aspect of Softerm Plus+ is its great Telnet client, however, the browser is pretty low-powered.

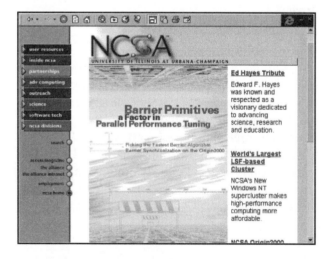

Mosaic

http://www.ncsa.uiuc.edu/

If you are nostalgic and would like to check out the granddaddy of Web browsers, check out Mosaic. Although development on Mosaic was recently halted, it boasts a few innovative features such as Web site crawler.

Chapter 9

BACK OFFICE PRODUCTIVITY

Introduction

When a firm is productive in the back office, it can have a stimulating result to the entire company. People aren't as frustrated with "things" going wrong and the well-oiled machine runs smoothly. This chapter will show you how you can utilize the Internet to improve your back office productivity.

Get a Leg Up on Software Support

There was a time when the only way you could get through to customer support was on the telephone. Wait times were (and still are) highly unreasonable, and some companies even charge a fee. Luckily, with the advent of the Web, our technical support headaches can be eased a bit. Substantially all software providers have as well as encourage interaction via E-mail. I have been very successful using E-mail to contact customer support and I have found the response times to be relatively quick for E-mail. To receive information on online support take a visit to Support Help at http://www.supporthelp.com/, which is a searchable directory of computer-related company addresses, technical support numbers, and Web sites.

Lately many hardware and software vendors are encouraging E-mail correspondence. Whether or not to use E-mail for a computer-related problem will depend on the issue itself and whether the problem you are experiencing prohibits you from using E-mail. If you decide E-mail is the way to go, check out these points to help get your solution ASAP.

Tips for a Quick Tech Response

- Before you compose your E-mail, quickly look over the Web site's FAQ pages to see if an answer to your question is posted. Maybe the FAQs will just give you more ammo because others are experiencing the same problem.

- See if the company has its knowledge base online (e.g., Microsoft and Solomon's WebTech). With Solomon's WebTech, users can plug their errors into a form for an immediate comparison to similar problems that have already been solved by Solomon technical reps.

- If you frequently work remotely or off-line, use the online Web site knowledge bases by downloading pages of interest (or E-mail the page to your E-mail account).

- Visit the company site and see if detailed telephone support information is available. For instance, the Lacerte site gives users real-time updates about the wait times for telephone support.

- Remember, the Web is open 24/7. Lots of people compose E-mail over the weekend. Try sending your request around midweek to avoid the Monday E-mail glut.

- Provide enough information so the tech rep will not have to play E-mail tag with you. For most inquiries one or two additional E-mails are not unreasonable.

Find Temporary or Permanent Employees

The Internet is a great resource for human resource information. From day one, employment agencies and temp firms have embraced the Internet as a way to connect the employee and employer. Although you may have to consider the geographical location of your prospective hire, the Internet has given talent-seeking employers another venue to announce their job offerings.

One way to find employees is to create a Careers or Job Opportunities section at your Web site. Most CPA firm Web sites include an area of this nature. Most contain general information; however, some have interactive forms for posting resumés, job announcements, and additional job-finding resources for recruits. Your firm size will more or less dictate how much you choose to invest in your careers area.

Job placement on the Internet is still catching on. It is much more popular with information technology professionals, since they are technologically savvy. You could always start out at the general career search engines such as Career Mosaic (http://www.careermosaic.com) or the Monster Board (http://www.monsterboard.com), but you may come away unfulfilled. However, there is hope for the accountant thanks to several Web sites targeted either exclusively or primarily toward placement of accounting professionals and accounting temps. You may find a more pertinent job posting (and more quickly!) at Robert Half (http://www.roberthalf.com), Accountemps (http://www.accoun-temps.com), or Accountants on Call (http://www.aocnet.com). You will find these sites classified by job function and cater to traditional accounting roles such as controller, accounts receivable, tax, and payroll.

Simplify with Web-Enabled Purchasing Applications

Purchase Order Processing (POP) modules are starting to evolve into Web-enabled interfaces in order to provide a quick and simple purchase requisitioning process. Purchasing application vendors such as Greentree Software, Inc. (http://www.

greentreesoftware.com/) are tapping into what the Web can offer with online purchasing modules.

Generally speaking, Web-enabled purchasing focuses around purchases made for internal consumption. Many companies are re-examining their purchasing function to determine ways to reduce their overall purchasing cost. The concepts around Web-enabled purchasing are still in a nascent stage, however, as vendors find proper applications for the Web, online POP modules will eventually become a standard business practice.

Spam—A Totally Useless Waste of Time and Bandwidth

Going through hordes of junk E-mail is a complete waste of time. The time it takes to hit the delete key today will multiply in the future if spam culprits continue their barrage of useless E-mails. Unsolicited Commercial E-mail (UCE) is overloading the Internet in a big way. You may feel helpless, but there are ways you can help prevent E-mail spam from clogging your in-box.

The most effective way to use your in-box is try to rid it of spam. You will have to spend some time maintaining your efforts in this cause, however, in the long run as others join in the battle, together we may be able to keep spam E-mail at a manageable level (or rid it altogether!). I will now walk you through some of the tricks of the trade to spam-proofing your in-box.

Methods to Get Rid of Spam

1. Filter your incoming E-mail. The goal here is to prohibit the E-mail from entering your in-box. This would greatly help your day-to-day activities since you won't have to even look at the junk. Most E-mail programs allow you to set up filters that will scan incoming message's domain names or other key words. For instance, James A. Cooley, an independent Internet consultant in Washington D.C., and cofounder of the Coalition Against Unsolicited Commercial E-mail (CAUCE, http://www.cauce.org), has set up a filter to automatically direct any incoming mail with "XXX" in the body directly to a folder called "Junk Mail." From time to time you should check your Junk Mail folder to make sure you had not inadvertently directed legitimate mail into your junk folder.

2. Contact your Internet service provider. You should ask your ISP exactly what it is doing to filter out spam. There is a regularly updated database called the Realtime Black Hole List that ISPs subscribe to which contains information about known spamming sites.

3. Unsubscribe from distribution. A number of unsolicited bulk-distributed E-mailers will include instructions at the bottom of their messages on how you can unsubscribe yourself from their distribution lists. Some bulk mailers actually remove you from their lists so it is worth a try. However, I have had a number of my "Remove" or "Unsubscribe" requests come back, so this doesn't always work. These E-mail lists are sold amongst bulk E-mailers so if you don't at least try to unsubscribe, you will exponentially be added to more useless distribution lists.

4. Hunt down the instigators. Forged or erroneous domain names and E-mail addresses make it difficult to track down the spammer. This is where Sam Spade (http://www.blighty.com/spam/spade.html) steps in. Sam Spade is a freeware program that determines the origins of the messages through a deciphering mechanism. The utility quickly finds the ISP that the message was sent from so you can send a copy of the spam to the original provider and any other intermediary ISPs you choose. Usually sending an E-mail to the ISP domain name with "postmaster@" or "abuse@" will get your message to the correct place. Many ISPs have policies to close the spammer's account. Working the ISP route may prove to be the most beneficial, as some people claim their spam problems became worse after directly complaining based on an E-mail address at the culprits' Web site.

5. Just delete the E-mail. If you only get one or two messages, this may be the best short-term solution. However, if most of your mail is junk, your in-box won't resemble anything good to look at. Spam is a community-wide issue for the Internet which needs community-wide action.

6. You can also try to find information about a particular spam E-mail. If the E-mail you received has a distinctive text string, try doing a search of the exact text at Dejanews (http://www.dejanews.com), the search engine for Usenet discussion groups. Oftentimes a discussion on the very E-mail you received will be going on among expert spam-trackers. You can check out what they have discovered. Replies of particular interest would be posted with the subject "help with decoding headers."

7. Be careful with newsgroup posts. If you make a post to a newsgroup, make sure you don't use your actual E-mail address in the reply header. Spammers harvest these E-mail names, and newsgroups are prime targets for this harvesting practice. Instead, use an obviously false reply header such as "NO SPAM," then include your actual E-mail address in your post for people to contact you.

8. Become a spam activist. Consider joining an anti-spam organization such as CAUCE (http://www.cauce.org) or Spam Abuse Net (http://www.junkemail.org/). CAUCE and other anti-spam groups favor a bill proposed that would extend the protection from junk-faxes to unsolicited bulk E-mail. In addition, the Federal Trade Commission (FTC) has released a report on its investigation into the problems created by UCE.

9. Report to the government. If you feel the spam is a potential fraud or misrepresentation, report it to the Federal Trade Commission. The FTC takes written requests via snail mail more seriously than E-mail, so if you feel especially strong about the spam you received, print off a copy and include a short cover letter asking the FTC to investigate potential fraud. Mail your request to: Federal Trade Commission, 6th Street and Pennsylvania Ave, NW, Washington, DC 20580.

Alternatively, you can submit your spam complaint to the FTC via an online form at the Spam Scam Page (http://www.junkcmail.org/spamscam/). The FTC accepts E-mail complaints about Unsolicited Commercial E-mail at uce@ftc.gov. Messages that seem potentially illegal can also be reported to the FBI (http://www.fbi.gov/) or the Attorney General.

Don't Flame—You May Pay

A questionable retaliation strategy is to flame back, where you send back dozens of copies of the offending E-mail. This approach has obvious drawbacks. First, you may not have found the correct E-mail address and you may be mail-bombing an innocent and unfortunate soul that had his/her E-mail address placed on a spam E-mail. Also, the drain on the ISPs will hurt other innocent individuals and companies. Furthermore, spammers usually have more sophisticated mail-bomb detecting software. Most importantly, you have just alerted spammers that you sent a mail-bomb and your E-mail address may be fodder for future attacks.

Use Web-Based Time and Expense Reporting Solutions

One of my least favorite activities is filling out paper time and expense reports. I have a funny feeling I'm in good company. However, there is some help out there to help you be more efficient when performing this bothersome although necessary task. Recently, many Web-based time and expense applications have surfaced to come to the rescue.

These Web-based applications have advantages that stand-alone applications do not provide. The basic advantage is the ability to access time and expense information online with 24-hour access from virtually any location in the world. Individuals on the go can access the status of their report from their hotels or client sites. Another advantage is its "bang for the buck factor." These programs are relatively cheap considering their interactivity features, giving many options for information status reporting and analysis. Since information is gathered and processed within seconds, the entire time and expense reporting workflow is speeded up, giving the opportunity to bill clients and reimburse employees quickly.

Companies that offer Web-based time and expense reporting products:

Vendor	Product	Web Site
ADP	e-XPENSE	http://www.adp.com/
Databasics	TimeSite	http://www.data-basics.com/
Extensity	Extensity Expense Reports	http://www.extensity.com/
Necho	NavigatER	http://www.necho.com/
Sage	TimeSheet Professional	http://www.timetracking.com/

SECTION 3

THE 1999 DIRECTORY OF ACCOUNTING AND FINANCE RESOURCES

INTERNET RESOURCES DIRECTORY BY DISCIPLINE

Accounting

AICPA

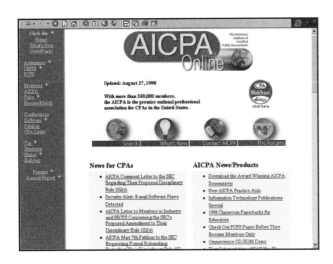

AICPA Online

http://www.aicpa.org/

The AICPA's Web site. Where do I begin? This should be one of the first Web sites you visit. You will find all kinds of resources under which you normally would have to dig out of a towering pile of literature on your desk. Spend some time at the home page itself, you'll find it is broken down into various sections. Toward the top of the page, you'll find news and items of current interest. Then a bit further down the page, you'll find the site directory which does not change and, therefore, lends itself to a consistent place you can start your research. Still feeling a little lost? Well, then check out the Web site tutorial the AICPA has provided (http://www.aicpa.org/tutor/index.htm). The tutorial starts out with "No, you don't get CPE credit for this!"

Directories

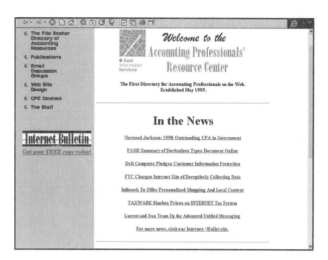

Kent Information Service

http://www.kentis.com/

On Kent Information Service's home page, you'll find current news stories for accountants. Kent hosts the Site Seeker Directory, a directory of accounting resources. In addition, it publishes the *Internet Bulletin for CPAs*. There are a few back issues archived for your viewing. They also publish *The Internet Bullet*. Its online archive version is purposefully one week behind so that our subscribers get the information first.

CPAnet

http://www.cpanet.com/

CPAnet is my very own Web site and as such, I'm a little biased. With that said, CPAnet is a Web site you can visit and use over and over again. With over one thousand indexed Web sites and the slogan, "start with us," CPAnet is a great starting point when trying to find Internet Web sites. In addition to its massive directory, CPAnet also hosts several discussion forums including client industry group forums.

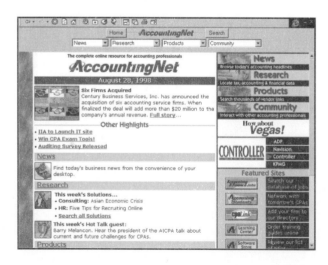

AccountingNet

http://www.accountingnet.com/

Known as a CPA's one-stop shop for marketing your Web site, AccountingNet is fully wired to get you connected, set up your Web site and market your Web site in its firm directory, CPALink. AccountingNet also has lots of directory resources including thousands of vendor links, a job search database, and research resources. Every week, AccountingNet updates its home page which includes lots of links to new content on its site.

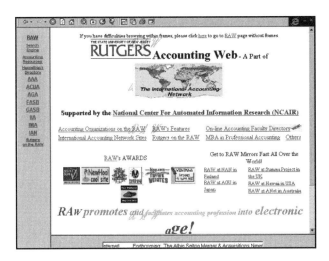

RAW—Rutgers Accounting Web

http://www.rutgers.edu/Accounting/raw.htm

One of the largest accounting sites (a.k.a. an accounting Supersite), Rutgers has information on just about every accounting topic you can think of. RAW is also home to several authoritative Web sites such as the FASB and the AGA. Although it's one of the largest, RAW is not the easiest Web site to navigate. In addition to checking out the organizations that are hosted at RAW, use this site to find some of the "harder to find resources."

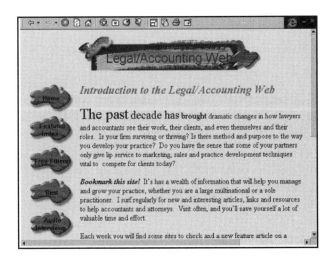

LAW—Legal/Accounting Web

http://www.users.cloud9.net/~kvivian/html/legal_
   accounting_web.html

LAW is a very interesting site I found not too long ago. Even though it's new to me, Kaye Vivian has been busy building content at her LAW Web site. Here you will find many articles and RealAudio interviews to read and ponder. In addition, she has provided several "newsletter filler" resources for you to include in your client newsletters for free! All you have to do is follow her reprint request.

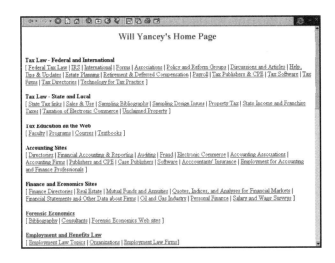

Will Yancey's Home Page

http://www.willyancey.com/

This home page is nicely organized, is easy to navigate, and does not include any graphics. This site is easy to use for these reasons, especially is you are using an older computer or are low on system resources. There are a few pages that address specific online resources for accountants such as forensic economics, employment and benefits law, evidence, and expert testimony.

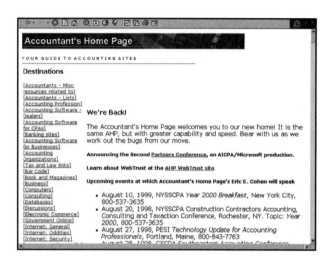

Accountant's Home Page

http://www.computercpa.com/

The Accountant's Home Page has a wealth of resources; you'll be here for a bit. It is a good place to start Web-based research. If you have an interest in learning more about E-commerce, visit its sister Web site on the topic.

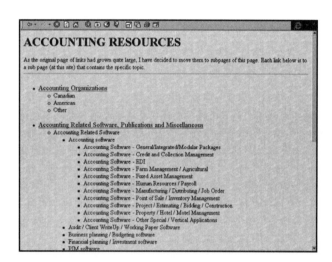

B.W. Hutton, CGA

http://icewall.vianet.on.ca/pages/hutton/account.html

This site isn't known for its good looks, but it is known for a quick place to get information on Canadian-related accounting resources. In addition, Bruce Hutton's has pried up several software Web sites to help you find those hard-to-find applications. The categories range from hotel management to point-of-sale.

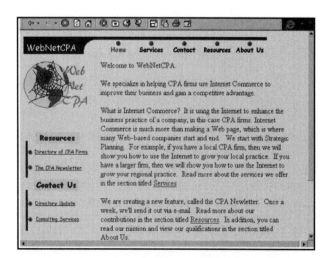

WebNet CPA

http://www.webnetcpa.com/

WebNet CPA is hosted by Dave Albrecht. He also is responsible for the excellent directory of CPA Firms at Bowling Green State University. Just recently the directory has branched out into its own domain name at http://www.cpafirms.com/. Mr. Albrecht's firms also perform consulting services and specialize in ways to best integrate Internet commerce into existing practices.

General

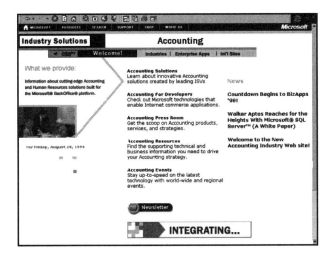

Microsoft's Industry Page—Accounting

http://microsoft.com/industry/acc/

Although this is a very Microsoft-heavy site, you may want to visit this Web site periodically to see what the software behemoth thinks accountants should know about. The site also features upcoming Microsoft events of interest. For example, just recently they hosted a free Microsoft CPA Technology Boot Camp.

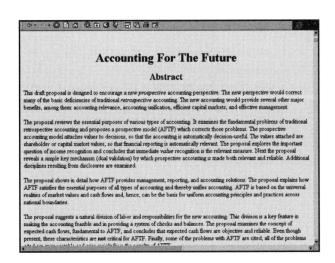

AFTF—Accounting for the Future

http://members.aol.com/heinichen1/AFTFweb.html

Proposal to value-added accounting by Humphrey H. Nash, PhD, FSA. As Mr. Nash states at his Web site, "This draft proposal is designed to encourage a new prospective accounting perspective." The AFTF proposal outlines several goals and includes an in-depth analysis of the accounting profession from Mr. Nash's perspective.

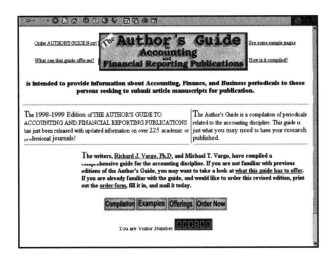

Author's Guide to Accounting Publications

http://www.lodinet.com/authguid/

The Author's Guide "is intended to provide information about Accounting, Finance, and Business periodicals to those persons seeking to submit article manuscripts for publication." You'll need to buy the guide, and it currently is not available for online download. The site does include some examples of what you will find in the Guide. Not much free stuff here, but since this is such a hard resource to find, it's worth mentioning.

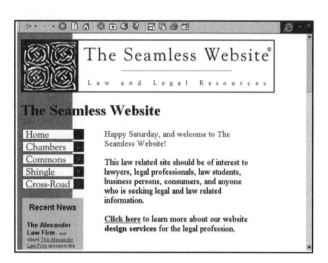

The Seamless Website—Law & Legal Resources

http://www.seamless.com/

Seamless was founded in 1994, and was the first commercial legal Web site. Seamless is linked from over five thousand other sites. Seamless is a free public service of Kevin Lee Thomason, Esq., a licensed attorney and Web designer. Seamless (through its client sites) contains thousands of pages of content and thousands of links to other legal Web sites.

The Spreadsheet Page

http://www.j-walk.com/ss/

There are resources for all of the major spreadsheet programs: Excel, Lotus, and Quattro Pro. Come here for news, FAQs, downloads, and tips. If you want to read about the history of the spreadsheet, it's here. This site even has spreadsheet jokes!

Resources from Big 5 and Large Firms

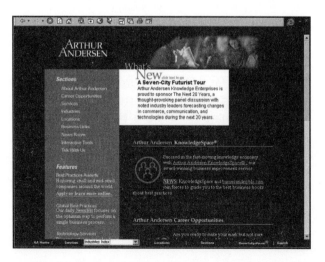

Arthur Andersen

http://www.arthurandersen.com/

The Big 5 Web sites are not just for clients. You can find some very interesting resources here you may otherwise overlook if you didn't know about the Big 5 sites. For example, the Arthur Andersen Web site has online assessment surveys which you complete online and compare your response on particular business issues with others. In addition, AA recently launched Knowledge Space, a subscription-based content resource which is organized by specific communities (i.e., business professional, CFO, internal audit).

Deloitte & Touche, LLP

http://www.dttus.com/

At the D&T site, go to News to find abstracts of its latest Web site articles, such as "Workers Comp Costs Dominate Public Sector" and "Worker Scarcity Worse by 2005." The News section also highlights new additions to its Web site. At the Publications page, you can view the *Deloitte and Touche Review* newsletter as well as various online surveys.

Ernst & Young, LLP

http://www.ey.com/

Ernst & Young, LLP has a heavy-duty download area, where you are encouraged to download more than two hundred magazines and newsletters (gratis!). The site has many interactive tools at the Web site, such as the Health Care Quiz and Retirement Contribution Analyzer. If you want a some information on how to best view the site, check out the Visitor's Center.

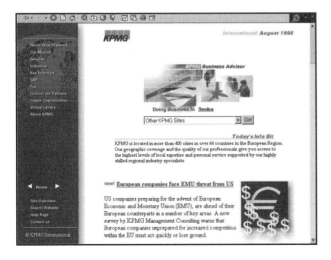

KPMG

http://www.kpmg.com/

KPMG has a nice virtual library which is searchable as well as indexed by month. If you visit this site often, you can just look at the month you haven't viewed yet. The U.S. KPMG site (http://www.us.kpmg.com/) offers even more surveys, publications, and news resources.

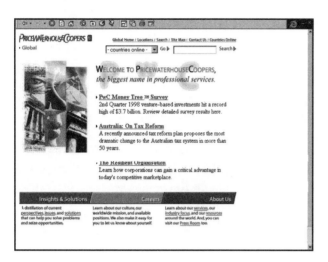

PricewaterhouseCoopers

http://www.pwcglobal.com/

The "newest" Big 5 Web site on the block is a result of the merger between Price Waterhouse and Coopers & Lybrand. You will find the best of each Web site at the combined global site. The site features management issue articles. I would check out its "1998 Software Business Practices Survey" and "Inside the Mind of the CEO."

Topic Specific Resources—Year 2000

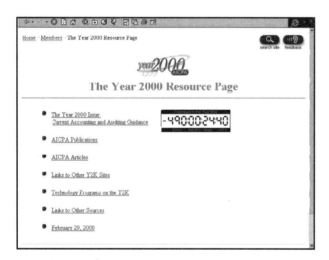

AICPA Year 2000 Resource Page

http://www.aicpa.org/members/y2000/index.htm

The AICPA's Web site for the Year 2000 is a great place to start researching Y2K issues. It has a listing of articles published by AICPA publications in addition to the Report "The Year 2000 Issue—Current Accounting and Auditing Guidance." The document is available in various formats. Links to Other Sources and Other Y2K Pages can be good starting points for additional Y2K resources.

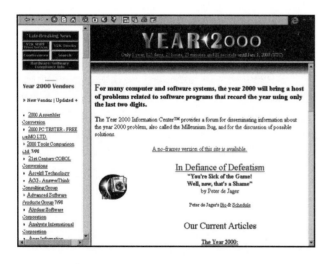

Year 2000 Computer Crisis Information Center

http://www.year2000.com/

This site should be considered the Y2K virtual community. You can be one of the 70,000 members who have signed up for its "low volume" E-mail update list. The Year 2000 Law Center focuses on "the legal, accounting and insurance aspects of the Year 2000 problem to avoid liability and maximize recovery." You can even check out the Y2K Stock Index!

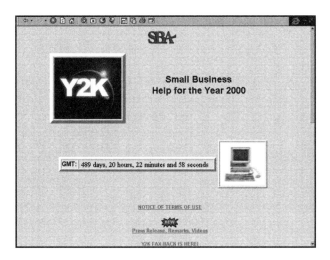

Small Business Administration: Help for the Year 2000

http://www.sba.gov/y2k/

A nice and concise resource for the Year 2000. Starting out with the definition of the Year 2000 problem published by the Office of the Chief Information Officer, visitors can find checklists and steps to take to help address Year 2000 Issues. The site also has a nice listing of other Y2K pages, in particular various SBA Y2K resources by state.

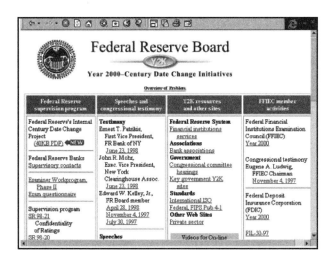

Federal Reserve Board Y2K Page

http://www.bog.frb.fed.us/y2k/

This site addresses what the Federal Reserve Board and affiliated agencies are doing about the Y2K problem. You can find both specific and general information at this site. The FRB hosts the interagency statements on this issue as well as full details on its supervision program. On the general front, the FRB has a consumer brochure and articles of general interest such as "How Computers Are Used in a Bank."

Tick, Tick, Tick Newsletter

http://www.tickticktick.com/

With a catchy domain name, the quarterly TTT Newsletter is entirely devoted to discussion of the Y2K problem. Although the newsletter is subscription-based ($40 per issue, via E-mail), the site also has a directory of regional user groups and online chat.

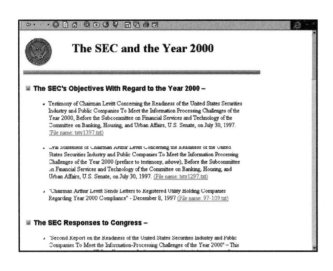

The SEC and the Year 2000

http://www.sec.gov/news/home2000.htm

The SEC has resources for Y2K preparation such as an article entitled "Questions for Investors to Ask About the Year 2000," as well as SEC Required Disclosures, Market Regulation and the SEC's Y2K Objectives.

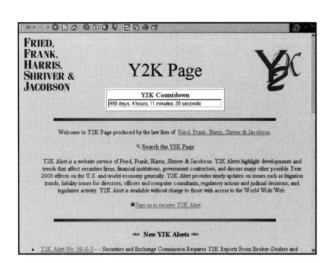

Fried Frank Y2K Page

http://www.ffhsj.com/y2k/y2kmain.htm

The firm that hosts this page has Y2K Alerts available via E-mail or online. The Alerts are made a couple times a month. A Year 2000 Compliance Checklist is also available. The site has a nice list of financial institution-oriented Y2K links.

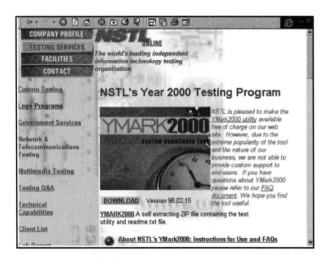

Ymark 2000

http://www.nstl.com/html/ymark_2000.html

NSTL provides a free Year 2000 testing utility program to ensure your computer is Y2K compliant. If you download the program, it is strongly recommended you check out NSTL's pages on Instructions for Using the Program and Frequently Asked Questions. The company also offers custom testing.

Topic Specific Resources—Other

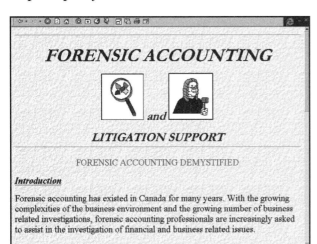

Forensic Accounting Demystified

http://www.forensicaccounting.com/

Topics covered include: what is forensic accounting; what is litigation support; what does a forensic accountant do and how to become a forensic accountant. This site is a nice overview and should be supplemented with Will Yancey's Forensic Resources page (http://www.willyancey.com/forensic.htm) for a deeper understanding.

LIFO Systems

http://www.lifosystems.com/

LIFO Systems is a commercial Web site by an accounting firm with over fifteen years of specialized LIFO accounting experience. Check out the News section for the last-in and the first-out of LIFO news (no pun intended). Under Learn LIFO, you can check out its LIFO glossary and FAQ.

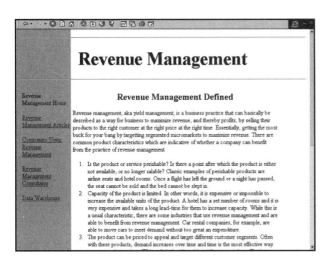

Yield Management

http://www.geocities.com/WallStreet/Floor/4921/

Revenue management, a.k.a. yield management, is used by companies with perishable assets in order to maximize their revenues by pricing for segmented markets. This GeoCities Web site provides some general information on the topic, in addition to references to detailed articles (online and off-line), listings of revenue management consultants and companies using it.

Periodicals, Publications & News

Electronic Accountant

http://www.electronicaccountant.com/

Brought to you by Faulkner & Gray, the Electronic Accountant is a great resource for accountants. It definitely is a full-service Web site, with news updated daily, Web site directory (links, vendors, etc.), forums and a handful of junior sites such as Career Center and Tax Center.

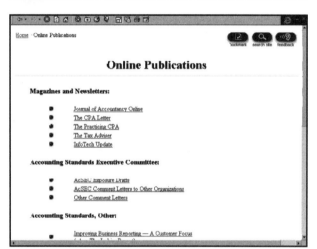

AICPA News Flash & Publications

http://www.aicpa.org/news/index.htm
http://www.aicpa.org/pubs/index.htm

The news and publication resources at the AICPA are rich and are more than worth mentioning more than once. The News Flash is updated on a periodic basis and is a one-stop page for all your AICPA news. *The CPA Letter*, *The Tax Adviser*, *The Practicing CPA*, and *Journal of Accountancy Online* are all available for your Web site–surfing pleasure. The *JOA* is not available online for three months after hardcopy publication due to advertising-related issues. However, once the publications come online, you may feel more comfortable recycling your hardcopies since there is an online version.

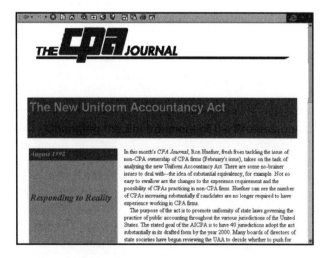

The CPA Journal

http://www.luca.com/cpaj.htm
http://www.cpaj.com/

The CPA Journal, sponsored by the New York Society of CPAs, wins the data conversion award. It has all issues dating back to 1989 in a searchable and by year format! With hundreds of articles in its database with titles such as "Understanding the Value of our Employees' Knowledge" and "Successful Selling for Introverts," plus lots of news. You can't go wrong with a visit to The CPA Journal.

CPA Wire

http://www.calcpa.org/

CPA Wire is the online publication from the California State Society of CPAs. The publication is well done with a good helping of articles applicable to all accountants, practicing in California or elsewhere. CPA Wire also hosts a town hall for discussion forums on specific topics and questions posed.

Authoritative Organizations

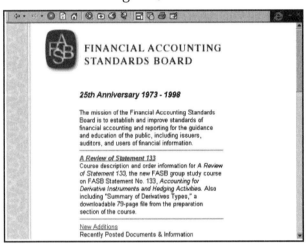

FASB—Financial Accounting Standards Board

http://www.fasb.org/
http://www.rutgers.edu/Accounting/raw/fasb/home2.html

The short FASB address is super easy to remember, but it will eventually route you to Rutger's Accounting Web (RAW). You will satisfy all your online FASB needs here. And if you can't find something, there is always an E-mail address close by. The FASB site has all Action Alert, Exposure Drafts, Statement Summaries, and Status and Available Publications and Documents for online viewing. When the documents are large, Word file downloads are available.

AcSEC—Accounting Standards Executive Committee, AICPA

http://www.aicpa.org/members/div/acctstd/index.htm

ARSC—Accounting and Review Services Committee and ASB—Auditing Standards Board, AICPA

http://aicpa.org/members/div/auditstd/index.htm

Two organizations that fall under the AICPA's authority are online and have information regarding announcements, technical status updates, documents, and reports. The Accounting Standards Team has the comprehensive report "Improving Business Reporting—A Customer Focus" (a.k.a. The Jenkins Report) available online.

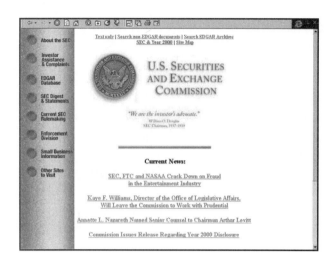

SEC—Securities and Exchange Commission

http://www.sec.gov/

An organization we are all too familiar with, the SEC's Web site is a wealth of information. Especially when you can find what you are looking for! Just recently, we have been rescued from the plight of losing ourselves at this site due to its new search function. You can now search the SEC as well as its popular database of SEC filings, EDGAR.

State CPA Societies—Top Picks

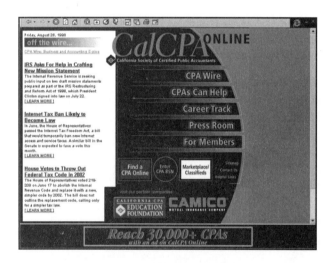

California

http://www.calcpa.org/

The CSCPA Web site is nicely designed and fast loading. The primary areas to visit are its *CPA Wire* newsletter, CPAs Can Help, Career Track, and the Press Room. In CPAs Can Help, you can link to its guide on "How to Choose and Use a CPA" from your Web site. *CPA Wire* hosts the CPA Town Hall, an interactive forum that submits questions to the CPA public for comment.

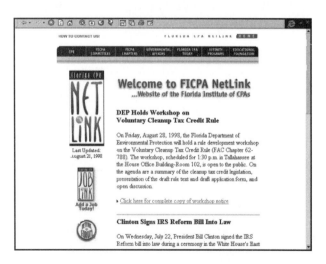

Florida

http://www.ficpa.org/

At FICPA Netlink, the News, Links, and IRS Sites are of interest to all. There is also the NetLink Forum for FICPA members. For CPE resources, the society has its CPE catalog available online. The FICPA site has recently been overhauled with added search features, governmental information, and archives of their award-winning monthly magazine, *Florida CPA Today*.

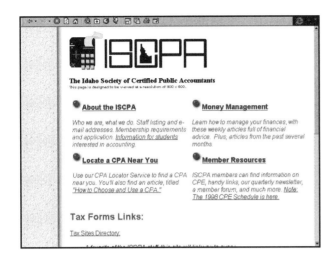

Idaho

http://www.idcpa.org/

The ISCPA has an ongoing series of articles under its Money Management column. Money Management is a weekly column on personal finance. A sampling of segments include "How to Keep Your Money in the Family" and "The Ins and Outs of Medical Savings Accounts." Under CPE, you can download the society's monthly newsletter, *The Envelope.*

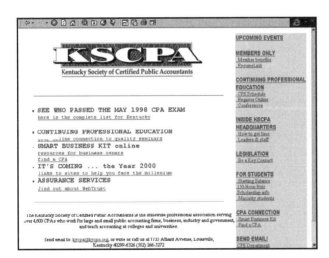

Kentucky

http://www.kycpa.org/

The Smart Business Kit has articles on over twenty subjects to help small businesses work smarter. At the CPA Connection pages you can find additional resources, especially the Weekly Tax Tip page, which has tax tips as well as additional tax resources. Under Future CPAs, you can check out the results of an entry-level salary survey.

Massachusetts

http://www.mscpaonline.org/

Just like the sites above, the MSCPA has a bunch of articles at its Newsstand. Visit its technology tip and tax tip of the week. There are also publications in Adobe Acrobat format for clients at the MSCPA such as "Business Disaster Recovery Planning" and the "Record Retention Guide."

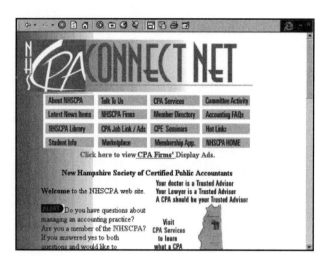

New Hampshire

http://www.nhscpa.org/

New Hampshire's society has additional Money Management tips. If you want to be notified of new tips, you can leave your E-mail address and be automatically notified. Under Accounting FAQ, you can find some technical Q&A resources.

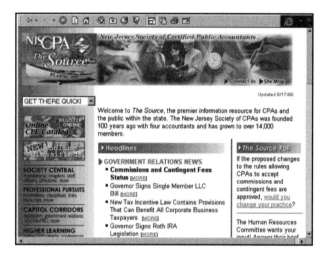

New Jersey

http://www.njscpa.org/

The NJSCPA has a For Your Information resource area with various articles. Each month's topic is something new and runs the gamut from retirement to Internet safety. Visit the Professional Pursuit section for resources for accounting professionals. If you navigate to the Technical Services, you will find lots of resources in its subsections including a Financial Reporting Check-list, sample audit letters, and brochures.

State and Territory CPA Societies—Web Site List

ALABAMA	CONNECTICUT	IDAHO
http://www.ascpa.org/	http://www.cs-cpa.org/	http://www.idcpa.org/
ARIZONA	DELAWARE	ILLINOIS
http://www.ascpa.com/	http://www.dscpa.org/	http://www.icpas.org/
ARKANSAS	DISTRICT OF COLUMBIA	INDIANA
http://www.arcpa.org/	http://www.gwscpa.org/	http://www.incpas.org/
CALIFORNIA	FLORIDA	IOWA
http://www.calcpa.org/	http://www.ficpa.org/	http://www.iacpa.org/
COLORADO	GEORGIA	KANSAS
http://www.cocpa.org/	http://www.gscpa.org/	http://www.kscpa.org/

KENTUCKY
http://www.kycpa.org/

LOUISIANA
http://www.lcpa.org/

MAINE
http://www.mecpa.org/

MARYLAND
http://www.macpa.org/

MASSACHUSETTS
http://www.mscpaonline.org/

MICHIGAN
http://www.michcpa.org/

MINNESOTA
http://www.accountingnet.com/
    society/mn/

MISSISSIPPI
http://www.ms-cpa.org/

MISSOURI
http://www.mocpa.org/

MONTANA
http://www.mscpa.org/

NEVADA
http://www.nevadacpa.org/

NEW HAMPSHIRE
http://www.nhscpa.org/

NEW JERSEY
http://www.njscpa.org/

NEW MEXICO
http://www.nmcpa.org/

NEW YORK
http://www.nysscpa.org/

NORTH CAROLINA
http://www.ncacpa.org/

NORTH DAKOTA
http://www.ndscpa.org/

OHIO
http://www.ohioscpa.com/

OKLAHOMA
http://www.oscpa.com/

OREGON
http://www.orcpa.org/

PENNSYLVANIA
http://www.picpa.com/

PUERTO RICO
http://www.prccpa.org/

RHODE ISLAND
http://www.riscpa.org/

SOUTH CAROLINA
http://www.scacpa.org/

TENNESSEE
http://www.business1.com/cpa/tn/

TEXAS
http://www.tscpa.org/

UTAH
http://www.uacpa.org/

VIRGINIA
http://www.vscpa.com/

WASHINGTON
http://www.wscpa.org/

WEST VIRGINIA
http://www.wvscpa.org/

WISCONSIN
http://www.wicpa.org/

WYOMING
http://www.wyocpa.org/

Other Organizations

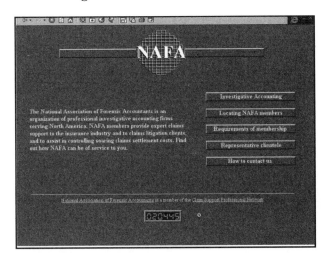

NAFA—National Association of Forensic Accountants

http://www.nafanet.com/

NAFA members provide claims support to the insurance industry and to claims litigation clients, and assist in controlling claims settlement costs. The site has general information about the organization, a brief description of claims accounting, and a listing of clients who use forensic accountants.

ACFE—Association of Certified Fraud Examiners

http://www.acfe.org/

ACFE is dedicated to fighting fraud and white-collar crime. ACFE publishes *The White Paper* and offers EthicsLine, a 24-hour hot line that enables workers the opportunity to anonymously report unethical behavior. Take a look at the "President's Report to the Nation on Operational Fraud and Abuse." An online directory of Certified Fraud Examiners is included at the site.

API—Accountants for the Public Interest

http://www.accountingnet.com/asso/api/

Accountants for the Public Interest is the national nonprofit organization whose mission is "to encourage accountants to volunteer their time and expertise to nonprofits, small businesses and individuals who need, but cannot afford, professional accounting services." At the site, you can find out how to become an API volunteer.

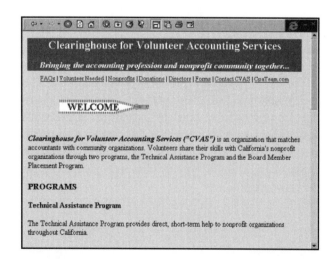

CVAS—Clearinghouse For Volunteer Accountants

http://www.cpateam.com/cvas.htm

CVAS is an organization that matches firms with community organizations in need. The site has general information about the matching program and has an active listing of community organizations needing volunteers. This hosting service and site maintenance is provided by Paul Glass, CPA, who also is responsible for the CPATeam.com Web site (http://www.cpateam.com/).

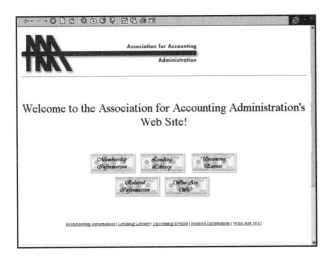

A.A.A.—Association for Accounting Administration

http://www.cpaadmin.org/

AAA is the voice of the accounting administration profession. The organization provides a Lending Library where members can pay a nominal fee to "check out" various hardcopy resources such as books and tapes. It has also developed a FaxNetwork program to help conduct topical surveys and convey the findings amongst the membership.

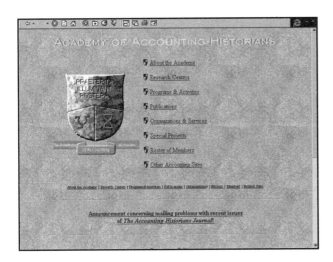

Academy of Accounting Historians

http://weatherhead.cwru.edu/Accounting/

Now *this* is an interesting site. The site features the full-text of accounting text classic *The Evolution of Cost Accounting to 1925* and appears to be the first online publication of a complete accounting text. To celebrate the 100th anniversary of the CPA Exam, the Academy published a copy of the first CPA examination offered by New York State on Tuesday, December 5, 1896. Gotta check it out! In 1998, Robert Mednick, partner, Arthur Andersen Worldwide, published a collection of his articles and speeches in a manuscript—and they are all here for the viewing.

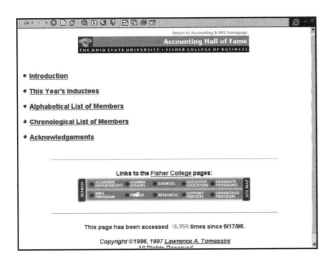

The Accounting Hall of Fame

http://www.cob.ohio-state.edu/dept/acctmis/hof/

The Accounting Hall of Fame (AHOF) Web site honors those who have made substantial and lasting contributions to accounting thought and practice. The page provides users with short biographies and pictures or sketches of the AHOF members. Also, you will find more detailed information about the most recent inductees there.

Assurance and Consulting

Assurance Resources

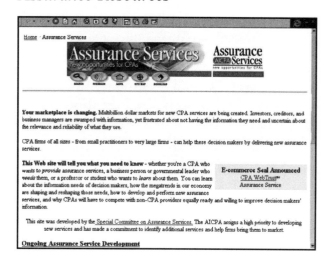

AICPA Assurance Services

http://www.aicpa.org/assurance/index.htm

Visit the impressive Site Map for the Assurance Division's Web site organization (http://www.aicpa.org/assurance/sitemap/index.htm). The assurance site is one of the better organized AICPA sites. It has a good balance of general and specific information. To find out about the future direction of assurance services, check out the Report of the Special Committee on Assurance Services at http://www.aicpa.org/assurance/scas/index.htm. To keep tabs on the latest in assurance, visit Ongoing Assurance Developments at http://www.aicpa.org/assurance/ongoing/eleccom.htm and http://www.aicpa.org/assurance/ongoing/eldcare.htm. The Assurance Services Executive Committee has the Special Committee on Assurance Services working in the assurance service areas of Electronic Commerce and Elder Care. Visit these Web pages for more information on the latest task force developments.

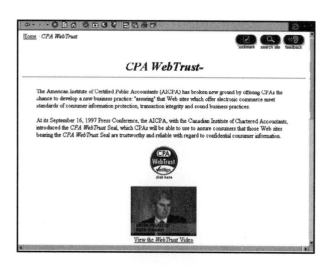

WebTrust—AICPA

http://www.aicpa.org/webtrust/index.htm

The AICPA's Web site for WebTrust is as you would expect for prospective CPAs who are offering or plan to offer WebTrust services. It has a snazzy WebTrust video which provides some general background information about WebTrust and its launch. Also, if you click on the WebTrust seal, you can view a WebTrust certificate.

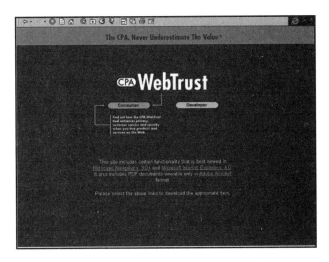

WebTrust—Commercial Site

http://www.cpawebtrust.org/

WebTrust's site is primarily an information resource for consumers and developers (two separate areas). The consumer area is set up to demonstrate how WebTrust enhances privacy, customer service, and security when buying products and services on the Web. The developer area teaches Web developers how the WebTrust Program can help build recurring Web sales.

Business Valuation Resources

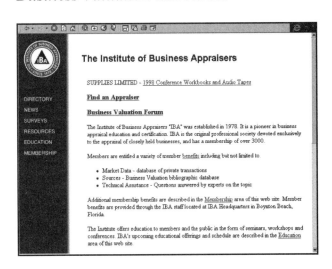

The Institute of Business Appraisers

http://www.instbusapp.org/

IBA has a directory of appraisers, workbooks and audio tapes. The Business Valuation Forum, which links to the Investment Network (http://www.nvst.com/), has lively discussions around valuation topics.

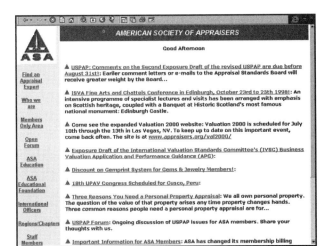

American Society of Appraisers

http://www.appraisers.org/asa/default.asp

The ASA has current forum discussions, education information and news announcements. Its new Web site, Valuation 2000 (http://www. appraisers.org/val2000/), is an alliance of appraisal professionals who will be meeting for a joint business conference in July 2000.

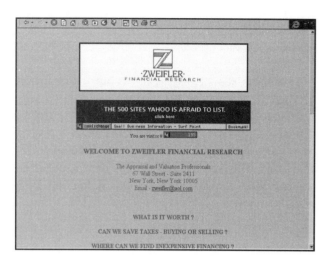

Zweifler Financial Research

http://www.zweifler.inter.net/

Zweifler specializes in appraisal and valuation research. The site offers seven topical guides with general information about stock option plans, buy/sell agreements, tax planning techniques, and maximizing equity ownership.

Consulting Resources

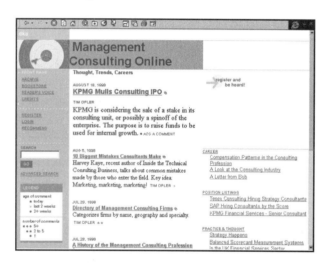

Management Consulting Online

http://207.240.64.186:8080/anon/z15/cover.dhtml

This successor Web site of the Ohio State University site by the same name has all kinds of resources for the management consultant. You'll find a complete directory, history, forum, and quizzes, all focused around management consulting. It's a nice place to get started.

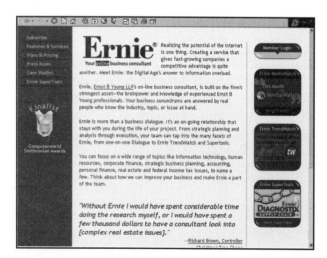

Ernie

http://ernie.ey.com/

Ernie is touted as "your online business consultant." Though this is a subscription-based site (hefty price, too), if you offer consulting services, you should be aware of what other firms, in this case Ernst & Young, are doing online. Ernie appears to be very user friendly, and there are samples for you to review.

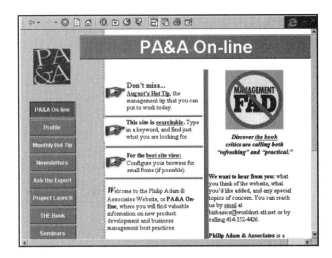

PA&A Online

http://www.bizbasics.com/

PA&A Online has monthly management tips such as "Critical Path Project Management" and "The Importance of Good Product Definition." Wisconsin-based consulting firm Philip Adam & Associates hosts this searchable resource. The firm publishes the newsletter *Ventures*, and the Web site has several consulting articles online for viewing.

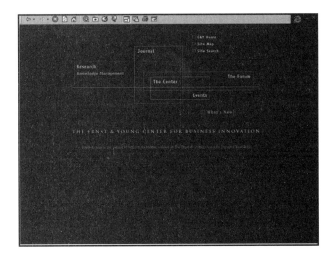

Center for Business Innovation

http://www.businessinnovation.ey.com/

The Ernst & Young Center for Business Innovation is "a source of new knowledge, insights, and frameworks for management." Visit the site map to begin your journey through this site, which is relatively new, so there should be more to come. The current issue of the Journal is the in-depth content feature for now.

Virtual Consulting

http://www.virtualconsulting.com/

A good resource for some in-depth articles on strategic planning, Virtual Consulting also provides consulting services for Visioning, Organization, and Training Development and Human Resource Management.

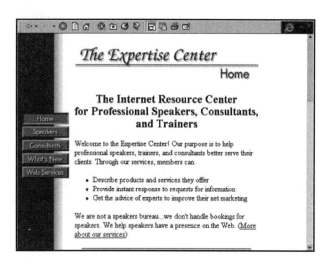

The Expertise Center

http://www.expertcenter.com/

The Center's purpose is to help professional speakers, trainers, and consultants better serve their clients through alliance. The Web site has a searchable database of consultants and professional speakers as well as an indexed listing of the weekly Speakernet and consulting chat session on America Online.

Periodicals & Publications

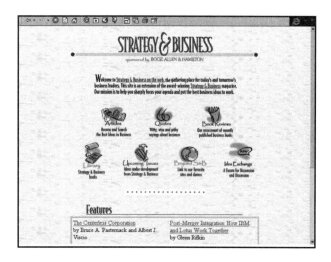

Strategy & Business

http://www.strategy-business.com/

Strategy & Business is sponsored by Booz, Allen Hamilton and is an extension of its award-winning quarterly publication. You'll find lots of interesting articles here as well as good resources such as reviews of recent strategy books and the Idea Exchange Forum. S&B also has a neat quote database that is searchable by keyword or author.

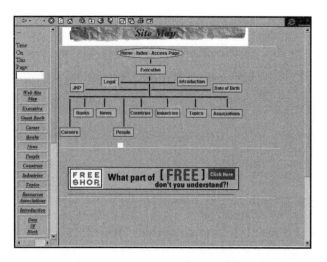

Harvard Business School Publishing

http://www.hbsp.harvard.edu/

Home of *Harvard Business Review* and HBS Publishing, this Web site has a wealth of knowledge available to you (albeit, not all of it is free). This site has lots of article abstracts, just enough to whet your appetite for the latest business topics. The site also supports online shopping. Snoop around a bit and you'll find the Web Sites for Managers page (http://www.hbsp.harvard.edu/frames/groups/newsletters/webmanager.html).

Sloan Management Review

http://web.mit.edu/smr-online/

MIT's management publication is online with abstracts a little more substantial in length than the HBS Review. Reprints are available for purchase. If you need a Sloan report, this is your site. Otherwise, there isn't much else here.

Research Resources

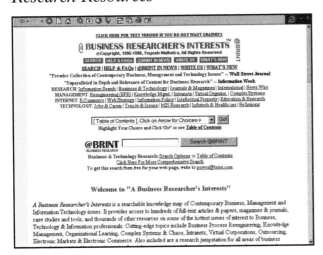

A Business Researcher's Interests

http://www.brint.com/interest.html

To quote a couple of known sources, this site is a "premier collection of contemporary business, management and technology issues" (*Wall Street Journal*) and is "unparalleled in depth and relevance of content for business research" (*Information Week*). It provides access to hundreds of full-text articles and papers, case studies and tools. You'll likely spend hours at this rich research resource.

Consulting Organizations

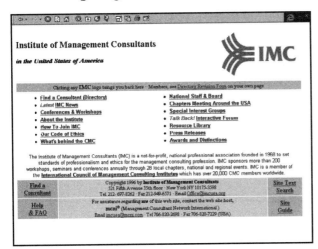

IMC—Institute of Management Consultants

http://www.imcusa.org/

The IMC publishes the *Management Consulting Times* and has the publication available for download. Also, the Strategic Interest Group Forum is available for consultants interested in using strategic alliances and affiliations to build virtual companies.

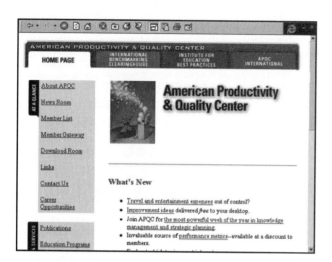

APQC—American Productivity & Quality Center

http://www.apqc.org/

The APQC has a monthly E-mail newsletter available for viewing, *APQC CenterView*. Every month the site features The Hot Topic of the Month where a topic is selected and a brief overview, bibliography and additional online resources are provided. A former month's topic was team-building.

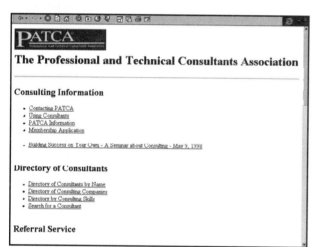

PATCA—Professional & Technical Consultants Association

http://www.patca.org/

Along with many of the other sites in this section, PATCA has a searchable directory of consultants. The site has almost two years of PATCA newsletters online.

Audit

Financial Accounting Audit Resources

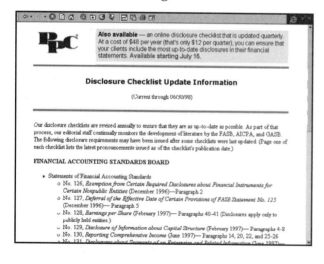

PPC's Disclosure Checklist Update

http://www.ppcinfo.com/disclo.htm

PPC has a nice and concise disclosure checklist update. The update is revised monthly. Check out its 5-Minute Update at: http://www.ppcinfo.com/5-min.htm to get the latest news on the latest pronouncements issued as well as other audit resources, such as downloadable sample client letters.

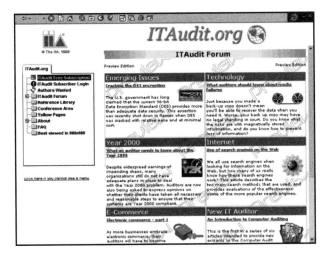

ITAudit.org

http://www.itaudit.org/

ITAudit.org is a very new site; but that doesn't mean there isn't much here. This site looks very promising. It had its launch in mid-August 1998 and it already has an extensive Resource Library, Discussion Forums, and Online Chat. Visit the IT Audit Forum for feature articles on emerging issues, technology, the Year 2000, E-commerce, and more.

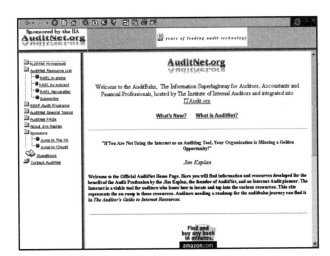

Jim Kaplan's AuditNet

http://www.auditnet.org/

AuditNet is *the* Internet resource for auditors. The site includes a section called Auditor Sharing Audit Programs (ASAP) with audit procedure programs from auditors around the world. Audit-Net also publishes *AuditZine* with articles on Internet for financial professionals, *FraudNet* with fraud policies, procedures and resources, and the *Audit-Net Resource List* (a.k.a. KARL). KARL provides links and descriptions for over five hundred sites of interest to financial professionals.

AuditWatch

http://www.auditwatch.com/

AuditWatch, Inc. provides the audit profession with training in audit efficiency. The company provides a number of services such as Audit Productivity Improvement and Data Extraction. Take a peek at AuditWatch's newsletter, *The Efficient Auditor.*

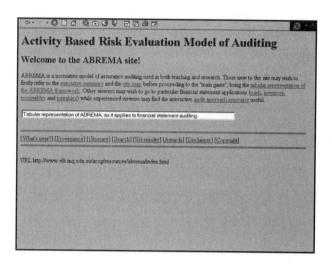

Activity Based Risk Evaluation

http://www.efs.mq.edu.au/accg/resources/abrema/

ABREMA is a normative model of assurance auditing used in both teaching and research. It is recommended that you refer to the executive summary and the site map before proceeding to the "main game." The site has a nice glossary of activity based risk terms and hyperlinked definitions.

Audit Serve

http://www.auditserve.com/

The Audit Serve Web site provides fifty-plus technical audit and Y2K articles. In addition, other research materials which support Y2K audit and conversions are available. Audit Serve publishes a free quarterly E-mail newsletter and *The Audit Vision Magazine* that contains technical articles relating to the EDP Audit and Security professions.

Government

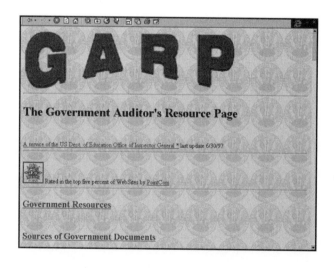

GARP—Government Auditor's Resource Page

http://www.trib.infi.net/~zsudiak/

The Government Auditor's Resource Page (GARP) is a service of the U.S. Dept. of Education Office of Inspector General. The site includes various government audit resources. All the links are on one page, so there isn't a lot of jumping around.

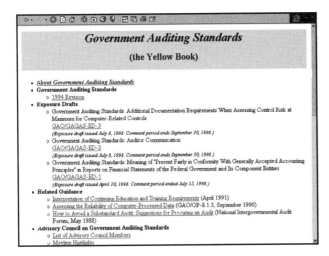

The Yellow Book

http://www.gao.gov/govaud/ybk01.htm

Government Auditing Standards (the "yellow book") contains standards for audits of government organizations, programs, activities, and functions, and of government assistance received by contractors, nonprofit organizations, and other nongovernment organizations. This site includes various Yellow Book resources such as exposure drafts and related guidance.

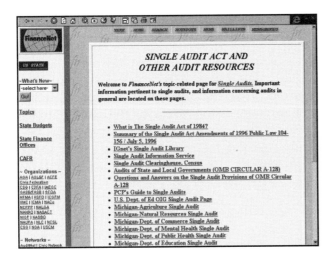

Single Audit Act

http://www.financenet.gov/financenet/state/sinaudit/
sinaudit.htm

FinanceNet's topic-related page for Single Audits includes important information pertinent to single audits, and information concerning audits in general. The site has links to state single audit pages as well as a listing of several states' CAFRs.

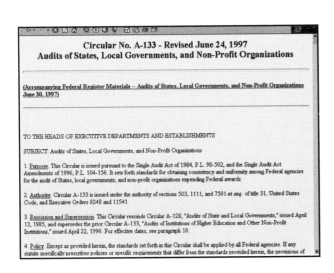

OMB Circular A-133

http://www.whitehouse.gov/WH/EOP/OMB/html/circulars/
a133/a133.html

Here you will find the text of Circular No. A-133 as well as accompanying Federal Register Materials—Audits of States, Local Governments, and Non-Profit Organizations.

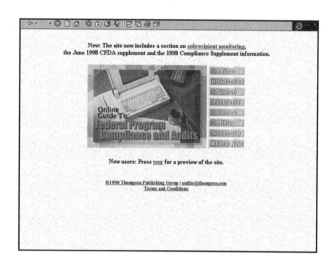

Federal Program Compliance and Audits

http://www.thompson.com/audit/

The Online Guide to Federal Program Compliance and Audits is designed to assist practitioners with performing audits of federal awards that meet the requirements of the Single Audit Act Amendments of 1996 and Office of Management and Budget (OMB) Circular No. A-133, Audits of States, Local Governments and Non-Profit Organizations. The Online Guide is available on a subscription basis.

Internal Audit

Internal Audit Online

http://www.columbia.edu/cu/ia/

One of the unique aspects of Internal Audit Online is its Go Ask Audit section. Columbia users are encouraged to submit anonymous questions regarding internal controls in our environment. The site also has a comprehensive Guide to Internal Control, checks lists, and resource links.

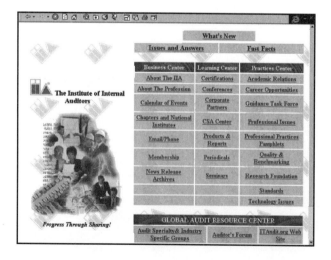

Institute of Internal Auditors

http://www.theiia.org/

The IIA is designed to provide information on the internal auditing profession. The Fast Facts section of its site lists all IIA offerings on a variety of subjects, including internal control, audit committees, management of the audit function, audit committees, and standards.

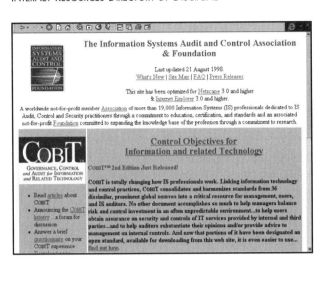

The Information Systems Audit and Control Association & Foundation

http://www.isaca.org/

The ISACA is "an association of more than 19,000 Information Systems professionals dedicated to IS Audit, Control and Security practitioners through a commitment to education, certification, and standards." It is the publisher of the *IS Audit* and *Control Journal*.

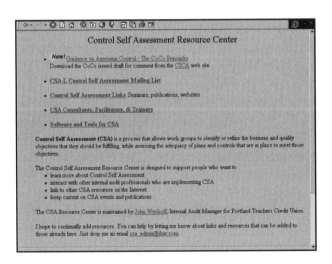

Control Self Assessment Resource Center

http://www.teleport.com/~jhw/csa/

The Control Self Assessment Resource Center is designed to support people who want to learn more about Control Self Assessment, interact with other internal audit professionals who are implementing CSA, link to other CSA resources on the Internet, and keep current on CSA events and publications.

Internal Control Primer

http://home1.gte.net/tateatty/ic.htm

This site provides a detailed account of the intricacies of Internal Controls. It walks you through the components of IC, discusses the audit/evaluation of internal controls, and provides a comprehensive list of Internal Control safeguards.

Government

Government Accounting Organizations

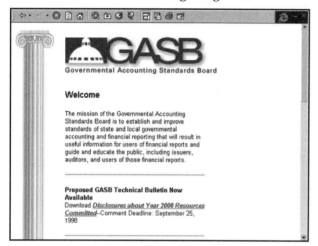

GASB—Government Accounting Standards Board

http://www.rutgers.edu/Accounting/raw/gasb/

Some of the features you will find at the GASB site are the quarterly plan of GASB projects, summaries and status of all GASB interpretations, proposed statements, interpretations, and technical bulletins. The GASB has provided a links page of all GASAC member organizations.

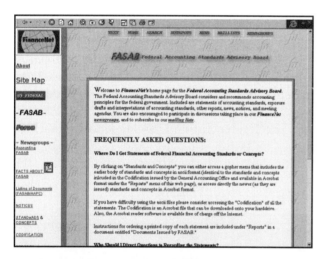

FASAB—Federal Accounting Standards Advisory Board

http://www.financenet.gov/fasab.htm

This site is hosted through FinanceNet. The FASAB started its newsletter online in early 1997. Check out the FASAB Interpretations and Exposure Drafts for the latest recommended accounting practices for federal government. The site has a forum and E-mail newsletter for further interaction and information.

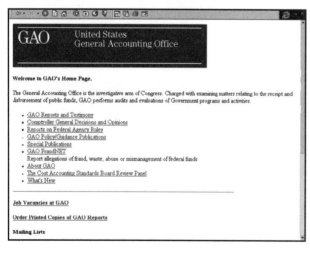

GAO

http://www.gao.gov/

The General Accounting Office is "the investigative arm of the Congress and is charged with examining all matters relating to the receipt and disbursement of public funds." If you are interested in what is going on at the GAO, you should subscribe to the Daybook and Decisions mailing lists. Look at the Special Publications section for the link to The Yellow Book and the Year 2000 Assessment Guide. To report allegations of fraud, waste, abuse or mismanagement of federal funds, visit GAO FraudNet. The What's New page lists the new posts to the Web site by date.

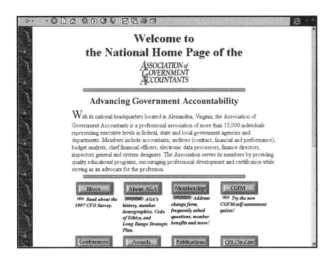

AGA—Association of Government Accountants

http://raw.rutgers.edu/raw/aga/

The AGA acts as an "educational organization dedicated to the enhancement of public financial management." AGA has the entire text of its survey "Preparing for Tomorrow's Way of Doing Business" online. There is also self-assessment quizzes for CGFM, the Certified Government Financial Manager and up to twelve hours of CPE online. Visit AGA's various publications and Web site resources for additional information.

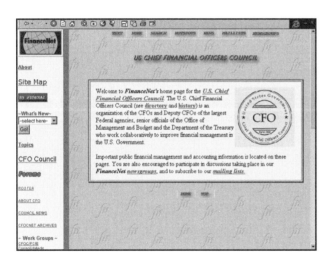

U.S. Chief Financial Officers Council

http://www.financenet.gov/cfo.htm

The U.S. Chief Financial Officers Council is an organization of the CFOs and Deputy CFOs of the largest Federal agencies, senior officials of the Office of Management and Budget, and the Department of the Treasury who work to improve financial management in the U.S. Government. The Council directory is available online.

NASACT—State Auditors, Comptrollers and Treasurers

http://www.sso.org/nasact/

Its goal is "to assure that government fiscal and financial management is effective, efficient, and professional." The site has current Washington news effecting state financial management officials. NASACT has links to many specific resources.

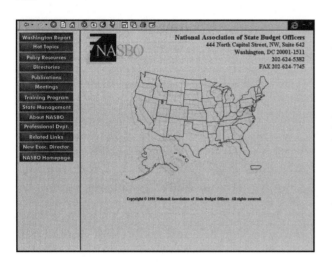

National Association of State Budget Officers

http://www.nasbo.org/

NASBO is "the instrument through which the states collectively are advancing state budget practices." NASBO publishes *Washington Report*, a weekly summary of federal legislative and regulatory happenings. Past issues are available online. The Hot Topics and Publications sections will give you additional news and in-depth resources.

Government Finance Officers Association

http://www.gfoa.org/

GFOA is "the professional association of state/provincial and local finance officers in the United States and Canada." Check out the What's New page first for timely updates to the site. Check out the Fact Sheets for interesting information on subjects such as derivatives, arbitrage, and Internet taxation.

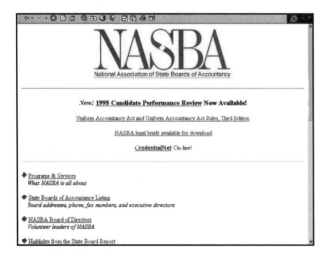

NASBA—National Association of State Boards of Accountancy

http://www.nasba.org/

NASBA's mission is "to enhance the effectiveness of state boards of accountancy." NASBA is the organization that publishes the report "Candidate Performance on the Uniform CPA Examination." The site lists all State Boards of Accountancy as well as information about the National Registry of CPE Sponsors.

Government Web Sites of Particular Interest

The White House

http://www.whitehouse.gov

After you check out the greeting from "Bill & Al," visit the Commonly Requested Federal Services section. There you will find links to major subsections within the site. At a minimum, visit the Benefits & Assistance, Employment & Taxes, and the U.S. Business Advisor subsections. Back at the home page, visit the Interactive Citizen's Handbook for additional U.S. Government resources.

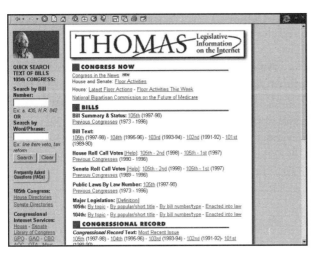

THOMAS

http://thomas.loc.gov/

An excellent resource brought to you by the legislative branch, THOMAS provides many resources. The site has substantial databases in the Congress Now, Bills and Congressional Record sections. In the Committee Information section, you will find committee reports and home pages. You can also find out about the entire legislative process through the site's guide on "How Our Laws are Made" and "Enactment of a Law." The directory of all Congress members (E-mail address and Web pages included) is also available at THOMAS.

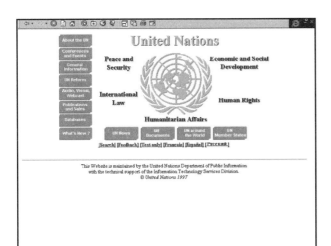

The United Nations

http://www.un.org/

Visit the UN in Brief for general information about what the UN does. For UN publications research, a documentation research guide is provided. Visit the Database section for statistical data. The UN media division has posted audio, television and photo resources for additional resources regarding UN activities.

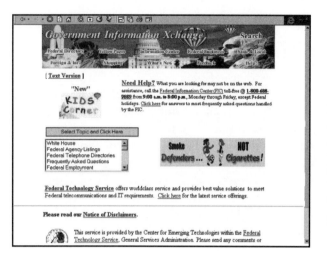

Government Information Xchange

http://www.info.gov/

The Center of Federal Technology Services produces GIX. Select a topic at the scroll box on the home page and you will be sent directly to the Web site addressing the topic. Go to the Federal Directory for a complete listing of all branches of federal government. The Information Center has detailed guides based on popular government topics. Each guide has many links to additional resources.

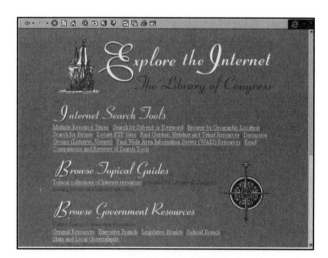

Explore the Internet

http://lcweb.loc.gov/global/

The Library of Congress has prepared an online resource to help you with your Internet experience. The site has various Internet search tools and resources for you to learn how to use the Internet. The Topical Guides it has prepared are very helpful. Browse through guides for copyrights, doing business on the Internet, and law.

U.S. Business Advisor

http://www.business.gov/

The U.S. Business Advisor exists "to provide business with one-stop access to federal government information, services, and transactions." The site has a nicely organized section addressing questions businesses frequently ask about the government. Here you will find answers about exports, the FCC, Social Security, and taxes. The other section to visit is the How-To Guides section.

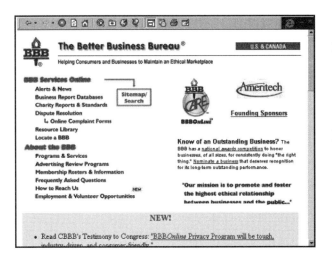

Better Business Bureau

http://www.bbb.org/

The BBB's site has the latest alerts and news about potentially fraudulent business practices, dispute resolution assistance, and online complaint forms. Visit the BBB Business Library for detailed information about scams and schemes targeted at businesses. Locate your local BBB office with the online directory.

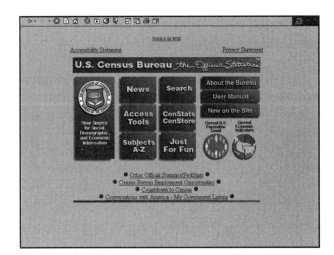

Census Bureau

http://www.census.gov/

If you need to use or represent certain statistical data, check out the Tools section for custom extract files, viewers and more. The home page has a User Manual (more like a section index). For a quick look at the U.S. Economic position, check out the Economic Clock which displays several economic indicators.

Smithsonian Institution

http://www.si.edu

To fill out your cultural repertoire, take a read of the *Smithsonian* magazine online (http://www.smithsonianmag.si.edu/). The magazine produces a book review page for further edification. Visit the What's New page for the latest additions.

U.S. Federal Government Agencies

http://www.lib.lsu.edu/gov/fedgov.html

For a virtual comprehensive listing of U.S. federal government, visit the Louisiana State University library site. The listing is all on one huge page which includes links to executive, judicial, legislative, independent agencies and more. Visit this page to access the states' web servers at http://www.state.me.us/states.htm.

Board of Governors of the Federal Reserve

http://www.bog.frb.fed.us/

For a complete reference of the Federal Reserve system, go straight to the complete online book *Purposes & Function*. You can also download the entire book, but the file is over 1MB. The monthly *Federal Reserve Bulletin* is online as well. Many additional resources are available such as speeches, testimony, press releases, and publications.

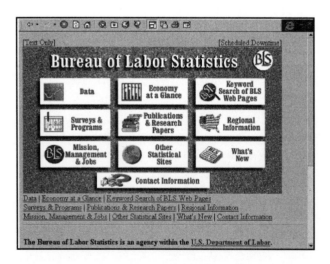

Bureau of Labor Statistics

http://stats.bls.gov/

The What's New page at the Bureau of Labor Statistics will give the latest issue of *Monthly Labor Review*, current compensation information, and newly posted articles. You can search the entire Web site and statistical database by keyword, select popular statistical data at the Data section, and read current surveys, and publications.

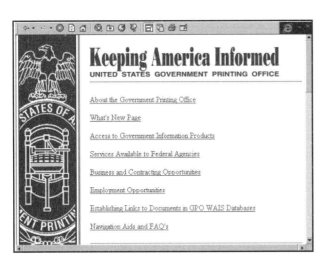

Government Printing Office

http://www.access.gpo.gov/

Start your research at this Web site with the About the GPO section. The section includes its mission, what's new and organizational structure. GPO is the home of the *Federal Bulletin Board* (http://fedbbs.access.gpo.gov/), the *Congressional Record*, *Federal Regulations*, and the *Federal Register*.

FedWorld

http://www.fedworld.gov/

The FedWorld Information Network provides a one-site search engine for many of the federal government's databases. The search results are given a score based on relevance to the key word entered. There is also a search for U.S. Government Reports, which includes a database of more than 420,000 reports in 375 categories from over 200 U.S. governmental agencies. Providing several additional services to the public, FedWorld includes a mirror for tax forms and Internal Revenue Bulletins (IRBs). Another site for government search is GovBot at http://eden.cs.umass.edu/Govbot/.

Government Nets

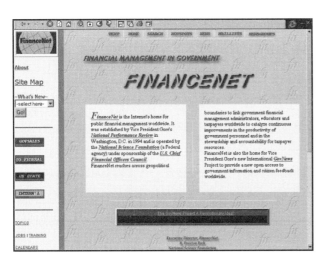

FinanceNet

http://www.financenet.gov/

According to the site, FinanceNet receives nearly 20 million "hits" per year, has over 50,000 Internet mailing list subscribers and hosts 225 government newsgroups. FinanceNet is one of the largest government administrative "Internetwork" sites in the world. FinanceNet has the dual missions of (1) providing the official U.S. government one-stop-shop Internet clearing site for information on the public sale/auction of some $6 billion/year of surplus government property, and (2) providing Internet communication tools to intergovernmental organizations. Visit the site map for the best organization feel for what this site can do for you.

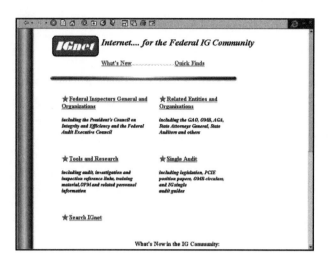

IG Net—Inspector General

http://www.ignet.gov/

Check out the Quick Finds area for IG Net's most popular features, in particular standards, legislation, and directory. Check out the Interactive Yellow Book Guide which is linked by chapter and includes a linked table of contents and linked keyword index. IG Net also provides a Single Audit section of legislation, PCIE position papers, and OMB circulars.

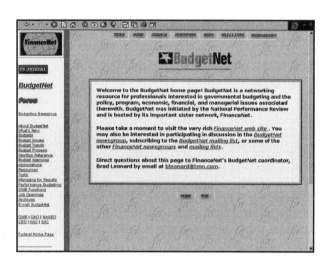

BudgetNet

http://www.financenet.gov/budget.htm

BudgetNet has been set up as "a networking resource for budget professionals, many of whom work for government, while others work for associations and other nonprofits, businesses, and educational institutions." The site has detailed pdf documents about the budget process for download. If you are involved in budgeting, visit the Tools section for techniques, software and materials used in budgeting.

Government Web Site Directory

Executive Branch

OFFICE OF MANAGEMENT AND BUDGET
http://www.whitehouse.gov/WH/EOP/omb

WHITE HOUSE OFFICE
http://www.whitehouse.gov

Executive Agencies

DEPARTMENT OF AGRICULTURE
http://www.usda.gov/

DEPARTMENT OF COMMERCE
http://www.doc.gov/

DEPARTMENT OF DEFENSE
http://www.defenselink.mil/

DEPARTMENT OF EDUCATION
http://www.ed.gov/

DEPARTMENT OF ENERGY
http://www.doe.gov

DEPARTMENT OF HEALTH AND HUMAN SERVICES
http://www.os.dhhs.gov

DEPARTMENT OF HOUSING AND URBAN DEVELOPMENT (HUD)
http://www.hud.gov/

DEPARTMENT OF THE INTERIOR
http://www.doi.gov/

DEPARTMENT OF JUSTICE (DOJ)
http://www.usdoj.gov/

DEPARTMENT OF LABOR(DOL)
http://www.dol.gov/

DEPARTMENT OF STATE
http://www.state.gov/

DEPARTMENT OF TRANSPORTATION
http://www.dot.gov/

DEPARTMENT OF VETERANS AFFAIRS
http://www.va.gov

DEPARTMENT OF THE TREASURY
http://www.ustreas.gov/

Department of Treasury Bureaus

INTERNAL REVENUE SERVICE
http://www.irs.ustreas.gov/

UNITED STATES CUSTOMS SERVICE
http://www.customs.treas.gov/

BUREAU OF ALCOHOL, TOBACCO AND FIREARMS
http://www.atf.treas.gov/

FINANCIAL MANAGEMENT SERVICE
http://www.fms.treas.gov/

UNITED STATES SECRET SERVICE
http://www.ustreas.gov/usss/

OFFICE OF THRIFT SUPERVISION
http://www.ots.treas.gov/

UNITED STATES MINT
http://www.usmint.gov/

OFFICE OF THE COMPTROLLER OF THE CURRENCY
http://www.occ.treas.gov/

FEDERAL LAW ENFORCEMENT TRAINING CENTER
http://www.ustreas.gov/fletc/

BUREAU OF PUBLIC DEBT
http://www.publicdebt.treas.gov/

BUREAU OF ENGRAVING AND PRINTING
http://www.bep.treas.gov/

FINANCIAL CRIMES ENFORCEMENT NETWORK
http://www.ustreas.gov/fincen/

Judicial Branch

U.S. FEDERAL COURTS FINDER
http://www.law.emory.edu/FEDCTS/

FEDERAL JUDICIAL CENTER
http://www.fjc.gov/

FEDERAL JUDICIARY
http://www.uscourts.gov/

SUPREME COURT DECISIONS
http://www.law.cornell.edu:80/supct/supct.table.html

U.S. SENTENCING COMMISSION
http://www.ussc.gov/

Legislative Branch

U.S. HOUSE OF REPRESENTATIVES
http://www.house.gov

U.S. SENATE
http://www.senate.gov/

LIBRARY OF CONGRESS (LOC)
http://lcweb.loc.gov/

GOVERNMENT ACCOUNTING OFFICE (GAO)
http://www.gao.gov/

GOVERNMENT PRINTING OFFICE (GPO)
http://www.access.gpo.gov/

OFFICE OF TECHNOLOGY ASSESSMENT
http://www.wws.princeton.edu/~ota/

STENNIS CENTER FOR PUBLIC SERVICE
http://www.stennis.gov

Independent Agencies

CENTRAL INTELLIGENCE AGENCY (CIA)
http://www.odci.gov/cia/

COMMISSION ON CIVIL RIGHTS
http://www.usccr.gov/

COMMODITY FUTURES TRADING COMMISSION
(CFTC)
http://www.cftc.gov/cftc/

CONSUMER PRODUCT SAFETY COMMISSION
(CPSC)
gopher://cpsc.gov/

DEFENSE NUCLEAR FACILITIES SAFETY BOARD
(DNFSB)
http://www.dnfsb.gov

ENVIRONMENTAL PROTECTION AGENCY (EPA)
http://www.epa.gov/

EQUAL EMPLOYMENT OPPORTUNITY COMMISSION
(EEOC)
http://www.eeoc.gov/

EXPORT-IMPORT BANK OF THE UNITED STATES
http://www.exim.gov

FARM CREDIT ADMINISTRATION
http://www.fca.gov/

FEDERAL COMMUNICATIONS COMMISSION (FCC)
http://www.fcc.gov/

FEDERAL DEPOSIT INSURANCE CORPORATION
(FDIC)
http://www.fdic.gov

FEDERAL ELECTION COMMISSION (FEC)
http://www.fec.gov/

FEDERAL EMERGENCY MANAGEMENT AGENCY
(FEMA)
http://www.fema.gov/

FEDERAL HOUSING FINANCE BOARD
http://www.fhfb.gov/

FEDERAL MARITIME COMMISSION
http://www.fmc.gov/

FEDERAL RESERVE BANK OF ATLANTA
http://www.frbatlanta.org

FEDERAL RESERVE BANK OF BOSTON
gopher://ftp.shsu.edu/11/Economics/FRB-Boston

FEDERAL RESERVE BANK OF CHICAGO
http://www.frbchi.org

FEDERAL RESERVE BANK OF CLEVELAND
http://www.clev.frb.org

FEDERAL RESERVE BANK OF DALLAS
http://www.dallasfed.org

FEDERAL RESERVE BANK OF KANSAS CITY
http://www.frbkc.org/contents.htm

FEDERAL RESERVE BANK OF MINNEAPOLIS
http://woodrow.mpls.frb.fed.us/

FEDERAL RESERVE BANK OF NEW YORK
http://www.ny.frb.org

FEDERAL RESERVE BANK OF PHILADELPHIA
http://www.libertynet.org/fedresrv/

FEDERAL RESERVE BANK OF SAN FRANCISCO
http://www.frbsf.org/index.html

FEDERAL RESERVE BANK OF ST. LOUIS
http://www.stls.frb.org/

FEDERAL RETIREMENT THRIFT INVESTMENT BOARD
http://www.frtib.gov/

FEDERAL TRADE COMMISSION (FTC)
http://www.ftc.gov/

GENERAL SERVICES ADMINISTRATION (GSA)
http://www.gsa.gov/

INTER-AMERICAN FOUNDATION
http://www.iaf.gov/

MERIT SYSTEMS PROTECTION BOARD
http://www.fpmi.com/MSPB/MSPBhomepage.html

NATIONAL AERONAUTICS AND SPACE ADMINISTRA-
TION (NASA)
http://www.nasa.gov/

NATIONAL ARCHIVES AND RECORDS ADMINISTRA-
TION (NARA)
http://www.nara.gov/

NATIONAL CAPITAL PLANNING COMMISSION
http://www.ncpc.gov/

NATIONAL CREDIT UNION ADMINISTRATION
(NCUA)
http://www.ncua.gov/

NATIONAL ENDOWMENT FOR THE HUMANITIES
(NEH)
http://www.neh.fed.us/

NATIONAL LABOR RELATIONS BOARD (NLRB)
http://www.doc.gov/nlrb/homepg.html

NATIONAL MEDIATION BOARD
http://www.nmb.gov/

NATIONAL RAILROAD PASSENGER CORPORATION
(AMTRAK)
http://www.amtrak.com

NATIONAL PERFORMANCE REVIEW (NPR)
http://www.npr.gov/

FINANCENET
http://www.financenet.gov/

NATIONAL SCIENCE FOUNDATION (NSF)
http://www.nsf.gov

NATIONAL TRANSPORTATION SAFETY BOARD
http://www.ntsb.gov/

NUCLEAR REGULATORY COMMISSION (NRC)
http://www.nrc.gov/

OFFICE OF GOVERNMENT ETHICS
http://www.usoge.gov/

OFFICE OF PERSONNEL MANAGEMENT
http://www.opm.gov/

OFFICE OF SPECIAL COUNSEL
http://www.access.gpo.gov/osc/

PANAMA CANAL COMMISSION
http://www.pancanal.com/

PEACE CORPS
http://www.peacecorps.gov/

PENSION BENEFIT GUARANTY CORPORATION
http://www.pbgc.gov/

POSTAL RATE COMMISSION
http://www.prc.gov/

RAILROAD RETIREMENT BOARD
http://www.rrb.gov/

SECURITIES AND EXCHANGE COMMISSION (SEC)
http://www.sec.gov/

EDGAR
http://www.sec.gov/edgarhp.htm

SELECTIVE SERVICE SYSTEM
http://www.sss.gov/

SMALL BUSINESS ADMINISTRATION (SBA)
http://www.sbaonline.sba.gov/

SOCIAL SECURITY ADMINISTRATION (SSA)
http://www.ssa.gov/

TENNESSEE VALLEY AUTHORITY
http://www.tva.gov/

TRADE AND DEVELOPMENT AGENCY
http://www.tda.gov/

UNITED STATES ARMS CONTROL AND DISARMA-
MENT AGENCY
http://www.acda.gov/

UNITED STATES INFORMATION AGENCY (USIA)
http://www.usia.gov/

UNITED STATES INTERNATIONAL TRADE COMMIS-
SION (USITC)
http://www.usitc.gov

UNITED STATES POSTAL SERVICE (USPS)
http://www.usps.gov/

State Government

ALABAMA
http://alaweb.asc.edu

ALASKA
http://www.state.ak.us

ARIZONA
http://www.state.az.us

ARKANSAS
http://www.state.ar.us/

CALIFORNIA
http://www.ca.gov

COLORADO
http://www.state.co.us/

CONNECTICUT
http://www.state.ct.us/

DELAWARE
http://www.state.de.us/

FLORIDA
http://www.state.fl.us/

GEORGIA
http://www.state.ga.us/

HAWAII
http://www.state.hi.us/

IDAHO
http://www.state.id.us/

ILLINOIS
http://www.state.il.us

INDIANA
http://www.state.in.us

IOWA
http://www.state.ia.us

KANSAS
http://www.ink.org

KENTUCKY
http://www.state.ky.us

LOUISIANA
http://www.state.la.us

MAINE
http://www.state.me.us

MARYLAND
http://www.mec.state.md.us/

MASSACHUSETTS
http://www.state.ma.us

MICHIGAN
http://www.state.mi.us/

MINNESOTA
http://www.state.mn.us/

MISSISSIPPI
http://www.state.ms.us

MISSOURI
http://www.state.mo.us

MONTANA
http://www.mt.gov

NEBRASKA
http://www.state.ne.us

NEVADA
http://www.state.nv.us/

NEW HAMPSHIRE
http://www.state.nh.us

NEW JERSEY
http://www.state.nj.us/

NEW MEXICO
http://www.state.nm.us

NEW YORK
http://unix2.nysed.gov/ils

NORTH CAROLINA
http://www.sips.state.nc.us

NORTH DAKOTA
http://www.state.nd.us

OHIO
http://www.ohio.gov

OKLAHOMA
http://www.oklaosf.state.ok.us

OREGON
http://www.state.or.us

PENNSYLVANIA
http://www.state.pa.us

RHODE ISLAND
http://www.state.ri.us/

SOUTH CAROLINA
http://www.state.sc.us

SOUTH DAKOTA
http://www.state.sd.us

TENNESSEE
http://www.state.tn.us

TEXAS
http://www.texas.gov

UTAH
http://www.state.ut.us

VERMONT
http://www.cit.state.vt.us

VIRGINIA
http://www.state.va.us

WASHINGTON
http://www.state.wa.us/

WEST VIRGINIA
http://www.state.wv.us/

WISCONSIN
http://badger.state.wi.us

Personal Financial Planning

Directories & Guides

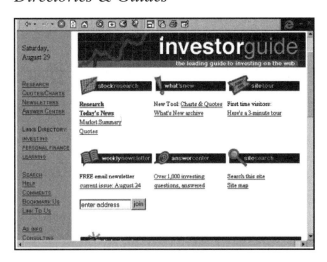

InvestorGuide

http://www.investorguide.com/

For first-time visitors, the Investor Guide has a three-minute tour. The Links Directory is the main attraction of this site, with links to thousands of investing sites, all organized by topic. Most links have a small write-up about what you'll find. IG provides *InvestorGuide Weekly,* an E-mail newsletter covering online investing. Check out the Answer Center, a collection of over one thousand investing questions, with links to their answers.

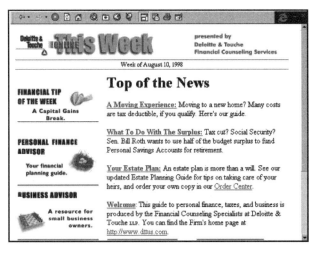

Mining Company—Personal Finance

http://pfinance.miningco.com/

Personal Finance has about five featured articles and lots of links in its directory. There are links to all sorts of resources for financial planning, "Crash Course in Wills and Trusts," "Debt Management," and "Options & Derivatives."

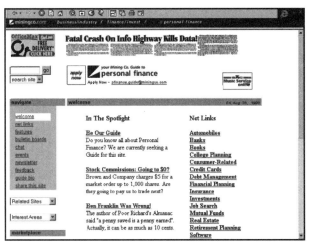

D&T Online—Personal Finance

http://www.dtonline.com/

D&T Online is organized into five major sections: Financial Tip of the Week, Personal Finance Advisor, Business Advisor, Tax News & Views, and The Library. The Personal Finance Advisor and Business Advisor sections are complete resource guides with articles covering various topics. The Library has additional guides that can be purchased from D&T.

Financenter

http://www.financenter.com/

The Financenter has several calculators; you will find them at the SmartCalcs section of its site. Each of the calculators is presented in the form of a question. The main SmartCalcs page has at least a hundred questions addressing various topics. Some of the questions asked at this site (along with accompanying interactive calculator) are "How do exchange rates affect my foreign stocks?" and "How much should I set aside for emergencies?"

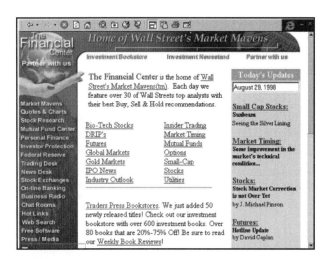

The Financial Center

http://www.tfc.com/

"Home of the Wall Street Mavens," The Finance Center has commentary you want to check into. At the Market Mavens section, fifteen investment sectors are covered by over thirty analysts. At the Financial Center, they are quoted each with their buy, sell and hold recommendations. Most of the analysts offer back issues of their newsletters.

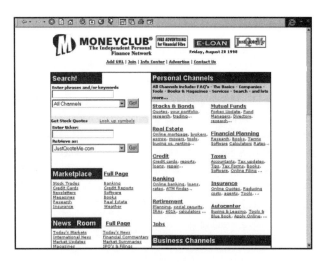

Money Club

http://www.moneyclub.com/

With a nicely organized home page, you might want to consider this your starting point for financial planning research. The page has a quotes search and when you venture to the Financial Planning sector, you'll find FAQs, links to several financial planning sites, and other investment tools.

Resources

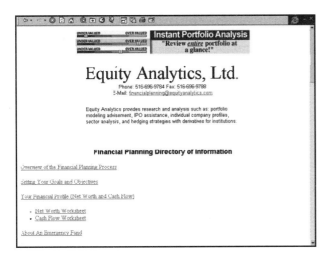

Financial Planning Process

http://www.e-analytics.com/fpdir1.htm

The Equity Analytics site is an excellent resource for financial planning. The Financial Planning Process guide is organized through a table of contents linking to lots of articles. The guide covers just about every planning topic from goals and objectives, stocks, bonds, and estate planning. Visit the Retirement Planning guide, too (http://www.e-analytics.com/insdir.htm).

Quicken Mortgage

http://www.quicken.com/mortgage/

Quicken Mortgage covers all stages of home ownership, addressing the planning, shopping, applying, and owning phases. The site calculates how much house a buyer can afford using given the current rates and available funds. Guest columnists are featured at the site and mortgage news is covered on a daily basis.

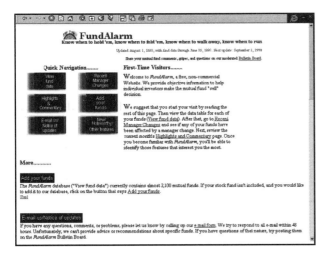

Fund Alarm

http://www.fundalarm.com/

This site has the motto of Kenny Rogers, "You gotta know when to hold 'em and know when to fold 'em." The FundAlarm "provides information to help individual investors make the mutual fund 'sell' decision." Come to this site to find out about recent fund manager changes, mutual fund news, and view fund data.

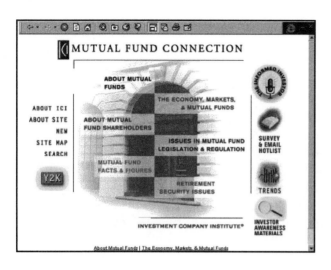

Mutual Fund Connection

http://www.ici.org/

Mutual Fund Connection is brought to you by the Investment Company Institute, the national association of the investment company industry. The site provides an in-depth view of mutual funds through its Mutual Fund Factbook and publishes the annual edition of its extensive *Directory of Mutual Funds and Other Investment Companies* via .pdf file format.

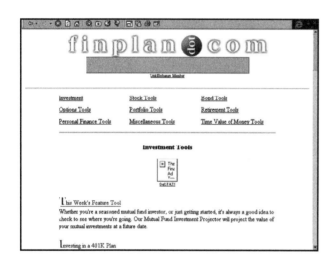

Finance Tools

http://www.finplan.com/finance/finmain.htm

Here is another Web site that features lots of calculators and financial analysis tools. Here you can use the car lease calculator, education needs planning tools, and time value of money calculators. The investment section can also be of value with the put/call parity calculator for options pricing and CAPM Beta calculator.

College for Financial Planning

http://www.fp.edu/

If you plan to become a Certified Financial Planner, this site may be of interest. The College for Financial Planning provides CFP courses to help CFP applicants fulfill the education requirements of the CFP distinction. The site provides information about the program offerings and has a form to order a complete catalog.

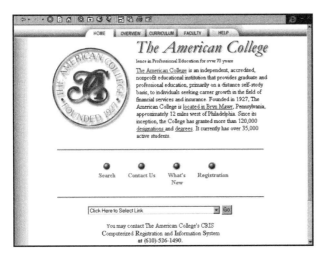

The American College

http://www.amercoll.edu/

The American College is another program that offers courses to help fulfill the CFP education requirement. The College offers various designation programs including CFP, ChFc (Chartered Financial Consultant) and REBC (Registered Employee Benefits Consultant).

Financial Planning Periodicals

Financial Planning Interactive

http://www.fponline.com/

If you aren't a subscriber of Financial Planning, never fear there are a few guest resources here. Guests can read the latest news at Newswatch, participate in eleven topic-based moderated discussion forums and browse through upcoming conference and events.

Money Magazine

http://www.money.com

Check out the Steps guides where you can explore tools, news and practical advice for each stage of a financial life. From Starting Out, to Raising a Family, Peak Earning Years and Retirement, these guides are practically mini-sites. Check out the Money Goals section for additional topic-based content. With all these resources, you may forget there is an entire monthly magazine at this site, too!

Smart Money Interactive

http://www.smartmoney.com/

The Answer Center has thirteen in-depth guides for you to read about. Each guide contains ten to twenty articles as well as worksheets, real life stories, and calculators. Back at the home page, the Tools section contains calculators and interactive analysis tools.

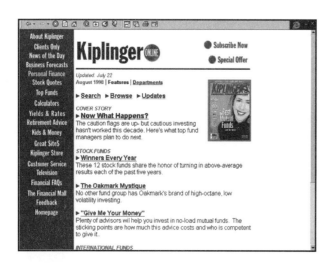

Kiplinger's Personal Finance

http://www.kiplinger.com/magazine/maghome.html

Personal Finance Online is Kiplinger's popular magazine Web site. The entire online magazine is available. The News section at the site is updated several times throughout the day. Like the other sites mentioned, Kiplinger's has many online calculators.

Mutual Funds Magazine

http://www.mfmag.com/

Once you sign up in the free registration area, you'll be entitled to visit all the areas of this Web site. At this site, you will find the entire text of the *Mutual Funds* magazine dating back to inception, November 1994. There is a weekly E-mail newsletter, fund performance calculators, and top performing fund announcements.

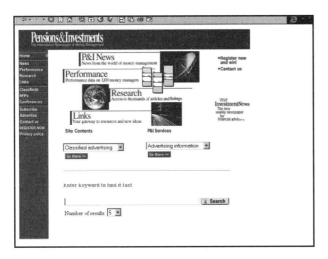

Pensions & Investments Magazine

http://www.pionline.com/

PI Online's major sections are generally search oriented. Therefore, at first blush it's somewhat difficult to determine what resources are available. However, there are many articles in its database as well as performance data and news. Plan a visit to Investment News, PI Online's sister site at http://www.investmentnews.com/.

Organizations

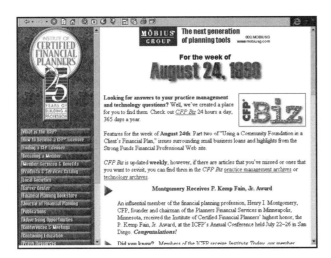

Institute of Certified Financial Planners

http://www.icfp.org/

ICFP "promotes the advancement of knowledge in financial planning, supporting programs that enable CFP members to better serve their clients, and ensuring the integrity and professionalism of its members." ICPF produces the *Journal of Financial Planning* and has a few articles online. You can also request a free issue. There are resources online on the CFP certification process.

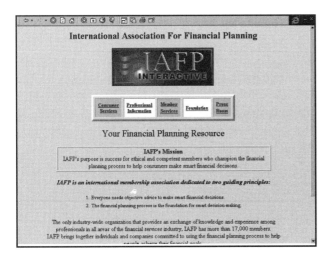

International Association for Financial Planning

http://www.iafp.org/

IAFP's purpose is "success for ethical and competent members who champion the financial planning process to help consumers make smart financial decisions." Visit the Consumer Services section for the Planning for Financial Success series, financial planning tip of the month, and free brochures. The Professional Information section has information on careers in financial planning, membership information, and more.

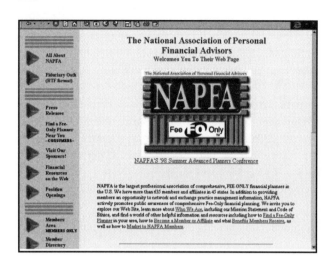

National Association of Personal Financial Advisors

http://www.napfa.org/

NAPFA's mission is to "promote the public interest through advancing the profession of comprehensive fee-only financial planning by enhancing the skills of NAPFA members, emphasizing NAPFA members' roles as fiduciaries, and educating the public about the financial planning process."

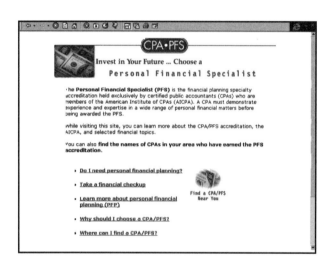

AICPA—PFS

http://www.aicpa.org/members/div/pfp/index.htm
http://www.cpapfs.org/

There are two Web sites associated with this write-up, a site for PFS professionals (AICPA site) and the CPA/PFS commercial site. At the AICPA site you can find out what the PFP membership section can offer you, information on CPA/PFS accreditation, and the white paper "Compensation and Disclosure Issues in PFP." The commercial site has general information about PFS and offers a financial checkup self-assessment.

International Society for Retirement Planning

http://www.isrplan.org/

The purpose of the ISRP is "to improve the quality of life of mature adults." The site has general information for its membership and links to other sources on retirement and life planning issues.

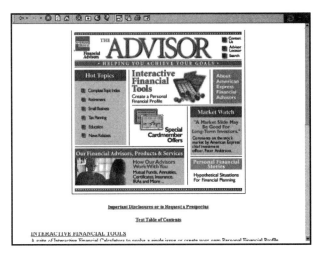

American Express Financial Advisors

http://www.americanexpress.com/advisors/

American Express' commercial site for financial advisors includes general information about its products and services. The site has interactive tools based on specific topics. Visitors can also create a personal financial profile based on specific sequenced steps.

Investment Adviser Resources

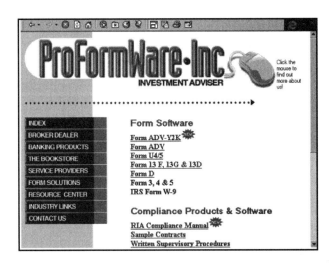

Investment Adviser

http://www.proformware.com/invest.html

ProFormWare has formed software for investment advisers. Under the Resources section, there are many links to investor adviser resources such as SEC Releases and Guidance for Investor Adviser Compliance.

INVESTools for Independent Investors

http://www.investools.com/

INVESTools is a great resource for newsletters and mailings lists. At the Newsletter section, you can sign up for more than twenty different newsletters offered through the site. The newsletters require a paid subscription. If you go to the pricing page, there will be a link to what is available for visitors of the site. The discussion groups are free of charge, although they require sign-up.

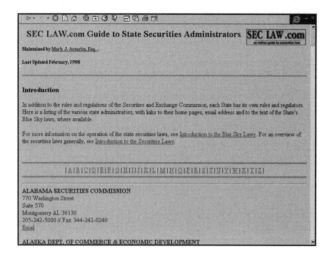

The Securities Law Home Page

http://www.seclaw.com/

SECLAW is maintained by Mark J. Astarita, Esq. He provides a monthly newsletter at the site for securities-related law issues and news. Several articles and an online events calendar are featured at the site. After Mark's signature, you will see sections entitled Arbitration, Corporate Finance, Brokers, Investors, and Related Links. Don't skip over these sections! Each section is chock-full of articles and additional resources. You might want to visit the Blue Sky Regulations (http://www.seclaw.com/bluesky.htm) and Security Law Rules Regulation and Information (http://www.seclaw.com/secrules.htm).

Private Industry

Resources

Business Researcher's Jumpstation

http://www.brint.com/Sites.htm

A gem of a Web site by @Brint. You can navigate the Jumpstation any way you choose via search, drop-down or complete index. The "must-see" areas of this site are the Discussion Forum on Knowledge Management (the Think Tank), Business Process Reengineering and Innovation, and Virtual Corporations & Outsourcing and E-commerce.

Controller's Web

http://www.ppcbusiness.com/

The Controller's Web, produced by Practitioner's Publishing Corporation, "provides solutions for Controllers, Consultants, Managers, and Financial Professionals." Each week the site features an Expense Reduction Tip and Technology Tip. Visit the Year 2000 Resources section for relevant information.

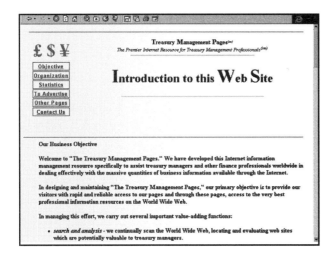

Treasury Management Pages

http://www.mcs.com/~tryhardz/tmpaa.html

The Treasury Management Pages' index is broken down into eight major areas of interest to the financial manager. Each area provides a directory of links to treasury resources. Areas of interest to a Corporate Treasurer are Treasury Administration, the Treasury Management Database, Banking and Corporate Finance, and Treasury Operations.

CEO Express

http://www.ceoexpress.com/

CEO Express is an excellent one-page (almost) directory of the best resources on the Internet. It has a portal look and feel which lends itself to "start page potential." The page has hundreds of links, and there are entire sections devoted to News & Information and Business Research.

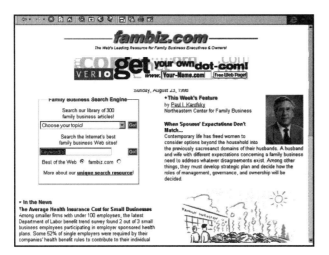

Family Business

http://www.fambiz.com/

The Family Business Web site has an impressive database of articles (over three hundred) relating to family businesses. Fambiz provides an E-mail service of its In the News articles and at the home page news is spotlighted in This Week's Feature.

Periodicals

CFO Net

http://www.cfonet.com/

A great read for those in private industry, CFO Net is the home of the *CFO Magazine* and the *Treasury and Risk Management Magazine*. The site has a discussion forum with several topics of interest to CFOs. Check out the Resources and Jobs sections where CFO Net has provided surveys, tools, and current job postings.

Business Finance Magazine

http://www.businessfinancemag.com/

This online magazine site was formerly known as *Controller Magazine*. Now it has a new name, new design, and same great content. The site provides selected magazine articles for online viewing. Visit the Vendor Directory, the Buyer's Guides for Back Office Accounting, and Innovations in Accounting and Finance Software.

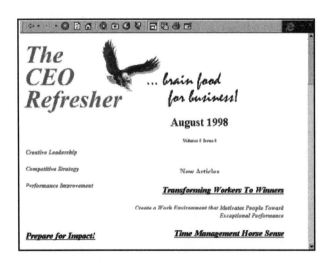

CEO Refresher

http://www.refresher.com/

The CEO Refresher provides "brain food for business." Each month this site brings a mixture of useful articles to the Internet. Former features have included subjects such as "Transforming Workers to Winners," "Time Management Horse Sense," and "Conditions for Change Management." The site also features upcoming executive conferences.

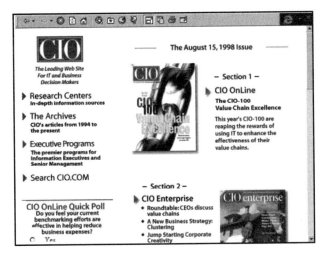

CIO

http://www.cio.com/

The CIO Web site is rich in resources for the chief information officer. The CIO Web site is brought to you by the publishers of *CIO Magazine*. You can search the entire site, which includes the full text of CIO articles dating back to 1994, or browse by topic or edition. There are several topic-based and in-depth Research Centers for Outsourcing, Electronic Commerce, IS Staffing, and more. You can even hear RealAudio webcasts at CIO!

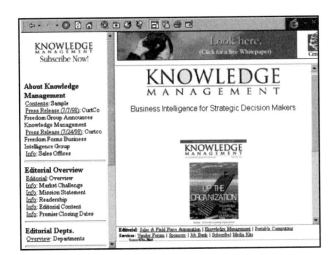

Knowledge Management Magazine

http://www.kmmag.com/

Knowledge Management is a new magazine that premiered in September 1998. The magazine's mission is to be "the definitive guide for executives to leverage their organization's information and intellectual assets." The Web site features a sample edition and editorial. At the site you can sign up for a free subscription.

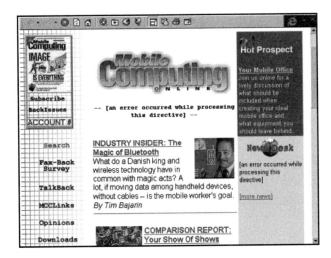

Mobile Computing Online

http://www.mobilecomputing.com/

Mobile Computing & Communications magazine focuses exclusively on portable technology being used in corporate applications. At its Web site several current articles are featured. The site hosts a Mobile Office forum and the posts looked pretty lively. News is featured at the site with announcements effecting the mobile computing industry.

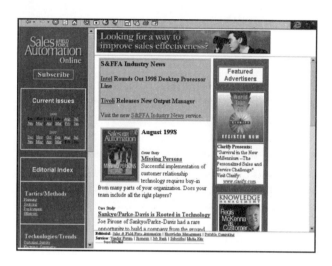

Sales & Field Force Automation Online

http://www.sffaonline.com/

In addition to the *Sales & Field Force* magazine, this site has resources to help you plan, source and deploy an automated sales force. In addition, there are various articles addressing technologies, trends, and industries. Visit the Vendors section for a complete online directory for hardware and software.

Organizations

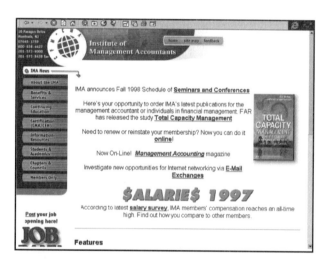

Institute of Management Accountants

http://www.imanet.org/

The IMA is devoted exclusively to management accounting and financial management. The organization publishes *Management Accounting* and offers its current issue online. The site includes information about the certification process for the CMA and CFM distinctions.

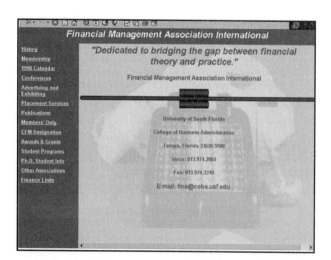

Financial Management Association

http://www.fma.org/

The mission of the FMA is to "broaden the common interests between academia and practitioners and to promote the development and understanding of basic and applied research and of sound financial practices." Past issues of the *Contemporary Finance Digest* are available online.

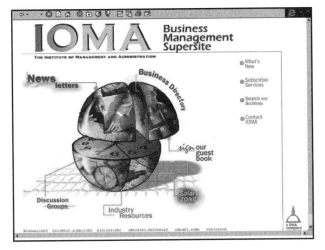

Institute of Management & Administration

http://www.ioma.com/

IOMA is a major publisher of business and management information. This site is rich in content. IOMA includes several articles from each of its recent publications as well as subscription information for all publications. The site also provides discussion forums, salary information, industry resources, and access to a substantial Business Directory.

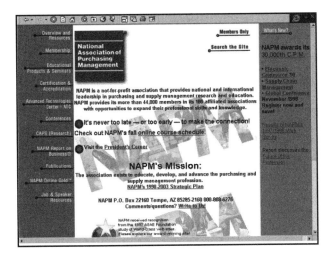

National Association of Purchasing Management

http://www.napm.org/

NAPM provides "national and international leadership in purchasing and supply management research and education." At the NAPM Web site you will find general information as well as NAPM's *Report on Business* and information about its other publications and its upcoming conferences.

Treasury Management Association

http://www.tma-net.org/

TMA provides its members and visitors access to past issues of the *TMA Journal* and highlights from its Electronic Commerce Report. In the Library and Research section, look for the TMA Discussion Forum, online resources, surveys, and studies.

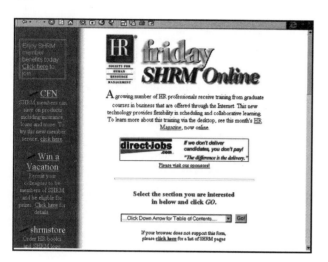

Society for Human Resource Management

http://www.shrm.org/

SHRM provides its members with education and information services, conferences and seminars, government and media representation, and publications. The best feature at this site is its extensive directory of links relating to human resource management. If you need to research an HR issue, you'll never regret visiting the SHRM Links Directory first!

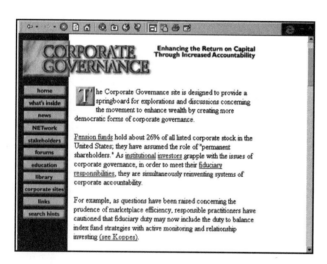

Corporate Governance Network

http://www.corpgov.net/

The Corporate Governance site is designed "to provide a springboard for explorations and discussions concerning the movement to enhance wealth by creating more democratic forms of corporate governance." The site provides chances to interact with others interested in corporate governance through its Discussion Forums, Commentary, and Conversation sections.

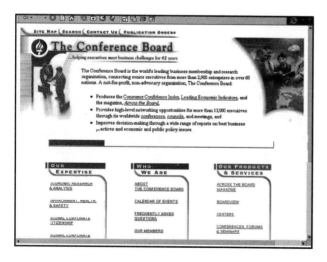

The Conference Board

http://www.conference-board.org/

The Conference Board produces the Consumer Confidence Index, Leading Economic Indicators, and the magazine *Across the Board*. The organization's Press Release section provides general insights regarding its findings. There are many publications generated from TCB, some have abstracts and sections online, others provide ordering information.

American Society of Corporate Secretaries

http://www.ascs.org/

ASCS was established to provide resources to those involved in duties normally associated with the corporate secretarial function. Its Web site is an extension of resources by providing members and visitors with articles of interest to corporate secretaries including "Best Tips for Proofreading your Annual Report."

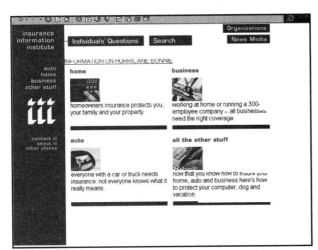

Insurance Information Institute

http://www.iii.org/

The III has many resources at its site. First, visit the News Media section for various articles and insurance information on topics such as worker's compensation, catastrophes, and finance. The Organizations section includes a listing and links to III member companies and state insurance associations.

Tax

Directories

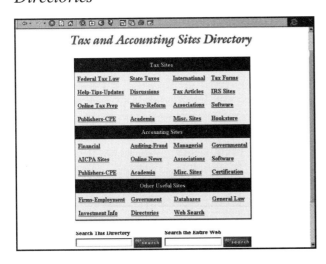

Schmidt's Tax Sites

http://www.taxsites.com

Dr. Dennis Schmidt's Tax Sites has plenty of tax resources in its extensive directory (over 2,000 links!). Tax Sites is well organized, easy to use, and is updated frequently. In addition to tax sites, it has a nice list of accounting, managerial accounting, and fraud resources.

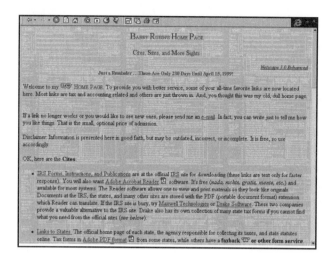

Barry Rubin's Home Page

http://home1.gte.net/brcpa/

Barry Rubin's page is the "official" home for the FAQ of the Usenet newsgroup misc.taxes.moderated (MTM). The FAQ offers basic tax information and links for a layperson. The links on his page are generally to noncommercial sites (IRS, fifty state DORs, and statutes, etc).

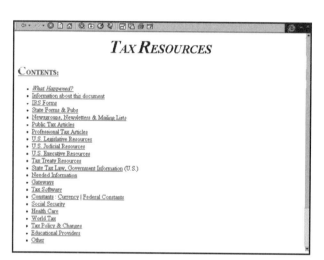

Frank McNeil's Tax Sites

http://www.taxresources.com/

Visit Tax Resources to tap into the area "What Happened?" It is a resource page that takes you to research sources to pick apart what happened in the U.S. income tax world today. The site also has FAQs, discussions of tax issues, and tax articles. Visit his state tax law page for helpful links to state forms, departments, and resources.

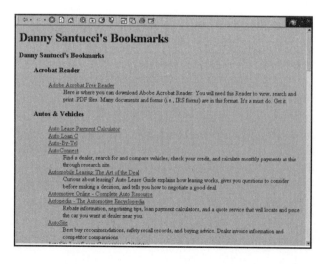

Danny C. Santucci, JD—Tax Attorney

http://members.aol.com/sdcpa/santucci/

Danny Santucci provides a listing to hundreds of Web site links. Many of his Web site links lead to hard to find resources and many are topic specific. His list is updated quarterly on the Web site but a free daily update is available to anyone by E-mailing sanpub@idt.net and requesting it.

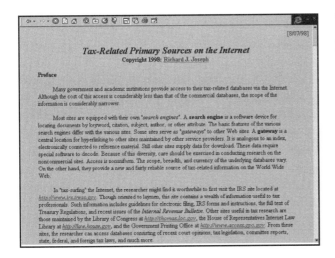

Tax-Related Internet Sources

http://www.bus.utexas.edu/~josephr/384/itaxsrcs.htm

This site is oriented exclusively to tax research. Tax-Related Internet Sources was designed by a tax research professor (and Prentice Hall's authority on tax research methodology). The site is alphabetized and organized by authority, not by source. This mode of organization facilitates the type of tax research conducted by CPAs and tax attorneys.

1040.com

http://www.1040.com/strev.htm

Visit the Taxing Subjects at the 1040.com Web site for helpful tax information. The site has a good state resource area that includes links to the various State Revenue Departments at http://www.1040.com/state.htm. 1040.com also houses the IRS BBS daily file and posts them in various viewing formats.

General Tax Resources

Tax Analysts

http://www.tax.org/

Tax Analysts is a great Web site. It has a subscription service (i.e., for TaxBase, etc.) and provides many resources in its free service area. To make the site even better, it recently underwent an entire revamp of design and content. Some of the areas to visit while at the Tax Analyst site are: The Tax Analysts Newswire, updated throughout the day to reflect breaking news, The Tax Lobbying Report, and the Tax Analysts newsgroups, offering more than twenty moderated discussions on various tax topics.

Tax Prophet

http://www.taxprophet.com/

Tax Prophet targets a specific audience, U.S. and foreign individuals and small businesses. It contains timely articles written in plain English on relevant income and estate tax issues, and the content is frequently updated. Check out the Cybersurfing page; it has an extensive list of links to other tax-related sources on the Internet.

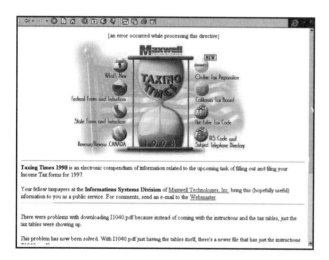

Taxing Times

http://www.scubed.com/tax/

Taxing Times 1999 is an electronic compendium of information related to the upcoming task of filling out and filing your Income Tax forms for 1998. Get the latest site updates at What's New or go straight to the Forms section. The site has information about its online tax preparation service, SecureTax.

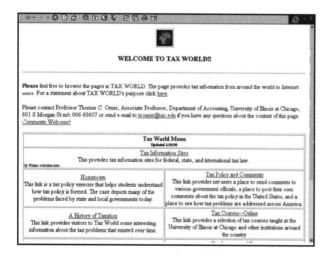

Tax World

http://omer.actg.uic.edu/

Tax World's most unique feature is its history of taxation section. Tax World's creator, a university professor, researched tax history since he is "always trying to show how taxes relate to the world no matter the time period." Tax World exists to provide a broad range of research resources to those seeking to understand more about the various tax systems in existence in today's economy.

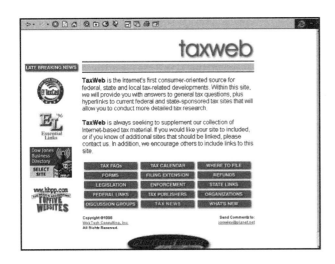

TaxWeb

http://www.taxweb.com/

This site is a commercial site for federal, state, and local tax news developments. The site includes FAQs, forms, extension and refund information, and various links. Visit the Legislation section for pending federal and state legislation. The state legislation is by state and the coverage is good.

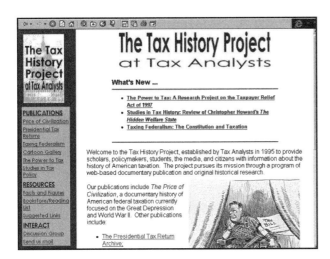

The Tax History Project

http://www.taxhistory.org/

The Tax History Project is a unique effort to shed light on the history of American taxation. It was established in 1995 to "provide scholars, policymakers, students, media, and citizens with information about the history of taxation." You will find copies of tax documents with historical significance here. On the lighter side, the site has old tax cartoons as well as a presidential tax return archive.

Roth IRA Web Site

http://www.rothira.com/

The purpose of this site is to provide technical and planning information on Roth IRAs to consumers and practitioners. The site includes articles, news, and archived content. Visit the Sites section for further sources of information on Roth IRAs.

Tax News & Publications

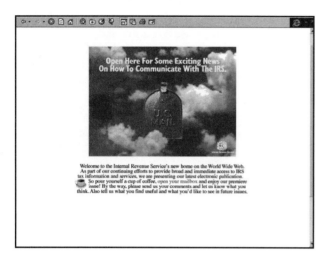

IRS Home Page

http://www.irs.ustreas.gov/

This site probably does not need much explaining. Therefore, I'll just mention some of the major areas you can find here. The IRS Web site is a very comprehensive site for federal taxation and it includes various resources such as a tax calendar, forms, publications, proposed regulations, news, and announcements.

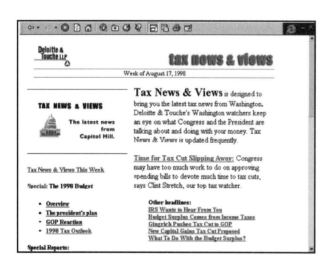

Deloitte & Touche's Tax News and Views

http://www.dtonline.com/tnv/tnv.htm

Tax News & Views is updated weekly and is designed to bring you the latest tax news from Washington. For the latest breaking tax news on Capitol Hill, D&T offers a free E-mail alert. In addition to tax news, the Web site features articles on various tax topics such as capital gains and tax reform.

E&Y—TaxCast

http://www.taxcast.com/

At the site's Knowledge Center, TaxCast has several tax-related publications online including the *Tax Information Reporting Newsletter* and *Tax News International*, among others. For clients, they can visit the Forum for over 20 tax-related discussions. View the E&Y Tax news and browse tax topics by date or by category. TaxCast also has a free Executive Edition that includes custom content which is available for its tax clients.

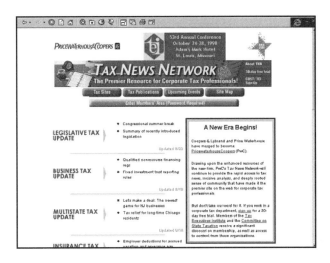

PwC—Tax News Network

http://www.taxnews.com/tnn_public/

The Tax News Network is brought to you by PricewaterhouseCoopers. Visit TNN for various tax updates for legislative, business, multi-state, benefits, global and insurance tax issues. The site also includes several online publications for viewing. TNN includes a members-only area and has a 30-day free trial membership to provide an opportunity to visit the private content and resources provided.

Washington D.C. Highlights

http://www.riatax.com/washdc.html

The RIA site hosts weekly tax news and provides timely updates to the latest in taxation. It also provides an article from the *Journal of Taxation* at its site. For another publisher that has updates (about every two weeks), check out PPC's Tax Action Bulletins at http://www.ppcinfo.com/5-min.htm.

Law Resources

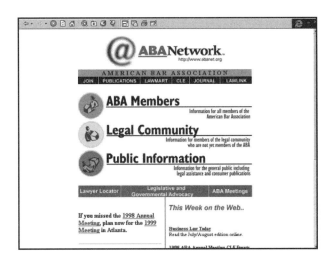

American Bar Association Tax Section

http://www.abanet.org/tax/

The ABA's Tax Section includes general information about the section, news, and a myriad of publications. You can view the publications via PDF, and the topics include Analysis of Current Consumption Tax Proposals, the State Tax Law Journal, the Property Tax Deskbook, and New State Tax Law Journal.

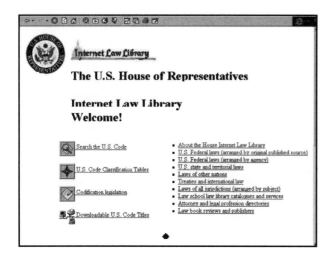

U.S. House of Representatives Internet Law Library

http://law.house.gov/

Search the United States Code at this site (http://law.house.gov/usc.htm). At the Code home page, visit the section on background information on the U.S. Code as well as the top twenty questions about searching the Code. The United States Code contains the text of current public laws enacted by Congress. In addition, the Library houses the federal court's decisions and rules (http://law.house.gov/6.htm).

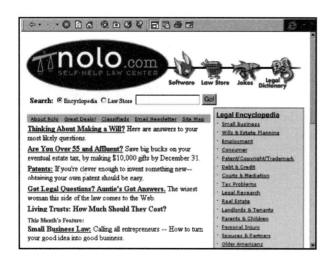

Nolo Press

http://www.nolo.com/

Nolo Press is a great resource for all kinds of legal information. Go to the Tax Problems section where you will find original articles regarding general tax concerns, audits, appeals and tax bills, filing returns, and small business tax concerns.

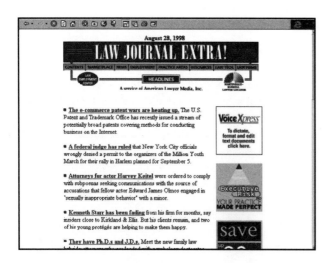

Law Journal EXTRA!

http://www.ljx.com/

The Law Journal EXTRA! is full of helpful law information. The site is broken up into the following categories: news, employment, practice areas, and resources. Visit the taxation resources in the practice section. In addition, the Law Library has many original articles.

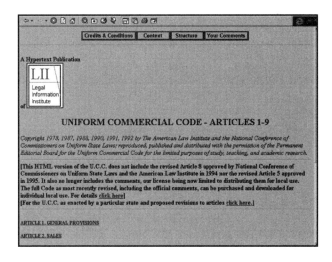

Uniform Commercial Code

http://www.law.cornell.edu/ucc/ucc.table.html

Cornell provides the U.S. Tax Code at http://www.law.cornell.edu/uscode/26/ and Supreme Court Decisions at http://supct.law.cornell.edu/supct/online.

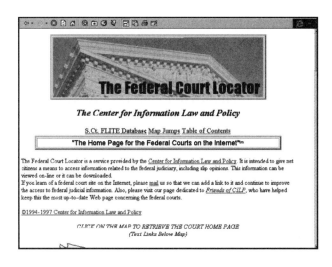

The Federal Court Locator (Villanova)

http://www.law.vill.edu/Fed-Ct/

This site has plenty of judicial system information available. The site hosts the Oral Arguments Archive and Federal Court Opinions and Rules. In addition, you will find links to the court of appeals, district courts, and federal courts. Visit Faris Law at http://www.farislaw.com/ for the Supreme Court International Bulletin.

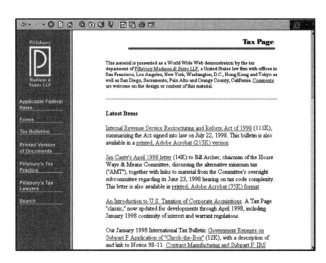

Pillsbury Madison & Sutro LLP Tax

http://www.pmstax.com/

Visit Pillsbury, Madison & Sutro for the various bulletins regarding international, corporate, partnership, general, and state and local tax issues. The site also has the published IRS Applicable Federal Rates, which are published monthly.

Foreign/International Tax

OZ TAX AUSTRALIAN TAXATION INDEX
http://www.law.flinders.edu.au/tax/

TAX ON AUSTRALIA
http://www.csu.edu.au/faculty/commerce/account/tax/tax.htm

TAXATION INSTITUTE OF AMERICA
http://www.taxia.asn.au/

DELOITTE TAX NET AUSTRALIA
http://www.deloitte.com.au/

REVENUE CANADA
http://www.rc.gc.ca/

HONG KONG GOVERNMENT TAX INFORMATION
http://www.info.gov.hk/info/taxinfo.htm

INDIAN TAX SYSTEM
http://sunsite.sut.ac.jp/asia/india/jitnet/india/ibeo/tax.htm

IRELAND CHARTERED ACCOUNTANTS TAXATION SUMMARY
http://www.icai.ie/catsmenu.htm

IRELAND REVENUE COMMISSIONERS
http://www.revenue.ie/

ITALIAN TAXATION SYSTEM
http://www.icenet.it/cosver/html/primer_uk.html

INLAND REVENUE—UK
http://www.open.gov.uk/inrev/irhome.htm

TREASURY DEPARTMENT—UK
http://www.hm-treasury.gov.uk/

Tax Topics

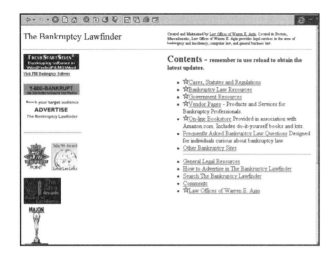

The Bankruptcy Lawfinder

http://www.agin.com/lawfind/

The Bankruptcy Lawfinder has cases, statutes, and regulations. There is a specific area that delves deeply into bankruptcy topics and provides many resources. Check out the FAQ on bankruptcy law questions.

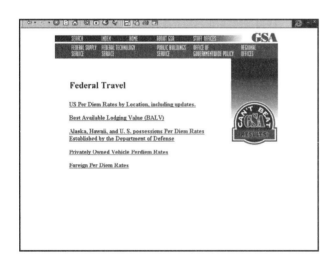

Per Diem Travel Allowances

http://www.gsa.gov/travel.htm

This site hosts the various federal per diem rates by location, including updates. On top of that check out the site for the Best Available Lodging Value, privately owned vehicle per diems, and foreign per diems.

Social Security Privatization

http://www.socialsecurity.org/

The Social Security Privatization site is sponsored by the CATO Institute's Social Security Project. The site has a Java calculator to run calculations under privatization, articles and opinion columns, speeches, video, Congressional testimony, and links to major supporters.

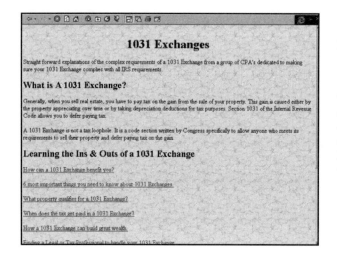

1031 Exchanges

http://www.exchangecpas.com/

This site walks you through the ins and outs of a 1031 Exchange. It covers the benefits, property qualifications, and the six most important things you need to know about 1031 Exchanges. For additional 1031 exchange information, visit Xchange Net at http://www.xchangenet.com/.

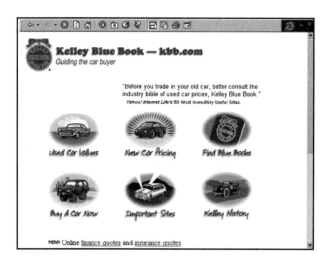

Valuation Kelley Blue Book

http://www.kbb.com/

Use the Kelley Blue Book online to perform your automotive tax valuations. The site is easy to use and uses interactive forms to calculate the precise value. You will have your completed value within seconds.

California Estate Planning and Trust Law

http://www.ca-probate.com/

This is a great resource to visit regardless of your location. Each state should have a resource this complete. Visit the Estate Planning & Probate Attorney List to perform searches. In addition, the creator of this site, Mark Welch, has a large list of law and estate planning sites for further research.

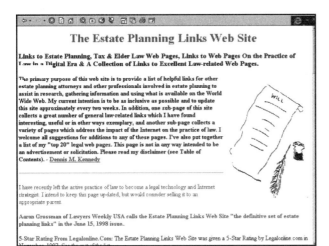

Estate Planning Links

http://users.aol.com/dmk58/eplinks.html

The primary purpose of this site is "to provide a list of helpful links for other estate planning attorneys and other professionals involved in the estate planning process." The site has a table of contents to easily guide you through the various link resources collected by Dennis Kennedy.

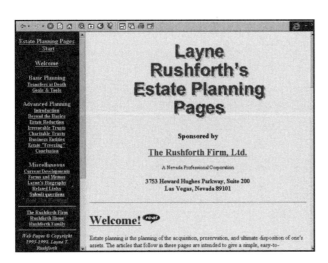

Layne Rushforth's Estate Planning Pages

http://www.rushforth.org/planning.html

Layne Rushforth's site is rich with original content. It is nicely organized via the navigation index which is broken out into the main categories of Basic Planning, Advance Planning, and Other. If you have an interest in the estate planning process, you should spend some time here.

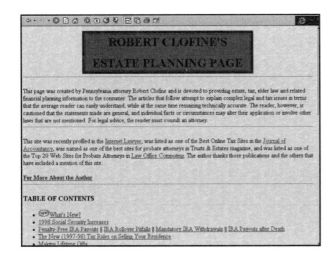

Robert Clofine's Estate Planning Page

http://www.estateattorney.com/

Another estate site with lots of content, Robert Clofine's site addresses issues such as Reducing Federal Estate Tax, Planning for Disability, Will Substitutes, Prenuptial Agreements, Nursing Care, and more.

Organizations Web Site List

ABA TAX SECTION
http://www.abanet.org/tax/

AMERICANS FOR TAX REFORM
http://www.atr.org/

CATO INSTITUTE
http://www.cato.org/

CONCORD COALITION
http://www.concordcoalition.org/

FLAT TAX HOME PAGE
http://flattax.house.gov/

CITIZENS FOR TAX JUSTICE
http://www.ctj.org/

CENTER FOR BUDGET AND POLICY PRIORITIES
http://www.cbpp.org/

CITIZENS FOR SOUND ECONOMY
http://www.cse.org/cse/

HERITAGE FOUNDATION
http://www.heritage.org/

JOINT ECONOMIC COMMITTEE
http://www.senate.gov/~jec/

NATIONAL BUREAU OF ECONOMIC RESEARCH
http://www.nber.org/

NATIONAL CENTER FOR POLICY ANALYSIS
http://www.public-policy.org/~ncpa/

NATIONAL TAXPAYERS UNION
http://www.ntu.org/

NATL. COMMISSION ON ECONOMIC GROWTH & TAX REFORM
http://www.townhall.com/taxcom/

TAX FOUNDATION
http://www.taxfoundation.org/

BUSINESS AND FINANCE RESOURCES

Business

Practice Development Resources

Accountants Marketing Secrets

http://www.mostad.com/

Mostad & Christensen provide accounting firms marketing solutions. M&C produces a variety of client newsletters and brochures for tax, financial planning, and client alerts. The Web site offers a marketing tip every month. If you want to receive some free stuff, fill out a brief form and get hard copy guides such as "No-nonsense Marketing Plan," "Marketing Reminder Calendar," and "27 Ways to Improve Your Marketing."

Parli.com

http://www.parli.com/

Rob McConnell Productions host the Parli.com Web site. This site gives you access to Parliamentarian by E-mail where you can receive various brochures, a periodic newsletter, and a chance to ask your Robert's Rules of Orders. Questions appear in Dear Parliamentarian.

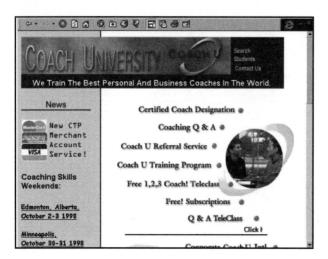

Coach University

http://www.coachu.com/

Coach U has an extensive Q&A section where you can find out more about coaching and what it takes to be a good coach. Coach U also supports the DailyCast Web site at http://www.dailycast.com/. At DailyCast you can start your day with a little knowledge in subject matters such coaching, communication, top ten business lists.

Malcolm Baldridge National Quality Program

http://www.quality.nist.gov/

Its mission statement sums up why you should take a peek at this Web site: "to assist U.S. businesses and nonprofit organizations in delivering ever-improving value to its customers, resulting in marketplace success, and improving overall company performance and capabilities." Make sure you check out the CEO survey and the Winners Showcase.

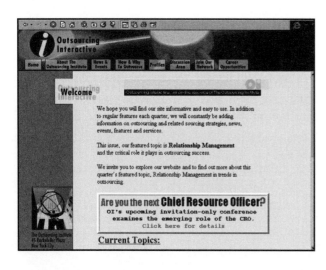

Outsourcing Interactive

http://www.outsourcing.com/

Outsourcing Interactive has regular features each quarter as well as periodic additions of related sourcing strategies, news, events, features, and services. This quarter's topic is relationship management and the critical role it plays in outsourcing success.

Personal Development Resources

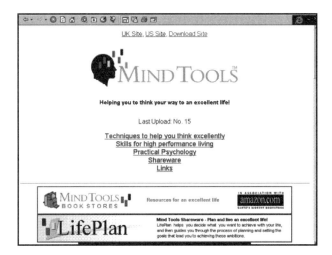

Mind Tools

http://www.mindtools.com/

Food for the mind. This site has "techniques to help you think excellently and skills for high performance living." I found many of the topics to have high relevance to my life. Check out Mastering Stress, Goal Setting, and Time Management. Don't miss the Links to Other Sites page for additional mind exploration!

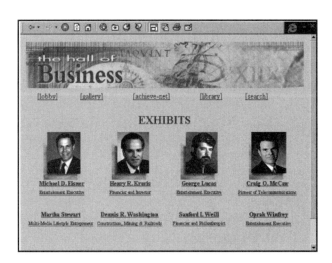

The Hall of Business

http://www.achievement.org/autodoc/halls/bus

Find out what makes successful business leaders tick. Visit the Achievement.org's Hall of Business. There you will find detail transcripts and audio feeds of interviews with its inductees. The leaders run the gamut from KKR's Henry R. Kravis to Oprah Winfrey.

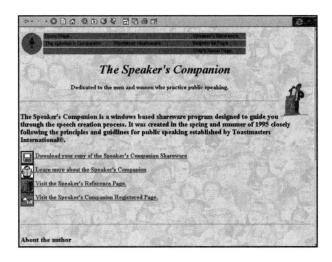

The Speaker's Companion

http://www.lm.com/~chipp/spkrhome.htm

Boy, if you are looking to improve your communication and speaking skills, do I have a site for you. Visit the Speaker's Companion Reference Page for tons of resources for you from Toastmasters to Tom Peters. There are articles such as "Power Speaking" and "Overcoming Speaking Anxiety" all for the reading. Ever wonder about the do's and don'ts of presentations with graphics? You can find the answers here.

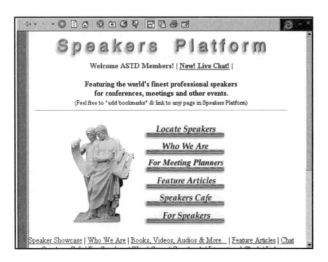

Speakers Platform

http://www.speaking.com/

The Speakers Platform Web site has many feature articles available via search or browse. Looking for a speaker? You can look here and find a speaker by browsing the large list of speaking topics available. The database has over two thousand speakers indexed. You can interact at this site through its active discussion forum or its new online chat feature.

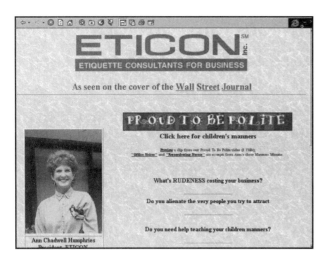

Etiquette for Business

http://www.eticon.com/

Ann Chadwell Humphries' Web site Eticon has some resources to help us all with our business etiquette. There is an article entitled "What's Rudeness Costing Your Business?" After you have had a dose of Ann's wisdom, watch her movie clip sample or read her business etiquette articles and sample columns. Last but not least, read "Overcoming Phone Fury."

Resources for Clients

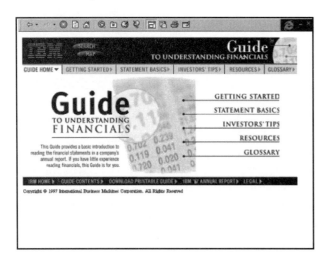

Guides to Understanding Financials

http://www.ibm.com/FinancialGuide/

IBM has prepared an easy-to-follow guide on understanding financial statements. The guide includes statement basics, investors' tips, resources, and a glossary. If you would like a pdf version of how to read a financial report visit: http://www.ml.com/pdfs/frhowtor.pdf.

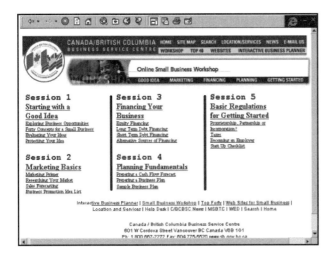

Online Business Workshop

http://www.sb.gov.bc.ca/smallbus/workshop/workshop.html

This is a very nice online business tutorial. The workshop covers topics such as Exploring Business Opportunities, Financing your Business, Basic Regulations for Getting Started, Marketing Basics, and Preparing a Business Plan. Please note this is a Canadian site, so some of the terminology may differ from U.S. practices.

Bookkeeping and Accounting from Start to Finish

http://www.onlinewbc.org/docs/finance/

Although this Web site is called the Online Women's Business Center, there is something for any client here—especially if they are starting out and need some guidance with basic accounting procedures. The site also has complete guides on managing and expanding business.

Planning Your Estate

http://ext.msstate.edu/pubs/pub1742.htm

A resource provided by the Mississippi State University Extension Service. The service includes a few other topics your clients may find of interest. For the "How to Get Out of Debt" publication, substitute pub1737.htm for pub1742.htm in the URL. The "Steps to Successful Money Management" article is pub1738.htm. The "Planning Your Estate" series run from pub1739.htm to pub1746.htm.

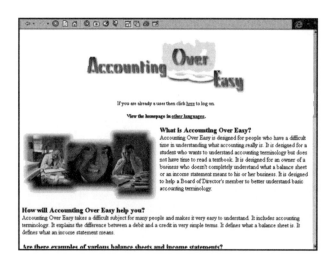

Accounting Over Easy

http://www.ezaccounting.com/

Accounting Over Easy (yes, those are eggs on the Web page) is "designed for an owner of a business who doesn't completely understand what a balance sheet or an income statement means to his or her business. . . ." Timothy Stewart, CPA, provides his service for a very low one-time fee. Once the fee is paid, the subscriber is entitled to enter the site. A demo is available.

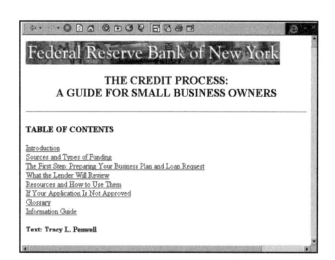

The Credit Process: A Guide for Small Business Owners

http://www.ny.frb.org/pihome/addpub/credit.html

The Federal Reserve Board of New York hosts this guide which investigates various aspects of the credit process. The guide covers types of funding, what the lender will review, resources and how to use them, and a glossary of credit terms.

Business Periodicals

Business Week

http://www.businessweek.com/

This is a weekly staple for the business world. Although there is a fee for nonsubscribers of the hard copy edition of *Business Week*, if you click on the current edition, there are several articles that have been selected for public viewing. The site also hosts RadioNet, an hourly audio update from BW's Ray Hoffman.

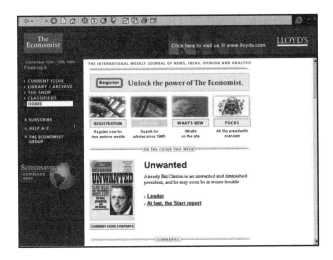

The Economist

http://www.economist.com/

This is an online version of the well-respected publication. There is a substantial "free for all" area. You can also join as a paid subscriber for additional benefits. One nice feature of the site is that this showcases some of the best pieces from previous issues. They have selections from early 1997.

Forbes Digital Tool

http://www.forbes.com/

The Digital Tool is a great business resource. The articles are always fresh and there's lots of content. For the latest, check out the Cool section. After you are done with the Cool and E-Business sections, go to the Toolbox. There you will find a nice indexed directory of popular guides and lists such as the Fortune 500 Listing.

U.S. News Online

http://www.usnews.com/

The online weekly features the latest news and has a "news you can use" article for various categories of interest from money to health to travel. U.S. News sponsors the .edu College and Careers Center which provides detailed rankings among various disciplines, including the popular MBA School Rankings.

Fast Company

http://www.fastcompany.com/

If you haven't had a chance to check out Fast Company, you better do it soon. This up-and-coming business and management publication is a breath of fresh air due to its unique journalistic approach and content. It touts itself as "the magazine about work and life in the new economy." To pique your interest about this new resource, there is the daily Random Factoid (and related article), selected articles of the popular magazine, and lots of discussion forums.

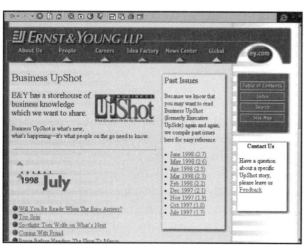

Business UpShot

http://www.ey.com/upshot/

Ernst and Young's Business UpShot Web site notes that E&Y would like to "share their storehouse of business knowledge." This site has a monthly edition with various articles of interest ranging from doing business in Zimbabwe to Japanese real estate. You can also download previous editions of UpShot for off-line reading.

Finance

Directories

E-Analytics Directory

http://www.e-analytics.com/

The E-Analytics site is truly an amazing Web site. You can come here and learn just about every finance topic. The site has in-depth guides and directories for general topics such as stocks, bonds, options, and commodities. Within each section there are articles on the basics as well as deeper analysis of various financial transactions. A visit to the Glossaries and the IPO Resource Center are a must.

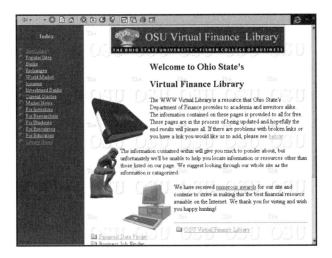

WWW Virtual Library Finance and Investments

http://www.cob.ohio-state.edu/dept/fin/overview.htm

Ohio State has done it again with another wonderful Virtual Library. Before you hunker down to check out the great resources here, check out its New Links page which will give you the latest finds and will help you stay on top of the site for subsequent visits. The index is easily navigated so you won't have a problem finding information on banks, markets, and exchanges. The site also has sections for researchers and executives.

Mining Company Finance

http://economics.miningco.com/

http://stocks.miningco.com/

The Mining Company's Stocks and Economics sections are chock-full of resources to help you. Both sections include features as well as impressive directories for researching finance and economic topics. The Economics section has an extensive listing of organizations and associations. Visit the Stock section for Web site reviews and stock analysis.

FinanceWise

http://www.financewise.com

The first and currently only search engine dedicated to Finance resources on the Internet. This search engine is considered a category search engine. Using the site's Smart Search, you can look up information by company name, type of organization, country, region, or language. You can also browse the site by topic.

Wall Street City

http://www.wallstreetcity.com/

Visit Wall Street City's Talk section for roundtable discussions, forums and newsgroups. The site also offers several newsletters, for which some are free and some are by subscription.

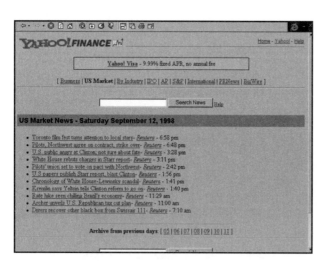

Yahoo! Finance

http://biz.yahoo.com/

This section would not be complete without a mention of the Yahoo! Finance site. Come here for the latest U.S. Market Summary, stock split announcements, economic calendar, and earnings surprises. Oh yeah, you can get stock quotes here, too.

General Finance Resources

CNN Financial Network

http://cnnfn.com/

CNNfn is a great source for general financial information. Its site has a similar Industry Watch section similar to Infoseek's. It also has a section devoted to market news, information, tools, and resources. Visit Digital Jam for the latest on the technology market.

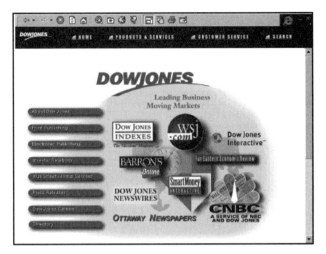

Dow Jones

http://www.dowjones.com

Visit the Dow Jones Web site to learn about DJ's latest products and services. The company also uses the Web site as a gateway to its various online offerings such as CNBC, the *Wall Street Journal*, and the *Wall Street Journal Report*.

The Motley Fool

http://www.fool.com/

The Motley Fool is here to educate, amuse, and enrich you. Check out the Fool's School at http://www.fool.com/school.htm to learn more about the methods to their madness. The site has very lively discussion forums and chats, so next time you are the neighborhood, check out the Fool.

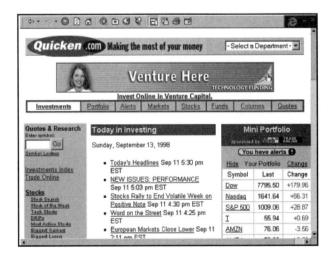

Quicken.com Investments

http://www.quicken.com/investments/

The Quicken.com provides an online portfolio if you choose to track a few stocks online. Or maybe track a stock watch list. Visit the Stock Columns section for columns by various investment specialists. The Alerts section provides details on major stock announcements or market movements.

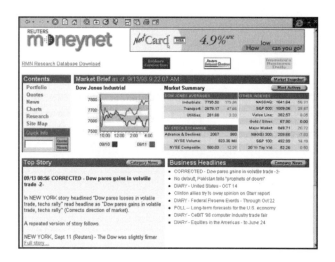

Reuters Moneynet

http://www.moneynet.com/

Reuters Moneynet provides the latest business and market news. The Inc.Link section contains company profiles on more than twelve thousand U.S. public companies. Visit the Research section for information on Hot Stocks and Fund Summaries.

TheStreet.com

http://www.thestreet.com/

TheStreet.com is a popular online resource with several new articles, commentaries, and advice posted daily. The majority of the content is subscription-based, however, the site does provide a thirty-day free trial membership. The free content areas include Market Update and Tools. The Market Update is well worth the visit.

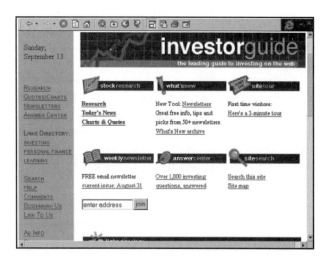

Investor Guide

http://www.investorguide.com/

Visit the Research section of this site and type in the ticker for America Online (AOL). The search results are pretty impressive giving you the option to venture off to several other Web sites where AOL is researched. The site also provides excerpts of several investing newsletters as well as its sister site InvestorWords at http://www.investorwords.com/ for the biggest and best investment glossary on the Internet. The glossary has over five thousand definitions and fifteen thousand links between related terms.

Silicon Investor

http://www.techstocks.com/

The top of the site in bold letters reads "SI Members have posted 5,581,374 messages," which is a testament to this site's popularity and inter-activity. Take a peek into the many Stock Talk groups. Visit the SI Spotlight section for stock results by category: features, big movers, volume, and highs/lows.

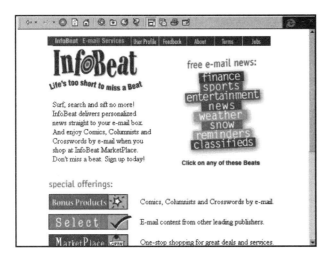

InfoBeat Finance

http://www.infobeat.com/

You can have free E-mail service pushed to your In-box. InfoBeat Finance offers several different E-mail newsletters such as Morning Call, Midday Updates, Alerts, Internet Daily, and Weekender. As you can tell by the titles, the newsletter updates are distributed at various times of the day, giving you more subscription options.

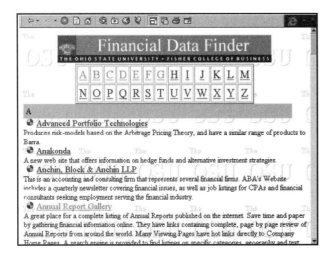

Financial Data Finder

http://www.cob.ohio-state.edu/dept/fin/osudata.htm

The Finance Department at Ohio State has prepared an extensive Web site full of research resources to help you find data. The various resources are listed alphabetically, so once you have figured out which sites you are interested in visiting, it will be easy to come back to the Data Finder and browse again.

Finance Periodicals

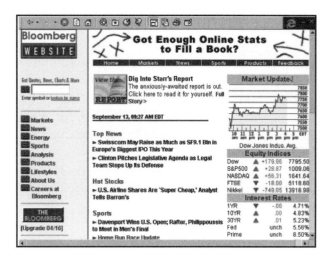

Bloomberg Online

http://www.bloomberg.com/

With a Web site reminiscent of its popular format of "information everywhere," Bloomberg Online does not disappoint. The site has a home page cover story, lots of news, and analysis tools. Visit the Hot Stocks section for a brief synopsis of the market movers. The analysis area has a handful of useful calculators.

Fortune

http://www.fortune.com/

Fortune Online has the same great online content and coverage you would expect from a great magazine. The entire online edition has many articles and they are all free for the picking. Follow the Daily Business Report for the latest.

Red Herring Online

http://www.herring.com/

The Red Herring is a great source for mainstream "insider" news (a bit of a misnomer, I may add). The Herring has a database of original content company profiles which you can search or browse. If you are a subscriber to *The Red Herring* hard-copy magazine, don't forget to visit the magazine's online supplement.

Upside Online

http://www.upside.com/

Upside magazine brings you its online version which brings you the latest in Internet industry financing. Upside Online is responsible for the Upside 100 list of up-and-coming technology-based entrepreneurs. You can easily browse through many of its past issues.

Topic Specific Finance Resources

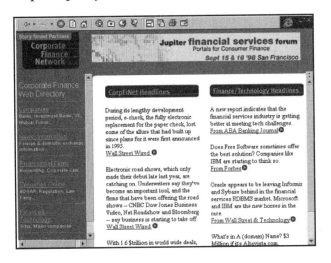

CorpFiNet—Corporate Finance Network

http://www.corpfinet.com

This site is a good place for those in private industry to start their Web research as it is pretty much a directory of resources. It focuses on areas of interest to those in corporate finance, such as banks, insurance companies, leasing companies, and investor relations resources. The site also includes a Finance Careers section.

Hedge Fund Home Page

http://www.hedgefunds.net/

This is the site for everything hedge fund. Did you ever wonder where you could participate in a hedge fund chat? Well, never fear, this is your site. The Hedge Fund Home Page has information about Hedge Fund accounting as well as legal issues and news. Visit the online bookstore for additional information.

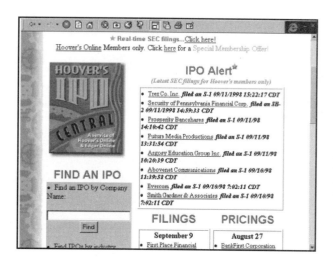

IPO Central

http://www.ipocentral.com/

IPO Central is a service of Hoover's Online and EDGAR Online. Visit its Beginner's Guide to IPOs for a good IPO primer. You can also browse or search the database of IPOs either by industry, underwriter, state, or metro area. Visit the IPO timetable for a comprehensive look at IPOs in the works.

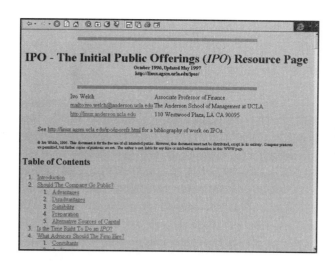

Initial Public Offering Resource Page

http://linux.agsm.ucla.edu/ipo/

This site is literally a page, but it's a big one. UCLA Associate Professor Ivo Welch has prepared a concise look at the IPO process. Here you can learn about IPO advantages, disadvantages, offer pricing, market reaction, and more.

Bondsonline

http://www.bonds-online.com/

Visit Bondsonline for news on various types of bonds, from treasuries, savings, corporate to municipals. Take a look at the Bond Professor for the most common bond FAQs. The site includes a nice listing of bond-related lines for further research.

Investing in Bonds

http://www.investinginbonds.com/

The Bond Market Association is the sponsor of the Investing in Bonds Web site. Visit its complete Investor's Guide to Bond Basics. You'll also find information on the bond market and an investor's checklist of questions to ask yourself when considering bond investments.

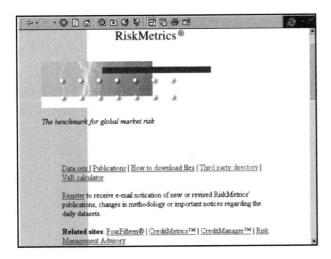

JP Morgan Risk Metrics

http://www.jpmorgan.com/RiskManagement/RiskMetrics/
RiskMetrics.html

RiskMetrics is "a methodology to estimate market risk based on the Value-at-Risk approach." At the site you will find general information about RiskMetrics, publications, and download files. The site includes a third-party directory of various consultants used to help develop the RiskMetrics methodology. Related Web sites are also listed at the site.

Riskview

http://www.riskview.com/html-inf/riskview_splash.html

Riskview.com allows you to look at investment return, estimate risk, and potentially improve your investment performance. Riskview is a free service (you get what you pay for). The program creates special risk charting and benchmarking output.

Company Research

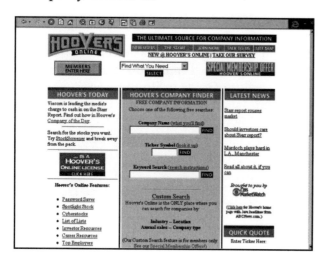

Hoover's Online

http://www.hoovers.com/

You can view more than thirty thousand Company Capsules at this Hoover's Online. The capsules are always free, and if your want a more in-depth profile, Hoover's offers both a monthly and yearly membership plan. For the latest on a company in the news, check in on the Company of the Day page.

Zacks Free Investment Research

http://www.ultra.zacks.com/free.html

If this is all the information you can get for free, I can imagine the mounds of resources that the paid subscribers get at Zacks. The free area is set up as a stand-alone site from the pay area. The full text of Zacks "Investing 101" publication is available for viewing. Don't forget to check out the details of Zacks free trial.

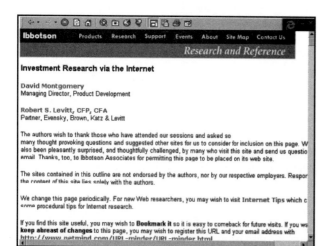

Investment Research via the Internet

http://www.ibbotson.com/Research/iafp96.htm

I gladly stumbled across this mega-page. The page is lengthy, but if you are planning to do a little finance-related surfing, start here. This site took me to interesting places for days. The page is broken out into sections to help with the navigation.

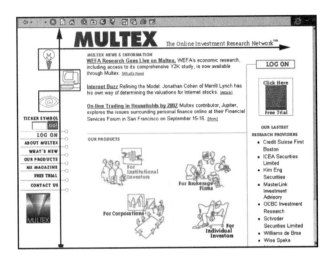

MultexSystems, Inc.

http://www.multexnet.com/

Multex is a provider of online investment research and information services designed for institutional investors, investment banks, brokerage firms, corporations, and individual investors. Multex has access to over 650,000 research reports and other investment information from more than three hundred leading investment banks, brokerage firms, and third-party research providers worldwide. A trial subscription is available.

Annual Report Gallery

http://www.reportgallery.com/

The Annual Report Gallery includes a complete listing of Annual Reports published on the Internet. Save yourself some time and paper by gathering the financial information you need online. The site provides links to Annual Reports from around the world. In addition, the Annual Report Gallery has links directly to the Company's home pages.

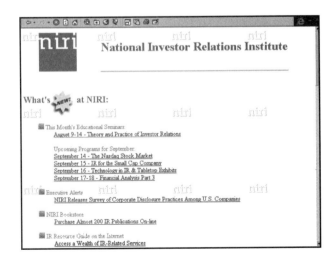

National Investor Relations Institute

http://www.niri.org/

When you arrive at the NIRI Web site, go straight to Investor Relations Resource Guide on the Web. You will find all sorts of Investor Relations (IR) resources such as: Financial Media Relations, Electronic Publishing, and IR Program Evaluation & Implementation.

The Public Register

http://www.annualreportservice.com/

The Public Register's annual report service has over 1,100 annual reports in its database and more are coming online every day. When you select a company, you will have the choice to view the online annual or to request hard copy. Some annual reports are in the Adobe Acrobat format (PDF).

SEC & EDGAR

SEC—Securities and Exchange Commission

http://www.sec.gov/
http://www.sec.gov/edgarhp.htm

Pick up information regarding the Securities Act of 1933 and Securities Exchange Act of 1934 at SEC.gov. The SEC's famous database EDGAR (http://www.sec.gov/edgarhp.htm) is currently under a major restructuring to make searches more dynamic and improve its update time. Under Investor Assistance check out the SEC's draft publication "Handbook of Plain English: How to Create a Clear SEC Disclosure" (http://www.sec.gov/consumer/plaine.htm).

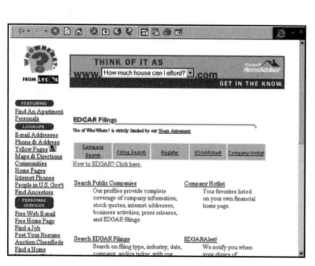

Who Where? EDGAR

http://www.whowhere.com/Edgar/index.html

At WhoWhere EDGAR, you can use its versatile search forms to access EDGAR filings, stock quotes, Internet addresses, press releases, and more. The Company Hotlist Feature allows you to store your favorites on a personal financial page, and the EDGARAlert! feature provides you with E-mail notifications of new filings.

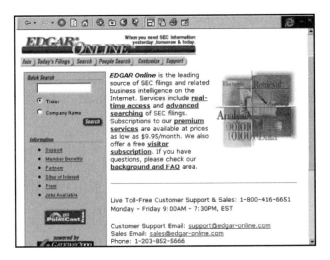

EDGAR Online

http://www.edgar-online.com/

EDGAR Online is a subscription-based service. It provides real time access to SEC reports. Everyone can visit the People tab at EDGAR Online where you can search the SEC proxy statements by individual name.

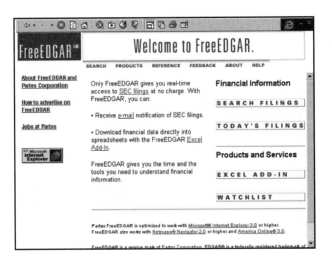

FreeEDGAR

http://www.freeedgar.com/

FreeEDGAR gives you real-time access to SEC filings at no charge. With FreeEDGAR, you can receive E-mail notification of SEC filings and download financial data directly into spreadsheets with the FreeEDGAR Excel Add-In.

Economics

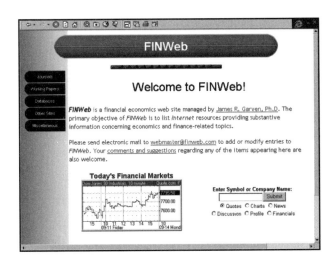

FINWeb—Financial Economics

http://www.finweb.com/

FINWeb is a financial economics Web site managed by James R. Garven, Ph.D. The primary objective of FINWeb is to list Internet resources providing substantive information concerning economics and finance-related topics. FINWeb provides resources on databases, journals, and working papers.

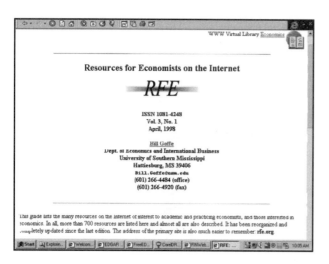

Resources for Economists

http://www.rfe.org/

There are several subsections to this site including, U.S. macro and regional data, various single subject sites, world and non-U.S. data, consulting and forecasting, and financial markets. In all, more than seven hundred resources are listed here and almost all are also described.

Calculators

OANDA Currency Converter

http://www.oanda.com/

OANDA has *the* #1 Currency Converter. Its converter has over two million conversion requests per month! The site houses current and historical exchange rates for 164 currencies. Plus it's free! This site gets better by the minute. Check out the new Interactive Daily Table and its FX Graphs and Tables.

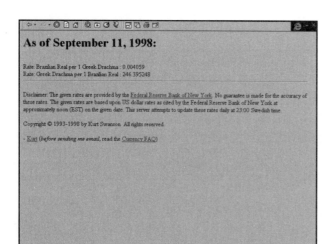

Kurt's Currency Rate Comparisons

http://www.dna.lth.se/cgi-bin/kurt/rates

For a simple currency rate comparison, visit Kurt. He has prepared a bare-bones interface. Click on your currency of choice and the currency you would like it to be compared to. The database is updated once daily.

Stock Quotes

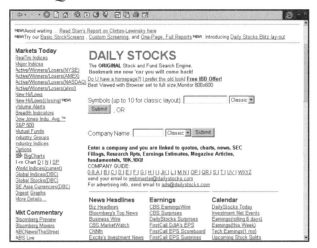

Daily Stocks

http://www.dailystocks.com/

The main index of Daily Stocks provides you with a laundry list of stock categories to choose from. Pick from market summaries, winners, losers, or check into the Daily Stock's links to an entire sheet of stock analysis information for a single company. Of course, the site includes stock quotes, which you can search for in various formats such as single stock or ten at a time. Input a company's symbol to get a Blitz Sheet which lists just about every site where the company is mentioned.

Thomson Real Time Quotes

http://www.thomsonrtq.com/index.sht

If you need your quotes in real time, visit Thomson. Once you sign up for your free membership, you will have access to up to fifty real time quotes per day. Along with your quote, you also get the Thomson TipSheet which contains Intraday and twelve-month charting, Current Investment Ratings from First Call™, Investnet, Innovest, and Key Measures for company and industry performance.

Stock Exchanges

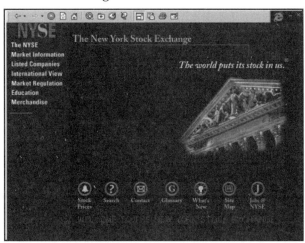

NYSE

http://www.nyse.com/

Visit the NYSE Web site to get the complete exchange company listing. Visit the International View section to obtain information on global investing, non-U.S. companies and raising capital. The Market Regulation section addresses surveillance, regulatory issues, and enforcement actions.

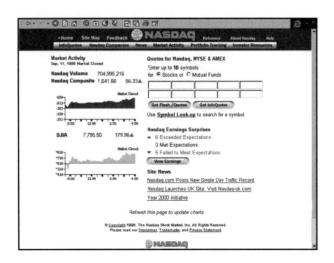

NASDAQ

http://www.nasdaq.com/

Along with the listing of companies on the NASDAQ, its site includes market activity from the major indices, the NASDAQ most active, and earnings surprises. If you like to get your information straight from the source, here's your chance. The NASDAQ also provides a pop-up window desktop ticker with mini-company logos.

Chicago Mercantile Exchange

http://www.cme.com/

The CME provides many resources at its site to further educate the public about the basics of CME futures and options. Visit the Getting Started section and take the futures intelligence quiz or the currency IQ quiz. Under the Prices section, it provides a variety of free price data to help you track the markets.

Organizations

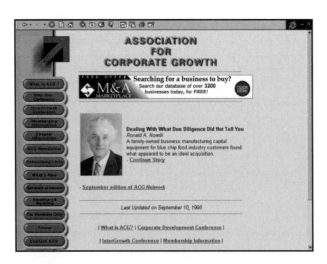

Association for Corporate Growth

http://www.acg.org/

The ACG is an international organization dedicated to fostering sound corporate growth. Its objectives concern "high quality performance, earnings and increasing corporate value." The organization publishes the *ACG Newsletter* and provides highlights from its current issue at the site.

IMAP—International Merger and Acquisition Professionals

http://www.imap.com/

Visit this site to read the *M&A Insider*. The *Insider* is a quarterly newsletter that covers stories such as "The Role and Strategy of an Industry Consolidator" and "Multiples Deceive When Valuing a Business."

Online Trading List

ACCUTRADE
http://www.accutrade.com/

AMERITRADE
http://www.ameritrade.com/

CHARLES SCHWAB E-TRADE
http://www.etrade.com/

LOMBARD
http://www.lombard.com/

Investment Banks List

BANKERS TRUST
http://www.bankerstrust.com/

BEAR, STEARNS & CO. INC
http://www.bearstearns.com/

BT ALEX. BROWN
http://www.alexbrown.com/

DEUTSCHE MORGAN GRENFELL
http://www.dmg.com/

DONALDSON, LUFKIN & JENRETTE
http://www.dlj.com/

FIDELITY
http://www.fidelity.com/

FURMAN SELZ
http://www.furmanselz.com/

GOLDMAN SACHS
http://www.goldman.com/

HAMBRECHT & QUIST
http://www.hamquist.com/

J.P. MORGAN
http://www.jpmorgan.com/

LEHMAN BROTHERS
http://www.lehman.com/

MERRILL LYNCH
http://www.ml.com/

MORGAN STANLEY
http://www.ms.com/

NATIONSBANC MONTGOMERY SECURITIES
http://www.nationsbancmontgomery.com/

PAINEWEBBER
http://www.painewebber.com/

ROBERTSON STEPHENS
http://www.rsco.com/

SALOMON SMITH BARNEY
http://www.salomonsmithbarney.com/

WARBURG DILLON READ
http://www.sbcwarburg.com/

TORONTO-DOMINION BANK
http://www.tdbank.ca/

Entrepreneur

General Resources

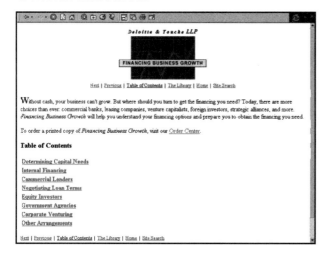

Financing Business Growth

http://www.dtonline.com/finance/bgcover.htm

A complete text provided by D&T, Financing Business Growth addresses issues such as determining capital needs, internal financing, commercial lenders, negotiating loan terms, equity investors, and corporate venturing.

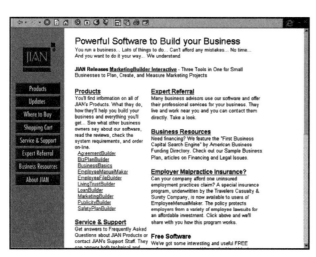

Building Business Agreements

http://www.jian.com/biz.html

The same company that produces the popular "Builder" and "Maker" series software, JIAN provides a few articles building various business agreements. The site also has a complete hyperlinked sample business plan.

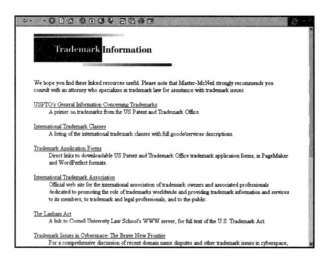

Trademark Information

http://www.naming.com/

Master McNeil specializes in strategic naming. Its site has a sampling of names that the company has created as well as a Glossary of Naming Terms. Take a look at the site's trademark information for several related Web sites.

The Interactive Business Planner

http://www.cbsc.org:4000/

From the Canada/British Columbia Business Centre, the Interactive Business Planner assists entrepreneurs with the preparation of a three-year business plan. In an interactive Q&A format, your business plan is created before your eyes. Sample business plans are also available online.

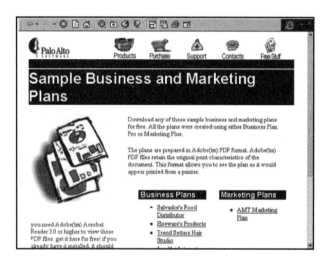

Sample Business Plans

http://www.bplans.com/

Palo Alto software has taken "free content resources for all" to heart. In addition to providing all the normal company information, it has included several sample business plans you can download. The complete plans are in PDF format. Did you ever wonder what a shaved ice company's business plan would look like? Look no further.

Directories

EntreWorld

http://www.entreworld.org/

EntreWorld's mantra: "Find what you need without wasting time looking for it. We search every corner of the Web and deliver the best resources, so you can devote your attention to your business." EntreWorld stays true to its word by providing a nicely annotated directory of resources. The site even color codes by type of article for easy spotting.

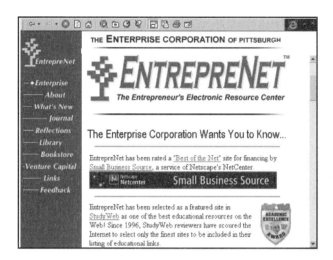

EntrepreNet

http://www.enterprise.org/enet/index.html

On the surface this site looks like your standard run of the mill organization site. However, check out the Library resources. The Library provides various documents to be more successful. Within the Library visit The Role of the Business Plan, Early Stage Company Valuation, and Elements of a Successful Promotional Strategy sections.

Smart Biz

http://www.smartbiz.com/

The Smart Biz site has an excellent directory of resources, with over sixty categories to choose from. In addition to this massive directory, the site hosts discussion forms and detailed category guides. For career information visit Resources for Job Seekers and Employers Guide.

Periodicals

Inc. Online

http://www.inc.com/

Not only will you find the complete version of *Inc.* magazine at this site, but you will no doubt find information on starting your own Web site, discussions at the Peer to Peer section, and Inc. Extra, a Web-only selection of original content.

Entrepreneur Weekly

http://www.eweekly.com/

Visit Entrepreneur Weekly for its articles. After you have checked out the current edition, head on over to the past issues where over fifty issues are archived. Many of the topics covered by this Web site are Internet and Web site development-based.

Entrepreneurial Edge Online

http://edgeonline.com/

Entrepreneurial Edge Online is a service of the Edward Lowe Foundation (http://www.lowe. org/), which is another Web site you should check out to visit its other online initiatives such as SmallbizNet. At Edge Online take a look at the Business Builders & Interactive Toolbox sections for useful stuff.

The Entrepreneur's Mind

http://www.benlore.com/index2.html

The EM is a Web resource that presents an array of real-life stories and advice from successful entrepreneurs and industry experts on the many different facets of emerging business. A previous real-life feature was Pete's Wicked Ale.

Entrepreneur Magazine

http://www.entrepreneurmag.com/

This site is home to many online magazines you are most likely familiar with: *Entrepreneur* magazine, *Business Start-Ups* magazine, *Entrepreneur's Home Office*, and *Entrepreneur International*. Just to make sure you haven't missed a popular feature, the site has a list of the most requested features on EntrepreneurMag.com this week.

Venture Capital Resources

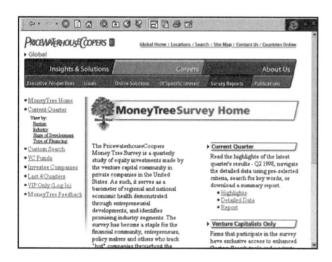

PwC Money Tree Report

http://www.pwcmoneytree.com/

The PwC Money Tree Report is the same as the well-respected C&L survey by the same name. Each quarter PwC posts the results from an in-depth survey conducted on venture capital activity. The survey has many output graphs and provides insight to trends in VC markets.

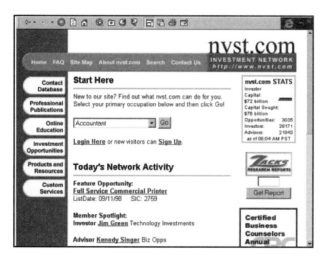

NVST Investment Network

http://www.nvst.com/

Read sample issues of *M&A Dealmakers Journal*, the *Corporate Growth Report*, the *Venture Capital Journal*, the *Business Valuation Update*, and *M&A Today*, and subscribe to these online journals. The site also allows you to post your professional profile with links to your company home page and professional association.

Organizations

National SBCD Research Network

http://www.smallbiz.suny.edu/

This site is dedicated to the provision of information deemed useful to the potential or ongoing entrepreneur. Take a look at the Information for Entrepreneurs section for a complete listing of regional SBDC's on the Internet. The same directory includes many listings for information about contracts, grants, trademarks, and legal.

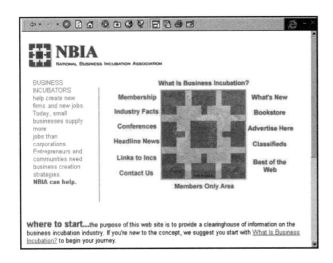

National Business Incubation Association

http://www.nbia.org/

The NBIA objective is to "provide information, research and networking resources to help members develop and manage successful incubation programs." Visit the Facts section for facts and figures regarding incubation. The Webmaster has started up a Best of the Web directory complete with review, rankings, and awards.

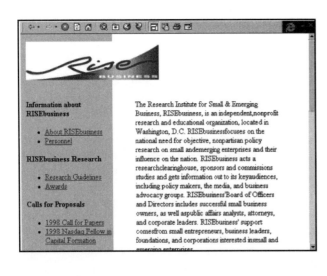

Research Institute for Small & Emerging Business

http://www.riseb.org/

RISE business focuses on the "national need for objective, nonpartisan policy research on small and emerging enterprises and their influence on the nation." The site is a repository of working papers, press releases, and information on projects the organization is spearheading.

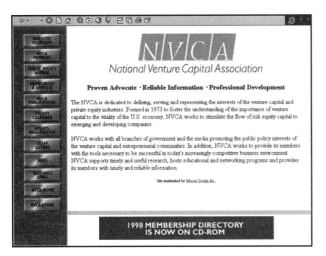

National Venture Capital Association

http://www.nvca.org/

The NVCA is "dedicated to defining, serving and representing the interests of the venture capital and private equity industries." Visit the Industry Overview section for a nice description of the VC Industry. The site also has information about upcoming events and provides a links page.

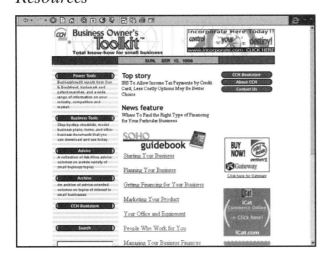

NASBIC—National Association of Small Business Investment Companies

http://www.nasbic.org/

The association acts as "the voice of the small business investment company (SBIC) industry before Congress and the Administration." NASBIC publishes several industry guides and provides samples and ordering information at its site.

Small Business

Resources

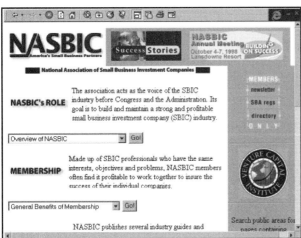

CCH's Small Business Toolkit

http://www.toolkit.cch.com/

The CCH Business Toolkit is an excellent resource for any small business. Check out the site to see everything that is available. Visit the Business Tools section for checklists, model business plans, forms, and other business documents available for download. In the Advice and Archive sections, check out the many articles available on topics such as Deciding to Make a Major Purchase, Leasing Your Equipment, and Accounting Terminology.

American Express Small Business Exchange

http://www.americanexpress.com/smallbusiness/

Like the CCH Toolbox, this site has many interesting topics to choose from. Select from the list of topics such as Start-Up issues, Incorporation & Business Structure, Finding More Customers, and Buying/Selling a Business. After you are done with the topics, visit the Expert Advice section for FAQs on the same topics.

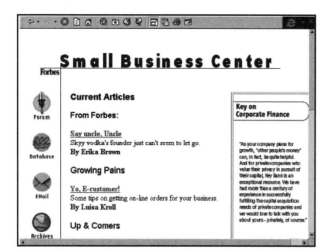

Forbes Small Business Center

http://www.forbes.com/growing/

The Small Business Center is an offshoot of the Forbes site. Here you will find a handful of articles specially tailored for small business issues. Check out the Forum for start-up discussions. Click on the database icon and you'll be taken to "The 200 Best Small Companies in America" edition. Browse the results in a number of ways.

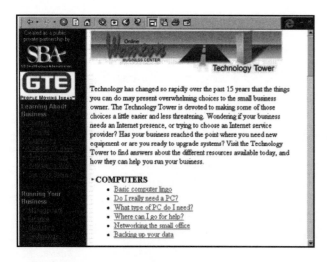

Online Women's Business Center

http://www.onlinewbc.org/

This site is not just for women. You will find hundreds of articles written about business, management, and technology issues. The Center has cross-indexed information and provides an index of resources based on the stage of business development you would like to research. Under the Finance section there are many resources you can share with clients.

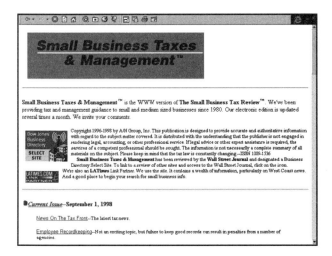

Small Business Tax Review

http://www.smbiz.com/

Small Business Taxes & Management is the WWW version of The Small Business Tax Review. The service has been providing tax and management guidance to small and medium sized businesses since 1980. The electronic edition is updated several times a month. Back issues and link collections are also highlighted at the site.

Small Business Administration

http://www.sba.gov/

The SBA site is organized in phases of business development and covers resources available from inception to growth. Information on the latest legislation and regulatory fairness are addressed at the site. Visit the Online Library for a detailed directory of online resources.

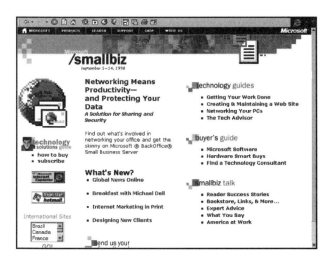

Microsoft's Focus on Small Business

http://www.microsoft.com/smallbiz/

Microsoft's Small Biz site includes a feature articles software resources for small businesses. The Technology Guides are helpful and cover topics such as creating and maintaining a Web site, networking your PCs, and the Tech Advisor. If you don't mind the Microsoft slant, Focus on Small Business has some useful information.

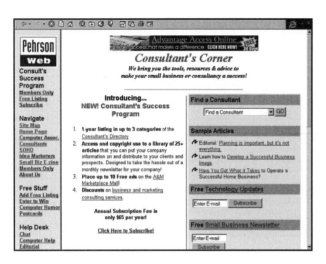

Consultant's Corner

http://www.pwgroup.com/ccorner/

Visit the site map first to get a good feel for what's here. Take a look at the latest articles supplied by the Small Business e-zine. Some resources here are for members-only such as the "Keeping Your Sanity in a Home Business" online course. You will find technology resources and news here, too.

Banking

Periodicals & Trade Journals

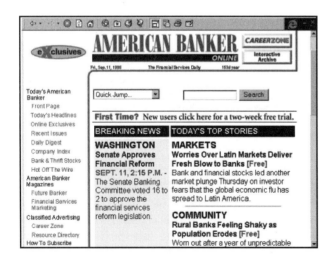

American Banker

http://www.americanbanker.com/

AB is a great banking resource and considers itself the financial services daily. I found lots of current content from news, articles, and publications. There are some areas that are for subscribers only.

Faulkner & Gray Publications

U.S. Banker
http://usbanker.faulknergray.com/

Financial Service Online
http://fso.faulknergray.com/

The Credit Union Journal
http://www.cujournal.com/

You will find here selected articles, discussion forums and the latest news on the banking, online banking, and credit union industries. This is a publication and online resource brought to you by Faulkner & Gray. The Web sites have an excellent listing of related F&G publications. Each site has a very consistent look and feel, so moving from site to site is a breeze. The resources are well integrated.

Banking Resources

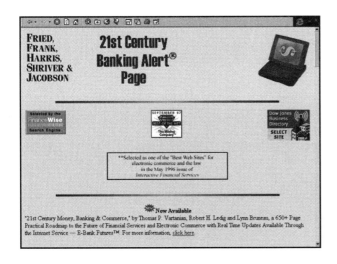

21st Century Banking Alert

http://www.ffhsj.com/bancmail/bancpage.htm

If you are interested in online banking and the future of financial services, you'll want to visit this site. There are a series of current Banking Alerts on the page as well as an E-mail alert ability. It also has connections to its related Web sites: 21st Money, Banking and Commerce Book, and Fried Frank Y2K Page.

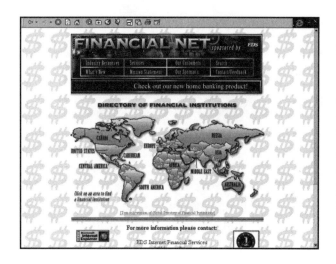

Financial Net

http://www.financial-net.com/

Sponsored by EDS, Financial Net is has a complete global directory of financial institutions. The listings are for banks, thrifts, credit unions, and mortgage companies. All institutions are listed regardless of their online status; however, if it has a Web site, there is a link to its home page. The industry resources page has a nice listing of links.

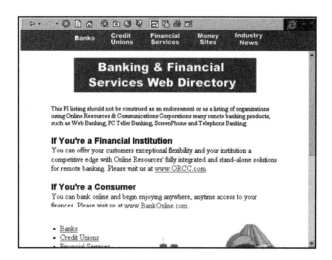

Online Banking and Financial Services

http://www.orcc.com/banking.htm

This site is primarily a directory. It is organized by the following categories: banks, credit unions, financial services, money sites, and industry news. The industry news page is a good one to visit since it has indexed various NewsPage categories for quick banking industry news.

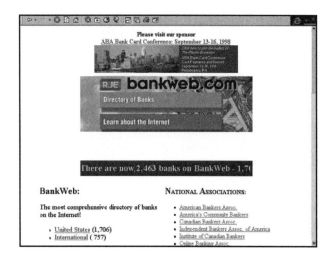

BankWeb

http://www.bankweb.com/

If you can't find your bank at the EDS supported site, try this one. BankWeb had 1,676 U.S. banks and 749 international banks in its directory at the time of this profile. In addition, it has a nice listing of state bank associations.

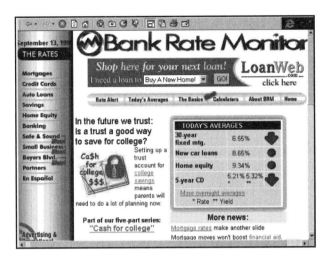

Bank Rate Monitor

http://www.bankrate.com/

Bank Rate Monitor provides hundreds of pages of mortgage, CD, and federal discount rate information. BRM also tracks ATM and checking account fees and online banking fees. It offers the Bank Rate Alert, a free E-mail newsletter which notifies subscribers of major rate movements. In addition, BRM reviews and rates the Web sites of financial institutions nationwide.

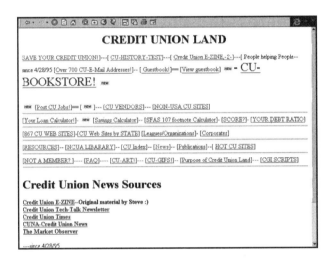

Credit Union Land

http://www.culand.com/

Credit Union Land is not a very pretty site, but it's what inside that counts. The site has all kinds of credit union information ranging from a newsletter to the history of credit unions. It even has a FASB Statement No. 107 Footnote Calculator.

Federal Organizations

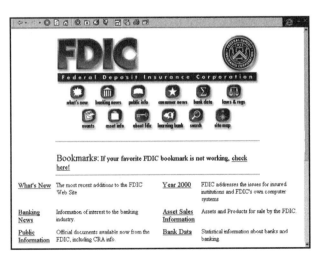

FDIC

http://www.fdic.gov/

The Federal Deposit Insurance Corporation's Web site has a wealth of useful information. Even if you are not involved with financial institutions, it would behoove you to visit this site. Search the site for rulings, check out the site map, and visit the Learning Bank for basic educational information.

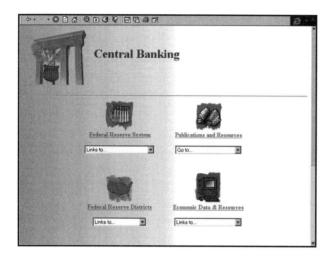

Federal Reserve Resources

http://www.frbsf.org/system/indx.sys.html

The Board of Governors' Web site is too heavily trafficked to be of much use. For your Federal Reserve needs, I recommend you start with the nicely organized Federal Reserve resources that the Federal Reserve Bank of San Francisco has provided. The drop-down menus make their Central Banking resources easy to navigate.

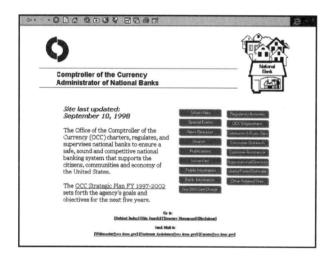

Office of the Comptroller of the Currency

http://www.occ.treas.gov/

The OCC charters, regulates, and supervises national banks. At the OCC Web site you will find the latest news and many of its advisory letters, alerts, and bulletins. Various forms are also available for download.

Organizations

ABA—American Bankers Association

http://www.aba.com/

When you visit this Web site, you should start out with a visit to its nicely displayed site map. ABA's subsite, BankersMart at http://www.bankersmart.aba.com/ features news, events, and the Monthly Spotlight.

Bank Administration Institute

http://www.bai.org/

At the BAI Web site, you will find the quarterly online newsletter *BAI Insights* and selected articles from *Banking Strategies* magazine. BAI also has a very informative Y2K section, Beating the Clock.

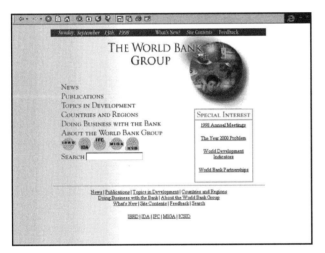

The World Bank

http://www.worldbank.org/

Of particular interest at the World Bank Web site is its News section. In News, you will find the full text of various speeches given by high-ranking World Bank directors, detailed world banking news, and the Bank's media schedule. The other area you should visit here is Topics in Development.

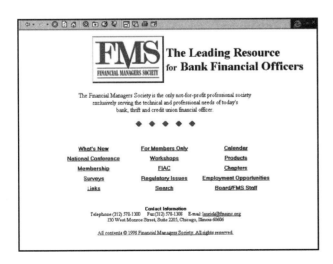

FMS—Financial Managers Society

http://www.fmsinc.org/

This Web site is for bank financial officers. At FMS, you can visit its surveys and results it has conducted on various topics such as FAS 125. FMS sponsors the FIAC, Financial Institutions Accounting Committee, which maintains an ongoing liaison with all of the various accounting regulatory and standard setting agencies which impact the operations of financial institutions.

INFORMATION RESOURCES

Information and News

Newswires

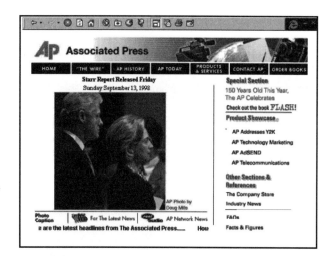

The Associated Press

http://www.ap.org/

Within the AP's Web site is the WIRE, the news Web site of the AP, its member newspapers, and broadcasters. It is arranged by geographical location drop down menus for easy navigation. The AP has an entire section devoted to the history of the AP, including a timeline, and a Staffer Memorial, dedicated to the twenty-three journalists who gave their lives while on AP assignments.

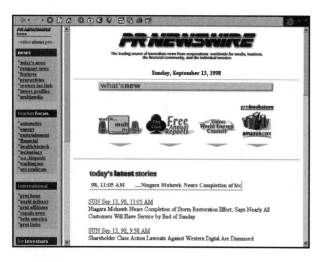

PR Newswire

http://www.prnewswire.com/

PR Newswire is a great resource for finding news from corporations. In Today's News, you will find a searchable database of all stories appearing within the last thirty days. Looking for news on a particular company? Go to Company News and search by company. I performed a search on PricewaterhouseCoopers and found at least twenty releases.

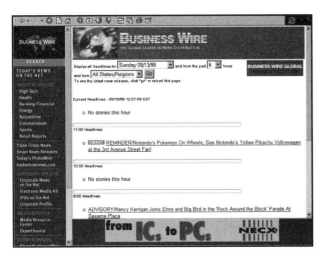

Business Wire

http://www.businesswire.com/

Business Wire specializes in worldwide media distribution of business news. The site is searchable and also has content organized by industry and company. Visit the Trade Ticker news section for editorial exclusives generated by industry trade publications.

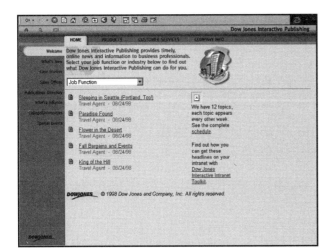

Dow Jones

http://bis.dowjones.com/

At the home page you can view the schedule of topics that "air" on Dow Jones. There are twelve topics that rotate through every other week. The topics cover industries such as media, financial, chemicals, and aerospace. The company also hosts the Dow Jones Business Directory, a free guide to high-quality business Web sites at http://bd.dowjones.com/.

Reuters

http://www.reuters.com/

At Reuters, the drop down navigation box at the left, really helps you navigate through the site. Much of Reuters' information is used as content on other Web sites. However, at the Reuters site you can find out where "Reuters content is playing." Reuters hosts the popular Moneynet Web site at http://www.moneynet.com/. You can find the Reuters' News Summary at Yahoo! (http://headlines.yahoo.com).

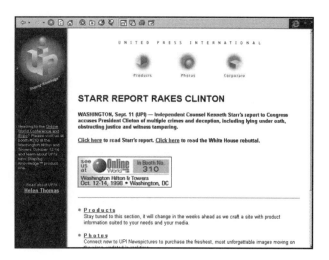

United Press International

http://www.upi.com/

UPI has its news picture photo gallery online with over thirty thousand high-quality photos. You can search and view online for free and if you choose to use a photo, you can add it to your shopping cart for a licensing fee payment. Like Reuters, much of UPI's content is located at other sites. In the upcoming months more content is expected at the UPI site.

Aggregated News Sources

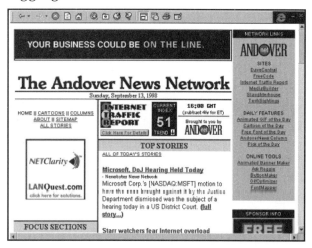

Andover News Network

http://www.andovernews.com/

ANA is a technology-focused Web site. The home page features the top tech stories and has links to its Focus Section categories. Some of the news categories include AOL, software, and Microsoft. Andover has some internal content as well via its weekly columnists. Recent columns include "Nuts & Bolts of E-commerce" and "Building Corporate Web Sites."

Periodical & News Directories

AJR NewsLink

http://www.newslink.org/

AJR NewsLink by the American Journalism Review can be enjoyed by a wider audience than just journalists. This site has received kudos from U.S. News and Global News Network as the "best online magazine and newspaper index" and "an essential resource." I recommend you spend a few minutes at this site to learn about all its offerings. Under the Sites section, there are several essential indices, including those for newspapers and periodicals, that will make your life much easier. If you go on to the Articles section, you will very interesting articles from the current *American Journalism Review*.

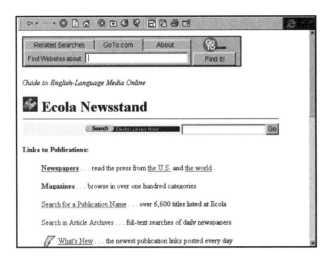

Ecola

http://www.ecola.com/

Ecola also has a massive newspaper, magazine, and periodical directory. At Ecola, you can search for a publication name with over 6,500 titles listed as well as search the articles archive of full-text daily newspapers. The Breaking News section is worth visiting to make sure you have the links to the most recent news sources. Its Bonus section has some fun sites to visit.

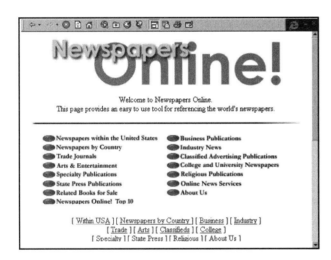

Newspapers Online

http://www.newspapers.com/

I like the home page interface of this site. Somewhat of a newspaper gateway or portal, this Web site allows you to quickly navigate to the newspaper of your interest. There are links to trade journals, specialty publications, state press publications, business publications, and more. The site posts its top ten list every week, which represents the top most used links from its Web site.

American City Business Journals

http://www.amcity.com/

An excellent resource to help you find online business journals. This site has about twenty-five of the top U.S. business journals by city. Your can either search by current issue or by back issues. The site's Extra Edge section has general topics such as small business, current politics, and industries.

MediaFinder

http://www.mediafinder.com/

MediaFinder is the source of a database containing over 95,000 publications and catalogs. The site has magazines, catalogs, newsletters, journals, and newspapers. You can search the database to request information or order your subscription online. Many publications also have their media kits online for further information. Interested in a trade show? MediaFinder has an extensive database for trade shows, too.

RealAudio

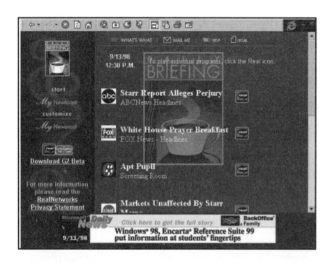

Daily Briefing

http://www.dailybriefing.com/

Daily Briefing is an awesome little Web site. It's your one-stop shop for picking up your daily dose of RealAudio. When you first arrive, go to "Customize My Newscast." There you can select the news you want, from ABC News, CNN, Fox News, various business reports, and more. Another nice feature of this Web site is that once you have customized your audio profile it will come streaming to your desktop one audio feed after another. No clicking around to find your next audio update.

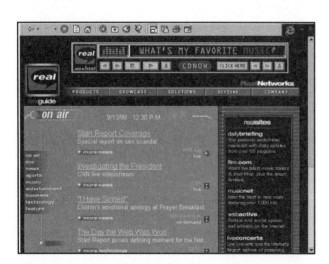

Timecast

http://www.timecast.com/

Timecast is the complete directory of RealAudio and RealVideo sites on the web. Brought to you by Progressive Networks, the site is searchable as well as broken down into Live, Audio/Video Sites, and Radio/TV stations. Checking under the Business heading in the Radio/TV section, there are more than ten programs to choose from.

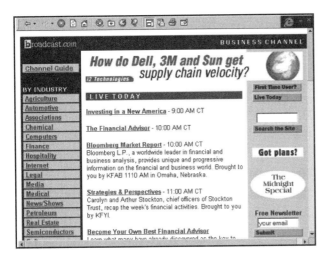

Broadcast.com—Business

http://www.broadcast.com/business/

Broadcast.com is the front-runner in web-casting. The site was formally named AudioNet. The site includes rich audio resources such as the CNBC/Dow Jones Business Report, NASDAQ Stock Exchange Report, CNN Audio Select, and BBC World Service. Several companies have flocked to Broadcast.com to cast their earnings releases, conferences, and press conferences out to the Internet public.

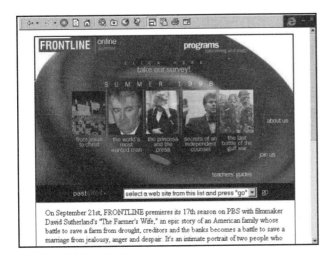

PBS—Online Newshour

http://www.pbs.org/newshour/realaudio.html

PBS—Frontline

http://www.pbs.org/wgbh/pages/frontline/

PBS has published audio content from two of their most popular business and economy programming through the Online Newshour and Frontline. Both sites are updated frequently, include archives, and contain text content as well.

News Radio

http://www.pcworld.com/news/newsradio/index.html

PC World hosts News Radio, an audio update on the technology industry. The site has features and interviews. Previous interviews features "E-trading," "Preparing for the Millenium," and "The Virus Writers." News Radio has a daily news update and includes pages with links mentioned in the news update.

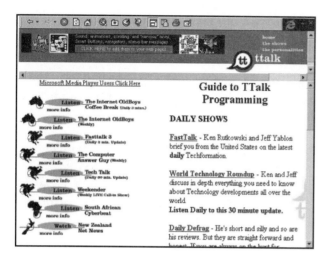

Tech Talk

http://www.ttalk.com/

This Web site has a myriad of affiliate tech programs from different spots in the world. Some feeds are updated daily and weekly. For an excellent taste of Internet news from down under, check out the "Internet Old Boys Coffee Break."

FlightTalk Interviews

http://www.flightalk.com/

Do you enjoy listening to the leader and company bios available on airlines? If you do, you'll spend hours at this Web site. I was quickly able to navigate to an hour-long program on Andrew Grove's book, *Only the Paranoid Survive*. Albeit, there are commercials here and there, and quite a prelude, however, with RealAudio you can easily jump ahead in the audio stream. For a little coffee break, there is also a nice list of celebrity interviews.

Popular Newspapers

Wall Street Journal

http://www.wsj.com/

If you don't have a subscription to Wall Street Interactive, what can you do here? Well, not too much, but here are a few pointers. If you download PointCast, you can view selected WSJ articles via PointCast's Business Network. A free service to check out is the WSJ Annual Report Service. It permits you to order annual reports in its database. A selection of all companies starting with the letter "A" had over one hundred companies listed!

Financial Times Online

http://www.ft.com/

If you don't have a subscription to the WSJ, you may want to consider joining Financial Times Online. Access to the site is free, but you are required to register first. The content at this site is plentiful and is updated daily. FT Online includes other resources than news, such as market data, special reports and industry information. Check out the Inside Track for a magazine within a newspaper.

The Washington Post

http://www.washingtonpost.com/

For a little of everything and a lot about the Hill and the House, visit the Washington Post Online. Twelve columnists are featured at the site and news highlights are always fresh. WP online has a detailed weekly calendar of events so you don't miss important coverage. Visit the Photo Gallery and view the eighteen exceptionally prepared galleries.

Nando Times

http://www.nando.net/

Install the Nando News Watcher to automatically bring you the latest news from around the world. The News Watcher has been programmed to continuously scan Nando's news pages and post the current headlines to the News Watcher for you to read. Visit the Business Section for the latest Nando business news. Techserver is another section to check out.

The New York Times

http://www.nytimes.com/

The Business Section includes all kinds of business articles, market information, and special subsections such as Industry News and Briefcase. The Technology section is just as content-rich and informative. You'll also want to check out the Forums at the Times. In particular, there are several financial forums and a forum for business travel.

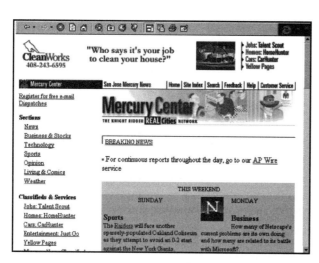

The Mercury News

http://www.mercurynews.com/

For all your technology news needs, the Mercury News Online is there for you. The "Merc" Online is searchable and you can register at the site for free E-mail dispatches. The Daily Dispatches cover the latest news headlines. On a quarterly basis, visit the Mercury's newsletter. The newspaper's columnists are featured at the site as well.

Television Broadcasting

CNN & CNNfn

http://www.cnn.com/
http://www.cnnfn.com/

Not only does CNN and CNNfn have the latest news, but both sites have some unique offerings to check out. Come to CNN to take the Daily News Quiz and test your current affairs knowledge. Visit the Daily Almanac for interesting tidbits about current and past events and milestones. The In-depth section offers a close look at top news stories. At CNNfn, visit Digital Jam, Industry Watch, and Push This.

ABCNEWS.com

http://www.abcnews.com/

The ABCNews.com Business Index provides the latest business news and many industry-related articles. Check out the ABCNews Dispatches area to see where the ABC Correspondents are around the globe along with accompanying articles. The site has gateways to all ABC news-magazine shows.

MSNBC & CNBC

http://www.msnbc.com/
http://www.cnbc.com/

I have the MSNBC page as my home page. It is quick loading and the interface can be easily navigated. I have also installed the MSNBC News Alert which keeps me in the news loop. The alerts are very timely and for breaking news the alerts pop up within minutes. MSNBC has lively discussion forums and many customization features. Don't forget to visit a MSNBC's sister site, CNBC, for all kinds of business resources.

CBS

http://www.cbs.com/

The Business & Money section of CBS's Web site has Stock Watch and Market Watch for your market needs. You must visit the Investor's Primer, a complete guide to investing. The sections include primers in Mastering Markets, Your Big Financial Picture and Tools of the Trade.

Professional Publishers—Authoritative Literature Sources

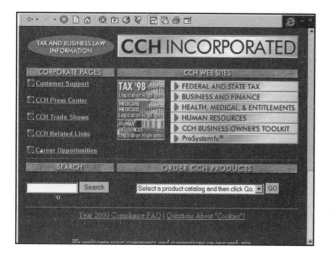

CCH Incorporated

http://www.cch.com/

CCH is a major publisher of tax and business law information and software. CCH has six separate Web sites addressing tax and business. The Business & Finance site hosts the newsletter, Insight, full product descriptions, and FAQs. At the Tax site, check out the Conference Room for announcements, a detailed tax calendar, and helpful research articles. The Business Owners' Toolkit is a must-visit site with hundreds of useful articles and downloads.

Faulkner & Gray

http://www.faulknergray.com/

Faulkner & Gray is a leader in business and professional information. It serves the payments, banking, mortgage lending, health care, and accounting sectors. Visit the Accounting products area for detailed descriptions of F&G's popular accounting publications, *Accounting Today* and *The Practical Accountant*, among others. Faulkner & Gray provides The Electronic Accountant at http://www.electronicaccountant.com/ as its online news service, providing accountants with substantial content, timely news, and discussion forums.

Harcourt Brace Professional Publishing

http://www.hbpp.com/

Harcourt Brace's Web site provides online CPE Testing available 24/7. The CPE testing available is based on its various publications. HBPP provides highlights of its *Executive Compensation* newsletter at their sister site, http://www.ecronline.com./. Its Health Niche Advisor site includes *Healthcare Accounting News Notes* online dating back to March 1996.

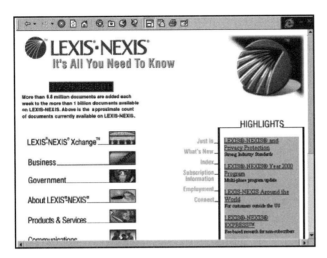

Lexis-Nexis

http://www.lexis-nexis.com/lncc/

If you have ever wondered how many documents are available on Lexis-Nexis, check out its Web site, complete with an online counter ticker. The highlights area will get you up-to-speed on the Web site's offerings, Lexis-Nexis products, and services. Although the Web site is primarily descriptions of the company's products, you can quickly identify which products you need through the Q&A filters used to help direct you to products of interest.

Irwin McGraw-Hill

http://www.mhhe.com/business/accounting/

From the major publisher of accounting texts, Irwin McGraw-Hill produces a newsletter, *Professor to Professor*. Check out the Accounting Showcase profiling its popular texts. Most of the texts featured in the showcase are like mini-Web sites, complete with instructors demos, resources for students, text updates, related Web sites, sample syllabi, and discussion forums.

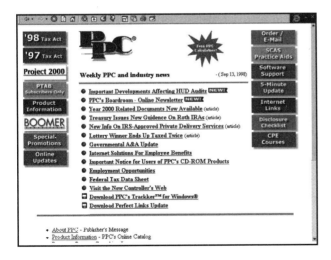

Practitioners Publishing Co. (PPC)

http://www.ppcinfo.com/

You will want to spend a few minutes acclimating yourself with this Web site; it has much to offer. Start with PPC's online newsletter, *Boardroom*. The newsletter contains the latest PPC news, success stories, and FAQs. Check out the 5-Minute Update for additional news. PPC offers many resources for accountants, including a wide range of guides, CPE courses, and software. You can find updates to all your favorite PPC publications at the site.

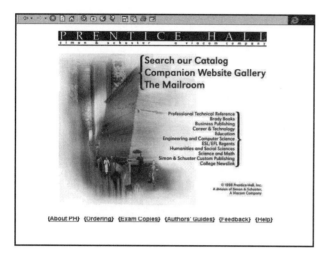

Prentice Hall

http://www.prenhall.com/

Prentice Hall has its entire catalog online in a flexible search or browse format. Check out the Business Publishing section. The section includes links to authors' home pages and text Web sites similar to McGraw-Hill's. If you are an author or a wanna-be author, visit the Professional Technical Reference section. The section includes detailed Author Guidance. Although all information is not applicable to accounting-oriented texts, you will surely find some good tips at this section.

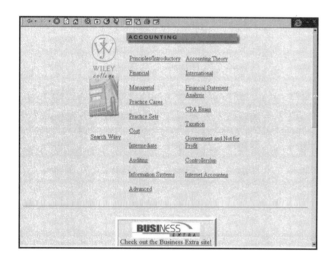

John Wiley & Sons, Inc

http://www.wiley.com/college/busin/accnt/

Wiley's accounting text Web site features the Accounting Resources for Students site (go to it even if you aren't a student!); the accounting Web link categories have hundreds of useful links. In addition, Accounting Resources includes feature articles on networking, controversies, and interview profiles.

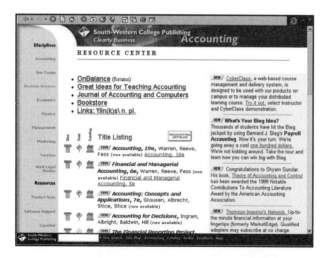

South Western College Publishing

http://www.swcollege.com/acct/accounting.html

This is another Web site with lots of accounting text resources, including Power Points slides and hot links. South Western is also affiliated with the news resource for case instructors CaseNet at http://casenet.thomson.com/. You may want to check out its other disciplines, especially Finance, Management, Business Communications, and Decision Sciences.

Bookstores

Amazon.com

http://www.amazon.com/

This is *the* Web site for buying books online. Amazon.com is not only an online store, it's an online community. Once you search for a book, you can read what others thought of the book. Many of the write-ups are insightful and give you a sense if you would enjoy the book highlighted. Amazon.com also suggests other books related to your search request.

AudioBooks

http://www.audiobooks.com/

For books on tape (new and used), Audio-Books is a good place to start. Be sure to visit News for the latest in bestsellers and for release information about audio books currently in production. Use the Navigate page as a quick way to access a wide variety of services available through Audiobooks.com.

Events & Conferences

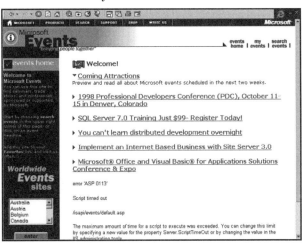

Microsoft Worldwide Events

http://events.microsoft.com/

For a complete listing of Microsoft events, check this site out. You can search the events database and create a custom events page. You can search the database by keyword or by location. A search on the word "accounting" for the next two months produced fourteen different events.

Trade Show Central

http://www.tscentral.com/

Go straight to the Finance, Accounting and Taxation Section for a complete listing of seminars and conferences. Since there are two separate listings for seminars and conferences, you'll need to check both listings individually. Both Seminars and Conference listings produced many events for the accounting professional.

Industry

Industry Information Sources

Infoseek Industry Watch

http://www.industrywatch.com/

Infoseek's Industry Watch is a creative use of technology. Infoseek covers several industries and provides article headlines. If you want to learn even more, just click on the headline and a pop-up window will appear with a complete article synopsis.

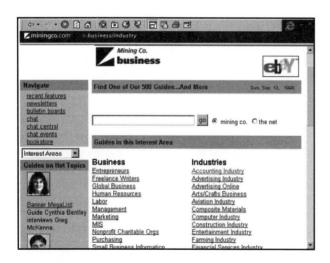

Mining Company Industry Pages

http://home.miningco.com/business/

The Mining Company currently has nineteen in-depth industry guides. Each guide is virtually a stand-alone Web site, each hosted and moderated by a guide who has expertise in the industry. There is even a guide for the Accounting industry. Check it out!

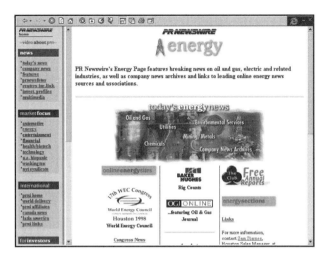

PR Newswire Market Focus

http://www.prnewswire.com/

PR Newswire's Market Focus sections each include a field to search on the latest industry news. Click on finance where you can search or visit the various industry-related link buttons the Newswire has posted. For example, the site hosts IPO News and Stats at the Finance Industry page and a video from the World Energy Council at its Energy page.

NewsPage from Individual

http://www.newspage.com/

If you are looking for industry news, News-Page is the place. The Web site includes a combination of free and pay-per-view articles. You can create your own NewsPage based on industries and key words. For a modest monthly fee, you can subscribe to NewsPage Direct, a daily E-mail of news topics based on your preferences. The E-mail includes a brief synopsis of each article and provides a hyperlink to the full story.

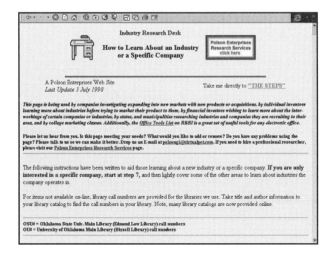

How to Learn About an Industry

http://www.virtualpet.com/industry/howto/search.htm

This is an excellent resource for researching a particular industry. The site is both an in-depth guide as well as a directory of industry links. The navigation isn't the best, so plan to spend a little time here to get the most of this site. Once you find a page you will need in the future, bookmark it, because this is the kind of site that has great stuff, but you may not be able to find it again!

IOMA Industry Resources

http://www.ioma.com/industry/

Another Web site with a wealth of information, IOMA has articles written for Corporate Finance, Import/Export, Insurance and Risk, Law, Manufacturing, and Public Accounting. Each area has hundreds of articles on just about every topic you can think of. For instance, in the Manufacturing section there are articles on customer service and fulfillment, supplier selection and management, and inventory reduction.

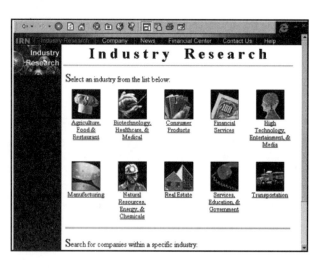

IRN Industry Research

http://irn.net/industry/industry.idc

IRN has information on ten different industries including Real Estate, Consumer Products, and Transportation. Each industry has links to market summaries from other sites, a news retriever (which you can modify the search period), and a listing of in-depth resources on select companies. In addition, its database has companies sorted geographically and you can click on the region of your choice to view a list of companies.

Specific Industries Resources

Aerospace & Aviation

AEROWORLDNET

http://www.aeroworldnet.com/

AEROSPACE.NET

http://www.aerospace.net/

AEROSPACE RESOURCES ON THE INTERNET

http://www.cranfield.ac.uk/cils/library/subjects/airmenu.htm

Agriculture

AGRICULTURE ONLINE

http://www.agriculture.com/

PRO FARMER
http://www.profarmer.com/

AGRIBIZ
http://www.agribiz.com/

FARM JOURNAL ONLINE
http://www.farmjournal.com/

Biotechnology & Pharmaceutical

BIOTECHNOLOGY INDUSTRY ORGANIZATION
http://www.bio.org/

BIO ONLINE
http://www.bio.com/

BIOSPACE
http://www.biospace.com/

Chemical

CHEMICAL INDUSTRY HOME PAGE
http://www.neis.com/

CHEMICAL ONLINE
http://www.chemicalonline.com/

Education

ACUA—ASSOCIATION OF COLLEGE AND UNIVERSITY AUDITORS
http://www.acua.org/

Energy and Oil & Gas

OIL & GAS JOURNAL ONLINE
http://www.ogjonline.com/

POWER MARKETING ASSOCIATION
http://www.powermarketers.com/

OILONLINE
http://www.oilonline.com/

Entertainment

HOLLYWOOD REPORTER
http://www.hollywoodreporter.com/

PAUL KAGAN FREE FEATURES
http://chaplin.pkbaseline.com/features.html

Healthcare

REUTERS HEALTH ELINE
http://www.reutershealth.com/frame_eline.html

HEALTHCARE FINANCIAL MANAGEMENT ASSOCIATION
http://www.hfma.org/

Insurance & Risk

NATIONAL ASSOCIATION OF INSURANCE COMMISSIONERS
http://www.naic.org/

RISKWEB
http://www.riskweb.com/

Manufacturing

INDUSTRY WEEK
http://www.iwgc.com/

ISO ONLINE
http://www.iso.ch/

Nonprofit

THE NONPROFIT TIMES
http://www.nptimes.com/

INTERNET NONPROFIT CENTER
http://www.nonprofits.org/

PHILANTHROPY NEWS DIGEST
http://fdncenter.org/phil/

Retail

NATIONAL RETAIL FEDERATION
http://www.nrf.com/default-java.htm

THE APPAREL STRATEGIST
http://www.appstrat.com/

Telecommunications

TELECOMMUNICATIONS INDUSTRY ASSOCIATION
http://www.tiaonline.org/

TELECOM INFORMATION RESOURCES ON THE INTERNET
http://china.si.umich.edu/telecom/

TELECOMMUNICATIONS LIBRARY
http://www.ntu.edu.sg/library/telecomm.htm

International

Primary International Organizations

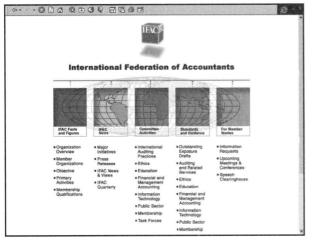

IFAC—International Federation of Accountants

http://www.ifac.org/

IFAC's objective is to "to develop the profession and harmonize its standards worldwide, to enable accountants to provide services of consistently high quality in the public interest." Its Web site helps them to further its agenda, with lots of resources under the Standards and Guidance section and Committee Activities.

IASC—International Accounting Standards Committee

http://www.iasc.org.uk/

The International Accounting Standards Committee (IASC) "is an independent private-sector body working to achieve uniformity in the accounting principles." Its Web site has over three hundred pages of information on standards and interpretation resources, news, and an IASC accounting quiz. Remember the quiz is under International Accounting Standards!

Africa

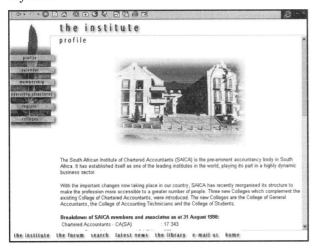

South African Institute of Chartered Accountants

http://www.saica.co.za/

The SAICA has three active forums for Small Practice, Commerce & Industry, and SAICA Students. Under the News section, the Institute lists its latest developments and employment opportunities. The Library section has many resources including related organizations in South Africa.

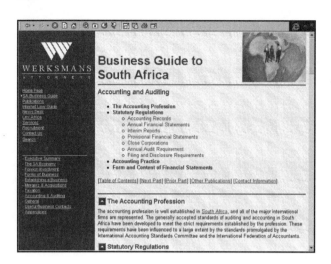

Accounting in South Africa

http://mbendi.co.za/werksmns/sabus07.htm#7.3

Accounting in South Africa is one of ten in-depth resources for doing business in South Africa and is produced by the Werksmans law firm. The Accounting Guide addresses the Accounting Profession, Statutory Regulations, Accounting Principles, and Form & Content of Financial Statements. Werksmans also has a Taxation section.

Asia

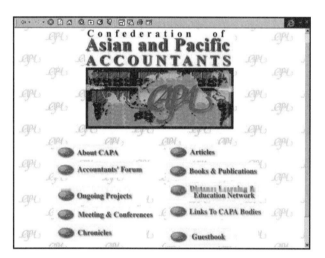

Confederation of Asian and Pacific Accountants

http://www.jaring.my/capa/

If you are doing accounting research on Asia, take a look at CAPA, especially the article archive. Here you will find articles such as "Tax System in ASEAN Countries," "Professional Accountants and the Asian Economy in the 21st Century," and "Value Added Tax Issues in China." There are many other resources here, too.

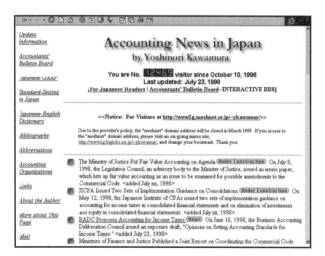

Accounting News in Japan

http://www2g.biglobe.ne.jp/~ykawamur/

Visit the Accountant's Bulletin Board for inquiries and information. If you need to look up information on Japanese GAAP, see the section by the same name. The site also has information on standard setting.

ABN—Asia Business News

http://www.abn.com.sg/

Sported as the CNBC Asia Homepage, ABN has the latest news from Asia. Check out the Business Traveller section for local transport information, advice on tipping, and recommended restaurants for business entertaining. Visit the Money Talks section for various articles with an Asian focus.

Australia/New Zealand

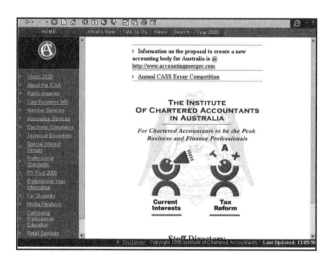

Institute of Chartered Accountants in Australia

http://www.icaa.org.au/

For information on the Australian technical accounting resources, visit the Technical Essentials section. Here you will find exposure drafts, updates, guidance statements, and audit programs. Back at the home page, check out the E-commerce, Online Publications, and Links sections.

The Australian Financial Review

http://www.afr.com.au/

To get the latest Australian news, check out AFR. The site includes in-depth special reports, daily news, and features. Under the Information section, there are even more articles. Visit the AFR Web Directory for a nice listing of Australian-related links.

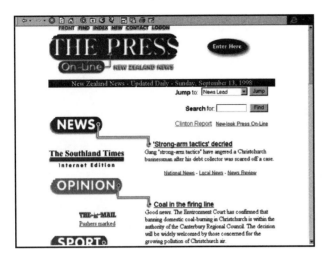

New Zealand Press Online

http://www.press.co.nz/

This site has a very comprehensive Business section. You can look up all your New Zealand business news here. The site offers an in-depth information on New Zealand's primary industry segments. Visit News Reviews for an in-depth look at New Zealand issues.

Europe

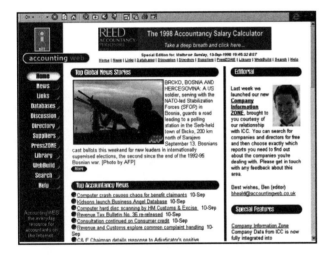

AccountingWeb

http://www.accountingweb.co.uk/

Your first stop in researching accounting and finance issues in the UK should be AccountingWeb. Under the Links section, find the page for Journals. The Journals page has a complete listing of UK journals and also tells you the percentage of content that is currently online. Under the Databases section, you'll find links to the top ten UK databases and resources for company and general research. AccountingWeb has many other sections worth exploring as well.

European Accounting Association

http://www.bham.ac.uk/EAA/

The EAA aims "to link together the Europe-wide community of accounting scholars and researchers, to provide a platform for the wider dissemination of European accounting research, and to foster and improve research." The EAA publishes the *European Accounting Review* and has recent article titles and online ordering of samples. The organization hosts an annual conference and has paper abstracts databases, findings, and other resources online.

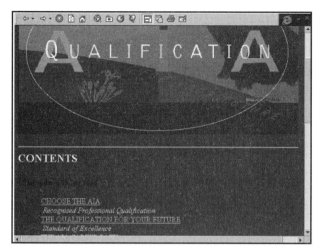

AIA—Association of International Accountants

http://www.a-i-a.org.uk/

AIA "promotes and supports the advancement of the accountancy profession both in the UK and internationally." The Contents at the home page directs you through the Web site via a series of articles on "The AIA Career Path," "Worldwide Choice," and "Passing the AIA."

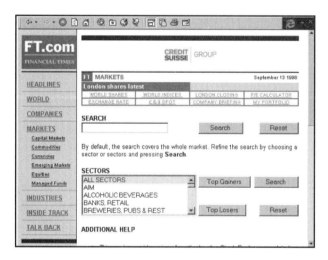

Financial Times Online

http://www.ft.com/

From the very popular print edition, the Financial Times Online does not disappoint. Access is free to the site, but you must register first. At a glance, you will find the latest financial headlines, press reviews and special reports. The site includes market data, from around the world as well as specifically London.

Russia Today

http://www.russiatoday.com/

Russia Today hosts news information in Video News and in a number of news updates, articles, and features. The site has an Opinion section as well as a Discussion Forum with many topics to choose from. Check out the Related Links for additional Russia research sources. Check out links to sister sites in China at http://www.insidechina.com/ and Central Europe at http://www.centraleurope.com/.

Middle East

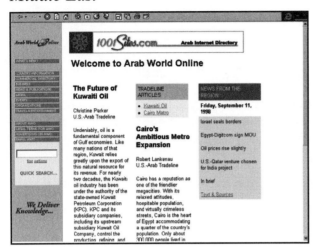

Arab World Online

http://www.awo.net/

For Arab news check out Arab World Online. The site has detailed information by country on each country's profile, government contacts, articles, and related links. Check out the Business section for information on the investment climate, U.S./Arab Trade and business travel links. The News & Publications sections have U.S.-Arab Tradeline Articles available online dating back to 1994.

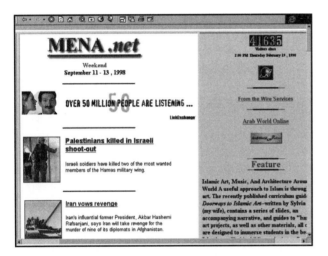

MENA.net

http://www.mena.net/

MENA.net has information about the Middle East and North Africa. Here you will find news, discussion, analysis, opinion, chat, and special reports. The site has multimedia resources such as the BBC Arabic Radio live and video streams of the latest news stories.

North America

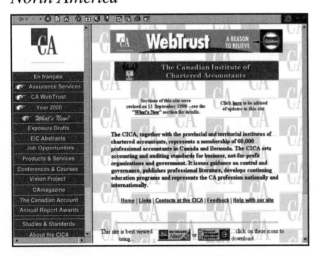

Canadian Institute of Chartered Accountants

http://www.cica.ca/

The CICA sets accounting and auditing standards for business, not-for-profit organizations, and government. The site includes exposure drafts, EIC Abstracts, Year 2000 resources, and WebTrust information. CICA publishes the *Chartered Accountant (CA)* and has many issues online for viewing.

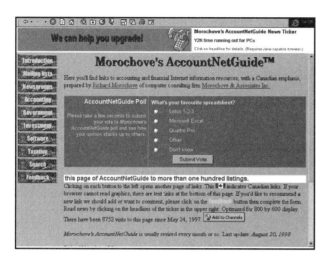

Morochove's AccountNet

http://www.morochove.com/netguide/

Morochove's AccountNet is a directory of Web site accounting resources in Canada. Here you will find detailed sections of links for mailings lists, newsgroups, government, accounting, investments, taxation, and more. Check out the AccountNetGuide news ticker for computer news.

South America

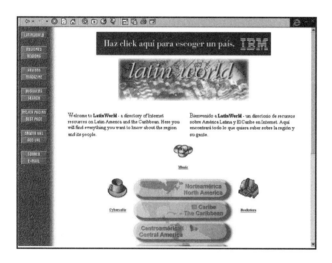

Latin World

http://www.latinworld.com/

Latin World is a directory of Internet resources on Latin America and the Caribbean. Here you will find everything you want to know about the region and its people. Visit the Regions section for specific country information. Latin World hosts the *Latinworld Magazine* which includes a feature article and articles on culture, economics and travel.

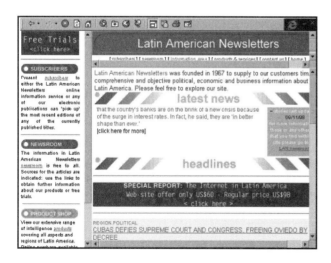

Latin American News

http://www.latinnews.com/

As a service to the public, the Newsroom section is available to all. It includes short excerpts of the latest news stories occurring in Latin America by country. Although you will need to navigate around the pay newsletters, Latin American News is one of the better news resources.

E-commerce

Directories & Resources

Mining Company—Electronic Commerce

http://ecommerce.miningco.com/

The Mining Company has done it again with another guide for you to check out. Electronic Commerce resources are popping up faster than you can keep track. So you may want to check out what the Mining Co. has already indexed for you. The site also includes some original content at In the Spotlight. A past spotlight was "Checklist for a Successful WebStore."

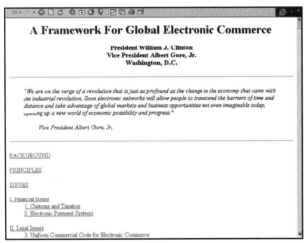

A Framework for Global Electronic Commerce

http://www.iitf.nist.gov/eleccomm/ecomm.htm

This is the discussion document by Bill Clinton and Al Gore on the future of Electronic Commerce. To give you a preview of what you will find in this document, here is a quote from Vice President Al Gore: "We are on the verge of a revolution that is just as profound as the change in the economy that came with the industrial revolution. Soon electronic networks will allow people to transcend the barriers of time and distance and take advantage of global markets and business opportunities not even imaginable today, opening up a new world of economic possibility and progress."

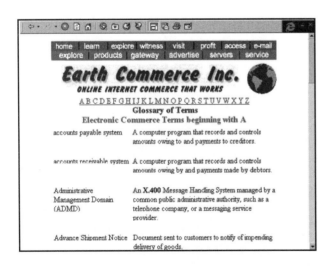

E-commerce Glossary of Terms

http://www.helpfindit.com/glossa.html

Not the prettiest site, but it does its job. This glossary has hundreds of E-commerce definitions from ACH Transfer to Value Added Network.

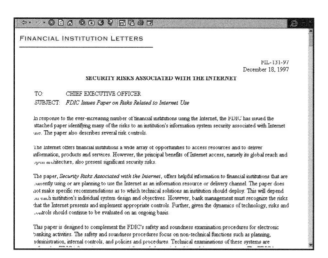

Security Risks Associated with the Internet

http://www.fdic.gov/banknews/fils/1997/fil97131.html

A FDIC Financial Institution Letter, "Security Risks," is a great overview document about high areas of concern when conducting commerce on the Internet. The report touches on risks such as privacy, viruses, data integrity, and authentication.

Organizations & Standards

Commerce.net

http://www.commerce.net/

CommerceNet's mission is to "make electronic commerce easy, trusted, and ubiquitous." This site has all kinds of information to help accomplish this goal. It publishes the *Buzz* newsletter and has all past issues archived at the site. In the Advocacy section, you will find many policy documents. The Research Center has a handful of E-commerce presentations, research reports, and demographic data.

RosettaNet

http://www.rosettanet.org/

RosettaNet was established to harness E-commerce potential "by developing, promoting, and leading the adoption of open and common electronic business interfaces." The site includes white papers such as Supply Chain Misalignments.

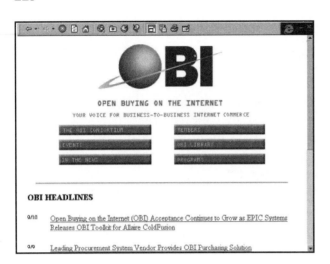

OBI Consortium—Open Buying

http://www.openbuy.org/

Another Web site promoting open standards, the OBI consortium has a comprehensive overview on "Open Buying on the Internet." OBI has also published the OBI Standard, which it is endorsing. There are also articles, publications, and a glossary relating to electronic commerce at the OBI Web site.

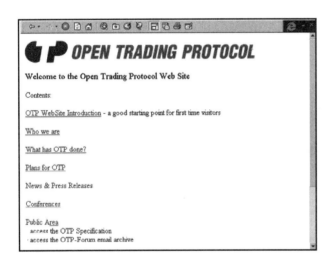

OTP—Open Transaction Protocol

http://www.otp.org/

This is yet another site for open standards. The public publications area has many documents both internal and external that are available for download and/or online viewing. OTP sponsors an E-mail server list for E-commerce standards and provides an E-mail archive.

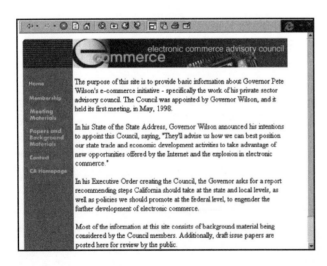

E-commerce Advisory Council

http://www.e-commerce.ca.gov/

The E-commerce Advisory Council was created by the State of California to advise the governor on how to position California's economic development activities as they relate to the Internet and electronic commerce. The site has papers and background materials on E-commerce and tax issues as well as statutes and legislation.

Articles & Publications

E Business

http://www.hp.com/Ebusiness/

E Business Magazine is a monthly publication by Hewlett Packard. For this month, E Business tackles features such as "Portal Madness" and "Europe's E-tailing Future." The site has other resources available in the Tools section and a specific section for E-commerce issues.

ZDNet—E-commerce User

http://www.zdnet.com/icom/e-business/

This site has a nice database of E-commerce articles. For each edition, there are at least fifteen articles, all relating to the latest E-commerce stories. This Web site is somewhat consumer-end–oriented, and is a great resource to help keep your finger on the pulse of the E-commerce consumer.

eMARKETER

http://www.emarketer.com/

eMarketer claims to be the online authority on business online. It publishes the eList, the top ten business sites online. In the eNews section there is usually a lead story with links to several other in-depth articles. An interesting section is eStats, covering the latest published statistics regarding the Internet and E-commerce. The site also has a few discussion forums to boot.

Companies Involved in E-commerce

BIZRATE GUIDE
http://www.bizrate.com/

iCAT
http://www.icat.com/

INTERSHOP COMMUNICATIONS
http://www.intershop.com/

INTRANET SOFTWARE
http://www.paybutton.com/

PANDESIC
http://www.pandesic.com/

VERISIGN
http://www.verisign.com/

Community Resources

General Discussion Forums

Deja News

http://www.dejanews.com/

Probably the most popular and comprehensive discussion forum directory, Deja News allows you to search the entire Internet for Web-based discussion forums. Deja News is where you can read, search, participate in, and subscribe to more than fifty thousand discussion forums, including Usenet newsgroups. Using My Deja News (free!) you can access your favorite forums from any computer and use its Web-based spam-free service. Also, check out "Interest Finder" for further customization features.

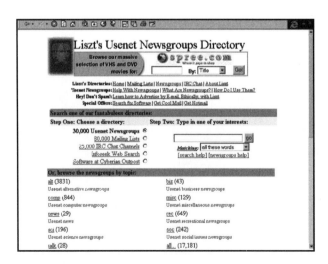

Liszt's Usenet Newsgroups Directory

http://www.liszt.com/news/

Although Liszt is mainly known for its massive listing of mailing lists, it can also be used as an excellent search resource for over thirty thousand usenet newsgroups. When you perform a search for a newsgroup, you receive an annotated results list. This is especially helpful since most usenet names are somewhat cryptic.

Reference.com

http://www.reference.com/

Reference.com is another search engine for usenet newsgroups, mailing lists, and web forums. At Reference.com you can read up on topics such as how to "Find, Browse, Search, and Participate" in the interactive features of the Internet.

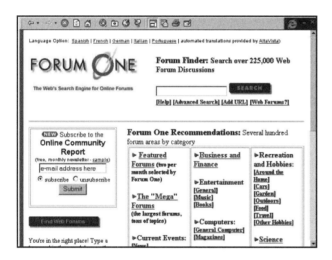

Forum One

http://www.forumone.com/

This Web site is the Web's search engine for online forums. It touts a database of over 210,000 web forum discussions. You can search its engine in five other languages. Or if you want to stay on top of the Web forum sector, subscribe to the *Forum One Report*, a monthly newsletter.

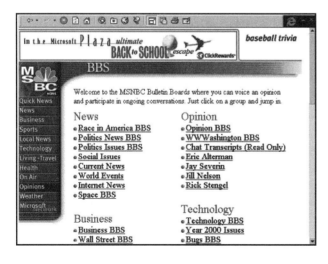

MSNBC Forums

http://www.msnbc.com/bbs/default.asp

If you want to discuss anything from Wall Street to the White House, MSNBC has a spot for you to post your opinions. With over fifty different forums, you can keep your finger on the pulse of America by lurking (this is a real tech-term!) through the latest public reaction and opinions to the latest news stories.

Pathfinder—Money and Business Forums

http://boards.pathfinder.com/cgi-bin/webx?14@@

This site features discussion groups from *Fortune* and *Money* magazines. Lots of current event discussion threads. Since some of the issues proposed at the discussion group sites are initiated by the magazines, there is some structure to what you will find at this Web site.

Specific Discussion Forums

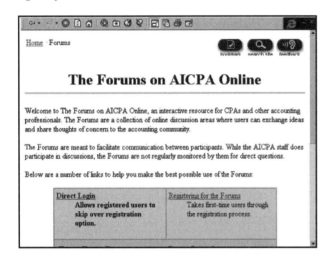

AICPA Forums

http://www.aicpa.org/forums/index.htm

This Web site has forums of interest to anyone in accounting. With WebTrust as a hot topic, there's a lot going on in the Assurance Services forum. However, much like other discussion forums, the loading and moving from page to page was slow. Patience is a virtue with discussion forums. The forum allows you to drill down to topics that interest you using its "containing keyword" filter option.

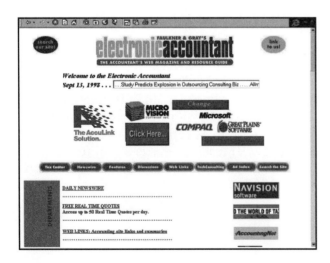

Electronic Accountant Forums

http://www.electronicaccountant.com/#discuss

From the publishers of the magazine by the same name, EA provides a handful of moderated discussion forums. At present, I noticed there weren't too many posts and they were primarily replied to by the moderator. However, with time more content should develop.

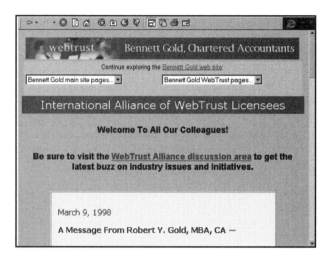

WebTrust Alliance Forum

http://www.webtrust.net/alliance/

Bennett Gold, Chartered Accountants hosts the WebTrust Forum. The forum is the main part of the Alliance, however, more resources are planned. When you enter the forum, go to the Announcements and Hot News posts for the latest information from the host. Among the posts, some WebTrust sites of interest are mentioned. If you are interested in WebTrust, interact and post here!

CalCPA Town Hall

http://www.calcpa.org/townhall/

The CalCPA Town Hall is a very cool forum format. Although it is not an open topic forum, its structure serves a purpose. Each of the forum sections includes a synopsis of the issue to be covered including some background information and links to additional resources. Once you are ready to "Be Heard," enter the discussion forum.

Ethnic/Gender Organizations

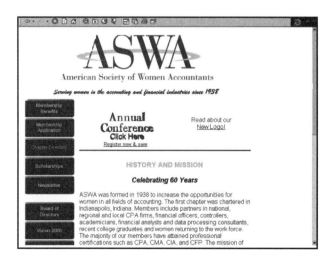

ASWA—American Society of Women Accountants

http://www.aswa.org/

ASWA was formed in 1938 to increase the opportunities for women in all fields of accounting. At the site in the Newsletters section you will find the results of a survey entitled "We've Come a Long Way in the Accounting Profession," which documents the profile of women in accounting since 1972.

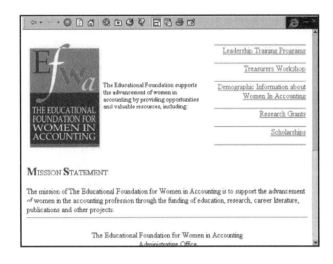

The Educational Foundation for Women in Accounting

http://www.efwa.org/

The mission of The Educational Foundation for Women in Accounting is "to support the advancement of women in the accounting profession through the funding of education, research, career literature, publications, and other projects." EFWA has demographic information about women in accounting.

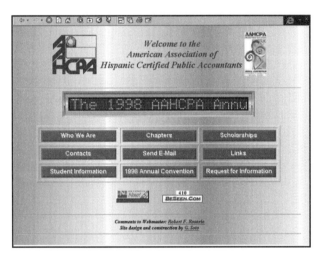

AAHCPA—American Association of Hispanic Accountants

http://www.aahcpa.org/

"The American Association of Hispanic Certified Public Accountants is a national organization with the primary purpose of helping Hispanic students, accountants, and CPAs enhance their professional capabilities while expanding Hispanic representation in the nation's work force." Check out the Links pages for additional resources for Hispanic accountants.

Firm Alliances

If you are a small to mid-size firm and are looking to join a firm alliance, you will want to research the various alliances currently available. Virtually all of these sites include the same information: general information about its alliance, services and resources provided, terms of arrangement, and contact information. Some alliances are more active than others. Due to book space limitations, I won't be able to profile each of these sites, but I felt a listing of Web sites would be most appropriate. Good luck with your alliance endeavors!

AGN—ACCOUNTANTS GLOBAL NETWORK–INTERNATIONAL
http://www.agn.org/

AAFI—ASSOCIATED ACCOUNTING FIRMS INTERNATIONAL
http://www.aafi.org/

ACPA—Affiliated Conference of Practicing Accountants
http://www.acpaintl.org/

BDO Seidman Alliance
http://www.bdo.com/

BKR International
http://www.bkrintl.com/

CPAAI—CPA Associates International, Inc.
http://www.cpaai.com/

HLB International
http://www.hlbi.com/

IA—Independent Accountants International
http://www.iai.org/

Inpact Americas
http://www.inpactam.org/

International Association of Practicing Accountants
http://www.iapa-accountants.com/

International Group of Accounting Firms
http://www.igaf.org/

JHI—Jeffreys Henry International
http://www.jhi.com/

Kreston International
http://www.kreston.com/

Moore Stephens North America, Inc.
http://www.msnainc.com/

NATP—National Association of Tax Practitioners
http://www.natptax.com/

Nexia International
http://www.nexia.com/

Summit International Associates, Inc.
http://www.siaglobal.com/

AFAI—Accounting Firms Associated, Inc.
http://www.afai.com/

NACPAF—National Associated CPA Firms
http://www.nacpaf.com/

Academia & University

Resources

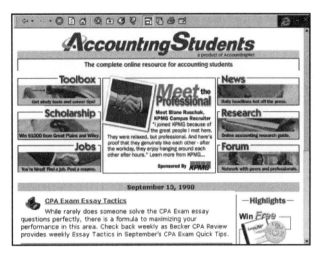

Accounting Students

http://www.accountingstudents.com/

Accounting Students is a Web site for students by the same individuals who developed AccountingNet. At Accounting Students, there are many resources to check into. Some resources are student-specific and others are general enough for everyone. For instance, the past feature was Networking Demystified. There is a Jobs section where you can search for available candidates. The site also hosts the Student Corner Forum.

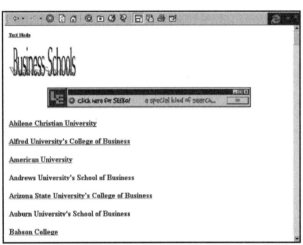

University Links

http://www-net.com/univ/

At University Links, check out the Find That School section for a listing of all business school Web sites. The links take you straight to the school.

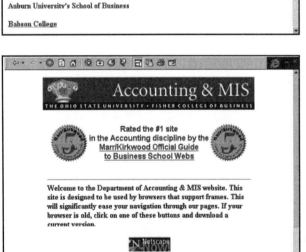

OSU AMIS Site

http://www.cob.ohio-state.edu/~acctmis/

This Web site was selected by Marr & Kirkwood as the #1 site in the Accounting discipline. It contains a vast array of course materials, research papers, and a quarterly e-zine. Once you enter, you will want to visit the Research section for directories, a research working papers and resource links.

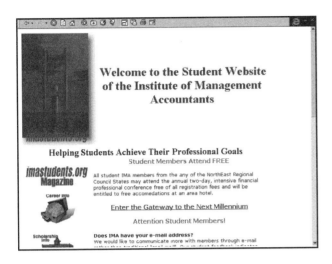

IMA Students

http://www.imastudents.org/

IMA Students Web site is a helpful resource for students considering a career in management accounting. The site features the *IMA Student Magazine,* the 1st Annual Bean Counters Bean Dip Contest, and Salary Survey. The site is hosting various student competitions as well.

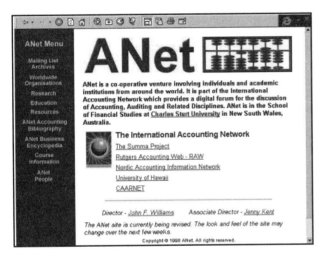

ANet Accountancy Network

http://www.csu.edu.au/anet/

ANet is a cooperative venture involving individuals and academic institutions from around the world. It is part of the International Accounting Network which includes the Summa Project, Rutgers Accounting Web, among others. Resources are still being added to this site. Currently the ANet Accounting Bibliography is complete.

The Summa Project

http://www.summa.org.uk/

The Summa Project is the European accounting research site. Visit the Recent Changes section first for new posts to the site. Most resources at this Web site are included in the Academia section. However, if you want to venture around more, use the Search/Index section and select the subject index.

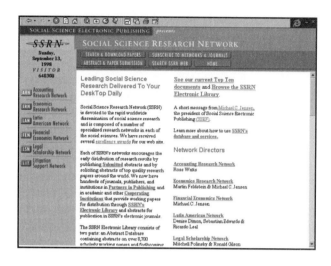

ARN—Accounting Research Network

http://www.ssrn.com/

ARN encourages the "early distribution of research results by publishing abstracts of research papers in its three journals: *Auditing, Litigation and Tax Abstracts*, *Financial Accounting Abstracts*, and *Managerial Accounting Abstracts*." At the Announcements section you can review the call for papers.

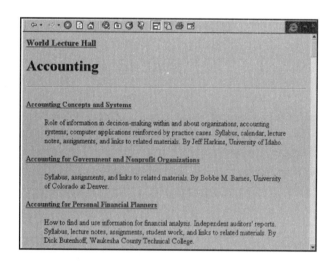

World Lecture Hall

http://www.utexas.edu/world/lecture/acc/

The University of Texas' World Lecture Hall (WLH) contains links to pages created by faculty worldwide who are using the Web to deliver class materials. The Accounting Page is organized by topic and includes various contributed resources such as syllabi, lecture notes, link resources, and assignments. The Business Administration Lecture Hall is worth a look as well at http://www.utexas.edu/world/lecture/ba/.

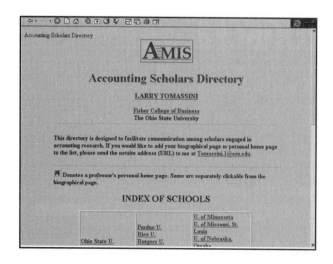

Accounting Scholars Directory

http://www.cob.ohio-state.edu/~tomassin/acc_sch/

The Scholars Directory links users to accounting faculty biographies and homepages at more than seventy major universities. This directory is designed to facilitate communication among scholars engaged in accounting research. It is also useful for students trying to learn about faculty members' interests at schools which they are considering attending.

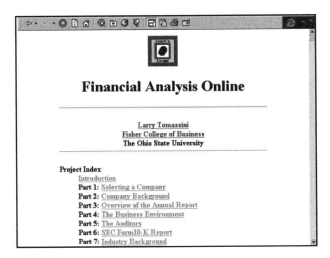

Financial Analysis Online Project

http://www.cob.ohio-state.edu/~tomassin/fanon.html

This Web site has a comprehensive project assignment that can be used to your ability to analyze financial statements. This project includes several assignments, each of which comprises a part of the analyst's task. An excellent introduction to financial analysis.

Publications

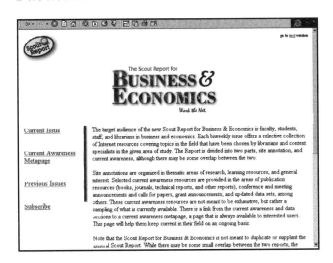

The Scout Report

http://scout.cs.wisc.edu/scout/report/bus-econ/

"Published every Friday both on the Web and by E-mail, the Scout Report provides a convenient way to stay informed of valuable resources on the Internet." The Scout Report has been providing this service for over three years and is a well-respected resource. The report itself contains about ten business and economics related Web sites complete with site review.

Journal of Finance

http://www.cob.ohio-state.edu/~fin/journal/

The complete text of the *Journal of Finance* is available online. The articles are broken down to in-depth studies and shorter articles. The contribution made in February 1998 entitled "Why Do Companies Go Public? An Empirical Analysis" is forty-six pages of information via .pdf format. The Journal is an excellent resource for in-depth research.

Organizations

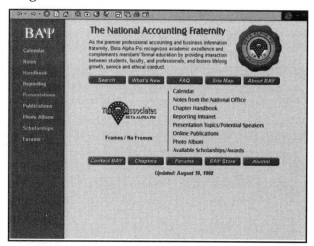

BAP—Beta Alpha Psi

http://www.bap.org/

The BAP home page includes general information about the honor fraternity, has a student discussion forum, and provides the BAP Handbook online. The schedule of activities and information about the Annual Meeting are available at BAP.

American Accounting Association

http://www.rutgers.edu/Accounting/raw/aaa/

AAA has several publications online. For accounting education news visit the quarterly edition of *Accounting Education News*. It also has abstracts of three other quarterly publications online, the *Accounting Review, Accounting Horizons,* and *Issues in Accounting Education.* On top of that, there are at least another ten online newsletters and journals contributed by AAA Sections.

Continuing Professional Education

CPE Top Web Sites

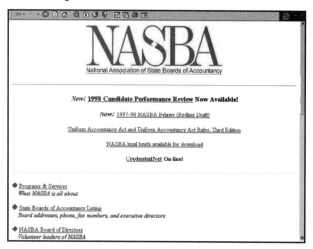

NASBA—National Association of State Boards of Accountancy

http://www.nasba.org/

NASBA is a not-for-profit membership organization of the fifty-four state boards of accountancy of the United States. It created the National Registry to assist its member boards in evaluating CPE sponsors and to assist accountants in selecting qualified providers of formal continuing education programs.

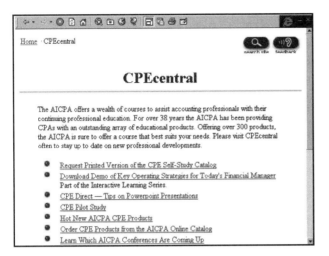

AICPA

http://www.aicpa.org/cpe/index.htm

Visit the CPEcenter for all your AICPA CPE needs. Order the catalog or read about the newest CPE products available. The AICPA has set up a virtual storefront for online purchasing. You will also find updates to the *Journal of Accountancy*'s CPE Direct here.

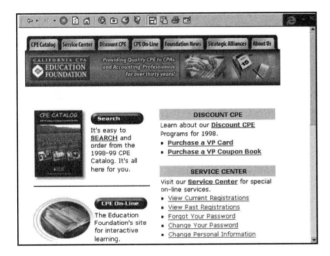

CPA Education Foundation

http://www.calcpaed.org/

California has some wonderful resort locations to obtain your CPE credits, and this site features these conferences. Its entire catalog is online for searching, and at current one online interactive course is offered (an ethics course). Visit Foundation News for CPE updates and read the monthly newsletter CPE Exchange.

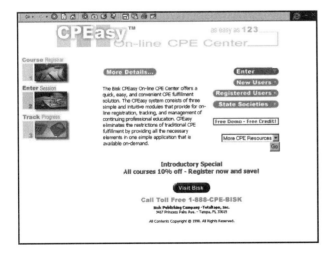

Bisk CPEasy.com

http://www.cpeasy.com/

Bisk CPEasy offers online CPE classes. Once you sign up, you can take the optional chapter quizzes to find out if you are ready to successfully complete the CPE quizzer for each program. The site automatically tracks your CPE credits, and new courses are added to the database as soon as they are written.

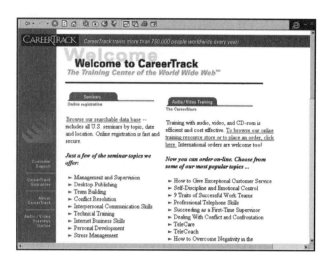

CareerTrack

http://www.careertrack.com/

CareerTrack is well-known for its extensive line of audio/video training products, public and on-site seminars, as well as custom seminar and consulting services for a wide variety of business-related and personal subject matter. Now you can view and hear extended clips of some of its more popular products and audio and video products online for free. The site also has a worldwide searchable database of CareerTrack seminars.

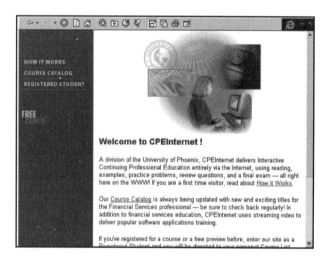

CPEInternet

http://cpe.uophx.edu/

A division of the University of Phoenix, CPEInternet delivers Interactive Continuing Professional Education entirely via the Internet. You are entitled to preview the first workshop and quiz of any course online. Currently CPEInternet has a nice selection of courses on the topics of Professional Development, Management, Accounting/Auditing, Taxation, Consulting, Specialized Knowledge, and Computer Training.

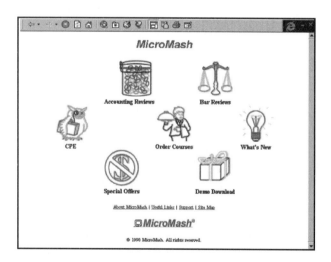

MicroMash

http://www.micromash.com/

At the MicroMash site you can find downloadable demos of all MicroMash reviews that are available. Two free hours of CPE credit are available from a MicroMash sample course. Check out the What's New section for updates and tax law updates.

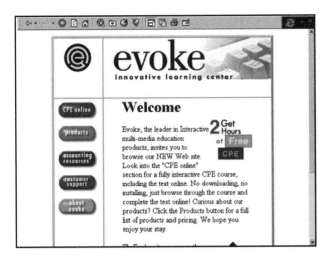

Evoke

http://www.evoke.com/

Visit Evoke for two free hours of CPE credit. Look into the CPE online section for a fully interactive CPE course, including the test online. Its courses include Tax & Financial Strategies for the High Income Individual and The Interactive Yellow Book on government auditing standards.

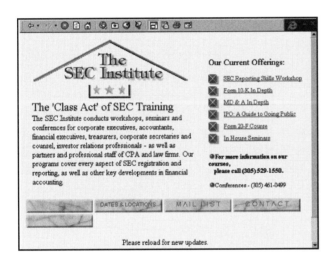

SEC Institute

http://secseminars.com/

The SEC Institute programs cover every aspect of SEC registration and reporting, as well as other key developments in financial accounting. The site has details on its current course offerings of IPO—Going Public, Form 10-K In-Depth, and M&A In-Depth. The site offers a mailing list for course update notifications.

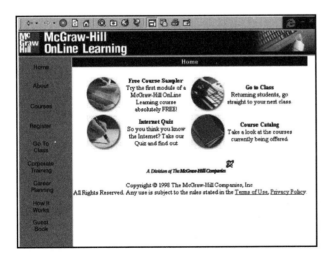

McGraw-Hill Online Learning

http://www.mhonlinelearning.com/

McGraw-Hill offers various Microsoft certification courses at its site. Visit the Free Course Sampler section where you can try the first module of a McGraw-Hill OnLine Learning course absolutely free. There are classes in Programming, Internet, Business, Management, and Computer Applications.

ValuED

http://www.valued.com/

ValuED provides self-study CPE classes. The new course offerings are highlighted at the home page. Check out the special discounts for promotions given to Web visitors only.

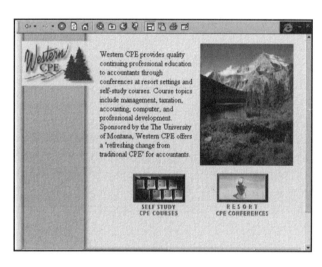

Western CPE

http://www.umt.edu/ccesp/wcpe/

Western CPE offers self-study and resort CPE classes. Both catalogs are online for browsing. Western offers courses and conferences in the areas of Management, Legal, Financial Analysis, Taxation, Accounting/Auditing, and Computers.

Other CPE Companies List

ACCOUNTING PROFESSIONALS
http://www.cpanews.com/courses.asp

ASCE—AMERICAN SOCIETY FOR CE
http://www.asce.com/

BUREAU OF NATIONAL AFFAIRS
http://www.bna.com/

CARSWELL—CANADA
http://www.carswell.com/

CCH—COMMERCE CLEARING HOUSE
http://www.cch.com/

CONTROLLER MAGAZINE
http://www.controllermag.com/

CPA ASSOCIATES, INC.
http://www.cpassoc.com/

CPE ACCOUNTING AND TAX INSTITUTE
http://www.cpecredit.org/

CPENET
http://uu-gna.mit.edu:8001/~compass/

FOUNDATION FOR CONTINUING EDUCATION
http://fce.org/

GLEIM PUBLICATIONS
http://www.gleim.com/

HARCOURT BRACE—ONLINE TESTING
http://www.hbpp.com/cpetest/

K2 ENTERPRISES
http://www.k2e.com/

KENT INFORMATION SERVICES, INC.
http://www.kentis.com/cpe.html

KRL CONSULTANTS & PUBLISHERS
http://www.poweradz.com/krlcp/cpe.htm

LEXIS-NEXIS COMMUNICATION CENTER
http://www.lexis-nexis.com/

PPC PRACTITIONERS PUBLISHING COMPANY
http://www.ppcinfo.com/cpe.htm

RIA—RESEARCH INSTITUTE OF AMERICA
http://www.riatax.com/elecsub.html

SURGENT & ASSOCIATES
http://www.surgent.com/

TAFT UNIVERSITY SCHOOL OF CE
http://www.taftu.edu/ce1.htm

WARREN, GORHAM & LAMONT
http://www.wgl.com/acct/acct.html

WISEGUIDES
http://www.wiseguides.com/

State Boards of Accountancy

ALASKA
http://www.commerce.state.ak.us/occ/pcpa.htm

ARIZONA
http://www.accountancy.state.az.us/

CALIFORNIA
http://www.dca.ca.gov/cba/

COLORADO
http://www.dora.state.co.us/Accountants

CONNECTICUT
http://www.state.ct.us/sots/SBOA/bdacc.htm

DISTRICT OF COLUMBIA
http://www.gwscpa.org/dcba/

FLORIDA
http://www.gwscpa.org/dcba/

IDAHO
http://www2.state.id.us/boa/

ILLINOIS
http://www.illinois-cpa-exam.com/

INDIANA
http://www.ai.org/pla/accountancy/

IOWA
http://www.state.ia.us/government/com/prof/acct/acct.htm

KENTUCKY
http://www.state.ky.us/agencies/boa/

MAINE
http://www.state.me.us/pfr/led/account/

MARYLAND
http://www.dllr.state.md.us/occprof/account.html

MISSISSIPPI
http://www.msbpa.state.ms.us/

MISSOURI
http://www.ecodev.state.mo.us/pr/account/

NEBRASKA
http://www.nol.org/home/BPA/

NEVADA
http://www.state.nv.us/boards/accountancy/

NEW JERSEY
http://www.state.nj.us/lps/ca/nonmed.htm

NEW YORK
http://www.nysed.gov/prof/cpa.htm

NORTH CAROLINA
http://www.state.nc.us/cpabd/

NORTH DAKOTA

http://www.state.nd.us/ndsba/default.htm

OHIO

http://www.state.oh.us/acc/

OREGON

http://www.boa.state.or.us/boa.html

SOUTH CAROLINA

http://www.llr.sc.edu/bac.htm

TENNESSEE

http://www.state.tn.us/commerce/tnsba/

TEXAS

http://www.tsbpa.state.tx.us/

UTAH

http://www.commerce.state.ut.us/web/commerce/
    dopl/dopl1.htm

VIRGINIA

http://dit1.state.va.us/dpor/acc_main.htm

WEST VIRGINIA

http://www.state.wv.us/wvboa/

WYOMING

http://www.wyocpa.org/borad.htm

Exams

CPA Exam

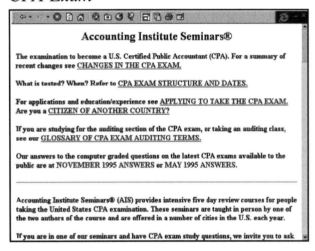

Accounting Institute Seminars

http://www.ais-cpa.com/

AIS has detailed information about the CPA Exam at its Web site. In addition, AIS's Web site has information about its intensive five-day review class. These seminars are taught in person by one of the two authors of the course and are offered in a number of cities in the U.S. each year.

Becker

http://www.beckercpa.com/

The Becker site has general information about its popular review program. It also provides information about its intensive program and CD-ROM resources. Visit the section entitled "Thinking About Becoming a CPA." The section gives you insights regarding the CPA profession, career, and salary information. Check out Exam Info for state-by-state resources.

CPAexam.com

http://www.cpaexam.com/

CPAexam.com is produced by Bisk-Totaltape (http://www.bisk.com/). At this site you will take a virtual journey to the summit of a huge mountain (so to speak). Using this analogy, CPAexam guides you through the Base Camp. Here you can pick up general exam information, take a diagnostic practice run, register for preparation classes, pick up supplies, and use the discussion forums. In case you get lost along the way, there are guides, resources, and first aid at your disposal.

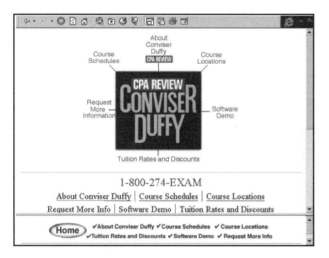

Conviser Duffy

http://www.conviserduffy.com/

The Conviser Duffy Web site primarily has information about its review course. After you are done checking out the course information, visit its software demo of the Conviser Duffy PassMaster software. The full version of PassMaster includes the last thirteen released CPA exams, including 3,800 multiple choice questions and over two hundred long essay-format questions.

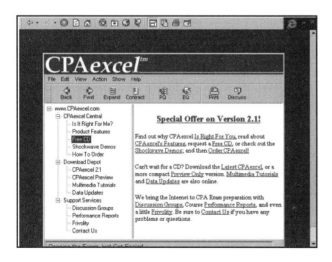

CPAexcel

http://www.cpaexcel.com/

CPAexcel's exam preparation software features an integrated suite of software tools and Internet support services along with study materials prepared by professors from the University of Texas at Austin. Although the Web site is primarily a software delivery mechanism at this point, it also has discussion groups and course performance reports available.

Gleim

http://www.gleim.com/

Gleim offers online updates in text format for all of its books. This is especially helpful for that "day before the exam anxiety." One good example of its update service is the new material posted for the CMA/CFM exam where several hundred interactive practice questions are included online.

Kaplan

http://www.kaplan.com/accounting/

Kaplan's site helps accounting and financial professionals understand the CPA exam; sample questions, scoring, test dates and interactive study tools are available. Extensive career information is available, too, including resumé advice, job search tips, and a fun mock job-interview game called "The Hot Seat." Kaplan also manages a Web site at http://www.kaplancpareview.com, which is dedicated to delivering streaming video, audio, and text-based course materials for enrolled students (some free stuff here too!).

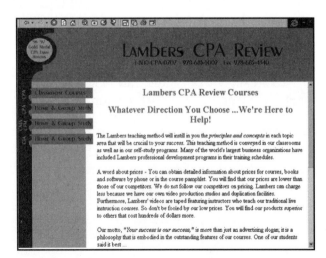

Lambers

http://www.lamberscpa.com/

The Lambers CPA Review home page has information about its classroom courses as well as its home and group study programs. At the site you can download a free demo and inspect a sample chapter of the Lambers review guide.

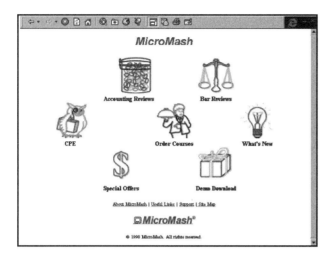

MicroMash

http://www.micromash.com/

At the MicroMash Accounting Review section, you can check out the Indicators section for information on MicroMash software that can help you gauge the possibility of passing the exam (other exams too!). Click on the CPA jelly bean and get information about the review program and download a demo of the CPA Review.

Tutorial Group

http://www.tutorialgroup.com/

The Tutorial Group provides a flashcard review program and has online ordering abilities for quick CPA Exam fixes. Click on CPA Coverage for a detailed listing of the areas covered in the flashcard review. The CPA Flashcard System provides over one thousand flashcards for the CPA Exam.

Wiley

http://www.wiley.com/products/subject/accounting/cpa/

The Wiley Web site has more online resources than most of the other sites. Visit Delaney's Tip of the Week for advice. Or if you are feeling luck, enter the drawing contest. The site has a guide on how to pass the exam as well as FAQs about the CPA Exam and a Review software demo you can download.

Other Exams List

Below, I have included the Web addresses of the sites that provide information on other exams of interest to accountants. I have not profiled any of these sites as these organizations have already been profiled elsewhere. I have noted the section where you can find the complete profile.

CMA—CERTIFIED MANAGEMENT ACCOUNTANT & CFM—CERTIFICATE IN FINANCIAL MANAGEMENT

http://www.rutgers.edu/Accounting/raw/ima/ (profiled in Private Industry section)

CFP—CERTIFIED FINANCIAL PLANNER

http://www.cfp-board.org/ (profiled in Financial Planning section)

CFE—CERTIFIED FRAUD EXAMINER

http://www.acfe.org/whatis.html (profiled in Accounting section)

CIA—CERTIFIED INTERNAL AUDITOR AND CPD

http://www.theiia.org/ (profiled in Audit section)

GMAT

http://www.gmat.org/ (not profiled elsewhere)

Exam Preparation Resources

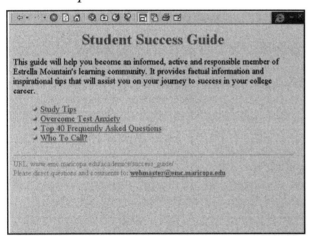

Test Success Guide

http://www.emc.maricopa.edu/academics/success_guide/

A quick test guide, this site includes sections on Study Tips, Sixteen Ways to Overcome Stress Anxiety, and Top Forty Frequently Asked Questions.

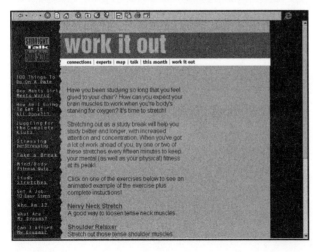

Study Break Stretches

http://www.balancenet.org/workout/stretch/stretch.html

Use the study break stretches as a chance to rejuvenate and reinvigorate yourself. This site has six exercises you can perform at the comfort of your desk (or near it!). Each stretch has an accompanying animated graphic to help you see the stretch in action.

Chapter 13

OTHER RESOURCES

The CPA Toolbox

Reference

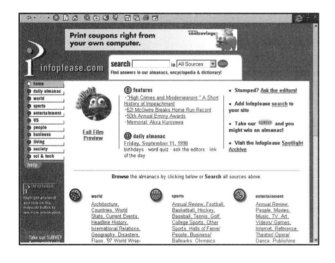

Information Please

http://www.infoplease.com/

Information Please is an excellent reference resource. Find answers in the almanac, dictionary, and encyclopedia. There are nine major almanac categories, the one you should check out first is Business. The Business Almanac provides information on the economy, taxes, personal finance, and general business.

Encyclopedia.com

http://encyclopedia.com/

Encyclopedia.com is a free encyclopedia. This site places an extraordinary amount of information at your fingertips with more than 17,000 articles from the *Concise Columbia Electronic Encyclopedia, Third Edition*. You can search the site or browse by encyclopedia volume.

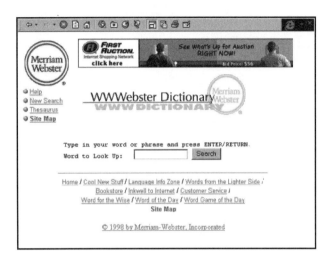

WWWebster Dictionary

http://www.m-w.com/dictionary

This is the online version of *Merriam-Webster's Collegiate Dictionary, Tenth Edition*. Visit the Help section for topics on how to effectively use the dictionary. Hit the Language Info Zone for the "Guide To International Business Communications," "Interactive Vocabulary Builder Quizzes," and "A Brief Look at the History of the English Language."

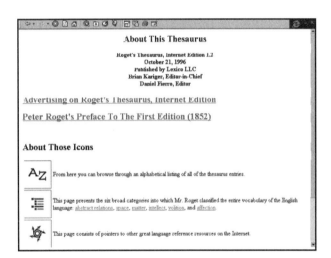

Roget's Thesaurus

http://www.thesaurus.com/

Roget's site has a simple interface that includes one search box at the home page. Just type in a word or phrase to search the thesaurus. Just like the hard copy of the book, the site is nicely organized and it's a snap to find related words. You can also use the site by browsing the alphabetical index. To really get into words, go to the outline format and view in detail the six main classes of words.

My Virtual Reference Desk

http://www.refdesk.com/

MVRD is a great resource by Bob Drudge. Visit the Table of Contents first to get familiar with the site. The site is a great portal site for reference sources and has links to facts, search engines, encyclopedias, almanacs, software downloads, and much more.

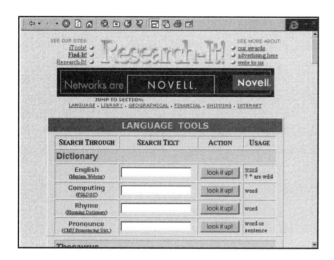

iTools

http://www.itools.com/

iTools is organized in a sleek search interface. Visit either Research-It or Find-It for a one-page entry form for searching. At Research-It, you can tap into various dictionary, thesaurus, and translator databases. You can also search for maps, people, and package shipping status. At the Find-It page, you can perform a search of several search engines.

Library Spot

http://www.libraryspot.com/

Library Spot has a complete directory of libraries on the web, from public, law, state, and school. The Reference Desk area includes links to various sources of reference information. For example, the acronyms page had links to six different acronym sites.

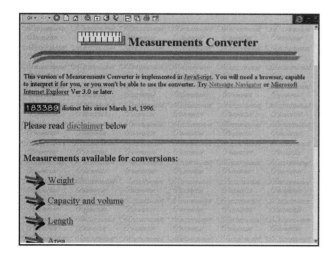

Measurement Units Translation

http://www.mplik.ru/~sg/transl/

This site has a quick and friendly measurements converter application using a JavaScript interface. The translator converts time, weight, area, speed, temperature, and more into different units. For more links visit Measure4Measure at http://www.wolinskyweb.com/measure.htm for a collection of interactive sites that "estimate, calculate, evaluate, and translate."

Acronym Finder

http://www.mtnds.com/af/

This is a quick search tool to find the meaning of acronyms. To find out how many acronyms are derived from certain words use the advanced search for results. The database has over 57,000 records.

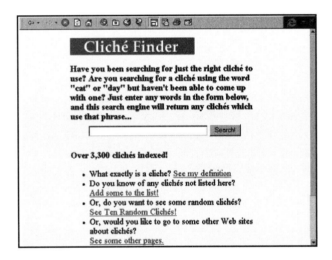

Cliché Finder

http://www.westegg.com/cliche/

Have you been searching for just the right cliché to use? Well, now you have an answer. This database has over 3,300 clichés indexed. The site can randomly generate ten clichés if you choose.

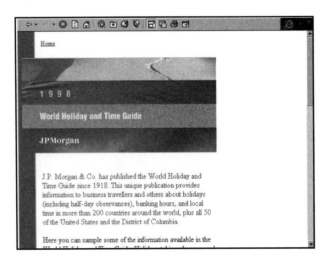

World Holiday and Time Guide

http://www.worldtime.com/

http://www.jpmorgan.com/cgi-bin/HolidayCalendar

J.P. Morgan & Co. has published the World Holiday and Time Guide since 1918. The site-searchable information is by country (and all the U.S. states) or by date. The entire guide is available in hard copy.

Computer Resources

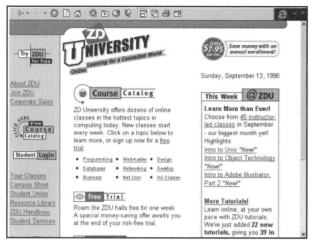

ZD University

http://www.zdu.com/

ZD University is an online community for computing technology. For a low monthly fee, you are entitled to enroll in the many online classes at ZDU. The classes are all in the format of discussion threads, and this site has mastered the method of instructing in this way. They have recruited instructors who have the most experience on the class topic. For example, for the class "Advertising on the Internet," the instructor/moderator was the author of the book by the same name, Robin Neff.

PC-Help Online

http://www.pchelponline.com/

The goal of PC-Help Online is "to give PC users the resources to solve their own problems." Instead of searching on the net for a hardware or software vendor visit this site first. PC-Help has organized its Web site so this kind of information is easy to find.

BugNet

http://www.bugnet.com/

BugNet is undisputedly the World's Leading Supplier of PC Bug Fixes. Have you had a computer crash lately? If so, check out BugNet for a potential fix. BugNet subscribers have access to the entire knowledge base. However, don't fear, there is a BugNet Freebies section which includes BugNet Alert, BugNet Top Ten and Search Free BugNet Site.

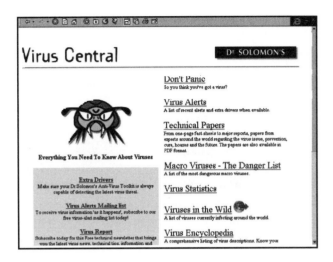

Virus Central

http://www.drsolomon.com/vircen/

Virus Central is virtually a one-stop virus shop. The top of the page has the reassuring words "don't panic." It gives visitors not only words of comfort but also solutions. Find details of a virus by visiting the *Virus Encyclopedia*. If you are current with your anti-virus program, then you can read the Virus Alerts for the latest in virus threats and hoaxes. Macro viruses are climbing in number and Virus Central has a section devoted entirely to these pesky critters.

Win Drivers

http://www.windrivers.com

If you are looking for a driver update, come to Win Drivers first. This massive site is produced and directed single-handedly by Scott Hermanson, a self-proclaimed supergeek and tech nerd. When you need drivers, someone of Scott's nerd-caliber is surely in order. Search for your driver by Company, Category, or FCC Id. The site has weekly tech tips, discussion forums, and installation guides.

Windows Resources

http://www.winfiles.com/

The purpose of the WinFiles.com site is "to provide explanations, software, and information about Microsoft Windows operating systems." The Web site interface is cleverly designed as a Windows 95 desktop and is very easy to navigate. Pick up a few pointers at Tips and Tricks or receive E-mail updates.

E-mail Spam Resources

Fight Against Spam

http://www.cauce.org/

CAUCE is made up of "Internet users and system administrators who have lost faith in the efficacy of technical or market-driven 'solutions' to junk E-mail." CAUCE promotes legislation—specifically H.R. 1748, "The Netizens Protection Act"—to ban junk E-mail on behalf of more than 11,000 members who have completed an online sign-up process.

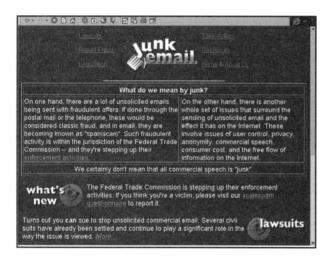

Junk E-mail Resource Page

http://www.junkemail.org/

Junkemail.org was created and is maintained by the Center for Democracy and Technology and the Voters Telecommunications Watch. Check out this site's Resources page for background information, articles, and tips. You can also report Scam Spam via interactive forms!

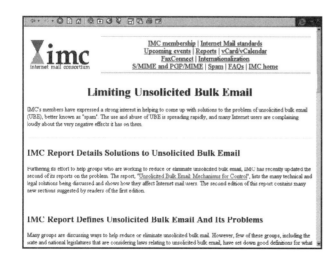

Limiting Unsolicited Bulk E-mail

http://www.imc.org/imc-spam/

Another organization active in the legislation of unsolicited bulk E-mail, the Internet Mail Consortium has published its findings of E-mail abuse in its second report, "Unsolicited Bulk E-mail: Mechanisms for Control." Its first report, "Unsolicited Bulk E-mail: Definitions and Problems," is also online.

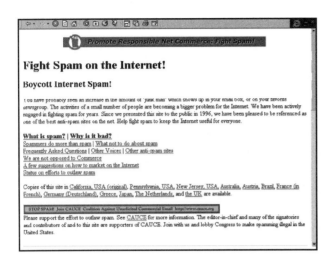

Spam Abuse Net

http://spam.abuse.net/

Spam Abuse Net has several articles to help you fully understand spam E-mail, how you can fight it, and how you can prevent it. Check out the explanation of the difference between commerce and spamming activities and the brief tutorial on how to complain to providers about spam.

Directories & Search

Directories

Broadcast.com

http://www.broadcast.com/

The Mother of Web-casting sites, Broadcast.com should be close to the top of your favorite bookmarks for audio content. You will find a myriad of audio feeds to tap into, ranging from complete seminars and interviews to corporate earnings and press conferences.

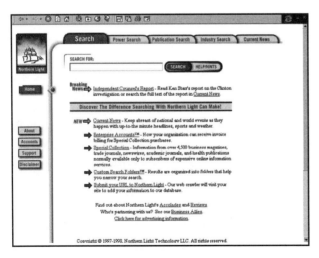

Northern Light Search

http://www.nlsearch.com/

Northern Light provides searches of its uniquely indexed content. Some of NL's content is hard to dig up elsewhere, some is free, and some is pay-per-view. Northern Light organizes its search results by creating folders of documents with similar subjects, sources, or types. These custom folders help guide you to a set of focused results.

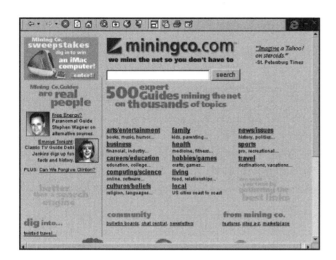

Mining Company

http://www.miningcompany.com/

With an extremely unique idea to create specialty guides, the Mining Company recruits guides to moderate an entire site (for example, Entrepreneur's or Internet Industry). These guides scour and mine the Web so you don't have to. Just pick your favorite areas and drop in every once in a while. Or ask to be notified when the section changes.

Essential Links

http://www.el.com/

Essential links is a quick and clean directory of Internet resources that is organized by category. EL does have some very in-depth guides; for instance, check out its guide on Taxes. But probably better known is its home page interface, one that is worthy of your start page.

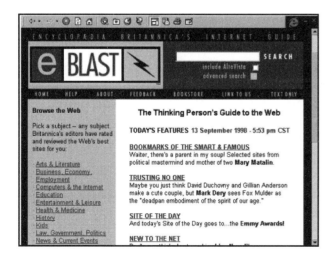

eBLAST—Encyclopædia Britannica's Internet Guide

http://eblast.com/

This is a directory of Web sites, from the publishers of Encyclopedia Britannica. The guide loads fast, has some nice results, and is a good alternative to Yahoo! Listings can be searched or browsed. A partnership with AltaVista provides searches beyond the guide's listings. The guide was launched Oct. 14, 1997.

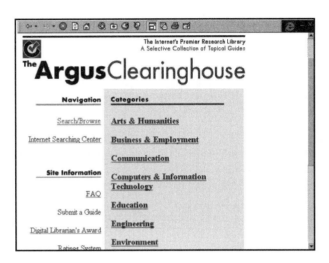

Argus Clearinghouse

http://www.clearinghouse.net/

Argus is a clearinghouse of Web site directories. It is responsible for indexing other index-based topical guides. The site provides a search tool to find related directories quickly. All guides submitted to Argus are reviewed prior to inclusion at its Web site. The clearinghouse provides ratings and reviews of the directories as well.

The Top Search Engines & Portals

Note: I decided to profile each of the major search engines. This isn't because I use all of them, I primarily use Yahoo!, AltaVista, and HotBot. However, if you plan to register your Web site with the major search engines, you should have a quick list you can refer to, hence the list below.

Yahoo!

http://www.yahoo.com/

We all know about Yahoo!. It goes without saying for browsing on the Web, Yahoo! has the easiest interface. Since real people index the primary directory (secondary links are co-branded by the HotBot search engine), there is a better chance you will find the right home page. Here are some Yahoo! categories you may want to visit, just search using the following keywords and you should be pointed to the appropriate subdirectory:

- CPA Exam
- Accounting_and_Auditing
- Year_2000_Problem
- Accounting Organizations
- Accounting Employment
- Taxes

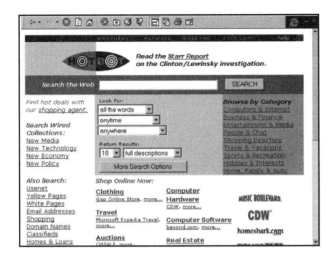

HotBot

http://www.hotbot.com/

HotBot has received praise for being one of the more accurate search engines. It has extremely flexible tools to help you narrow down your search and make special queries that would be otherwise very difficult to handle with other search engine interfaces. The returned information is very flexible as well, giving you the choice to see ten to one hundred Web sites per page and the choice of full or brief description format. For another site powered partly by HotBot's company, Inktomi, visit Snap! at http://www.snap.com/.

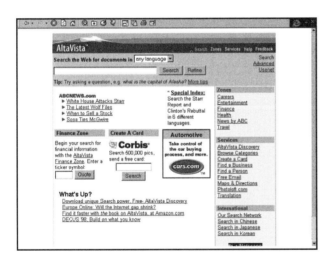

AltaVista

http://www.altavista.com/

One of the largest depositories of indexed Web pages, AltaVista has started to branch out as a Web portal and now has various Zones you can visit. The search engine includes other interactive features such as a foreign language translator and a personal version of AltaVista you can place on your desktop for searching through your own PC.

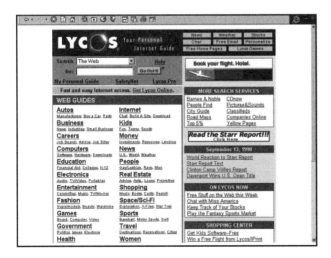

Lycos

http://www.lycos.com/

Lycos has been working on becoming an even more prominent and useful search engine by adding several features to its site such as free E-mail, personal page, chat, and a number of Web-directory topic guides. Lycos provides a listing of related categories when it displays its search results.

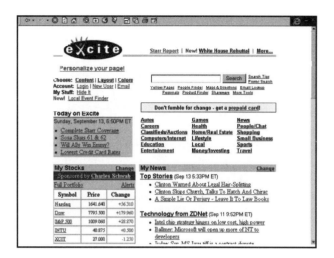

Excite

http://www.excite.com/

Excite has been ranked as the most functional search engine of all the top alternatives. Its speed, ease of use, and relevant results are all characteristics that have put Excite on top. The AOL NetFind site (http://www.aol.com/netfind/) is powered by Excite.

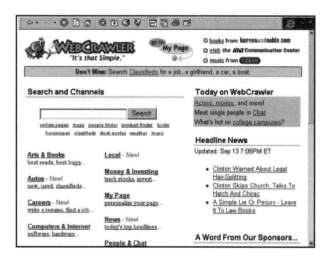

Webcrawler

http://www.webcrawler.com/

Although Excite owns Webcrawler, it is an independent search engine with an associated directory of reviewed sites, WebCrawler Select.

Infoseek

http://www.infoseek.com/

In addition to its status as a top search engine, Infoseek has really made a good showing as a Web browser. The site has created extensive channels for browsing or searching. Sites are listed by topic, and editors pick the sites that appear. Search.com (http://www.search.com/) is powered by Infoseek.

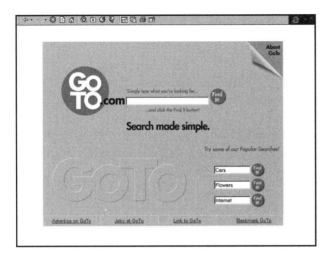

Goto.com

http://www.goto.com/

Goto has an interesting business model. The search engine gives priority ranking to companies who pay a very small fee such as $.01 per viewer. To fill in the gaps, Goto selects various Web sites to be included in its directory, free of charge.

LookSmart

http://www.looksmart.com/

LookSmart's interface has received many kudos for its browsable folder format. Look-Smart hand picks its directory submissions, similar to Yahoo!, after the primary search results. Additional results are powered by AltaVista.

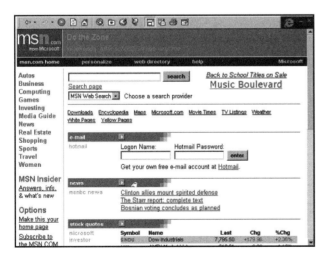

MSN

http://www.msn.com/

Microsoft has released its plans to turn MSN into a full-fledge search engine/Web portal. The site's search component is planned to be powered by Inktomi, the makers of HotBot.

Netscape Netcenter

http://www.netcenter.com/

You will find much more than Netscape resources at the Netcenter. The Netcenter is a browsable topic-guide and a fully functional search engine. The site has several personalization features to make your searching experience more effective.

Other Search Engines

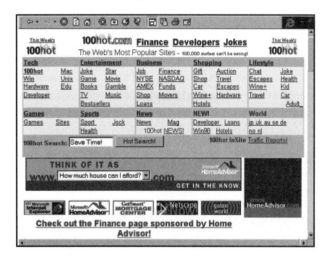

100hot.com

http://www.100hot.com/

100hot.com is a site that indexes its Web site picks in a series of Top 100 lists. The site has topic-based categories such as finance, news, technology, and international sites.

EuroSeek

http://euroseek.net/

This is a European-based search engine which covers the globe. If you are looking for international Web sites and resources, check out EuroSeek.

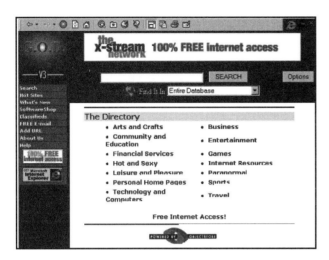

GOD

http://www.god.co.uk/

If you didn't find what you needed at EuroSeek, then try the Global Online Directory (GOD). GOD is a well-known international search directory and has been around since the Web's early days. It is UK-based and covers the globe.

Top Metacrawlers & Metasearch Engines

MetaCrawler

http://www.metacrawler.com/

MetaCrawler is one of the oldest meta search services and has been around since 1995. Its interface is basic with a single search box to perform your META search.

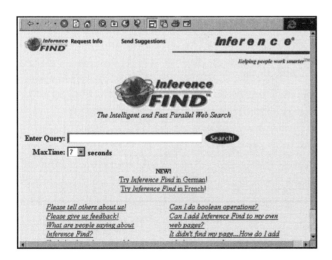

Inference Find

http://www.inference.com/ifind/

An alternative to typical metacrawlers, Inference lists results grouped by subject, rather than by search engine or in one giant list. Inference Find utilizes AltaVista, Excite, Lycos, WebCrawler, and Yahoo!

Dogpile

http://www.dogpile.com/

It sends a search to a customizable list of search engines, directories, and specialty search sites. Once a search is performed, Dogpile presents a detailed listing by search engine of its search results.

Internet Sleuth

http://www.isleuth.com/

Internet Sleuth permits you to choose which search engines you would like it to consecutively search. The site even includes a timer that shows you the maximum search time involved, which depends on how many search engines you select. IS touts over three thousand searchable databases.

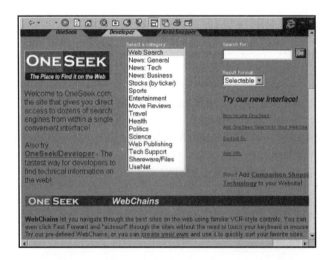

OneSeek

http://www.oneseek.com/

OneSeek is a metacrawler that displays the results from two or three search engines side-by-side. Depending on your search purposes, this interface may be preferred. The site also offers a "WebChains" service that lets you move between related sites using a control panel (similar to Web Rings).

Other Interesting Search Sites

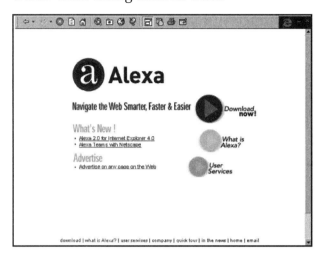

Alexa

http://www.alexa.com/

Alexa is a site discovery application that works with your browser. You don't perform the Alexa software for searches. Instead, it monitors sites you visit while on the Web and provides suggested related sites.

Ask Jeeves

http://www.askjeeves.com/

Ask Jeeves is a human-powered search service that aims to direct you to the exact page that answers your question. If it fails to find a match within its own database, then it will provide matching Web pages from various search engines.

Search Resources

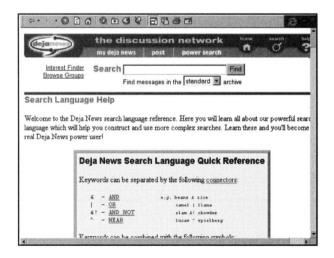

Search Language Help

http://www.dejanews.com/help/help_lang.shtml

A general search language guide is included at the Dejanews site. It includes basic search concepts such as keyword separations (that is, AND, OR) and various Boolean connectors.

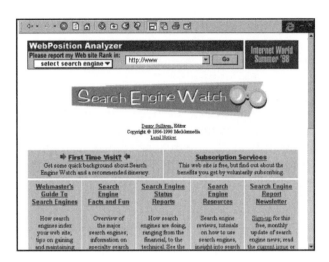

Search Engine Watch

http://searchenginewatch.com/

For metacrawlers and metasearch engines, you can go to http://searchenginewatch.com/facts/metacrawlers.html. Unlike search engines, metacrawlers don't crawl the Web themselves to build listings. Instead, they allow searches to be sent to several search engines all at once. The results are then blended together onto one page.

Statistical Sources

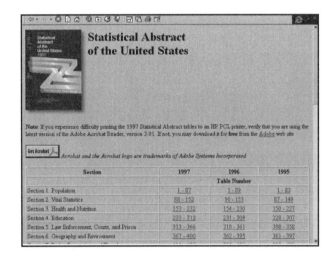

U.S. Statistical Abstract

http://www.census.gov/prod/www/abs/cc97stab.html

The U.S. Statistical Abstract is a product of the U.S. Census Bureau. At the site you will find PDF hyperlinks that will take you to statistical data and results of components of the census such as population, vital statistics, elections and labor force, employment, and earnings.

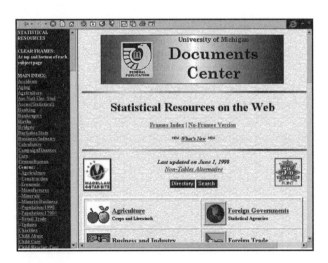

Statistical Resources

http://www.lib.umich.edu/libhome/Documents.center/frames/statsfr.html

The University of Michigan has an amazing directory of statistical information. Navigate its main index to select your category of choice, such as bankruptcy, births, business and industry, and unemployment. The site will return a list of sites to visit that house the requested statistical data.

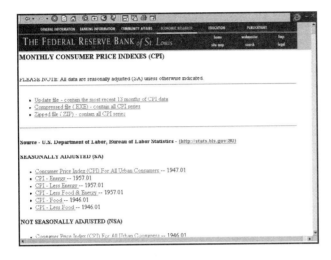

FRED—Consumer Price Indexes

http://www.stls.frb.org/fred/data/cpi.html

This site has extensive information about the CPI. The figures are presented both in the seasonally and not seasonally adjusted indices for the overall CPI as well as energy and food.

Job Search

Online Job Search Companies

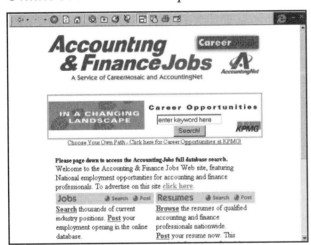

Accounting & Finance Jobs

http://www.accountingjobs.com/

At Accounting & Finance Jobs site over three thousand new jobs are posted each month. This site is a partnership between CareerMosaic and AccountingNet. It offers users access to jobs plus the ability to post resumés. And once a job is posted on the Accounting & Finance Jobs site, it can be automatically accessed through CareerMosaic's site at no extra cost. The site is free to job seekers, including a guide to finance and accounting resources on the Web.

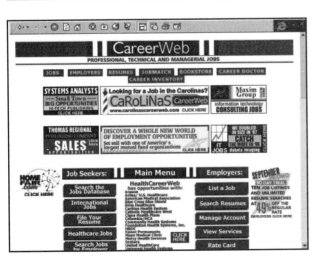

CareerWeb

http://www.careerweb.com/

CareerWeb is an online job search company that assists professional, technical, and managerial jobs. Other resources you will find at this site include original articles at the Career Doctor, and an interactive Career Inventory quiz. The quiz covers issues to help you determine if you are doing all that you can to find a good job.

Accountants on Call

http://www.aocnet.com/

Accountants on Call specialize in temporary employment opportunities. The company also runs the Accountant Executive Search program. Other resources at this site include a salary guide and help landing the perfect job at the Career Guide.

Accountemps

http://www.accountemps.com/

Accountemps is another online recruiting company that specializes in temporary employment. It provides an online job search function and the extensive career resources made available to job seekers. Visit the Resumania section to improve your resumé writing skills.

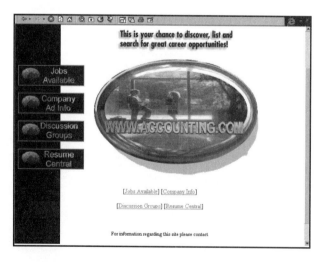

Accounting.com

http://www.accounting.com/

Like many of the online job search sites, you can upload and edit your resumé online. In addition, Accounting.com provides a discussion group to discuss career issues. The site has links to many of the employees that recruit at accounting. com.

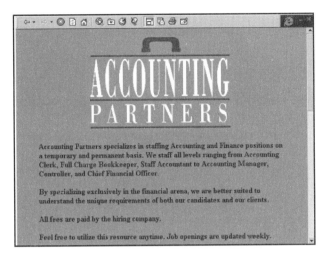

Accounting Partners

http://www.apartner.com/

Accounting Partners specializes in staffing temporary accounting and finance positions. The job opportunities are posted by geographical location. Visit the job hunting tips for articles on resumé and interviewing tips, commonly asked questions and reference information.

AICPA ResuméMatch

http://www.resume-link.com/society/expl.htm

ResuméMatch is the searchable resumé database comprised of AICPA and Participating State CPA Society member resumés. Employers may subscribe to the ResuméMatch database, regionally or nationally, for three months, six months, or one year to locate qualified CPAs. For those employers needing to fill a single position, Resumé-Link will search the database and forward matching resumés.

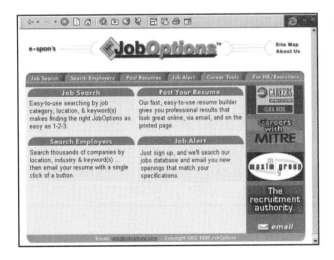

JobOptions

http://www.joboptions.com/

JobOptions (formerly known as eSpan), is in the process of re-launching its JobOptions Web site. Minimal information was available at this time.

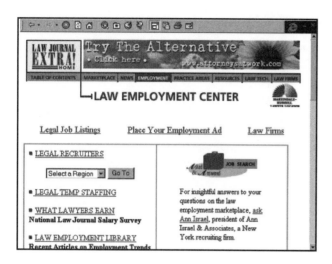

Law Jobs

http://www.lawjobs.com/

For those of you with a law background, take a visit to Law Jobs to obtain salary survey results, legal job listings a discussion forum, and many original articles. Visit the Practice Areas for links to its affiliate site the Law Journal Extra! page.

Michael Page International

http://www.michaelpage.com/us/

Michael Page has various recruiting divisions such as finance, law, and technology. Its site primarily serves as a means to market MPI's services. However, some additional resources include listings of job openings and the ability to submit your resumé.

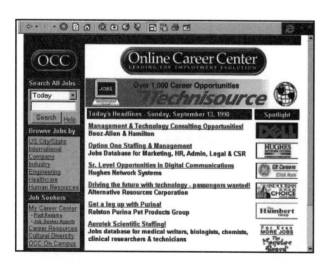

Online Career Center

http://www.occ.com/

At the OCC site job seekers can post and edit their resumés free of charge and watch it become instantly available to OCC's member companies. In addition, you can create your own personalized profile, which includes useful information such as relocation preferences and salary requirements. At OCC, you can track how often member companies view your resumé.

Robert Half

http://www.roberthalf.com/

Visit the Robert Half Career Center for Interviewing Tips, the Hiring Index, Free Resources, and RHI books. The Free Resources section provides order form details for a complimentary edition of RHI's "1998 Salary Guide" and "How to Get Ahead in Accounting, Finance and Banking."

Career Resources

WSJ Careers

http://careers.wsj.com/

The *Wall Street Journal* produces an excellent career resource. At WSJ Careers you can tap into various guides and articles on the topics of Job-Hunting Advice, Succeeding at Work, and HR Issues. The site also hosts the entire text of the WSJ's career columnists. The site has many archived articles for deeper research into a topic. There's even more here, so you better check it out soon!

Career Magazine

http://www.careermag.com/

Career Magazine's site is rich with content and chances to interact. In addition to its magazine publication, check out the Articles and News sections to help you plan and execute your networked career search. The site also has a moderated career forum, a resumé bank, and employer profiles.

Hard@Work

http://www.hardatwork.com/

This site takes a whimsical approach to career resources. At the top of the Web page is a to-do list for the week which has areas of the Web site you should visit soon. Then it's off to the Water Cooler for forums on interoffice communications and then to the Back Office for lots of articles on career insights from the Hard@Work staff.

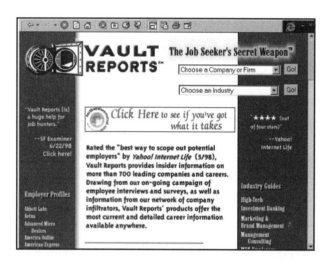

Vault Reports

http://www.vaultreports.com/

Vault Reports provides independent in-depth knowledge of over seven hundred companies across all industries and job functions. You can find lots of free online profile capsules for over six hundred companies. Vault Reports also publishes its monthly newsletter, the *Vault Reports Career Newsletter*. Information includes job strategies, career and salary trends, and sample interview questions.

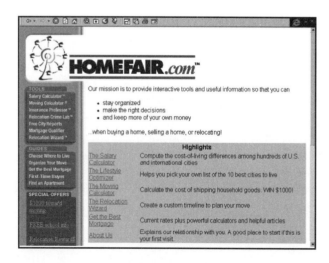

Homefair Relocation Resources

http://www.homefair.com/

The highlight of this Web site is the International Salary Calculator. Go ahead and compute the cost-of-living differences among hundreds of U.S. and international cities! You might as well check out the Lifestyle Optimizer while you are at it. The Optimizer helps you pick your own list of the ten best cities to live in. Gotta move some stuff? Check out Homefair's additional relocation resources such as The Moving Calculator and The Relocation Wizard.

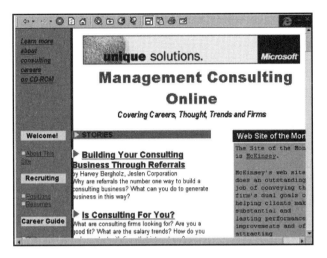

Management Consulting Jobs

http://www.cob.ohio-state.edu/~opler/cons/mco.html

An excellent site by Professor Tim Opler. The site has a detailed guide on careers in consulting and has a complete directory of firms both alphabetically and by consulting function. Visit the recruiting section for recently posted positions and selected resumés. Check out its selected directory of links for additional consulting information.

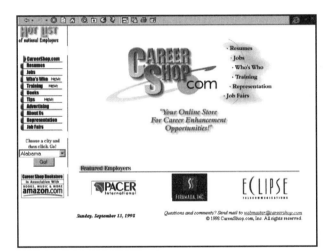

Career Shop

http://www.careershop.com/

The Career Shop has an online Career Fair that has listings by city. They currently have information on forty-eight U.S. cities. The site houses a resumé database where you can add and edit your resumé. Check out the guide on preparing for a job interview or visit the Salary Survey.

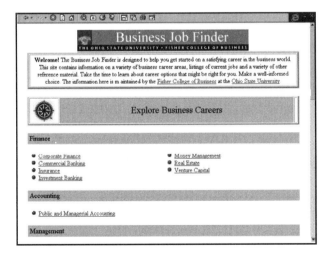

The Business Job Finder

http://www.cob.ohio-state.edu/~fin/osujobs.htm

This is another great site from Ohio State University. You can research the business job of your choice in the areas of Finance, Accounting, and Management. Each section is rich with career information, from Skills & Requirements, Print Resources, Salaries & Trends, and Facts. The site also includes a nice listing of other career sites and career articles.

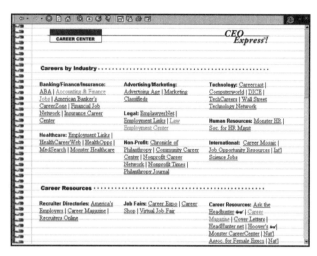

Career Center

http://www.ceoexpress.com/hr.htm

This site is primarily a directory of links to other Web sites, but here you can find links that take you to career resources by industry. Currently the industries covered are banking, finance, insurance, advertising, marketing, technology, legal, healthcare, and nonprofit. International job resources are also available at the Career Center.

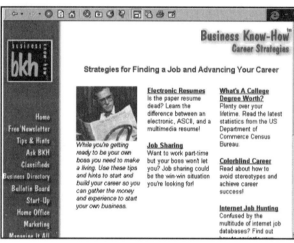

Career Strategies

http://www.businessknowhow.com/bkhcareer.htm

Career Strategies is part of the Business Know How Center. Here you will find original articles on strategies for finding a job and advancing your career. Current features include Electronic Resumés, Job Sharing, and Internet Job Hunting.

Travel Resources

Booking Resources

Expedia

http://expedia.msn.com/

Expedia is Microsoft's online travel resource and reservation Web site. To get the most out of Expedia, check out the Help section. It will get you on the right track as it has a nice hyperlinked listing of the major sections at the site. You can also take the site tour of the site. A few of the site's features include a weekly magazine, fare tracker E-mails, and detailed maps.

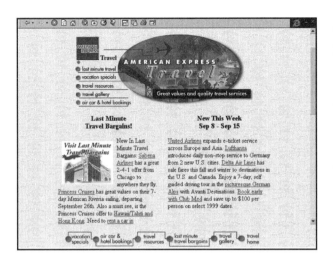

American Express Travel

http://www.americanexpress.com/corporateservices/

The *American Express Business Travel Review* is online, a source to help corporations compare their travel expenditures against industry averages. In the News Room, check out "T&E Management Directions," a quarterly report which highlights new trends and announcements that affect the travel industry. You can also book and ticket your travel plans through its Web site.

Biztravel.com

http://www.biztravel.com/

A cool feature of the Biztravel site is the ability to track your frequent flyer and stayer programs. You will find this feature in the bizMiles resource section. In addition to booking travel arrangements at this site, you can also take a read of its travelzine, bizTRAVELER and get information on chartered flights.

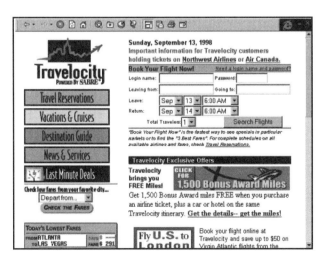

Travelocity

http://www.travelocity.com/

Travelocity reservations are powered by the popular Sabre travel reservation network. You can pick up last-minute deals at all of the sites mentioned in this Booking Resources section and Travelocity is no exception. Other features at the site include a newsletter, E-mail fare notifications and a flight information pager service.

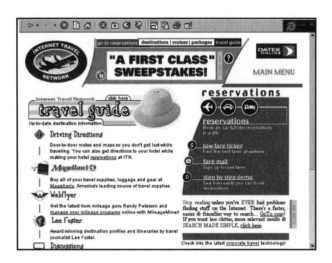

Internet Travel Network

http://www.itn.net/

At ITN you can view information about airlines via its sister site, Airlines, on the Web at http://www.4airlines.com/. Or if you are in a real hurry and just want a 1-800 number, check out http://www.princeton.edu/Main/air800.html. ITN has a discussion forum for you to discuss and share travel information.

Preview Travel

http://www.previewtravel.com/

Preview Travel has a special section for business travelers; so check it out. In the Business Travel Section you will find tips, information, links, and the business travel newswire. At the home page click onto the Destination Guides for hotel, restaurant, and currency information. Preview Travel has partnered with Fodor's to provide this resource.

The Trip

http://www.thetrip.com/

For real time flight tracking visit the section by the same name at The Trip. Since it is real time flight data, the tracker only shows flights that are flying, have recently flown, or are about to take off. You can also track the flight visually! You gotta love technology. The Trip is the first Web site to show flight status with topographic maps. The Trip features tips and strategies for airports and ground transportation.

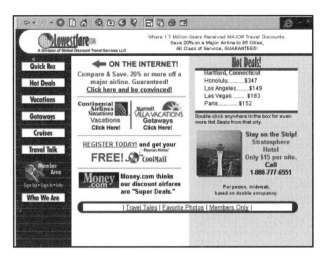

LowestFare.com

http://www.lowestfare.com/

Just like the Web site name says, this site tries to get you the lowest fare. I have successfully used this Web site to get a good fare. The pages load fast and the interface is easy to use. Visit the Travel Talk section for message boards, chats, and weekly columns.

Resources

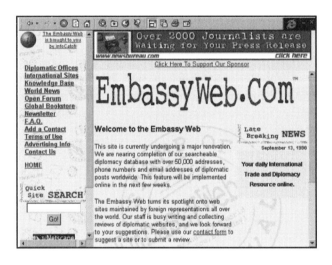

EmbassyWeb

http://www.embpage.org/

This site provides information about diplomatic offices worldwide and related information on international affairs, trade, travel, and policy. Visit the Knowledge Base for specific resources such as visa information and travel safety in particular countries. At EmbassyWeb you can order currency before you leave so you can have some change on hand when you arrive to your foreign destination.

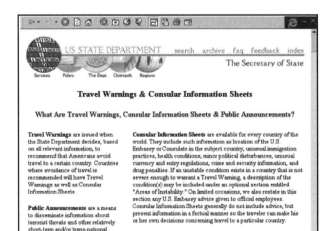

Travel Updates

http://travel.state.gov/travel_warnings.html

The U.S. State Department provides a Web site with travel warnings, consular information sheets, and public announcements. Resources can be found via search or by country index. The site also includes a nice FAQ section. At the bottom of the travel warnings page, you will find a link to the Consular Affairs home page which includes a wealth of consulate information.

Foreign Currency Converter

http://www.oanda.com/

The Oanda converter is considered the best currency converter on the Web. Check out the Currency News for up-to-date information. If you are on the move, definitely check out the Cheat Sheet, a wallet-size table of currency exchange rates for travelers. Visit the FX Playground for customized graphs, historical exchange rates, and cross-rate tables.

MapQuest

http://www.mapquest.com/

MapQuest has a great interface with a list of Fast Track areas such as Find a Place, Driving Directions, International Cities, and Plan your Move. The map search engine is very easy to use; just enter the address, city, and state. Visit the FAQ and What's New pages for additional information.

Fodor's Travel Online

http://www.fodors.com/

At the Fodor's travel site you can create your own mini travel guide, from a selection of ninety cities worldwide. Visit the Resource Center for information on customs and duties, electricity, language, and visas. The site also has a moderated forums which are organized by world destination.

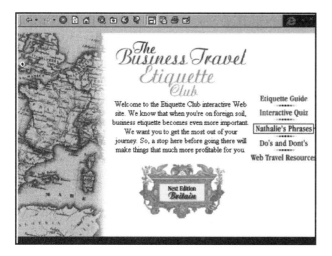

Business Travel Etiquette

http://www.traveletiquette.com/

At the Business Travel Etiquette Club you will find all the resources you need to keep yourself in line while traveling to France. With varying cultures and traditions, it's easy to make an etiquette *faux pas* without even knowing it. At the site, go straight to the Business Etiquette Guide; it is a rich resource that covers several important topics. Read the do's and don'ts for extra coverage. When you think you're ready, take the interactive quiz. More countries will be added in the future.

HotelView

http://www.hotelview.com/

HotelView is a database of virtual hotel tours. It uses RealPlayer (audio and video) technology. The audio streams over just fine; you can listen to a few minutes of general information about the hotel. It is also accompanied by video, although the current Internet video technology still does not lend itself to a clear picture.

The Weather Channel

http://www.weather.com/

Before you leave on a business trip, you may want to check out the weather forecast. Visit the Weather Channel's Business Travel Wise section to learn whether your airport is experiencing any delays. A map of the U.S. is shown with different colors representing various delay times. The site also has safety tips and a weather glossary.

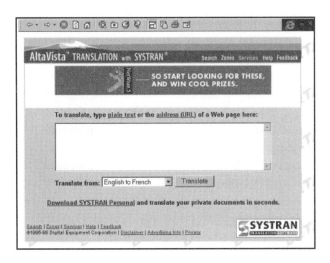

AltaVista Translator

http://babelfish.altavista.digital.com/

AltaVista is providing a free online translation service. With a fairly large text box, you can copy and paste the text you would like to have translated. The languages currently supported are English, Spanish, French, German, Italian, and Portuguese. *C'est une trouvaille merveilleuse!* Translation . . .

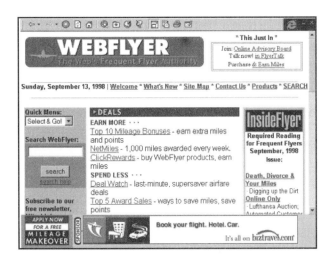

WebFlyer

http://www.webflyer.com/

This site is all about frequent flyer programs. To the right on the home page, there is a required reading box which features articles from the current online publication InsideFlyer. The site is organized by Deals, Programs, Interact, and Extras categories. In the Interactive section you can apply for a free Mileage Makeover.

The Subway Page

http://www.reed.edu/~reyn/transport.html

Looking for a subway map? Are you heading to Milan? Just look it up on the home page directory, click on a link, and check it out. Resources vary by destination on this page since most of the content has been contributed by various sources. If you know you are short on time or have a tight connection once you arrive, you can at least try to find your way around before you leave.

Microsoft TerraServer

http://terraserver.microsoft.com/

The TerraServer is a huge repository of aerial photographs and satellite images. Go to the Map Search to click on the interactive map. Go to the Find a Spot on Earth page and search based a specific place. For information on how to search, check out the page on how to use the site. There is also a section for famous places.

Runzheimer International

http://www.runzheimer.com/

Runzheimer is an international management consulting firm specializing in transportation, travel, and living costs. It produces several surveys and is the developer of Runzheimer Standard Cost Reimbursement Systems. At the site, click on the Publications section for past surveys and current samples. Its News Release section contains useful findings from the company's analysis and surveys.

Guides

Foreign Languages for Travelers

http://pathfinder.com/travel/language/

Located at the Pathfinder site, you can select one of the thirty-three language guides. After you have selected the language you would like to learn, the guide further narrows your request for either basic words, numbers, travel, directions, and places. Once you have made your selection, you are taken to a page of that has sound clips of the words to learn. After you are done listening to the words, you can then take a short quiz. This is a nice interactive site.

Duty Free Shopping & Tax Free Shopping

http://www.webscope.com/duty_free/

Alexander Dun & Sons provides a general guide with the basics of duty free shopping. It addresses duty free shopping now and in the future as well as allowances and origins. For more resources visit Duty Free International's home page at http://www.dutyfreeint.com/.

Entertaining

Zagat Dining Guide & Zagat Survey

http://www.zagat.com/

The popular Zagat reviews are now online. Visit the Zagat's survey partners' sites for reviews from the top U.S. cities. Or if you choose, you can take the Zagat New York City survey, view the Top Lists, and read the latest Zagat press releases. An order form is available if you want to buy any of the Zagat books.

Playbill Online

http://www.playbill.com/

The official Playbill is online. The Web site includes information about theatre happenings in New York City and London and listings of the latest Broadway plays and musicals. Theatre seating charts, show awards, and critic features will help you make the best theatrical decisions.

Internet

Resources

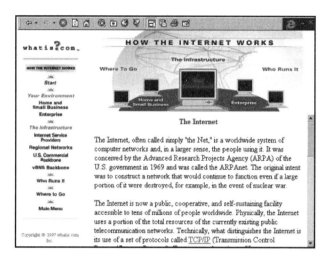

How the Internet Works

http://www.whatis.com/tour.htm

This site has an excellent overview of how the Internet functions. The guide discusses the infrastructure of the Internet, who runs it, and what services are available. In addition, the guide has many hyperlinks which take you to various definitions of Internet components to further your knowledge.

The List

http://www.thelist.com/

The List is one of the most comprehensive Internet Service Providers (ISP) listings around. The list currently has 4,228 ISP listed in its database and you can perform searches by area code. The List also provides ISP news and a reference directory of ISP-related resources.

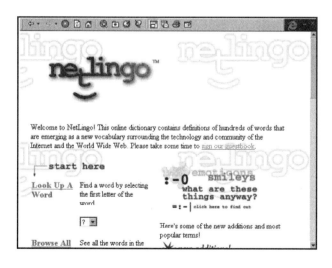

NetLingo

http://www.netlingo.com/

NetLingo is the online dictionary of Internet terms. The site has an emoticons directory as well as a floating dictionary which is comprised of a javascript pop-up screen that follows you as you surf the Web. NetLingo provides search and browse capabilities.

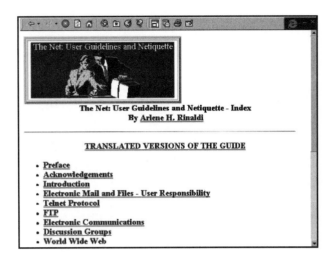

The Net: User Guidelines and Etiquette

http://www.fau.edu/rinaldi/net/index.htm

The formulation of Arlene Rinaldi's netiquette guide was motivated by the need of general guidelines to ensure Internet users conduct themselves in a responsible fashion. This site is popular among netiquette endorsers. Excerpts of this guide are included in the Appendix.

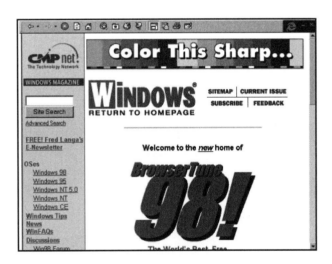

Browser Tune

http://www.browsertune.com/

Browser Tune is an online browser test and tune-up site. Browser Tune tests three hundred separate browser features and functions. There is a classic version available for older browsers. The site also contains other resources and hot links.

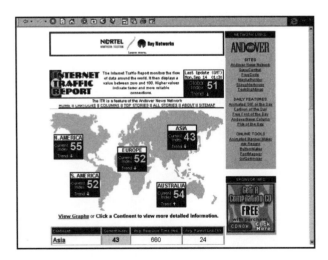

Internet Traffic Report

http://www.internettrafficreport.com/

The Internet Traffic Report monitors the flow of data around the world. It then displays a value between 1 and 100. Higher numbers indicate faster and more reliable connections. Click on the geographical interface to connect to your region of choice.

David J. Farber's Home Page

http://www.cis.upenn.edu/~farber/

This University of Pennsylvania professor is a mover and shaker in Internet development. He is the originator of the popular E-mail newsletter *Interesting People*. The site includes links to working papers and ongoing projects.

Organizations

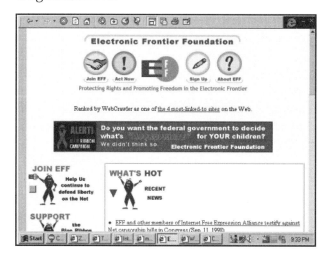

Electronic Frontier Foundation

http://www.eff.org/

EFF, the Electronic Frontier Foundation is a nonprofit, nonpartisan organization working in the public interest to protect fundamental civil liberties, including privacy and freedom of expression. The site houses a Beginner's Guide to the Internet as well as The Unofficial Smiley Directory.

Periodicals

InternetWeek

http://pubs.cmpnet.com/internetwk/

InternetWeek is a popular trade magazine for the Internet industry. The site is updated very frequently and is commonly a source of breaking news. The current feature at the site addresses VPNs incorporating DSL technology.

[clip] for the Internet Insider

http://www.compaq.com/clip/

[clip] has interesting original content such as the recent interview conducted featuring the big players in the Internet industry. In addition, the site has resources on various knowledge tools.

CIO WebBusiness

http://webbusiness.cio.com/

The *CIO Magazine* site is rich with content. Visit any of the six Research Centers: Electronic Commerce, Human Behavior/Web, Intranets, Knowledge Management, Remote Computing, and Web Careers.

Internet.com

http://www.internet.com/

Mecklermedia's internet.com Web site has much to offer in the way of Internet information. Visit its sister site, Internet News, for the latest industry stories at http://www.internetnews.com/. The site has several other links which jump you its many mini-sites.

Web Site Development

Web Site Development Resources

Note: Several general Web site development resources were discussed and featured in Chapter 15. Please see Chapter 15 for more information or see the below list to tap straight into these excellent Web site development sites.

BUILDER.COM
http://www.builder.com/

DEVELOPER ZONE
http://www.projectcool.com/developer/

HTML GOODIES
http://www.htmlgoodies.com/

SITE BUILDER NETWORK
http://www.microsoft.com/sitebuilder/

DEVEDGE ONLINE
http://developer.netscape.com/

WEB DEVELOPER
http://www.webdeveloper.com/

WEBREFERENCE.COM
http://www.webreference.com/

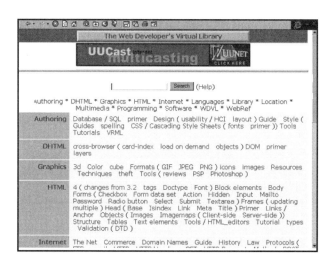

Web Developers' Virtual Library

http://www.stars.com/Index.html

The Web Developers' Virtual Library is a comprehensive topical index to Web development. It covers authoring, graphics, software application resources, and reference. This site can be a good starting point to your Web development efforts. The links will take you to in-depth guides on topics such as databases, graphic formats, and design.

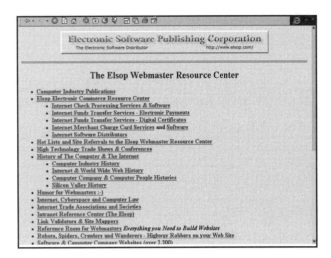

Elsop's Webmaster Resource Center

http://www.elsop.com/wrc/refroom.htm

The Reference Room does not stop at HTML. It covers many subjects and issues that Webmasters encounter when developing Web pages. For instance, this directory provides resources for link validators, Internet law, cookies, scripts, domain names, and password authentication. Visit the home page for more interesting resources for Webmasters.

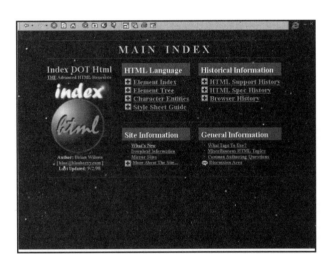

Index Dot HTML

http://www.blooberry.com/html/

Looking for information on a particular HTML tag? Index Dot HTML is a great reference guide to all tags. Visit the HTML Index for an alphabetical listing of tags or visit the element tree which lays out tags based on its Web page hierarchy.

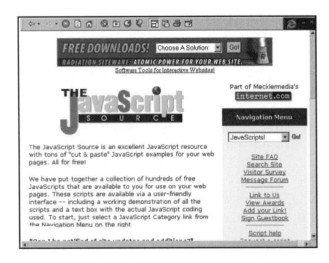

JavaScript Source

http://www.javascriptsource.com/

The JavaScript source is an excellent resource with lots of cut and paste JavaScript examples for your Web pages. These scripts are available for free and the site uses an easy to use interface by showing the code itself and providing interactive examples of the code's effect.

Jasc Paint Shop Pro

http://www.jasc.com/

If you are thinking about building a Web site or you have a Web site and want to spruce it up with graphics, rush on over to Jasc's Web site for an evaluation copy of Paint Shop Pro. Many webmasters got their newbie feet wet (myself included!) on the graphics front by using this very easy program. Long live Paint Shop Pro!

Resources

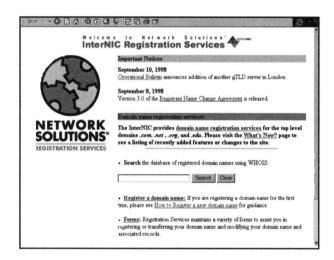

InterNIC

http://www.internic.net/

Come to the InterNIC's Web site when you need to visit its WhoIs database to check out which domain names are already taken and which domain name can be yours. When you have decided on a domain name, the site provides you with detailed instructions on how to register your new domain. The InterNIC also provides forms to help you maintain your domain name administrative information.

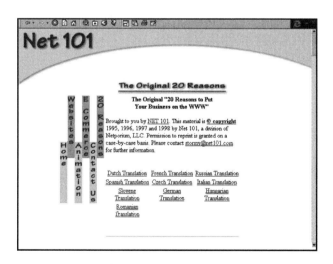

20 Reasons to Get on the Internet

http://www.net101.com/20_1.html

If you are still not sure about why you should be on the Internet, visit The Original 20 Reasons. The guide gets to the point by proving a one-paragraph explanation for each reason.

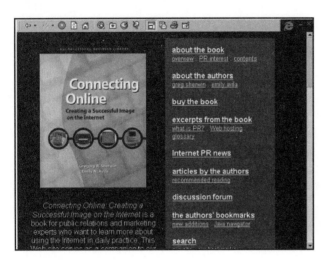

Connecting Online

http://www.connectingonline.com/

Connecting Online is the Web site for the book entitled *Connecting Online: Creating a Successful Image on the Internet*. Here you will find online reference material for the book, which is helpful whether you have the book or not. Visit the Overview section for an illustration of some of the key principles behind Web site image creation. There are also excerpts to the book here as well as other articles written by the authors.

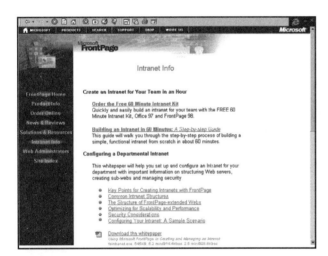

FrontPage Intranet Guide

http://www.microsoft.com/frontpage/intranet/

The FrontPage's intranet resource page contains an offer for the free guide, *Building an Intranet in 60 Minutes.* You can also view the entire guide online. Download the document, "Using Microsoft FrontPage in creating and managing an Intranet." The paper covers common intranet structures, optimizing the scalability and performance, and a sample scenario of intranet configuration.

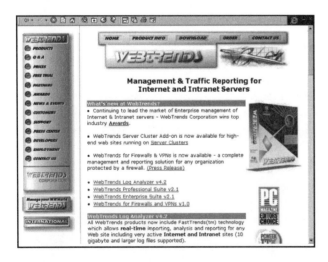

Web Trends

http://www.webtrends.com/

Web Trends is one of the more popular software packages available to provide Web site traffic management and reporting. Visit its Web site for general product information and for your free trial.

Web Site Marketing & Promotion

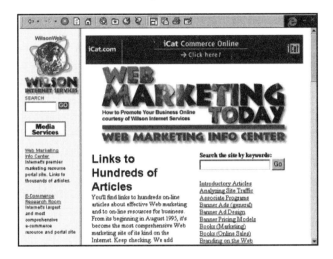

Web Marketing Today

http://www.wilsonweb.com/webmarket/

Wilson Internet Services provides the epitome of excellent free Internet content. At Web Marketing Today you will find practically all the information you need to market and promote your site. Visit here first and take a look at a few of its popular newsletters. You can also subscribe via E-mail, but the site has a great HTML enhanced version online. If you are interested in E-commerce, visit Web Marketing Today's sister site, Web Commerce Today at http://www.webcommercetoday.com/wct/.

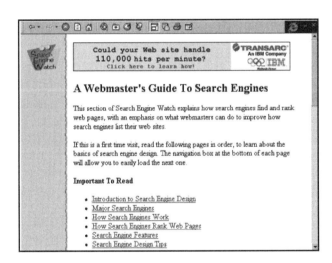

A Webmaster's Guide to Search Engines

http://searchenginewatch.com/webmasters/

This is a special guide from the excellent Web site, Search Engine Watch. The guide addresses search engine issues as they relate to Webmasters. You will find resources on how to register and how to prepare your Web pages for the best search engine results.

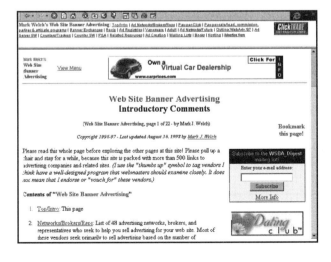

Web Site Banner Advertising

http://www.markwelch.com/bannerad/

If you are considering banner advertising, or if you just want to learn more about it, this site is an absolute must. I have been using this site for over two years now and it has been a very helpful resource. If you don't want to post a commercial banner at your site consider a public service announcement (PSA) banner. The site includes an entire section devoted to socially conscience banners.

VirtualPROMOTE

http://www.virtualpromote.com/

Another great Web marketing and promotion site, VirtualPROMOTE provides all sorts of resources including a very good E-mail newsletter, information on discussion forum promotion, and a forum regarding search engine promotion.

Organizations

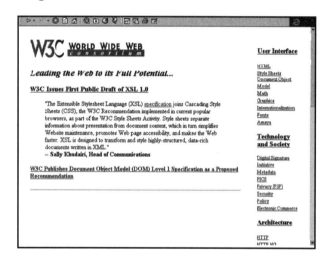

W3C World Wide Web Consortium

http://www.w3.org/

The W3C was founded in 1994 to lead the World Wide Web to its full potential through its promotion of common protocols. Read the online version of the *World Wide Web Journal,* a newsletter designed to help people implement open systems. The current version's articles are "WebSecurity: A Matter of Trust" and "Transfer Protocols: Plumbing the Web."

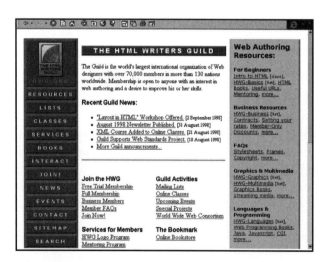

HTML Writers Guild

http://www.hwg.org/

The HTML Writers Guild has over 70,000 members from 130 countries. Membership is available to anyone interested in Web authoring and the desire to improve their skills. The Guild's site includes many resource guides, authoring tips and FAQs. The organization hosts classes, too.

Java Break

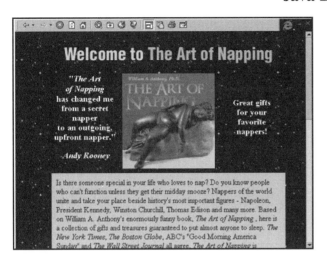

The Art of Napping

http://www.napping.com/

If you consider your java break as a chance to catch a few winks, you'll want to visit this Web site before you doze off. The Art of Napping site takes a comical look at the "habit of nap," my husband's favorite pastime. Stroll through the Napthanaeum, take the Napping Vocabulary Quiz, or divulge personal information at the Napping Workplace Survey.

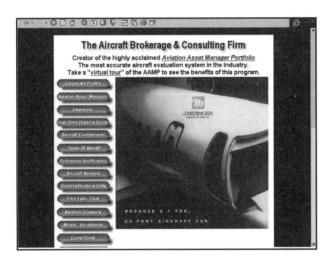

Jet Sales Comparison

http://www.jetsales.com/

In case you are strapped for time and need to do a little jet shopping during your coffee break, here's a resource you can use. Or, if you are just a jet aficionado, you can just drool. It's just a fun Web site to park yourself in front of for a few minutes. The Comparison's byline is "Because all aircraft are not created equal." You can check out the First Time Buyer's Guide or participate in the aviation chat room.

The Comic Zone

http://www.unitedmedia.com/comics/

For some laughs, visit the Comic Zone. Hit the bull's-eye for Today's Comics. This is the home of Dilbert and Snoopy. For some career advice, visit Catbert's Anti-Career Zone. There you can find resources at Resumania and try to survive the Interview with the Evil Resources Director.

The Bathrooms of Madison County

http://www.nutscape.com/

Looking for a nice vacation spot? Visit the Bathrooms of Madison County for some travel plan ideas. This site is "a love story, in seven short web pages." Yep, it's about a trip to Madison County that involved more views of johns than bridges. The story is narrated throughout. Pictures included (G-rated).

The Straight Dope

http://www.straightdope.com/

The Web site from the syndicated column that has appeared in alternative newspapers since 1973. In addition to the weekly column, there is a FAQ area as well as an archive of previous columns. This week's column answers the question: when will average people be able to afford commercial space flight?

Easter Eggs

http://www.eeggs.com/

Have you ever wondered what a software Easter egg was or maybe where you can find more? Well, if you are interested in software Easter eggs, this is the site for you. Check the New Hatches for the latest, search the Egg Catalog by application and visit the Egg-Related Links.

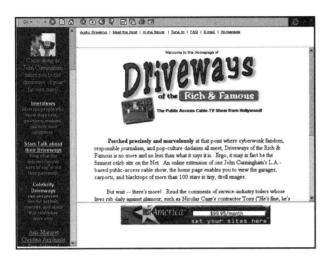

Driveways of the Rich & Famous

http://www.driveways.com/

This Web site is an extension of a public-access television show (can you believe it!). Actually, John Cunningham has a pretty impressive list of celebrities and their driveways. If you want to delve deeper into lives of the rich and famous, read the interviews from those who know them best, gardeners, mailmen, and next-door neighbors. There are a few interviews from the stars themselves, check out the "Madonna 'you are in my driveway' interview!"

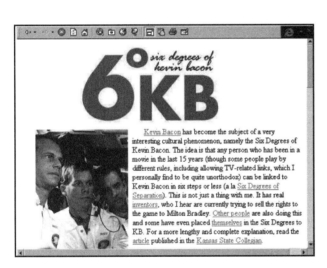

6 Degrees of Kevin Bacon

http://www.wjh.harvard.edu/~minga/sdokb/

If you have heard of the game, you have to go to the Web site that started it all. 6°KB and its inspiration, Kevin Bacon, has become the focus of an interesting phenomenon. The general basis is that "any person who has been in a movie in the last fifteen years can be linked to Kevin Bacon in six steps or less (à la *Six Degrees of Separation*)". Good luck with the game!

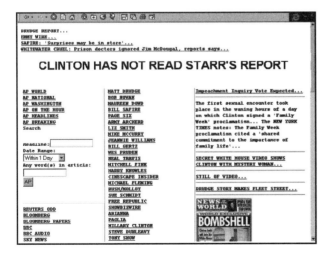

Drudge Report

http://www.drudgereport.com/

Another cultural icon of late is the Matt Drudge Report. I checked out this guy's counter; he is getting tons of hits, so someone is listening! I'd pop into this Web site now and then for a little "political edification." If you aren't interested in reading Drudge, the site is still extremely useful as it provides direct links to many newspaper columns.

Hollywood Stock Exchange

http://www.hsx.com/

This is the site where you can "trade virtual millions in MovieStocks—real films assigned a value based on buzz and box office—and Star-Bonds: from triple-A superstars to aspiring C-graders." This site is pure fun, although the guys that run this site are actually mining the data they collect on HSX trades. That's ok, I guess they deserve something, where else can you find a ticker of the Hollywood Exchange Stocks & Bonds!

Blue Mountain Animated Cards

http://www.bluemountain.com/

I'm starting to feel like Blue Mountain has invented a few holidays since they started up this site, but nonetheless, Blue Mountain Animated Cards are free and they are fun. Blue Mountain adds new cards to their site frequently. I have checked out several E-mail card sites and this one is great if not the best. Lots of the cards include music and many have animation.

Slate

http://www.slate.com/

Although *Slate* magazine online is now a subscription-based publication, there are still a few free items to pique your interest and while away a few minutes of your day. In the Free Today at Slate area is the Keeping Tabs article, reply all: an E-mail novel, Today's Paper.

Eating Well

http://www.eatingwell.com/

What? Healthy Living is not a fun break topic? Oh well, I guess we all need a reality check now and then. If you looking for a new and healthy recipe for dinner tonight, check out this site. After you visit the calorie counter and the article on How to Determine your Fat Intake, you'll be ready to return to the daily grind of work!

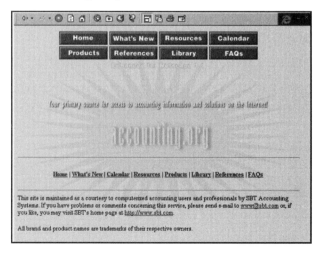

Reader's Digest World

http://www.readersdigest.com/

Reader's Digest World is the interactive version of the ever-popular publication. Each online edition features Laugh Lines, Word Power, Join the Debate, and a special feature article. An archive is also at the site.

Software & Hardware

Accounting Software Resources

Accounting.org

http://www.accounting.org/

Accounting.org is the primary source for access to accounting information and solutions on the Internet. At this site you will find listings of accounting packages which are currently on the market, including contact information and links to accounting sites. The site also includes comparisons of the accounting products, a list of educational resources, accounting services, and accounting professionals.

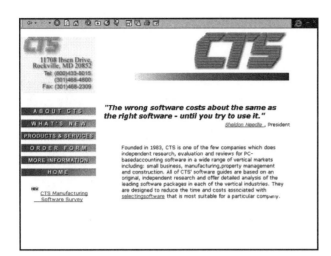

CTS Guides

http://www.ctsguides.com/

CTS is the publisher of independent accounting software reviews and ratings. In addition to its needs assessment program, CTS also provides detailed narrative descriptions of the software products. You can view a sample chapter online for an example. It also produces several other industries.

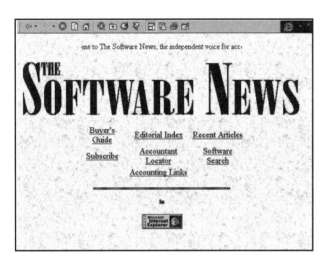

The CPA Software News

http://www.cpasoftwarenews.com/

The CPA Software News Buyer's Guide is a quick and effective way to find accounting-related software. Plus, it is a good source for software that you may want to recommend to business clients. A software search costs $75 for nonsubscribers and $59.95 for subscribers.

Software Resources

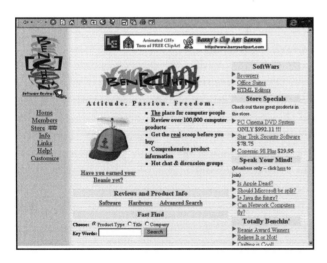

Benchin Software Review

http://www.benchin.com/

Benchin's Web site has over 100,000 reviews to computer products. You can search or browse through the product database. Under the Business Software category you can retrieve comprehensive product information and obtain the contact information to make a purchase. The site also has software discussion forums.

SoftSearch

http://www.softsearch.com/

Softsearch has a search engine interface which contains a software database of over 110,000 indexed software products and 22,000 software developers. Visit the FAQ page to get familiar with the best ways to search. You have to pay for the service which consists of a detailed report and a listing of related articles and reviews on the software product. If you don't have the time to conduct preliminary software research, SoftSearch may be a solution.

ZDNet Software Download Library

http://www.hotfiles.com/

This Ziff Davis site is an easy-to-use resource. Search the demo, shareware, and free-ware database based on keyword. There are legend icons to indicate review rating. Click on the software link for additional information and software synopsis. One nice feature is its download basket. You don't need to download right away since you can search for all your software and then visit your basket to conduct your download.

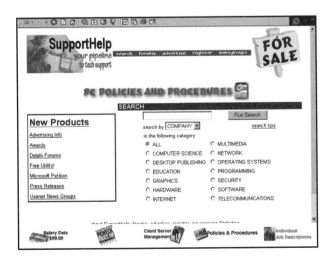

Support Help

http://www.supporthelp.com/

Looking for a one-stop Web site for technical support information? Or maybe you can't seem to find the phone number to a software vendor. Check out Support Help for some answers. Search the site based on keyword. The results will provide company name, address, phone number, Web site home page, and Web site address to technical support.

Hardware

Maven Computer Buying Guide

http://www.maven.businessweek.com/index.htm

Before you delve too deep into the buying guide, check out the page on how Maven performs its testing. Then visit the Getting Started section. In this section Maven will walk you through the basics, with such pages as How to Use Maven, What Should I Buy, and Glossary of Terms. The site has a listing of newly rated products as well as several detailed topical articles to check out.

Computer Discount Warehouse

http://www.cdw.com/

When shopping around for software and hardware, it is a good idea to check the prices of these products via traditional avenues as well as the Internet. For price checks visit CDW. On a handful of products I have found CDW has cheaper prices than the "brick and mortar" stores.

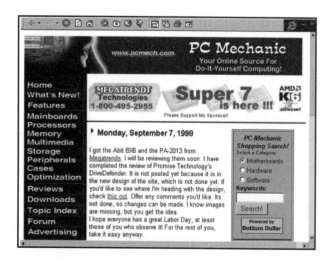

PC Mechanic

http://pcmech.pair.com/

PC Mechanic wants to be "your online source for Do-It-Yourself Computing." In the Features section, PC Mechanic has provided a tutorial to help you build your own PC as well as a computer troubleshooting guide. Visit the various hardware section to get hardware basics, installation information, and detailed resources. The Reviews and Forums sections are worth a look.

CREATING A PRESENCE ON THE INTERNET

Chapter 14

DESIGNING AN INTERESTING WEB SITE

Introduction

Ok. By now you should be connected to the Internet. Ready for more? How about starting up your own Web site? Section 4 of this book is designed to do just that. First, we will walk through the planning steps of designing your Web site. Then you will have to decide if you plan to jump off the HTML abyss and create the site yourself or outsource the site development. Lastly, we'll go through the Web site registration process to find out what it takes to be noticed in a sea of fifty million Web pages.

Determine Your Web Site Objectives

The amount of time and money you spend on your Web site should be directly correlated with the objectives you establish for your site. Some objectives will be more costly than others. This section addresses some of the potential objectives you may have as well as help you figure out what you really want to do with your Web site.

Choose from the laundry list, add to your list, and prioritize to establish your objectives. Several objectives are valid for both an organization or individual.

Possible Objectives for Your Enterprise Site

- Sell services from your Web site.
- Interact with your clients.
- Educate your employees.
- Say you are on the Internet.
- Create an online community.
- Provide information about your company.
- Build informative content.

- Make the Internet a better place.

- Explore how to create a home page.

- Create a source of reference on a particular topic.

Form Your Concept

Spend some upfront time just thinking about your Web site and what features you would like to include. Don't forget to think of your time horizon. What do you want to see at your Web site for its launch to the public, and how do you see the content at your site evolving over time? This section provides you with items to consider when creating your Web site concept.

The Golden Rule—Know Your Audience

At the beginning, ask yourself, "If I visited my Web site, what would I like to find?" Defining your audience and determining what they want to see will help you plan your site's content, style, structure, and navigation.

Design for your audience. If you don't design for your audience, they may visit, but they won't come back. If you are writing to an audience that wants fast loading pages, don't create a Web site with the latest bandwidth-consuming animations and graphics. Also, try to get a feel for what browser and display size your audience is using. Recently, I checked my site statistics logs that tell me which browsers my viewers are using. I was surprised to see the fast adoption of Navigator 4.0 and Internet Explorer 4.0. This early adoption trend may continue as people get in the new browser release loop.

Plan the Style

In most cases, your Web site is an extension of you and your company. If you are designing a company's Web site, it is likely there is already an "image" established and reflected through its logos, advertising, and other materials. However, if you are trying to convey a bit of an updated "tech" style (it is cyberspace after all!), you may want to consider tweaking your image a bit.

Take a look at what others are doing on the Web. Find styles or parts of styles you think emulate the image you are trying to convey. Also, take note of sites you don't want to be like and remember them as your Web site evolves. Try to stay true to your style.

Everything on your page is a visual element, even the font you choose for your text. Therefore, take some time determining what kind of visual element styles you would like to incorporate at your site, specifically:

- Blocks of text and how they will be arranged

- Font sizes, styles, and colors

- Graphic images to be used for navigation
- Graphic images to be used for color and "atmosphere"
- Open space usage

Don't worry, if you don't think you are much of an "artist," there are some design resources at the end of this chapter. In addition, you could always outsource this aspect of your Web site to a professional Web designer. For a fee, of course.

Domain Name Considerations

Another important aspect of your Web site is the domain name that visitors will diligently type in to reach your site. Put some thought into your domain name, however, do not analyze the various domain alternatives so much that it paralyzes you from deciding on one.

How do you get a domain name? Well, first you start out by determining if the domain name you want is taken. Visit the InterNIC's Web site and perform a WhoIs search to find out (http://www.internic.net/). Once you find a name that is not taken, visit the area at InterNIC's site that walks you through the intricacies of obtaining a domain name.

If you choose, you can conduct the entire registration process via online forms and E-mail correspondence. Currently, InterNIC is the only organization that assigns and coordinates the DNS (domain name system) for the biggest top-level domains: .com, .org, .net, and .edu. As discussed earlier in this book, this situation will change shortly and additional options will be available.

I think the jury is still out whether the proposed top-level domains will be well-received. If the domain name of your choice is available in the .com domain, claiming it would be a safe bet. However, as the domain name saga plays out, I think it would be prudent to keep an eye on the situation, especially if the .firm domain takes off. You may see accounting firms claiming names, however, they will probably keep their .com names, too.

Craft Your Content

Content is key. For the accounting profession, snazzy graphics and the latest JavaScript tricks alone will not an audience make. You should have a fair amount of original content at your site if you plan to have people visit more than a couple times a year. However, don't bog yourself down at the beginning either. If you choose your content wisely, it can build itself into a great Web site. This section will give you some ideas on digging up existing content as well as creating new stuff.

Possible Sources of Content

You may be surprised to find you already have a fair amount of content available for your Web site. After you identify what to place at your site, determine if you plan to use it as is (that is, scanned) or to convert it to HTML. The following are possible sources of content:

- Company literature (for example, pamphlets, fact sheets).

- Presentations. Text transcripts and Power Point presentations can easily be converted for your site.

- Company press releases and news articles.

- Descriptions of services available.

- Watermarks. Usually watermarks created with popular word processing packages can be converted to HTML.

- Firm directory of personnel. You may decide to place an abbreviated version at your site.

- Published articles. You will have to get permission to reprint. Check to see if your material is included at the publisher's Web site. If so, you can always provide a link to the article.

Create Unique Content

Existing hard copy content will get you off to a great start as well as provide you with needed general information about your organization. However, you also need to think about creating some original content. Keep in mind, whatever original content you decide to produce, craft it so your audience will return to your site time and time again. Here are some ideas to consider:

- Center of expertise. Provide articles about a topic you have great knowledge in. Upload a short tip every week, original articles every two weeks, and in-depth features once a quarter. You might want to turn your concept into a column where you have a firm member turned Web site "personality" contribute the content.

- Directory of additional Internet resources. Help your audience find helpful information on the Internet by including a nice directory. You may decide to create your directory based on your area of expertise. I have also seen directories focused on the firm's geographical location, providing useful links to city and/or state government, community resources, and local attractions. To further embellish your directory, annotate your link listing or provide Web site reviews.

- Discussion forums. Invite questions and provide answers and suggestions via a moderated discussion forum. If you still haven't chosen your ISP or Web host, make sure to ask what discussion forum options are available. Some forums give the readers nice options as well as the ability for you to break up messages, move, and categorize your threads. The better the discussion forum, the better chances you have to build good content.

- Provide software and hardware tips. If you have a tip that you think others would like to know about, write it up and get it on your Web page. If you create a rich resource of tips, clients will remember they can always check your site before venturing off to the rest of the Web. In addition, if you support certain accounting software packages, provide Web pages for your clients to read about the latest software changes, links to patches and support utilities, and links to the software company's latest product press releases.

- Invite guest contributors. Ask well-respected specialists to contribute content to your site. This may be in the form of asking a governmental official to provide information about upcoming legislation or an organization representative to discuss the latest ISO requirements for a particular industry. Make sure you provide a disclaimer that the views of your guests may not necessarily be the views of your firm.

Web Site Execution Pointers

Plan to create your pages for viewing by multiple browsers and multiple browser versions. There are many HTML validation programs and services on the market to make sure your pages look consistent. In addition, if you use JavaScript or applets, users may receive errors, and it is crucial to weed out as many issues before your Web site launch. Another way to test your pages is to ask others to check out the site with their computers and browsers. You may find lower-end HTML coding elements, which may be a good trade-off for the peace of mind of knowing users can view your site.

Schedule out your Web site launch. When you have determined you have a fair amount of content at your site, register your site with the search engines. Don't wait! Some search engines take weeks to register your site. How do you know you have enough content? It should be enough to keep the interest of your viewer, albeit at this stage, you won't keep his or her interest for long. This may involve a simple home page and a couple content pages. Don't create one of those disdainful "hi, we are under construction" pages, with no content and a construction zone graphic. These pages are irritating and clutter up the Web. Create just enough to look at and then register.

Once you are online, encourage feedback. Just as you would elicit feedback on a work project, you should do the same for your Web site. You need feedback especially when your site is new or you have just launched a redesigned version. If your site is new, the feedback you receive will help you make improvements, troubleshoot errors, and most importantly find out if people like the site.

Web Site Design Resources

To make sure you properly design and plan your Web site, tap into these online resources for more Web site design information.

High Five

http://www.highfive.com/

High Five is a weekly design zine that is known in the industry for both the quality of its selections as well as the publication's design biases.

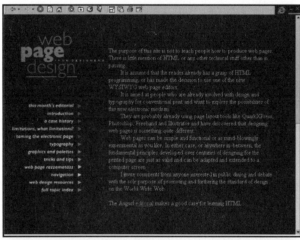

Web Page Design for Designers

http://www.wpdfd.com/

Web Page Design for Designers is aimed at people who are already involved with design and typography for conventional print and want to explore the possibilities within the Web.

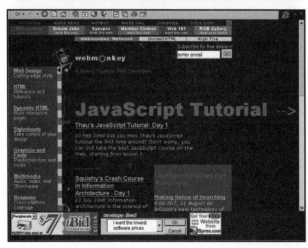

Web Monkey

http://www.hotwired.com/webmonkey/

Hotwired's Webmonkey is a resource that focuses on information and tutorials with a slant toward the leading edge of Web page design.

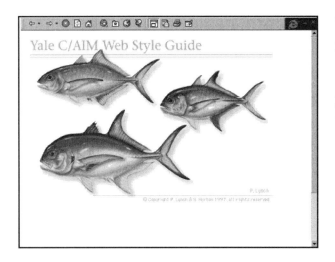

Yale C/AIM Web Style Guide

http://info.med.yale.edu/caim/manual/

The purpose of the Yale Style Guide is to provide some lessons the Yale development team experienced when designing the Yale site. The Guide covers interface, site, and page design.

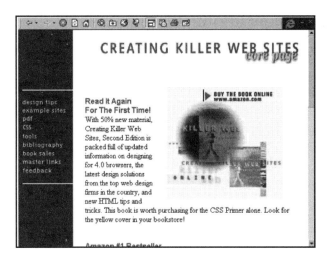

Creating Killer Web Sites

http://www.killersites.com

Visit the Web site or buy the book bearing the same title. Either way you'll have a great resource to tap into. The Web site provides Web site examples and design tips. You will also find links to recommended software tools.

CREATING A GREAT WEB SITE ON YOUR OWN

Introduction

If you are the inquisitive sort and would like to start up a Web site on your own, this chapter is for you. However, you need to come to one realization if you intend to create your own site: You need to make a commitment to your project (or intense hobby) and create a site people will want to visit. The first portion of the chapter will go over a few of the popular WYSIWYG (What You See Is What You Get) Web page creation packages. The second portion is for those who want to know how HTML works.

Easy Programs with Maximum Impact

Coding HTML is not an impossible task to learn. However, with the emergence of easy Web site publishing packages based on a WYSIWYG interface, you don't need to know the inner workings of HTML to launch a site. Even experienced Webmasters are flocking to these programs that use wizards, templates, and sophisticated HTML editing tools.

Microsoft FrontPage

http://www.microsoft.com/frontpage/

I have tried just about every Web authoring package and have happily found a product that does just about everything I need: FrontPage 98. FrontPage 98 uses an Explorer-type interface that allows you to easily navigate through your Web site, especially if you are a current Windows user. There are three different "modes" you can enter: Normal mode for WYSIWYG Web editing, HTML mode for direct HTML code editing, and Preview mode to view how your pages will look in a Web browser.

You can also conduct site management easily. Import and export functions are available as well as drag and drop ability. To do a quick check on your hyperlinks visit the Hyperlink Status area. I really like this feature, and although it isn't as powerful as stand-alone programs, it is definitely a welcomed feature to quickly check for broken links.

If your ISP supports FrontPage extensions, you can tap into some excellent "bot" features such as adding search or using Page Include to minimize the work necessary to include the same text on multiple pages (i.e., site index and navigation links, etc.). FrontPage has many additional features not mentioned in this short synopsis. Check out the FrontPage Web site to get the full details.

Microsoft FrontPage 98 currently sells for $149, and $60 for the upgrade version.

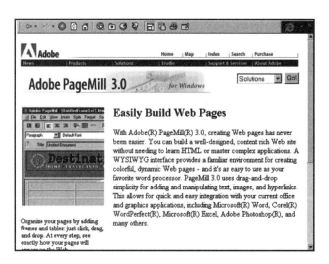

Adobe PageMill

http://www.adobe.com/prodindex/pagemill/

Adobe PageMill is well-known for its excellent foundation upon which to build a Web site, with over ten thousand images, sounds, and video clips at your disposal. Like FrontPage, PageMill includes customizable templates and style sets. PageMill uses a view-as-you-create interface.

Similar to FrontPage, PageMill has various site management features. When you rename or rearrange files, links are updated automatically. When you're ready to post your site, you can transfer it directly to the Web using the built-in Uploader.

Adobe PageMill currently sells for $99, and $49 for the upgrade version.

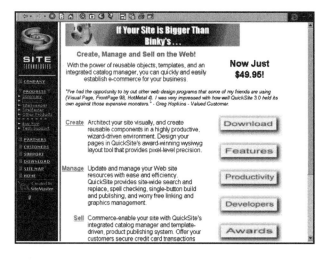

Site Technologies QuickSite

http://www.sitetech.com/

The key to QuickSite is its complete automation. The program has a built in FTP utility (so does FrontPage, but I opt to control the FTP on my own), and is known for its automatic guidance from creation, layout, and publish. If you don't need to have easy access to the HTML code and want to create a simple site without any of the latest bells and whistles, you may want to check out the QuickSite demo.

The program starts you out with its Site Wizard, which prompts you to answer lots of questions, which in turn produces an entire Web site!

Use the Style Wizard to change the look of a page or use QuickSite's Catalog Builder to create forms, catalogs, or to import existing databases.

QuickSite currently sells for $49.

Bare, Bare Bones HTML

This section is geared toward the souls who have to know how things work behind the scenes. Due to the release of several very good Web site wizard and template-based programs, such as the resources discussed in the previous section, learning HTML code is not a necessity to create a great Web page. However—one caveat for programs like Front Page—the more you know about the inner workings of the HTML source, the better you will be able to troubleshoot when you don't like what you see in the preview screen. This section will show you some of the basics, so when you go to "View Source," you won't become immobilized.

Learn the Basics

What Is HTML?   HTML (Hypertext Markup Language) is the set of "markup" symbols or codes inserted in a file intended for display on a World Wide Web browser. The markup tells the Web browser how to display a Web page's words and images for the user. The markup codes are referred to as "tags" which you will see in various forms throughout this section.

Basic HTML Rules   A good place to start is to explain the four basic rules for HTML tags that always hold true:

1. An HTML tag is always surrounded by brackets (for example, <TITLE> or <B> tags).

2. Most tags come in pairs to designate the beginning and end of the tag. For example <TITLE> represents the start of the TITLE tag and </TITLE> represents the end of the TITLE tag. All the information included between this tag is affected by the tag itself. (This will become more clear later.)

3. Tags are embedded; they must form a nested structure. This is best illustrated by the examples below:

   CORRECT: <TITLE><BODY>This example shows the proper use of tags.</BODY></TITLE>

   INCORRECT: <TITLE><BODY>This example shows the improper use of tags. Compare the tag sequence in the two examples.</TITLE></BODY>.

4. Many tags include additional options to further tailor the text between the tag. For instance, you can use the paragraph tag <P> as is or you can align the paragraph following the tag <P ALIGN=CENTER>. By the way, the end tag does not include the options; it is displayed merely as </P>.

Preparing a Page

Now that we have some of the basics down, it's time to take a breath and work out some HTML details interactively. We are going to prepare a sample page and render it into your browser so you can see how the HTML source code converts to a Web page. Let's start out by opening a basic Notepad (text) file.

1. Once you have a text file open, set up your page with the HTML tags that are required for every Web page you will ever create. Type in the following text:

   <HTML>

   <HEAD>

   <TITLE>Title will show up in title window</TITLE>

   </HEAD>

   <BODY></BODY>

   </HTML>

2. Now notice the nesting structure you have just created. For instance, all HTML codes and text for the entire page will be nested between the <HTML></HTML> tag.

3. Save the page out as an HTML file. Use test.htm as the file name. Now view the Web page you just created by opening your browser and use the File/Open command on your toolbar to browse to your file. Click on Ok when you have found the file, and presto, you have your page! The page shouldn't be too much to look at. Only the text "Title will show up in title window" should appear at the top of your browser.

A Few More Tags

I won't walk you through all the exact particulars since there are so many excellent online resources you can tap into for full-blown tutorials. Instead, I have given you some sample code to add to your Web page. Add each of the exercises below separately so you can see the individual effect.

To view your HTML code and continue working, select View and then Source from the browser toolbar and it will bring up your .htm page in a notebook format. This way you can make changes and simply refresh your Web page in your browser.

Add Text

- Add the following between your <BODY></BODY> tag:

  This test represents the body of my Web page.
When I see a Web page in my browser, all the text I see is included between the BODY tag.<P>This is the end of the Add Text test.<P>

- As you can see, I added a couple of new tags to the text, the <BR> and <P> tags. The <BR> tag is used to break text onto a new line and the <P> tag is used to create a new paragraph.

- You may notice I did not include the end code (i.e., the code with the / before the tag) for the <BR> and <P> tags. These tags do not require the end code and are a couple of the few tags like this.

Add Links

- Append to the above information by adding a link. Directly after the words "Add Text test" insert the contents of the <A HREF> tag. The <A HREF> tag is used to add links to Web pages:

  Visit <A HREF="http://builder.cnet.com/Authoring/Basics/"> Cnet's Know the Code</a> for the complete tutorial on HTML for beginners!</a>.<P><B>This is the end of the Add Links test.</B><P>

- You might have noticed, I slipped in the code for bold text, <B></B>.

Add a Hyperlinked Image

- You are almost done! Now we are going to add an image. In order for an image to appear you must link to a path where you know an image is present. In this case, I'll use the path to my CPAnet logo. Since the code below will be linking to an active page on the Internet, you'll have to be online to see the full effect. Insert the following after the Add Links test and before the </BODY> tag:

  <CENTER><B>Visit CPAnet!</B>
<A HREF="http://www.cpanet.com/"> <IMG SRC="http://www.cpanet.com/images/cpalogo.gif"></a></CENTER> End of Add Images test.<P>

Change Background Color

- Since the graphic doesn't look too good on a gray background, complete out your Web page test with a change to the <BODY> tag:

  <BODY BGCOLOR="white">

You Are Done!   Albeit, it's not the greatest looking page. You can now see how the HTML source code is interpreted by your Web browser, and you have successfully completed this abbreviated tutorial.

See Illustration 1.1 and 1.2 for the completed source HTML code and Web browser views. In Illustration 1.1, I have included extra spacing between the various HTML tags to provide a better view of each tag. With HTML code, you can use whatever spacing you choose.

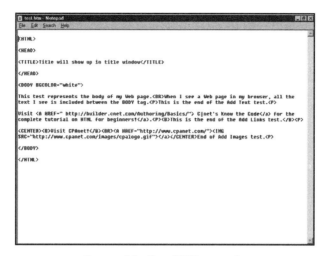

Illustration 1.1—View of HTML source code.

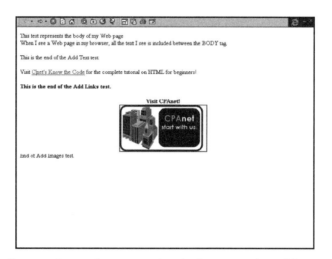

Illustration 1.2—View of HTML source code rendered in Internet Explorer Web browser.

To Learn More About HTML

C|net's Know the Code: HTML for Beginners

http://builder.cnet.com/Authoring/Basics/

Visit this site for the skinny on HTML coding. Nicely organized with lots of examples, the C|net site will hold your hand through each step. The site also has a nice listing of basic HTML tags. If you would like a more complete listing of HTML tags, visit HTML Goodies at http://www.htmlgoodies.com/html_ref.html.

Raggett's Ten Minute Guide to HTML

http://www.w3.org/MarkUp/Guide/

Visit this site, a very quick and easy guide, especially if you feel you need to take HTML coding really slow. It just hits the basics—no more, no less. If you are overwhelmed by the C|net guide, visit Raggett's.

A Few Design Tips

http://builder.cnet.com/Authoring/Htmltips/

This site section addresses specific tips you should be aware of when designing your Web site. It covers general tips such as keeping your site small and clean, knowing your audience, and testing your Web pages. On top of general tips and tricks, the site includes various specific design issues from setting font sizes to making your tables colorful. At Builder.com, C|net also provides advanced HTML Tips and Tricks.

Uploading Your Site for All to See—An FTP Primer

What is FTP?

File Transfer Protocol, or FTP, is the protocol or standardized way computers exchange files using the Internet as its transfer mode. The file transfers take place when a computer either uploads or downloads a file to another computer. The terms "download" and "upload" are considered common FTP terminology, so it is a good idea to get an understanding of the difference between the two terms. When you download a file, you request a file to be transferred (or "served up") from another computer to your computer (the "client"). On the other hand, in a file upload, you request a file to be transferred from your computer to another. That's about all there is to it.

FTP Software and Configuration

In order to do all this file maneuvering, you must have a special software program. In addition, you will need to configure the program in order to communicate with other computers. The freeware program I use is WS_FTP32 (http://www.ipswitch.com/downloads/). There are many other free programs available, but this program has been very dependable.

Once you have installed the program, you need to create your session profile. When you use a public FTP site, you should use an anonymous login (type anonymous for user ID). Use your E-mail address for the password. The screenshot figure shows you a typical anonymous FTP session profile. If you want to search for a particular FTP address, access the Archie Services Web site at http://www.nexor.com/archie/.

Ready to FTP

Once you have configured your profile you are ready to connect and FTP. Just make sure your Internet connection is open and then open your FTP program. Connect to the host you have selected. Ok, now that you are connected, let's assume you would like to download a file (vs. upload). The window on the left represents the files on your hard drive. The window on the right represents the files on the FTP server.

If you need to determine which file(s) you would like to download, take a look at the index or readme file. When you select your file, you must also select the transfer type. Select "ASCII" for text and "Binary" for graphics and programs. Use the arrow button in the center to move a selected file onto your hard drive. You have officially "FTP'ed."

HTML Validation

This section discusses Web page consistency. Through your design efforts, you can make sure there is a consistent look and feel among your Web site pages, but what about how your pages look on different browsers and browser versions? You can control the code you want to consistently work across a wide variety of browsers as well.

This is where the fun starts. Validating your HTML against different browsers can be a somewhat frustrating task. Although browsers try really hard to interpret your HTML code, sometimes they aren't geared to read the latest tags and some browsers aren't as forgiving when your code turns out a little cryptic. This section is intended to take some of the mystery out of HTML validation.

HTML Validation Resources

What does HTML validation involve? Well, if you want to pursue a very tedious process, you can pour over the latest W3C specification (http://www.w3.org/MarkUp/). Luckily, there are several HTML resources available to automate an otherwise painful task. The following are HTML resources you may want to check out:

Web Site Garage

http://www.websitegarage.com/

In the latest reviews by Clnet, Web Site Garage received the Editors Choice pick and kudos for being the most comprehensive and easy-to-use HTML validation tool tested. Web Site Garage has a browser-compatibility check, which gives you advice about where your HTML code may have problems when viewed in various browsers. You can check your pages for free. Web Site Garage also provides more in-depth reporting and consulting services for an extra fee.

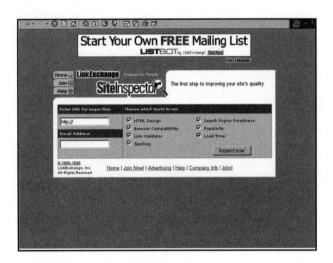

SiteInspector

http://www.siteinspector.com/

The company that created LinkExchange, the reciprocal link marketing tool, has now created SiteInspector. The interface is very simple. Just enter the URL you want to check and select the tests you want to run. There is one item you ought to be aware of, however. SiteInspector does not differentiate between flat-out errors and warnings.

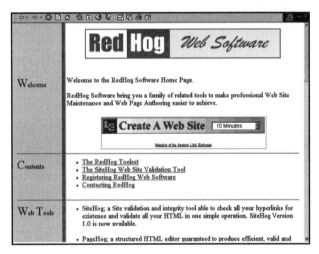

SiteHog

http://www.redhog.com/redhog/

SiteHog separates errors, warnings, and browser issues. The inspection reports are useful in its format, the code appears in an editable window, while the list of errors and warnings appears below in a separate pane. SiteHog works only with local files, which can be a drawback.

Easy Additions to Enhance Your Web Site

Serve Up a Splash Page

Creating a splash page is super-easy. If you don't know what a splash page is, it's when you visit one page and it jumps you to another page after a few seconds (in this example, five seconds). The trick to the HTML code is using the META tag refresh option. Here's the code that will have you jumping in no time!

```
<META HTTP-EQUIV="Refresh" CONTENT="5;URL=mainpage.html">
<BODY>
<IMG WIDTH="250" HEIGHT="110" ALT="splash screen" SRC="splash.gif">
</BODY>
```

You will need to change the "mainpage.html" text to the page you want to jump to and the "splash.gif" to the name of your splash graphic.

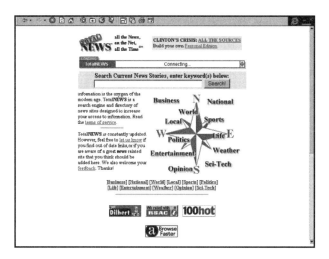

Add a Custom News Ticker

http://www.totalnews.com/

For instant news on your Web site, create a news ticker. TotalNews, gives users the ability to create a profile of various news sources to compare articles. You can then add the ticker to your Web page.

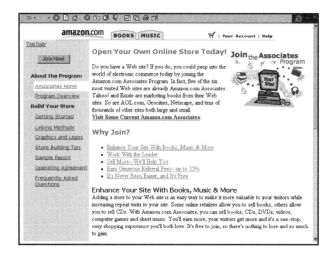

Become an Amazon.com Associate

http://www.amazon.com/

Join the Amazon.com Associate's program to provide Web visitors book resources that you can recommend. Base your bookstore on your areas of expertise. The Associate's section on Amazon's site offers resources to get your bookstore up and running. Amazon.com provides you with a commission for each book sold that was referred from your Web site.

Create a Slide Show

Using the same HTML code concepts as in the splash page example, you can create a slide show using the following HTML. Insert the following HTML at the first page of your slide show:

```
<META HTTP-EQUIV="Refresh" CONTENT="3;URL=slide2.html">
```

Next, open slide2.html, and add the following to the code to make the next slide pop up after three seconds and so forth:

```
<META HTTP-EQUIV="Refresh" CONTENT="3;URL=slide3.html">
```

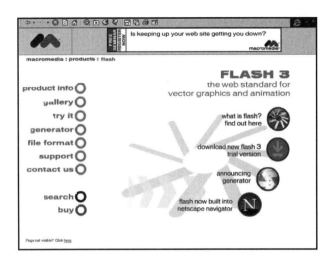

Give Your Site Some Flash

http://www.macromedia.com/

Macromedia's new animation creation tool, Flash, is receiving much praise for its stunning effects, small file sizes and easy interactivity. In addition, Flash animations will come straight to Internet viewer's browsers without any plug-in downloads (with the next versions of Navigator and Internet Explorer).

The effects are comparable to animated GIFs, but you can also insert audio and create mouse interactivity. To create Flash files, you need the Flash Generator. Since the viewing component is integrated into the browser, there is no cost to viewers.

Spice It Up with Dynamic HTML

Dynamic HTML (DHTML) is a collective term which encompasses the latest HTML standard, style sheets, and programming that allows you to create more animated and interactive Web pages. Both Netscape Navigator 4.0 and Internet Explorer 4.0 support DHTML.

However, the biggest roadblock for overall DHTML acceptance is that many individuals are still using old browser versions that cannot accommodate DHTML. Therefore, for now if you want to use DHTML, it is recommended that you use DHTML with caution. To play around with DHTML and give your site a little extra interactivity, create two versions of your home page. Then, when DHTML becomes the standard, you'll already be ahead of the curve, and you can then add DHTML to all your pages.

For more on DHTML visit:

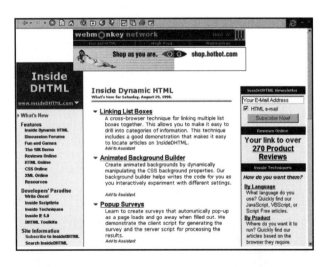

Inside DHTML

http://www.insidedhtml.com/

This Web site, created by one of MSIE's lead engineers, covers CSS and DHTML in the Microsoft IE4 style.

Free Home Page Resources

Tripod

http://www.tripod.com/

Tripod is one of the most popular community of personal home pages. All you need to do for your free home page is visit the site and supply your E-mail address (for verification purposes). Tripod has an easy home page builder that automatically uploads your pages if you don't care to FTP. Of course, the automatic builder does not have all the functionality you would have if you made the pages with an HTML program such as FrontPage. Tripod is a nice way to get your feet wet building a Web page.

Inc. Magazine Business Directory

http://www.inc.com/createsite/

Inc.'s Business Directory gives you a free home page to either create your company's Web site or provide information about the site you have already established. I took up *Inc.* on the offer and created my own "mini-site" for my Web site and used lots of links to reference to the major sections of my Web site.

GeoCities

http://www.geocities.net/

GeoCities is another popular home page community and is similar to Tripod. Both Tripod and GeoCities have ads that pop up when someone visits your Web site. However, with Tripod you can pay a nominal fee and have the ads removed from your site. GeoCities does not currently offer this option.

Comprehensive HTML Resources for the Basic Mechanics

For those interested in the mechanics of Web page creation.

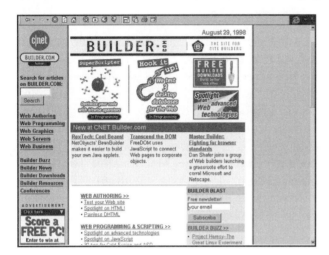

Builder.com

http://www.builder.com/

Builder.com is a weekly zine targeted at professional web builders. One look at it and you'll know that it comes out of Cnet and that you'll find plenty of content and regular columns.

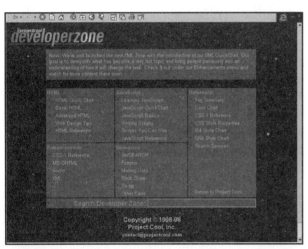

Developer Zone

http://www.projectcool.com/developer/

Project Cool's Developer Zone features easy "no geek speak" tutorials ranging from the most basic just-getting-started HTML information to advanced topics such as JavaScript, CSS, and DHTML.

HTML Goodies

http://www.htmlgoodies.com/

HTML Goodies claims that if it can be done in HTML, you can find it there. I don't know about that claim, but it does hold much information and many tutorials.

Site Builder Network

http://www.microsoft.com/sitebuilder/

Microsoft's Sitebuilder is the MS resource covering Web building and publishing. You should check out the Sitebuilder section as well as the Workshop.

DevEdge Online

http://developer.netscape.com/

Nearly everything you need to know about developing Web sites using Netscape's products can be found at DevEdge.

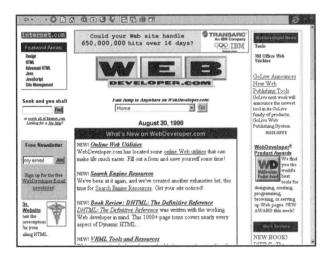

Web Developer

http://www.webdeveloper.com/

Formerly a print magazine, Web Developer now only exists in its online incarnation; its stories cover events relevant to Web developers.

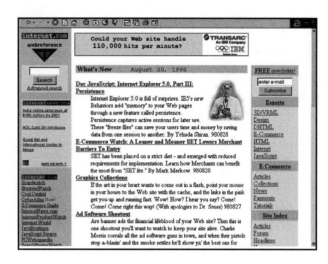

WebReference.com

http://www.webreference.com/

Another Mecklermedia Web site with columns and tutorials geared at Web page building.

Chapter 16

HIRING OUT: WEB HOSTING OPTIONS

Introduction

Finding a good Web host can be very tough. The Web hosting sector is extremely fragmented with lots of companies competing for your business. I know from experience that Web hosts are not perfect. However, it is imperative to avoid the really bad Web hosts, the ones that will cost you dearly in bucks and in business. This chapter is designed to walk you through the various factors you should consider when outsourcing your Web site to a Web host.

Determine What Services You Want to Outsource

The service a Web host provides greatly varies. You need to decide if you want the Web host to merely host your content (i.e., provide you with space so you can upload and maintain your Web site) or if you want the host to design, maintain and host your Web site. You could also retain a separate firm to outsource any of the components of your Web site (i.e., layout, design, graphics).

Obviously as a general rule, the more you outsource, the more control you lose. Furthermore, you pay a premium for their expertise. However, if you lack the skills internally, you will probably save money and wind up with a more professional product.

Learn from Others—Reasons to Switch Web Hosting Companies

Ok. So let's say you did all your homework and you found what you thought to be the perfect Web host. Then, you notice once you are signed up for the service, your E-mails and phone calls go unanswered. What you have just encountered is the start of a very bad relationship. It's better to get out of the situation right away; it will only get worse. Surely, you can ask for a good explanation and give them a second (or third) chance, but proceed with caution.

Here are some of the main reasons why businesses switch hosting companies:

1. Unanswered E-mail and/or phone calls

2. Unexplained charges

3. Slow servers (the "I can never get into your Web site" problem)

4. Congested lines

5. Failed or missing backups

6. Company moves files around without notification (i.e., causes FTP nightmares)

7. Unscheduled/unannounced server shut-down

> ➡ **Quick Note: QuickTip!**
>
> Because of the instability of some Web hosts, it is extremely important that you obtain your own domain name. By doing so, you have the flexibility to move from one host to the another without losing visitors. Albeit, this is not a headache-free process, but at least you won't have a coronary.

Talk to Others!

The single best way to find out if a prospective Web host has symptoms of a not-so-great host is to talk to others. Talk to individuals you know who have used Web hosting services. How do they like their current Web host? What features do they have? Have they ever switched? If so, why? And whom did they switch from? (This one is a freebie—one more company off your host list!)

If you don't know of anyone using Web hosts, ask your prospective Web hosts for referrals; E-mail or call each and every person. Make sure your questions are consistent so you have comparable answers. You will find by investing the time up front to find out as much as you can about your future Web host will save you a lot of potential headaches.

> ➡ **Quick Note: A Quick Web Host Guide**
>
> Before you hitch up with a Web host, take heed of some of these aspects:
>
> 1. Ask yourself, "What do I need the space for?" If the answer is graphics or application intensive, you'll need lots of space.
> 2. Conduct a good survey. Ask the company about its customer support policies and the reliability of its service.
> 3. Visit the Top Hosts site at http://www.tophosts.com/ and check out the Web host's connection.
> 4. Make sure you coordinate the change over of any domain names with InterNIC. Do not let the Web host perform these procedures. If you do and you have to switch hosts, it may be a difficult switch.
> 5. Think about going with a company that you believe to be reliable and that other sources are already using and are satisfied.
> 6. Ask if they have a money-back guarantee. If all else fails, at least you won't lose a bundle of money.

Primary Objectives When Retaining a Web Host

At the end of the day, you are looking for the following characteristics in a Web host. Again, it is important for you to analyze what is more important to the success of your Web site. Depending on what plans you have for your site, there may be some trade-offs involved such as a higher Web host fee for maximum security.

- Excellent Reliability—Web host servers are fast, seldom down and accurately direct technical support response quickly to requests.
- Excellent Security—username/password protection, secure physical assets, latest E-commerce technology.
- Excellent Technology/Infrastructure—Web host houses the latest technology, keeps you apprised of future technological enhancements.
- Excellent Technical Expertise—intelligent technical support group, Web host's Web site proves to be a useful source of technical information, quickly answers questions and maintains appropriate follow-up.

➡ Quick Note: The Top 10

The Ultimate Web Host List has a published listing of the Top 25 Web hosts. Included below are details on the Top 10. Visit its Web site for complete ranking and rating details: http://www.webhostlist.com/

1. Hiway Technologies—http://www.hway.net/
2. Dynamic Web—http://www.dynamicweb.net/
3. CI Host—http://www.cihost.com/
4. ConcentricHost—http://www.concentric.com/
5. TABNet—http://www.tabnet.com/
6. Netcom—http://www.netcomi.com/
7. Tri Star Web—http://www.tristarweb.com/
8. WebAxxs—http://www.webaxxs.net/
9. WEB 2010—http://www.web2010.com/
10. Alabanza—http://www.alabanza.net/

The Laundry List—Components of Web Host Service

Web host packages may or may not include the below features. However, it is important for you to prioritize what is imperative for your Web site to be successful. For instance, if you plan to offer RealAudio at your Web site, you should look for a Web host with the highest speed lines, affordable RealAudio services, and high data transfer limits.

- High speed server connection (T3 or T1)
- 20MB + of server space

- High data transfer limits (better yet—unlimited!)

- FTP update capability

- CGI-BIN programs and access

- Multiple E-mail accounts (also check into E-mail alias and auto-responder features)

- Secure server (for E-commerce—SSL is the current standard)

- Interactive services (i.e., discussion groups, chat, video-conferencing)

- Front-Page extensions (very important if you plan to use Microsoft's FrontPage)

- Spam protection

- Streaming audio and video (i.e., RealAudio)

- Low customer per server ratio

- Disaster recovery plans

- Good server statistics

- Technical support (try to get 24/7)

- Web site statistics

- Firewalls, digital certificates, and encryption (if E-commerce will be conducted)

- Internet fax (an emerging technology)

- Virtual Private Network (VPN—important if considering an EDI tunneling/extranet)

Web Host Resources

Top Hosts

http://www.tophosts.com/

This site provides a searchable directory of Web hosts. It claims to be an independent source and does not provide Web hosting services. You can also test your potential host connection before you decide to take the plunge with them.

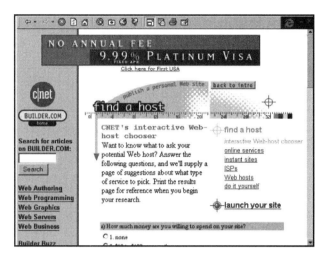

Interactive Web Host Chooser

http://builder.cnet.com/Servers/Publish/Personal/ss01a.html

Clnet supplies the questions, you fill out the questionnaire, and Clnet will provide the answers to your Web host preferences.

The Ultimate Web Host List

http://www.webhostlist.com/

This site includes the review of the top twenty-five Web hosts. Visit the Yellow Pages for various Web host listings. If you are extremely satisfied or dissatisfied with an existing Web host, help others out by registering and using the Voting Booth section.

HostSearch

http://www.hostsearch.com/

HostSearch lets you search for a Web host by price and server space needed. It provides Web host reviews and hosts an online discussion forum. The Buying Guide has a few tips about selecting a host.

Yahoo!

http://www.yahoo.com/

Type in "Web_Services/Hosting/" to find Yahoo!'s indexed directory of Web hosting resources.

SECTION 5

MARKETING YOUR SERVICES

ON

THE INTERNET

Chapter 17

REGISTERING YOUR WEB SITE

Introduction

You have now created your Web site and you are ready to let others know about it. Start early with your submissions to the search engines. Many are extremely bogged down with Add URL submission requests and many take a number of weeks before your Web site is listed in its engine. This site is designed to give you some pointers on how to register your Web site with the major search engines.

How Search Engines Rank Web Pages

Well, sort of . . . it's hard to tell how some search engines register sites. Search engines primarily rank based on location of keywords in the search query to the Web page as well the frequency these keywords are mentioned at the site.

Before You Register: Use Search Engine Design Tips

Pick Your Strategic Keywords

Make sure each page in your site includes different keywords. This increases the probability your site will turn up in a search request. Your strategic words should always be at least two words long.

Positioning of Keywords

Place your keywords on crucial locations of your Web pages. The title is the first place to consider, since a search engine will look at the titles first before searching Web page contents. Your chances are much better to include these words in the title or the first paragraphs of your Web page. Also, keep in mind the use of tables can "push down" your text down further on the page thus making key words less relevant. For example, if you picked a two-column page, the contents of the first column would be listed, then the second. If you happen to have used the first column for spacing, you have pushed down your chances of a good search ranking.

Have Relevant Content

Your keywords need to be reflective of your page's content. Otherwise, it is considered search engine spamming. If you have text that is relevant to the topic, do not present the information in graphics as the text in graphics will not be picked up by the search engines. On the plus side, some search engines index the ALT text in a graphic hyperlink.

Use META Tags

The following section includes several rules to help improve your submissions to search engines. With a little up-front work, you may produce better chances of a higher search engine result listing.

Follow the META Tag Rules

Rule #1: Use <META> tags.

You need to use the <META> tag in your HTML to include a description of your Web site and the keywords you develop (see Rule #2).

Rule #2: Develop Useful Keywords.

Visit the top search engines and enter your keywords individually. Visit the sites that are high on the results list. Look for new keywords. Make sure when you enter your keywords into your <META> tag that they are in the plural form (it gives you better chances of selection, whether singular or plural).

Rule #3: Use Lower Case in Keywords

Regarding case sensitivity, some people try to include every case variation in the META tags. However, these repetitions may alert the search engine's spam detector and disqualify your keywords. As such, you should use lower case only in your keywords since almost all individuals search in the lower. Plus only two search engines are case sensitive. The table below shows a real example of the keywords used to lead to a Web site. The generic word "name" was used for confidentiality reasons.

Variation	# Click-Throughs	Percentage
name	1011	82%
Name	128	10%
NAME	86	7%
Other variation		1%

Rule #4: Develop Precise Titles.

When a search engine receives a search request, it will search the <TITLE> tag first for possible matches. However, don't load up on keywords in your title. Make your title concise and precise and include only a few of your most compelling keywords.

Rule #5: Add Keywords in Comments Tag.

Not all search engines recognize <META> tags, so it is imperative to get your keywords near the top of your page.

Incorporating the "Before You Register" Rules into HTML:

<HEAD>

<TITLE>Make sure your title is descriptive and includes keywords here</TITLE>

<META Name="Description" Content="give a description of your Web site's offerings here">

<META Name="Keywords" Content="list the keywords you developed here">

</HEAD>

<BODY>

<!—"list the keywords you developed here as a comment">

Registering Your Site with the Top Sites

When you register your Web site, please start with the "Top 10." There are so many search engines out there; you will never reap the same benefits as registering wisely with the Top 10. On the following page is a list of the URLs to the submission forms of the Top 10 search engines:

ALTAVISTA

http://www.altavista.com/av/content/addurl.htm

EXCITE

http://www.excite.com/Info/add_url.html

HOTBOT

http://www.hotbot.com/addurl.html

INFOSEEK

http://www.infoseek.com/AddUrl?pg=DCaddurl.html

LYCOS

http://www.lycos.com/addasite.html

OPEN TEXT

http://index.opentext.net/main/submitURL.html

STARTING POINT

http://www.stpt.com/general/submit.html

WEBCRAWLER

http://www.webcrawler.com/WebCrawler/SubmitURLS.html

YAHOO!

http://add.yahoo.com/fast/add?

Registration Follow-up

Verify and Maintain Your Listing

Check back with the search engines and make sure your Web site has been properly listed. Once you have your site listed with the search engines, check back and re-verify every two weeks. Sometimes strange things happen. Furthermore, resubmit your site any time you make significant changes. Some search engines do not revisit and re-index sites as often as they should.

Checking Your URL Ranking

Would you like to see where you rank with the search engines? There are many resources available to do just that. Some services are free while others are free for some tests and a premium for extended services. The table on the next page includes information about some of the Web site addresses to URL checking services:

Vendor	Web Site	Features
PositionAgent	http://www.positionagent.com/	Free service allows checking with twelve top search engines based on your URL and keywords.
WebPosition	http://www.webposition.com/	45-day trial available for check on three search engines. Commercial version supports ten search engines.
ScoreCheck	http://www.scorecheck.com/	Free service check for two search engines, paid fees for more. Results are delivered via E-mail
InterNetGain	http://www.internetgain.com	Free service is standard (that is, same as above). Paid service includes checklist of deficiencies and suggested corrective action.
Rank This	http://www.rankthis.com/	Free service allows URL and keyword check, provides top two hundred results. Paid services available.
The Informant	http://informant.dartmouth.edu/	Free service provides check and results for top ten results. Results delivered via E-mail.
Did-It	http://www.did-it.com/	Free URL check. Paid service checks presence once a month. Keyword monitoring is not available.

Checking Links to Your Site

How would you like to know which sites are linked to yours? There are a few resources available to do just that, and they are available at the top search engines. The following are the sites that offer reverse searching:

AltaVista Enter your URL like this: link:cpanet.com. If you want to narrow the directory to search, select the directory you want the check to be performed on. To eliminate pages within your Web site that you don't care to have listed in your port, you can now exclude them by submitting the following query: link:cpaneet.com-host:cpanet.com.

HotBot Enter your URL in the search box and change the drop down checklist from "all of the words" to "links to this URL."

Infoseek From the Infoseek home page, click on Ultraseek. From there you can perform a URL Search.

UNDERSTANDING YOUR MARKET

Introduction

This section reminds me of an IBM print ad I read one day. The ad had a guy with a goofy grin parachuting out of a plane and the caption read, "the 'yippeeee, we're on the Internet! Now what?' solution." Well, the "now what" for *you* should be to let people know you are on the Internet with some creative Internet marketing. This chapter will address who is actually on the Internet, how you can potentially create a niche market, and how you can market yourself.

The World Is Your Oyster

If you don't think there are many people on the Internet, think again. When did you have the potential to reach over 153 million people? Grant it, due to geographical constraints it does not necessarily make sense for someone in Africa to retain a CPA in the U.S. (I'm sure it has happened, though). However, if you just look at the U.S. and Canada Internet population of 87 million, that should still be plenty big to pique your interest. The following is the breakdown of the world online population:

World Total	153 million
USA & Canada	87 million
Asia/Pacific	26.5 million
Europe	33.5 million
South America	4.5 million
Africa	1 million
Middle East	.78 million

Source: *How Many Online*, Nua Internet Surveys, January 1999 (http://www.nua.net/).

The numbers look fairly appealing. It was recently reported that over one-third of the entire U.S. population is online. But really, who are these people who are online? What are their preferences? Why do they go on the Internet? Are they online only to use E-mail or do they use the Web as well? These are all valid questions to ask and to help you try to narrow down what market segment you would like to cater to in the virtual world. The next section profiles several Internet surveys where you can answer some of these questions.

Group Dynamics and Demographics of the Internet

Since your Web site's audience is the entire online world, it is important you gain awareness as to the demographics of the Internet. The online population trends are changing quickly, so it's equally important you stay apprised of the latest online segments. This is also why I won't go into heavy detail about the latest Internet statistics. Instead, I will provide some general facts about the current Internet users and point to the myriad of Internet demographic surveys that are available on the Internet. The surveys are updated frequently, so by visiting a survey sponsor's site, you are guaranteed the most accurate profile of the typical Internet user.

Who Uses the Internet?—Some General Facts

- One of the current Internet trends is the shifting of gender on the Internet. Women are approaching parity on the Internet, accounting for about 40 percent of the online population. According to NetSmart Research, women will make up 60 percent of the online population by 2005.
- 93 percent use the Web on a daily basis.
- 40 percent have provided false information to a site when registering.
- 66 percent spend more than ten hours a week on the Internet.
- 62 percent have concerns regarding online anonymity.

Source: GVU Survey, October 1998 (http://www.cc.gatech.edu/gvu/).

- Small business constitutes 40 percent of Internet business users.
- 27 percent made online purchases in the past twelve months.
- Three out of four adult users are dependent on the Internet.
- 60 percent of these users use the Web daily, mainly for business.
- 27 percent of these users made online purchases in the past year.
- 39 percent of these purchases were made after clicking online ads.

Source: FIND/SVP 1997 American Internet User Survey (http://etrg.findsvp.com/).

- 70 percent are more concerned about privacy on the Internet than they are about information transmitted by traditional media, such as phone and mail.

- 41 percent left Web sites when asked to provide registration information.

- 27 percent provided false personal information on registration forms.

Source: Boston Consulting Group (http://www.bcg.com/)

Internet Survey Resources

The Internet was designed as a decentralized system, so it's hard to measure Internet demographics. Web users are much like television viewers—we know very little about what they actually watch. The best we can do is take a statistical sample of the population and extrapolate our results to the population. Since the commercial Internet came into existence, researchers have been busy attempting to size up the typical Internet user as well as the Internet's market potential. The following resources point out the various surveys conducted on the Internet industry.

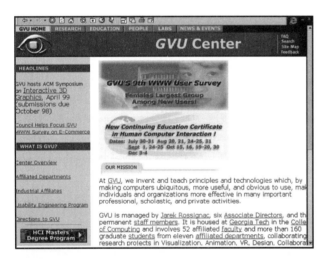

GVU Web User Survey

http://www.cc.gatech.edu/gvu/

Georgia Tech University's Graphics, Visualization & Usability Center sponsors this survey and it is conducted every six months. This survey does not ensure a representative population, as its surveys are distributed via the Internet. Users of this survey will find some of its questions interesting, such as "How did you learn HTML?" and "Why do you save Web pages?"

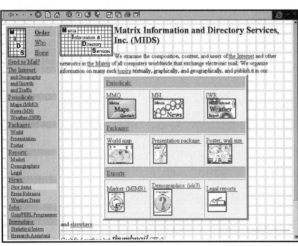

MIDS Survey

http://www.mids.org/index.html

This survey conducted by John Quarterman's Matrix Information and Directory Services takes a much more thorough approach than the GVU survey. MIDS sends questionnaires to ISPs and requests them to profile their users. MIDS incorporates standard statistical analyses of the data.

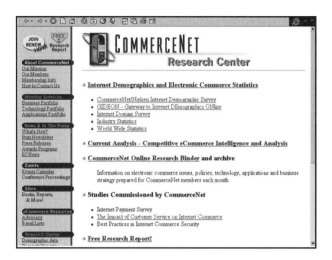

Nielsen-CommerceNet Survey

http://www.nielsenmedia.com/demo.htm

The Nielsen survey employs rigorous polling methods to determine the number and profile of online users. The method of survey is random telephone poll interviews and therefore includes Internet users as well as non-users. Some claim this may be the most accurate survey available to the public.

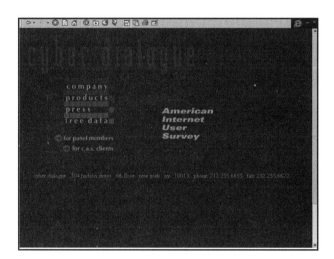

FIND/SVP Survey

http://etrg.findsvp.com/

The FIND/SVP survey incorporates factual measurements as well as conceptual questions into its random telephone surveys. Prior surveys have unveiled some interesting statistics about commercial online services.

➡ **Quick Note: Yahoo!**

To obtain more information about Internet statistics and demographics, visit Yahoo! and type in Internet/Statistics_and_Demographics. You will be taken to Yahoo!'s category on the topic.

Other Demographic Resources

These sites do not conduct surveys, however they do follow the demographic trends of the Internet:

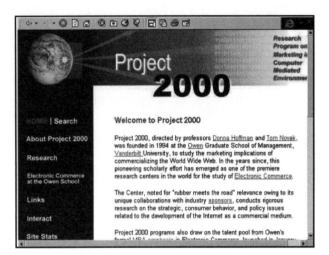

Project 2000

http://www2000.ogsm.vanderbilt.edu/

Project 2000 was founded in 1994 at the Owen Graduate School of Management, Vanderbilt University, to study the marketing implications of commercializing the World Wide Web.

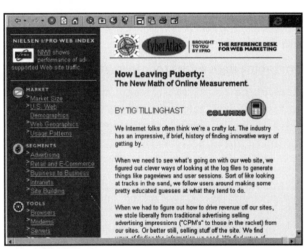

CyberAtlas

http://www.cyberatlas.com/

CyberAtlas considers itself the reference desk for Web marketing. The site includes various market and segment resources, columns, and news from around the Web.

Creative Internet Marketing

Devise a RVP—Repeat Visitor Plan

- Change your content often. Decide to develop content from what you are known for and have expertise in.

- Provide an E-mail newsletter. You need to come up with ideas to communicate with your visitors on an ongoing basis. The more you communicate, the better the chance your visitors will build a loyalty to your site. It regularly brings the business of your firm to their minds. Additional future contact could lead to gaining information on these visitors by conducting surveys and building a database profiling your visitor's characteristics and preferences.

- As your site grows, navigation will become increasingly important. Consider designing a good-looking site map.

- Have a good amount of free resources. Whether it be content, news or links/reviews to other Web site resources, Web surfers expect to see something other than a commercial at your site. If all they see is a hyped-up advertisement for your services, you can guarantee the chances of a second visit are very slim.

- The bottom line is the more you get people to visit, the more they will think about your site as a great resource and their praise will travel to others via word of mouth.

Gather Information about Your Web Site Visitors via Forms

More ISPs are providing form support for their customers. If this feature is available to you, or if you have a server, you may want to consider setting up a page to gather information about your Web site visitors. Below are some tips on how to make your form a success:

1. Keep the form short. Visitors get discouraged when they see a lengthy Web site form and may not sign up or provide you feedback.

2. Try to gather psychographic data. Psychographic date refers to information about lifestyle or personality. Sometimes demographic information (i.e., income, city, etc.) is not the way to gather useful information about how to target your visitors' interests. Questions such as, what is your favorite Web site and what topics are you interested in may be more useful use of a short form.

➡ **Quick Note: Twelve Ways to Market Your Site**

1. Request links on industry sites.
2. Include Web site address on letterhead, business cards, and firm literature.
3. Include Web site address in display advertising and traditional media efforts.
4. Develop a free service to market.
5. Request reciprocal links.
6. Issue news releases.
7. Request links from business sites.
8. Ask visitors if they would like periodic Web site updates and to obtain their E-mail addresses.
9. Publish an E-mail newsletter.
10. Include Web site address and pertinent site information below your E-mail signature.
11. Actively participate in discussion forums.
12. Announce a scholarship or a contest.

Differentiating Your Web Site

Look at Others' Web Sites—Do It Different

Look to see what your competing firms and Web sites are offering at their sites. If they are providing value at their site and you think it's unbeatable, think of a way you can emulate the benefits and put a spin on it. Think creatively when competing against the offerings at other Web sites.

Also, look to see if other sites have gaps in their service. If you are good at what they are lacking, jump onto the Web with full vengeance in your area of expertise. Leverage your strengths to differentiate yourself. By demonstrating that you are a specialist supplier, you will stand out from all the other "me too" sites. Furthermore, you are likely to gain some good alliances with firms that are lacking in areas you are strong. Firms will find innovative ways to make themselves "complete or whole" on the Web.

Don't Get Lost in the Crowd

In order to stand out from all the other sites, you need to offer something different. Do you have expertise in a particular field which is not yet heavily exploited on the Internet? Or maybe, there *are* players in your particular niche field, however, maybe you could find a different market segment to which you can tailor your service.

Finding your "Internet-worthy" niche will help you become different on the Web. Stick to what you do extremely well, and plan to discover new market areas in which you could dominate.

Thinking Out of the Box

Keep in mind if you solicit feedback or conduct surveys at your site that the research material you gather in this process may uncover demand for new or modified services within an existing market. Make sure you keep an open mind during this process. Pursuing certain services may not have made sense in the bricks and mortar world, but it may make perfect sense for the Internet.

Additional Marketing Resources

The Internet Marketing Plan: A Practical Handbook for Creating, Implementing and Assessing Your Online Presence by Kim M. Bayne.

Here is an Amazon.com synopsis: "With this guide, consultant Kim Bayne brings coherence and integration to Internet marketing and general marketing practice. She provides in a hands-on workbook format the means to set up a marketing blueprint which readers can use to effectively design, implement, and evaluate their Web sites."

Chapter 19

DRUMMING UP PUBLICITY

Introduction

Ok, now you have created your Web site and you have registered your site with all the major search engines. But what should you do now? How do you tell everyone that you are online as well as notify appropriate individuals of new features and significant Web site improvements? You can keep you fingers crossed and hope people stumble upon your site and the new content, or you can take the matter into your own hands and publicize your Web site.

The latter approach is more proactive and your action will reap benefits. This chapter will walk you through approaches to publicity that will help you effectively promote your Web site.

Promoting a Web Site

There are various ways to specifically promote a Web site. This section will address some of the more popular means used to contact clients and the media about your site. The promotion method you choose to use should depend on what you would like to publicize in addition to what subsequent action you would like your reader to take.

News Releases

Use news releases to inform the media of anything you think warrants some form of press coverage. News releases for the Internet are communicated through E-mail and are much shorter than fax or snail-mail versions. Keep your news release to three or four paragraphs. Past history has shown that online news releases result in higher press coverage than traditional means. Be advised, as Internet technology evolves, the tables could turn.

Announcements

An announcement is posted to discussion groups, both Web-based discussions and Usenet newsgroups. The goal is to entice individuals of the discussion group's community to request additional information or visit your Web site. You need to be careful when you craft online announcements. Later in this chapter, I will give you some pointers on how to approach this issue.

Links

Conducting a link campaign can be a very effective and a cheap way to get others to visit your Web site. If you have a differentiated site, many niche-topic Web site directories will be more than happy to include your site in their listings of links.

A link campaign is different from registering your site with the major search engines (which is also a must), since you will be nicely asking, via a concise E-mail, each Webmaster to consider a link to your site. However, use your time wisely, choose Web sites for which you have an affinity, have an excellent reputation, and is targeted to the same audience you cater to. If you follow these guidelines, your campaign will most likely be a success.

Not only can you perform a link campaign to ask others to link to your site, but you can also submit to detailed directories and create additional Web sites that link to your site. For example, *Inc.* Magazine (http://www.inc.com/createsite/) offers a free home page site and listing in its directory. You can create a mini site with the goal of promoting your business and Web site. The purpose of *Inc.*'s service is not to substitute for your site since the easy to use forms include a field to link to your main site. Another resource that provides a link to your site is firm directories. At the CPA Firms (http://www.cpafirms.com/), AccountingNet (http://www.accountingnet.com/), and CPAnet (http://www.cpanet.com/) Web sites, you can submit a free firm listing and link to your Web site.

Newsletters

The online newsletter should be a staple item for your online promotion efforts. It is a wonderful opportunity to provide clients a value-added service as well as provide various media contacts with important update information about your firm's products and services. Online newsletters can be distributed for a fraction of the cost of their snail-mail counterparts.

Online newsletters via E-mail should be no longer than a few paragraphs. If you have more in-depth information to cover or provide, include hyperlinks where your readers can visit the Web pages they are interested in. Online newsletter options are changing to an HTML-based format, whereupon subscription readers can select, if they would like, a text version or HTML newsletter version. I already receive several newsletters in HTML. I suspect in the future a substantial percentage of online newsletters will be announced via an E-mail which will include a link to visit the entire newsletter online or that will take you straight to the Web-based newsletter.

Online Library

By creating an online publicity library, you will establish a one-stop shop where media contacts can easily find information about your firm and its services. Journalists are frequently dealing with time-sensitive topics and need quick access to your information. As such, media contacts will be more likely to give you press coverage if you make the fact-finding process easier on them.

In the online library, you will want to include all announcements and news releases to the public. In addition, you can include any hard-copy brochures (you can scan them in or convert them to HTML, although converted is the preferred method), press clippings, answers to frequently asked questions, interview transcripts, online chat transcripts, firm mission, strategic plan and objectives, and key employee's bios.

Public Appearances

Don't discount the impact of physical public appearances when promoting your "virtual" world. If you are at an event, mention your Web site. Individuals who are interested in the unique features of your site will jot down your address and will take a look at your site. Many people still receive their "new Web sites to visit list" pushed to them via word of mouth. To make an even more powerful impact, include your Web site and E-mail addresses on your business cards.

You can also make public appearances on the Web. If you participate as a guest in an online chat, you have in essence made a public appearance. If you properly publicize your online chat, you can simultaneously reach thousands of online chat visitors in one fell swoop. Make sure you do your homework in advance so you can make an excellent impression.

Promotions

Online promotions in the form of surveys, quizzes, and the like may have a place on an accounting Web site, although I recommend using some discretion. A great way to help out others and maybe obtain some press coverage in the process is to offer student scholarships and conduct the process via the Web. Another appropriate application for promotions would be to rally the troops for a conference or event.

Ongoing Public Relations

To fully utilize the publicity vehicles mentioned in the previous section, some general and ongoing public relations maintenance activities must be performed. For starters, someone in your firm should be responsible for gathering a database of appropriate media contacts you plan to contact on an ongoing basis as well as for special or specific announcements. To obtain E-mail addresses for mainstream media contacts, I have included some search resources at the end of this chapter. For accounting specific contacts, gather media contact information to popular trade magazines and your local CPA society.

Have a designated person in your organization troll popular accounting news Web sites and discussion forums looking for potential promotion opportunities. By doing so, you will stay abreast of topics making news and you may be able to pitch a follow-up that ties to your firm's services and/or Web site. In addition, every once in a while visit the popular search engines and perform a search of your firm name or organization to look for new Web pages where your name is mentioned.

Publicity via E-mail

With the advent of Spam E-mail, conducting publicity functions via E-mail is an extremely touchy topic and should be approached with much trepidation. At least that's how I treat it. I take every measure to avoid criticism about how I conduct my business on the Internet. As a general rule of thumb, I only E-mail individuals who I think would want to hear from me. If you can put yourself in your recipients' shoes and honestly say you would like to receive the E-mail, then send it.

This section discusses some of the do's, don'ts, and tips of conducting E-mail-based promotion. Below are some guidelines you should follow when conducting promotion activities:

- Never make your promotion sound like a commercial, or, worse yet, an infomercial. Get to the point.

- Consider using the space below your signature as a place to include information about your Web sites' latest features.

- Use your intuition before you make your contact. Know your audience and have empathy for their busy schedules.

- Start out your E-mail with a sincere compliment, by praising the recipient's accomplishments or Web site content and design.

- Consider sending E-mail to fellow Web site neighbors to introduce yourself. Mention the hope of future networking opportunities.

- Think about your recipient's in-box inflow. Target your audience carefully and only approach media if the topic is appropriate. Get to know your media contacts via networking opportunities to help target and tailor your releases. Try to personalize your E-mail as much as possible.

- Provide your best possible copy to ensure accurate, timely, and possibly verbatim use of your release. Make sure you have addressed the questions "who, what, where, when, why."

- When sending your E-mail release to multiple recipients, never use the Cc field. If you use the Cc field, many unfortunate recipients will receive your entire distribution list, which can take up a large portion of your thread (they may not even scroll down to your message!). Furthermore, it is not proper netiquette to send such a lengthy header. If you have to use the Bcc (blind carbon copy) field or better yet, prepare individual E-mails (my preferred method).

Publicity via Discussion Forum

Active involvement with discussion forums and Usenet can prove to be an excellent way to promote yourself, your Web site, and your firm on an interactive and ongoing basis. This section provides the best way to use discussion forums to your advantage.

- Participate. Choose a handful of discussion forums and maintain an active presence by posting. Your forum action should be in the form of both answering as well as asking questions. This interactivity will surely bring some exposure to your Web site and your firm.

- Provide valuable content. When you make a post to a discussion forum, provide content that others will appreciate and will refer to. Maybe you have resources posted on your Web site that will answer a poster's question. Instead of merely providing a link to your page, include some content at the forum such as background information, the general solution, and where the reader can receive a more in-depth explanation (i.e., your Web site).

- Consider promotion information only in signature. This is the approach I have chosen when I interact at discussion forums. For me, discussion forums should be used to provide information and should never be used to blatantly advertise your wares (see the last pointer for how to avoid flames). When you provide helpful content, readers will often look for your signature to see who contributed as well as visit your Web site for additional information. Signatures should include your name, E-mail address, Web site address, and can include a very brief description of your business.

- Moderate. When you are chosen to moderate a discussion forum, you are granted instant credibility. When a Web site organization bestows this honor on you, you should not pass up this opportunity. Yes, there is a time commitment, however you stand to bring potential business your way. In addition, you will be a virtual inductee into a select group of professionals that is helping to mold and form the accounting and financial Internet community. Even though you won't be advertising your wares in this capacity, you will be building name recognition among your peers. Most formal moderated discussion forums provide a brief bio of each moderator and usually include a link to the moderator's Web site.

- Find appropriate groups. Don't waste your time lurking among discussion groups that are either inactive or inapplicable to the services you provide. Also, consider the purpose you are trying to accomplish when visiting a forum. For example, a forum of your own peers is an effective way to build your network. Interacting at a commercial site could potentially bring you new clients, or at another professional site (e.g., American Bar Association) could help you build relationships with other professionals.

- Avoid flames. The possibility of a flame should always remain in the forefront of your mind. Consider those who will be reading your post. If you were them, would you enjoy reading it, or would your be put off? To avoid flames, exercise care when making a post. If you are new to the forum, lurk (read but do not post) for a while to get a flavor for the posts made to date. Double-check the subject matter. Does your posting fit in? Are there similar posts that may be construed as redundant? Keep your messages concise, and when replying, only include the portions of the reply thread you plan to address in your post.

Publicity via Content Submission

Another way to drum up publicity about yourself is to offer your talent in the form of content submissions. Many Web sites, niche portals, and online newsletters provide articles contributed by those in the accounting and financial community. Write an article that hasn't been covered and is a topic in which you have expertise. Tap into your online network to offer your article in exchange for a short bio and a link to your Web site. Once your article is published online, you should provide the article in your online library to show your media contacts where you have been published.

Publicity Resources

The following resources are geared to help you learn more about online publicity and find potential media contacts.

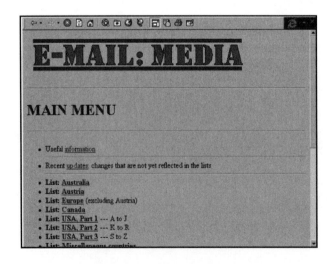

Peter Gugerell's Medialist

http://www.ping.at/gugerell/media/

This site is from Vienna, Austria, and is an excellent listing of E-mail addresses of the media. It includes hundreds of U.S. addresses.

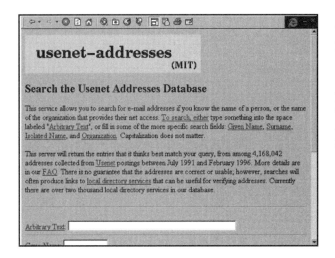

MIT Usenet E-mail Addresses

http://usenet-addresses.mit.edu/

This resource helps you track down the E-mail addresses of mainstream media contacts. The search for E-mail addresses is via Usenet postings. Try searching nbc.com and look at what you get.

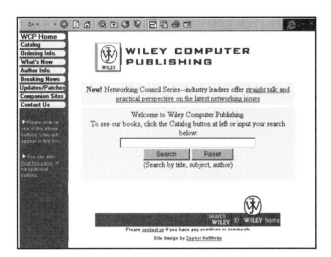

Publicity on the Internet

http://www.wiley.com/compbooks

This is a Web site that publishes updates and resources for the Steve O'Keefe book, *Publicity on the Internet*.

CREATING MAXIMUM PRODUCTIVITY AND INTERCONNECTIVITY

HIT THE EFFICIENT FRONTIER WITH AN INTRANET

Introduction

So you are all set for the Internet. Now it's time to explore the possibility of an intranet. This chapter will guide you through the intranet maze and answer questions as to what is involved, how much it costs, how you set one up, what the common pitfalls are, security issues, and most importantly, what you can do with an intranet.

Firms small and large are considering intranets. Some think intranets are just for large firms, however, in the near future intranets will be an integral part of an accounting firm's processing of information and will prove to be a powerful and cost-effective addition to your in-house resources.

What Is an Intranet? What Is an Extranet?

An intranet is like a local- or wide-area network that allows users to navigate through network information in a browser environment. Intranets are based on Internet technology, so employees that are familiar with browsing on the web should feel very comfortable in an intranet environment. However, some of the connection issues are different than the Internet. Next we will explore what is involved in establishing an intranet.

Basically, an intranet involves building a library of resources. It's one giant repository for your employees and, if you choose, your clients to access. It involves special software and hardware, and also a sense of organization, simple design, and quick access to accurate information.

When organizations extend part of its intranet to users outside the company, it is referred as an extranet. Extranets can be established to share information among clients, vendors, and other business partners. Companies can use extranets to conduct EDI (Electronic Data Interchange) transactions, share exclusive product catalogs and price lists among customers, and perform joint collaboration efforts with other business partners. For more information on extranet development, read the "Extranet

White Paper" prepared by OneSoft Corporation at http://www.onesoft.com/ and "Extranet—a reference page" at http://www.netg.se/~kerfor/extranet.htm.

Can You Afford an Intranet?

Before you start adding zeros behind the cost of your intranet, you must first decide how dedicated your organization is to not only initiating this venture but maintaining an ever-growing body of content. Change is difficult to manage and some are reluctant to learn new technologies. However, with the appropriate level of investment, both in time and money, you can reap big benefits from using an intranet. The following demonstrates the potential costs savings phases you may encounter when building and further developing your intranet:

Phase 1

Post company information that was previously printed and/or mailed to employees such as phone directories, policy manuals, newsletters, and internal reports.

Phase 2

Connect your intranet to the Internet. Capabilities: E-commerce, virtual private networks (VPN's), Internet EDI, and virtual business alliances. Higher costs are incurred at this level primarily due to security needs.

Phase 3

Communication and information sharing. Booz, Allen & Hamilton International has documented that using its intranet to acquaint new hires has been more successful and much quicker than traditional training methods.

You may wonder how much an intranet will cost you. The boilerplate answer is it depends. The cost will largely depend upon how much traffic you expect, your desired intranet configuration, and your future expected capacity requirements. Use the Intranet Suggested Configurations Chart and the Intranet Uses Laundry List which appear later in this chapter to help you with the cost/benefit trade-off analysis you will need to perform and to pin down your actual intranet development cost.

Obstacles and Pitfalls to Intranet Development and Maintenance

Before you build and implement your intranet, you should be cognizant of the typical roadblocks that stand in your way:

Common Development Obstacles and Opportunities

Roadblock	Opportunity
• Inability to convince employees to use the intranet consistently to improve performance.	• Opportunity to engage in dialogue with potential end-users during the design stage about what they need from the system.
• Lack of management buy-in support.	• Opportunity to understand from a manager's perspective what internal and external forces are driving change within the organization and how managers perceive their ideas.
• Cultural barriers.	• Opportunity to identify what is required to improve the organization's current work culture (i.e., from a "knowledge-hoarding" to a "knowledge-sharing" culture).
• Pressure to demonstrate short-term success.	• Opportunity to start small and demonstrate value, instead of overcommitting and underperforming. • Opportunity to use metrics and measurements to demonstrate need, and then to assess whether you have created a value-added system.

Source: Clnet, *Intranet Development Road Map* (http://builder.cnet.com/).

Common Implementation Pitfalls

- Not necessarily a pitfall, developing applications for an intranet may be a little trickier than buying the software and hardware. Most intranets start out as "read-only" and eventually evolve into programs and forms that are more interactive.
- Not carving out resources for the management and maintenance of the intranet. Once it has been built, that is only the beginning. Just like any Web site you visit online, it's only as good as its content.

Internet and Intranet Servers: Suggested Configurations

Finding the right server for the right job can be half the server-acquisition battle. The below table provides you with a configuration match-based on your traffic and budget level:

	Low Traffic Low Budget	**Medium Traffic Moderate Budget**	**High Traffic Big Budget**
Minimum CPU(s)	Pentium Pro-200 or Pentium II-233	2 to 4 Pentium II-233s; or at least one Alpha-300; or at least one SPARC-150	At least 4 Pentium II-300s; 1 to 6 Alpha-500s; 1 to 64 SPARC-200s
Cache	512K	512K per CPU	512K to 1MB per CPU
RAM	64MB to 128MB	64MB to 128MB per CPU	128MB per CPU
Storage Devices	One 4GB or larger SCSI drive	2 to 4 GB SCSI drives	One or more RAID-5 10GB or larger SCSI array(s)
Networking	10 or 100 mbps Ethernet	100 mbps Ethernet	100 mbps Ethernet, FDDI, ATM, or faster
Power	Single power supply	Single power supply with redundant backup	Multiple power supplies with redundant backups
Remote Tools	None	Performance metrics, error notify, remote reboot, dial-up access	Performance metrics, error notify, remote reboot, dial-up access, separate power source (battery), power cycling, temperature probe
Other	Local backup device	Backup scheme local or over network	Network-based backup scheme

Source: Clnet, *How to Buy a Server* (http://www.computers.com/).

Firewalls and Security Issues

Many firms are reluctant to build an intranet due to reasonable security concerns. Although it's always important to be conservative, especially when approached with the prospect of providing access to very confidential and firm-precious information, it is also important to start checking into several security options that are available. The next section will discuss the risks involved with intranets and what you do when you want to mix the Internet and an intranet.

A firewall is "a set of related programs, located at a network gateway server, that protects the resources of a private network from users from other networks" (Source: whatis.com). A firewall works behind the server's router program to filter all network packages. The firewall applications determine to forward or reject the packages.

To fully understand the issues that face accountants from a security standpoint, you will need much more than what is contained in the pages of this book. As such, I would like to point you in the direction of two book resources especially tailored for accounting and finance professionals.

CPA's Guide to Intranets by John Graves, Kent Information Services *Synopsis:* Co-published with the AICPA, this title shows CPAs how an Intranet site can enhance corporate administration and cut costs. The CD-ROM contains all the software necessary to construct an intranet site, along with videos that take users step by step through the process.

It is available at Amazon.com and the AICPA.

CPA's Guide to Information Security by John Graves, Kent Information Services *Synopsis:* This book not only describes information security risks and threats, but also provides tools for protecting information assets. The CD-ROM contains exclusive video content on using the wisely available PGP encryption tool to protect information assets, plus PGP and other standard Internet software packages.

It is available at Amazon.com and the AICPA.

Additional Firewall Resources Keeping Your Site Comfortably Secure: An Introduction to Internet Firewalls at http://csrc.ncsl.nist.gov/nistpubs/800-10/; Internet Firewalls Frequently Asked Questions at http://www.clark.net/pub/mjr/pubs/fwfaq/; General Firewall White Paper at http://www.ntresearch.com/firewall.htm.

Introduction to Virtual Private Networks

A Virtual Private Network, or VPN, is a private data network that utilizes the public telecommunication infrastructure. A VPN can be compared to that of owned or leased telephone lines where companies entrust the security of their telephone communications networks to outside parties. Companies today are looking at using private virutal networks for both extranets and wide-area intranets.

VPNs are more complex than establishing a firewall in that it uses "end-to-end tunneling," a methodology that ensures safe passage of the entire packet payload (data contents) through Internet encryption in addition to securing the source and destination addresses. One of the primary distinctions is that a firewall filters technology whereas VPNs use next generation encryption technology. For more information on VPNs, read Daniel Gasparro's article, "Charting the Data VPN Movement," at http://www.teledotcom.com/.

> **➡ Quick Note: The Intranet Uses Laundry List**
>
> Here's a laundry list of what you can do with an intranet:
>
> - Link together satellite offices
> - Give remote access to field staff
> - Offer telecommuting options
> - Store personnel manuals
> - Access forms
> - Access articles
> - Publish firm calendar
> - Provide interactive firm directory
> - Launch an extranet or VPN (see below)
> - Provide document retention and management
> - Store client databases
>
> - House audit policy, workpapers, and QC documents
> - Webcast tax updates
> - Conduct data mining (see Chapter 21)—extract useful management reports and discover trends from large volumes of financial data
> - Administer 401(k) plan management
> - Create employee bulletin boards
> - Scan and store newsletters from trade associations
> - Create interactive tax return approval process
> - Provide billing reports and contact management
> - House Power Point presentations
> - Maintain checklists library

Additional Research Resources

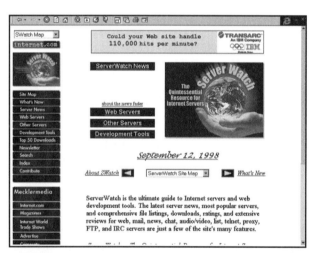

ServerWatch

http://serverwatch.internet.com/

ServerWatch is a complete guide to Internet servers and Web development tools. The site includes the latest server news and provides reviews of the most popular servers and server software applications.

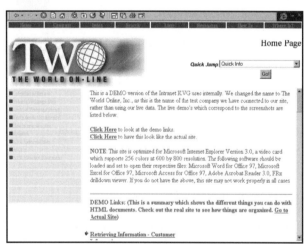

KVG—Knight, Vale & Gregory, CPA's

http://207.220.114.50/Intranet/

KVG provides an excellent intranet demo. This site is a great way to see what an intranet can look like and its potential functionality.

Chapter 21

IDEAS TO HELP YOU WORK FASTER AND SMARTER

Introduction

This chapter may be a bit of a misnomer. I think you would agree that things are moving pretty fast these days, including yourself, so how could you possible move faster? I don't think I could. But every once in a while I find a tool that helps me work smarter which usually generates faster results. After all, one of my primary objectives to working smarter is to save time. Maybe some of the ideas in this chapter will enable to you spend more time doing what you want to do (golf anyone?).

Untraditional Networking

Ideas and information flourishes on the Internet. Why don't you supplement your current networking endeavors and tap into this online wealth of knowledge and contacts by networking on the Internet?

One easy way to get started is to visit some of the accounting and Web sites in the Directory and join their discussion forums and chats. It's true that online networking is faceless, but as a supplement to your normal networking efforts, it can enrich your network of contacts.

E-mail is another way to network. Meet people at events and conferences and follow-up with E-mails. There are also formal E-mail directories online. For instance, the AuditNet E-mail Directory (http://www.cowan.edu.au/mra/home.htm) helps auditors find individuals in their area of interest or industry including, credit union, airline, healthcare, pension, and others.

Intranets as a Knowledge Base

There is a current interest in company knowledge management, which refers to exploiting aggregated and new information about competitors, customers, technologies, and themselves to its competitive advantage. Companies such as WavePhore (http://www.wavephore.com) are sprouting up to help businesses incorporate the technology necessary to create Knowledge Bases on their intranets.

You will hear the term knowledge management more and more in the years to come as companies attempt to explore their internal knowledge capabilities and best practices. Firms will be using knowledge management as a competitive advantage as well as a way to differentiate themselves. Intranets enable the sharing of information, a key ingredient to successful knowledge base.

Client Resource Center

Sometimes clients want to be able to quickly access the information they need without talking to you (yes, this can happen). Decide on which resources are best suited for minimal client interaction and provide this information in a client-only password protected portion of your Web site. Start with content you currently mail to them via snail-mail. You may opt to still mail this information, but what about including more value by having the information online as well? Start with an online version of your firm's client newsletter. You can make it even more interactive than just uploading the text by including hyperlinks to the resources referenced throughout your newsletter.

Create a client-only discussion forum. Get together professionals from other fields (e.g., law) and disciplines and provide clients a place to network and ask questions. You can invite industry experts to join your discussions as needed. Consider appointing various individuals within your firm to moderate certain aspects of the forum in order to tap into their expertise and elicit overall firm participation.

Webcasting for Information Dissemination

If you have time-sensitive information you need to share with many individuals, either internally or externally, you may want to consider Webcasting alternatives.

To reach those at your firm, incorporate Webcasting with your intranet. There are several Webcasting products available on the market (see Chapter 4) that load onto your Web server. Usually these programs use a channel-type interface, and you can determine which channels to pre-select. To conduct your own Webcasting, the programs guide you through the development of your own channels through which you can then "push" firm news, client industry information, and your region's business environment. By Webcasting meaningful information through the Firm's intranet, you can provide a consistent message to all and provide information each individual would have had to find on his/her own.

You can also use Webcasting to reach the general public. Companies are starting to use a specific form of Webcasting called Reportcasting. Reportcasting involves using financial report information for reuse and distribution to a selected audience (i.e., inter-department, auditors, vendors, customers, etc.). Below is the how the Reportcasting workflow might look like:

1. Define and save financial report formats for reuse.

2. Bundle reports into "packs" if required for specific audiences.

3. Schedule production of reports/packs to audience needs and subscription preferences.

4. Output reports to HTML or other Web-compatible format.

5. Move reports to intranet server and into specific channel locations.

6. Use push channel to notify clients of new reports and to view content, or

7. Use subscription to automate file download and view reports off-line.

Reportcasting will most likely become an acceptable and preferred method of disseminating periodic financial information. Its flexibility, tailoring features, and Web-based format will provide a venue in which any user will be able to easily navigate and analyze financial results. You'll need the following software resources to perform Reportcasting, including a push-enabled report writer, Web browser (IE 4.0 and Netscape Communicator 4.0 are both push-enabled), and Push software (for example, PointCast and Castinet). To obtain more information about push-enabled report writers, visit the following vendors:

Vendor	Product	Web Site
Actuate Software Corp.	Actuate Reporting System 3.0	http://www.actuate.com
Seagate Software Inc.	Crystal Info 5.0	http://www.seagatesoftware.com
SQRIBE Technologies	SQRIBE, Power SQRIBE	http://www.sqribe.com

Source: "Tuning In to Web-Based Push Reporting," *Controller* magazine, May 1998.

Legacy Data Wizards

Companies big and small still have legacy data issues. If you have worked with mini computers such as IBM AS/400s, then you know what it is like to use terminal emulation. Finding that one bit of data for which you have been looking can take what it seems like forever, when paging through layers of emulation screens.

Good news! Help is on the way. The reign of the green screen may be over. There is a myriad of next generation terminal emulation software that allows screen changes to be made in minutes, not hours, and a few of these resources allow you to access your legacy data from a browser. If you are looking for additional information about this software, read on.

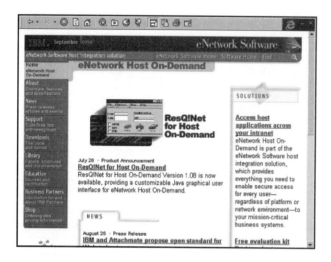

IBM Host on Demand

http://www.software.ibm.com/enetwork/hostondemand/

With Host on Demand, each type of session has a template to help you set up a new session. The software supports scaleable fonts and incorporates an easy-to-use, flexible, and customizable user interface.

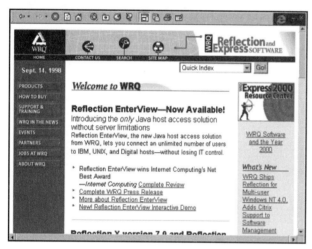

Walker Richer and Quinn Reflection InterView

http://www.wrq.com/

Reflection InterView is known for its ease of deployment and ease of use. An HTML generator gives administrators the ability to tie legacy data to the companies' Web pages.

PalmPilot Internet Resources

3Com's PalmPilot has really taken off. And rightly so, this small piece of hardware can be your window to the world when you are in remote locations without access to a computer. The latest version, the PalmIII, has integrated E-mail composition and viewing, and with its modem add-on accessory, you can retrieve E-mail from remote locations. Earlier versions of the PalmPilot require special software and a modem for E-mail functionality.

The Palm Computing Platform has an extremely strong software development following. You can get software applications that allow you to send faxes or browse the Web. With additional hardware you can even surf the information highway wirelessly. Looking for a little reading material? There is a substantial amount of text available for installation onto your PalmPilot, ranging from CNN Daily News to full-text books. I haven't even mentioned the hundreds of Web sites devoted to sharing PalmPilot applications, tips, and resources.

For additional Palm Pilot resources, visit 3Com's PalmPilot page at http://www.palm.com. In addition, check out The Pilot Zone (http://www.palmpilotzone.com) for over five hundred free applications that include calculators, communication, productivity, reference, and utility tools.

Mining Your Data

Extracting data from your system or data mining is quickly becoming a popular way to get more from your financial information. Data mining can be an effective way to perform automated analysis and provide value to other departments in your organization. This section explores the two types of mining software that is now the market to help you strike gold.

There are two types of data mining software: database mining software and report mining software. Database mining software queries large-volume transactional databases whereas report mining software is designed to create analytical and summary reports derived from interrogated data.

Report data mining utilizes conditional statements (i.e., if (rule)/then (action) statements) as well as constraints. An example of this would be if an item on-hand falls below an established level, and E-mail would be sent to the purchasing manager.

Data mining can be used to extract useful management reports and discover trends from large volumes of financial data, namely building profiles (e.g., bad risk customers), establishing correlations (e.g., between sales and season), and predicting behavior (e.g., which products sell first in economic downturn). Report mining is likened to the statistical analysis of data. This technology can also be used with legacy systems, which is a big plus since many legacy systems can only store and print particular files and analysis features are minimal. Using data mining software rule-driven agents can analyze report print files and extract predetermined into flexible databases and files.

Most accounting software has no specific data mining capabilities built in (at least for now); you'll have to settle on stand-alone software to tap into your data mine:

Data Mining Product	Vendor	Website
KnowledgeSEEKER	Angoss Software	http://www.angoss.com/
Scenario, 4Thought	Cognos	http://www.cognos.com/
DataMind Data Cruncher	DataMind	http://www.datamindcorp.com/
Intelligent Miner	IBM	http://www.software.ibm.com/
Darwin	Thinking Machines Corp.	http://www.think.com/
Report Analysis		
Cambio	Data Junction Corp.	http://www.datajunction.com/
Monarch	Datawatch	http://www.datawatch.com/
DataImport	Spalding Software	http://www.spaldingsoft.com/

Meetings Without Walls

There will always be a need and a function for meeting face to face. However, under some circumstances, long-distance flights, scheduling nightmares, and an overtaxed travel budget don't seem to make sense. Furthermore, late-breaking issues and the need for immediate decisions do not always give the luxury of a face-to-face discussion. New technologies are rapidly evolving which make online conferencing and paging more of a practical reality. These products are providing new ways to remotely conduct group meetings, file sharing, brainstorming sessions, and networked calendaring.

The following table provides a quick look at the various collaborative software resources on the market. A few of the applications mentioned have not merged onto the Internet, however, each of the technologies below will eventually be primarily Web- or intranet-based to incorporate full remote functionality.

Product	Vendor	Web Site	Use/Application
File Exchange/Application Sharing			
Face to Face	Crosswise	http://www.crosswise.com	A cross between application sharing and whiteboarding.
Internet Conference Suite	VocalTec Ltd.	http://www.vocaltec.com	Application sharing and Internet telephony.
Netopia	Farallon Communications	http://www.farallon.com	Client-based point-to-point file exchange, application sharing, and chat.
Whiteboarding			
Ibid	MicroTouch Systems, Inc.	http://www.microtouch.com	Whiteboard distribution of brainstorming sessions.
Microsoft NetMeeting	Microsoft Corp.	http://www.microsoft.com	Multiple-use product that includes whiteboarding, Internet telephony, application sharing, and file transfer.
Simplicity	Paradise Software Inc.	http://www.paradise.com	High-end whiteboard solution. Also handles videoconferencing, and includes necessary hardware.
Groupware/Document Management			
GroupWise	Novell Inc.	http://www.novell.com	Includes E-mail and document management.
Livelink Intranet	Open Text Corp.	http://www.opentext.com	Supports project home pages that include document control and threaded messaging.
Lotus Notes Corp.	Lotus Development	http://www.lotus.com	Currently has calendaring, E-mail, and whiteboarding features.

Source: "Meetings Without Walls," *Internet World*, October 1997.

Appendix

NETIQUETTE GUIDE

This guide is based on excerpts from *The Net: User Guidelines and Netiquette* by Arlene Rinaldi, Florida Atlantic University. You can find the complete guide at: **http://www.fau.edu/rinaldi/netiquette.html**. The self-proclaimed "I'm Not the Miss Manners of the Net" had received several awards for her useful resource on the do's and don'ts of Internet etiquette.

Electronic Mail and Files

The content and maintenance of a user's electronic mailbox is the user's responsibility:

- Check E-mail daily and remain within your limited disk quota.
- Delete unwanted messages immediately since they take up disk storage.
- Keep messages remaining in your electronic mailbox to a minimum.
- Mail messages can be downloaded or extracted to files then to disks for future reference.
- Never assume that your E-mail can be read by no one except yourself; others may be able to read or access your mail. Never send or keep anything that you would mind seeing on the evening news.

The content and maintenance of a user's disk storage area is the users responsibility:

- Keep files to a minimum. Files should be downloaded to your personal computer's hard drive or to diskettes.
- Routinely and frequently virus-scan your system, especially when receiving or downloading files from other systems to prevent the spread of a virus.
- Your files may be accessible by persons with system privileges, so do not maintain anything private in your disk storage area.

Anonymous FTP—File Transfer Protocol

- Users should respond to the PASSWORD prompt with their E-mail address, so if that site chooses, it can track the level of FTP usage. If your E-mail address causes an error, enter GUEST for the next PASSWORD prompt.

- When possible limit downloads, especially large downloads (1 Meg+), for after normal business hours locally and for the remote FTP host, preferably late in the evening.

- Adhere to time restrictions as requested by archive sites. Think in terms of the current time at the site that's being visited, not of local time.

- Copy downloaded files to your personal computer hard drive or disks to remain within disk quota.

- When possible, inquiries to Archie should be in mail form.

- It's the user's responsibility when downloading programs to check for copyright or licensing agreements. If the program is beneficial for your use, pay any authors' registration fee. If there is any doubt, don't copy it; there have been many occasions on which copyrighted software has found its way into FTP archives. Support for any downloaded programs should be requested from the originator of the application. Remove unwanted programs from your systems.

Electronic Communications

(E-mail, LISTSERV groups, Mailing lists, and Usenet)

- Under United States law, it is unlawful "to use any telephone facsimile machine, computer, or other device to send an unsolicited advertisement" to any "equipment which has the capacity (A) to transcribe text or images (or both) from an electronic signal received over a regular telephone line onto paper." The law allows individuals to sue the sender of such illegal "junk mail" for $500 per copy. Most states will permit such actions to be filed in Small Claims Court. This activity is termed "spamming" on the Internet.

- Never give your user ID or password to another person. System administrators that need to access your account for maintenance or to correct problems will have full privileges to your account.

- Keep paragraphs and messages short and to the point.

- When quoting another person, edit out whatever isn't directly applicable to your reply. Don't let your mailing or Usenet software automatically quote the entire body of messages you are replying to when it's not necessary. Take the time to edit any quotations down to the minimum necessary to provide context for your reply. Nobody likes reading a long message in quotes for the third or fourth time, only to be followed by a one-line response: "Yeah, me too."

- Focus on one subject per message and always include a pertinent subject title for the message; that way the user can locate the message quickly.

- Don't use the academic networks for commercial or proprietary work.

- Include your signature at the bottom of E-mail messages when communicating with people who may not know you personally or broadcasting to a dynamic group of subscribers.

- Your signature footer should include your name, position, affiliation, and Internet and/or BITNET addresses and should not exceed more than four lines. Optional information could include your address and phone number.

- Capitalize words only to highlight an important point or to distinguish a title or heading. Capitalizing whole words that are not titles is generally termed as SHOUTING!

- *Asterisks* surrounding a word can be used to make a stronger point.

- Use the underscore symbol before and after the title of a book, e.g., _The Wizard of Oz_.

- Limit line length to approximately 65–70 characters and avoid control characters.

- Never send chain letters through the Internet. Sending them can cause the loss of your Internet access.

- Because of the international nature of the Internet and the fact that most of the world uses the following format for listing dates, i.e., MM DD YY, please be considerate and avoid misinterpretation of dates by listing dates, including the spelled-out month, e.g., 24 JUN 96 or JUN 24 96.

- Follow chain of command procedures for corresponding with superiors. For example, don't send a complaint via E-mail directly to the "top" just because you can.

- Be professional and careful what you say about others. E-mail is easily forwarded.

- Cite all quotes, references, and sources and respect copyright and license agreements.

- It is considered extremely rude to forward personal E-mail to mailing lists or Usenet without the original author's permission.

- Attaching return receipts to a message may be considered an invasion of privacy.

- Be careful when using sarcasm and humor. Without face-to-face communications your joke may be viewed as criticism. When being humorous, use emoticons to express humor. (Tilt your head to the left to see the emoticon smile.) :-) = happy face for humor.

- Acronyms can be used to abbreviate when possible, however messages that are filled with acronyms can be confusing and annoying to the reader. Examples: IMHO= in my humble/honest opinion; FYI = for your information; BTW = by the way; and Flame = antagonistic criticism.

Listservs, Mailing Lists, and Discussion Groups

Some mailing lists have low rates of traffic, others can flood your mailbox with several hundred mail messages per day. Numerous incoming messages from various listservers or mailing lists by multiple users requires extensive system processing which can tie up valuable resources. Subscriptions to interest groups or discussion lists should be kept to a minimum and should not exceed what your disk quota can handle, or you for that matter.

- When you join a list, monitor the messages for a few days to get a feel for what common questions are asked, and what topics are deemed off-limits. This is commonly referred to as "lurking." Only when you feel comfortable with the group, should you start posting.

- See if there is a FAQ (Frequently Asked Questions) for a group that you are interested in joining. Veteran members get annoyed when they see the same questions every few weeks, or at the start of each semester.

- Follow any and all guidelines that the listowner has posted; the listowner establishes the local "netiquette" standards for her/his list.

- Keep in mind that some discussion lists or Usenet groups have members from many countries.

- Don't assume that they will understand a reference to TV, movies, pop culture, or current events in your country. If you must use the reference, please explain it.

- Don't assume that they understand geographical references that are local or national.

- Don't join a list just to post inflammatory messages; this upsets most system administrators and you could lose access to the net ("mail bombing").

- Keep your questions and comments relevant to the focus of the discussion group.

- If another person posts a comment or question that is off the subject, do *not* reply to the list and keep the off-subject conversation going publicly.

- When someone posts an off-subject note, and someone else criticizes that posting, you should *not* submit a gratuitous note saying, "Well, I liked it, and lots of people probably did as well, and you guys ought to lighten up and not tell us to stick to the subject."

- When going away for more than a week, unsubscribe or suspend mail from any mailing lists or LISTSERV services.

- If you can respond to someone else's question, do so through E-mail. Twenty people answering the same question on a large list can fill your mailbox (and those of everyone else on the list) quickly.

- Use discretion when forwarding a long mail message to group addresses or distribution lists. It's preferable to reference the source of a document and provide instructions on how to obtain a copy. If you must post a long message, warn the readers with a statement at the top of the mail message. Example: WARNING: LONG MESSAGE.

- If you cross-post messages to multiple groups, include the name of the groups at the top of the mail message with an apology for any duplication.

- Resist the temptation to "flame" others on the list. Remember that these discussions are "public" and meant for constructive exchanges. Treat the others on the list as you would want them to treat you.

- When posting a question to the discussion group, request that responses be directed to you personally. Post a summary or answer to your question to the group.

- When replying to a message posted to a discussion group, check the address to be certain it's going to the intended location (person or group). It can be very embarrassing if they reply incorrectly and post a personal message to the entire discussion group that was intended for an individual.

- When signing up for a group, it is important to save your subscription confirmation letter for reference. That way if you go on vacation, you will have the subscription address for suspending mail.

- Use your own personal E-mail account; don't subscribe using a shared office account.

- Occasionally subscribers to the list who are not familiar with proper netiquette will submit requests to SUBSCRIBE or UNSUBSCRIBE directly to the list itself. Be tolerant of this activity, and possibly provide some useful advice as opposed to being critical.

- Other people on the list are not interested in your desire to be added or deleted. Any requests regarding administrative tasks such as being added or removed from a list should be made to the appropriate area, not the list itself. Mail for these types of requests should be sent to the following respectively:

  LISTSERV GROUPS—LISTSERV@host

  MAILING LISTS—listname-REQUEST@host or listname-
     OWNER@host

For either Mailing Lists or LISTSERV groups, to subscribe or unsubscribe, in the body of the message include:

  SUBSCRIBE listname yourfirstname yourlastname (To be added to the
     subscription) or UNSUBSCRIBE listname (To be removed from the
     subscription)

World Wide Web

- Do not include very large graphic images in your HTML documents. It is preferable to have postage-sized images that the user can click on to "enlarge" a picture. Some users with access to the Web are viewing documents using slow speed modems and downloading these images can take a great deal of time.

- It is not a requirement to ask permission to link to another's site, though, out of respect for the individual and his or her efforts, a simple E-mail message stating that you have made a link to the site would be appropriate.

- When including video or voice files, include next to the description a file size, (i.e., 10KB or 2MB), so the user has the option of knowing how long it will take to download the file.

- Keep naming standards for URLs simple and not overly excessive. Some users do not realize that sites are case-sensitive. They might receive URLs verbally where case sensitivity is not easily recognizable.

- When in doubt about a URL, try accessing the domain address first, then navigate through the site to locate the specific URL. Most URLs begin with the node address of WWW followed by the site address, for example, http://www.ibm.com and http://www.fau.edu.

- A URL that includes only an image map and no text might not be accessible to those users who do not have access to a graphical Web browser. Always include the option of text links in your URL documents.

- W3 connections can be *very* high bandwidth consumers. With graphical web browsers, when graphic images are not necessary to obtain information, it is a good idea, both in terms of the speed of the session, and to conserve bandwidth, to set the options to "turn off" or "delay" inline images.

- URL authors should always protect their additions to the Web by including trademark (™) or copyright (©) symbols in their HTML documents.

- URL authors should include an E-mail address at the bottom (or in the address area) of all HTML documents. Because of the nature of HTML links, a user can automatically link to your HTML document and have questions about it, but will not know who to contact if the E-mail address is not available.

- Including the actual URL in the document source, preferably after the <Address> tag, will allow users who print out the information to know where to access the information in the future, e.g., URL—http://www.fau.edu/rinaldi/net/web.html.

- URL's authors should always include a date of last revision, so users linking to the site can know how up to date the information has been maintained.

- Infringement of copyright laws, as well as obscene, harassing, or threatening materials on Web sites can be in violation of local, state, national or international laws and can be subject to litigation by the appropriate law enforcement agency. Authors of HTML documents will ultimately be responsible for what they allow users worldwide to access.

The Ten Commandments for Computer Ethics

Below is a list of commandments from the Computer Ethics Institute:

1. Thou shalt not use a computer to harm other people.

2. Thou shalt not interfere with other people's computer work.

3. Thou shalt not snoop around in other people's files.

4. Thou shalt not use a computer to steal.

5. Thou shalt not use a computer to bear false witness.

6. Thou shalt not use or copy software for which you have not paid.

7. Thou shalt not use other people's computer resources without authorization.

8. Thou shalt not appropriate other people's intellectual output.

9. Thou shalt think about the social consequences of the program you write.

10. Thou shalt use a computer in ways that show consideration and respect.

GLOSSARY OF INTERNET TERMS

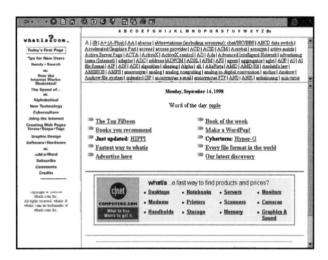

Internet Terms by whatis.com

http://whatis.com/

Whatis.com has graciously authorized the reprint of several of its Internet term definitions for this glossary. Whatis.com, an online encyclopedia of information, has over 1,500 recently written definition/topics and over ten thousand hyperlinks. It combines the approach of an electronic "pocket reference" with user-controlled knowledge views. I used whatis.com throughout the creation of this book and have found it to be an excellent resource. I highly recommend that you visit it as well as place it in your bookmark list for frequent visits. If you hear a new Internet buzzword, now you know where to go!

anonymous FTP　Using the Internet's File Transfer Protocol (FTP), anonymous FTP is a method for giving users access to files so that they don't need to identify themselves to the server. Using an FTP program or the FTP command interface, the user enters "anonymous" as a user ID. Usually, the password is defaulted or furnished by the FTP server. Anonymous FTP is a common way to get access to a server in order to view or download files that are publicly available.

applet　An applet is a little application program. Prior to the World Wide Web, the built-in writing and drawing programs that came with Windows were sometimes called "applets." On the Web, using Java, the object-oriented programming language, an applet is a small program that can be sent along with a Web page to a user. Java applets can perform interactive animations, immediate calculations, or other simple tasks without having to send a user request back to the server.

Archie Archie is a program that allows you to search the files of all the Internet FTP servers that offer anonymous FTP access for a particular search string. Archie is actually an indexing spider that visits the anonymous FTP sites, reads all the directory and file names, and then indexes them in one large index.

ASP An ASP (Active Server Page) is an HTML page that includes one or more scripts (small embedded programs) that are processed on a Microsoft Web server before the page is sent to the user. An ASP is somewhat similar to a server-side include or a Common Gateway Interface (CGI) application in that it involves small application programs that run on the server, usually tailoring a page for the user. The method or convention for passing data back and forth between the server and the application is called the *common gateway interface*. It is part of the Web's HTTP protocol.

backbone In a network, a backbone is a larger transmission line that carries data gathered from smaller lines that interconnect with it. There are generally two levels of backbone. (1) At the local level, a backbone is a line or set of lines that local area networks connect to for a wide area network connection or within a local area network to span distances efficiently (e.g., between buildings). (2) On the Internet or other wide area network, a backbone is a set of paths that local or regional networks connect to for long-distance interconnection. The connection points are known as network nodes or telecommunication data switching exchanges.

bandwidth Bandwidth most frequently means how much data can be transmitted how quickly over a telecommunication path. A synonym is data rate. Formally, the bandwidth of a transmitted communications signal is a measure of the range of frequencies the signal occupies.

boolean The term "boolean," often encountered when doing searches on the Web, refers to a system of logical thought developed by the English mathematician and computer pioneer, George Boole (1815-64). In boolean searching, an "and" operator between two words or other values (e.g., "pear AND apple") means one is searching for documents containing both of the words or values, not just one of them. An "or" operator between two words or other values (e.g., "pear OR apple") means one is searching for documents containing either of the words.

bot A bot (short for "robot") is a program that operates as an agent for a user or another program or simulates a human activity. On the Internet the most ubiquitous bots are the programs, also called spiders or crawlers, that access Web sites and gather their content for search engine indexes. A chatterbot is a program that can simulate talk with a human being. One of the first and most famous chatterbots (prior to the Web) was Eliza, a program that pretended to be a psychotherapist and answered questions with other questions. Shallow Red is a program that can be customized to answer questions from users seeking service for a product. Shopbots are programs that shop around the Web on your behalf and locate the best price for a product you're looking for. There are also bots such as OpenSesame that observe a user's patterns in navigating a Web site and customize the site for that user.

browser   A browser is a program that provides a way to look at, read, and even hear all the information on the World Wide Web. "Browser" originated prior to the Web as a generic term for user interfaces that let you browse text files online. When the first Web browser with a graphical user interface was invented (it was called Mosaic), the term seemed to apply to Web content, too. Technically, a Web browser is a client program that uses the Hypertext Transfer Protocol (HTTP) to make requests of Web servers throughout the Internet on behalf of the browser user.

burn rate   In venture investing and new company development, the burn rate is the rate at which a new company is spending its capital while waiting for profitable operation. Typically, a new company, especially in new, fast-growing fields such as Internet commerce or publishing, expects in its early stages to spend money faster than it can take in revenue.

chatting   Chatting is talking on the Internet in real time. Usually, this "talking" is the exchange of typed-in messages requiring one site as the repository for the messages (or "chat site") and a group of users who take part from anywhere on the Internet. In some cases, a private chat can be arranged between two parties who meet initially in a group chat. Chats can be ongoing or scheduled for a particular time and duration. Many chats are focused on a particular topic of interest and some involve guest experts or famous people who "talk" to anyone joining the chat. Chats are conducted on online services (especially America Online), by bulletin board services, and by Web sites. Several Web sites exist solely for the purpose of conducting chats. Some chat sites allow participants to assume the role or appearance of an avatar in a simulated or virtual reality environment. Many sites use a system called Internet Relay Chat (IRC).

cookie   A cookie is a special file that a Web site puts on the user's computer hard disk to remember something about that user. The Web's Hypertext Transfer Protocol (HTTP) has no way itself of remembering previous requests. For that reason, it sends the information about the user that it will need later back to the user's own computer for future reference. Web users must agree to let cookies be saved for them, but, in general, it helps Web sites serve the user better. See "Cupcakes" for a newer approach.

cracker   A cracker is someone who breaks into someone else's computer system, often on a network. A cracker can be doing this for profit, maliciously, for some altruistic purpose or cause, or because the challenge is there. Some breaking-and-entering has been done ostensibly to point out weaknesses in a site's security system.

cupcakes   Cupcakes is the name of a technology that allows a Web user to create personal information (name, occupation, professional interests, and so forth) that can be shared with any Web site the user wants to share it with. Like cookies, cupcakes keeps information about you on your own computer's hard disk. However, unlike cookies, you create the file yourself and are always aware of who has permission to look at your personal information and how much they can look at. Cupcakes is made possible by the Open Profiling Standard (OPS), which defines a standard format and content for a user profile.

cybercitizen   A cybercitizen is a "citizen of the Internet" or a member of the "cyber-community." A synonym is netizen.

cyberspace   Cyberspace is the total interconnectedness of human beings through computers and telecommunication without regard to physical geography. William Gibson invented or popularized the term in his 1984 novel, *Neuromancer*.

data mining   Data mining is the analysis of data for relationships that have not previously been discovered. e.g., the sales records for a particular brand of tennis racket might reveal a seasonal correlation with the purchase by the same parties of golf equipment. Data mining results include: (1) Associations, or when one event can be correlated to another event (beer purchasers buy peanuts a certain percentage of the time), (2) Sequences, or one event leading to another later event (a rug purchase followed by a purchase of curtains), (3) Classification, or the recognition of patterns and a resulting new organization of data (e.g., profiles of customers who make purchases), (4) Clustering, or finding and visualizing groups of facts not previously known, and (5) Forecasting, or simply discovering patterns in the data that can lead to predictions about the future.

digital cash   Somewhat similar to prepaid telephone cards, digital cash is electronic money that, after purchase from a bank, is downloaded to your computer's hard disk storage from which it can be then spent incrementally. Theoretically, the money could be spent in very small increments, such as tenths of a cent (U.S.) or less. Two major digital cash systems are Digital Cash and Cybercash.

digital certificate   A digital certificate is an electronic "credit card" that establishes your credentials when doing business or other transactions on the Web. It is issued by a certification authority (CA). It contains: your name, a serial number, expiration dates, a copy of the certificate holder's public key (used for encrypting and decrypting messages and digital signatures), and the digital signature of the certificate-issuing authority so that a recipient can verify that the certificate is real. Some digital certificates conform to a standard, X.509. Digital certificates can be kept in registries so that authenticated users can look up other users' public keys.

domain name   A domain name locates an organization or other entity on the Internet and provides a name for the Internet address that is easier to remember than the Internet address number. For example: www.totalbaseball.com locates an Internet address for "totalbaseball.com" (which is really Internet host 199.0.0.2) and a particular host server named "www." The "com" part of the domain name reflects the purpose of the organization or entity (in this example, "commercial") and is called the top-level domain name. The "totalbaseball" part of the domain name defines the organization or entity and together with the top-level is called the second-level domain name. The second-level domain name maps to and can be thought of as the "readable" version of the Internet address.

downloading   Downloading is the transmission of a file from one computer system to another, usually a smaller computer system. From the Internet user's point-of-view, to download a file is to request it from another computer (or from a Web page on another computer) and to receive it.

Easter egg   An Easter egg is an unexpected surprise, perhaps a message, an image, or a sound, hidden in a Web site or in an application program. Netscape's Navigator browser has hidden a number of Easter eggs behind or among the "About" pages you can get to from the Help pulldown menu. Among these are pictures of Netscape's mascot, Mozilla. Over the years many application developers have hidden more than their names behind rarely-clicked Credit buttons.

E-business   "E-business" ("electronic business," derived from such terms as "E-mail" and "E-commerce") is the conduct of business on the Internet, not only buying and selling but also servicing customers and collaborating with business partners. IBM and other major companies use the term to suggest that the world of business has been changed by the Internet, which is now a place where companies and customers can market products and services, buy supplies from other companies, and especially offer products and take orders online.

E-commerce   "E-commerce" (electronic commerce or EC) is the buying and selling of goods and services on the Internet, especially the World Wide Web. In practice, this term and a new term, E-business, are often used interchangeably. For online retail selling, the term E-tailing is sometimes used.

egosurfing   Egosurfing is looking to see how many places on the Web your name appears. On AltaVista, you can also see how many times it appears in Usenet postings. Simply enter your name surrounded by double quotes in the search field like this: "Clarence McGillicuddy" and you may be surprised to discover that you're a celebrated personage on someone's Web page or that the local task force report you helped write got put on the Web.

emoticon   On the Internet in E-mail, chatting, and posted messages, an emoticon (sometimes referred to as a "smiley") is a short sequence of keyboard letters and symbols, usually emulating a facial expression, expressing a feeling that supplements the message. Most of these emoticons use several symbols to create a small face with an expression such as a smile, wink, or turned-down mouth.

extranet   An extranet is a private network that uses the Internet protocols and the public telecommunication system to securely share part of a business's information or operations with suppliers, vendors, partners, customers, or other businesses. An extranet can be viewed as part of a company's intranet that is extended to users outside the company. The same benefits that HTML, HTTP, SMTP, and other Internet technologies have brought to the Internet and to corporate intranets now seem designed to accelerate business between businesses. An extranet requires security and privacy. These require firewall server management, the issuance and use of digital certificates or similar means of user authentication, encryption of messages, and the use of virtual private networks (VPNs) that tunnel through the public network.

FAQ The FAQ (frequently asked questions, pronounced "fack") or list of "frequently asked questions" (and answers) has become a feature of the Internet. The FAQ seems to have originated in many of the Usenet groups as a way to acquaint new users with the rules.

firewall A firewall is a set of related programs, located at a network gateway server, that protects the resources of a private network from users from other networks. (The term also implies the security policy that is used with the programs.) An enterprise with an intranet that allows its workers access to the wider Internet installs a firewall to prevent outsiders from accessing its own private data resources and for controlling what outside resources its own users have access to.

flamebait On the Internet, flamebait is a "posting" or note on a bulletin board, a Usenet newsgroup, a Web site, or other public forum that is intended to elicit the extremely strong responses characteristic of flaming and active public discussions. To be effective, flamebait should be a bit subtle (but not too subtle) so that potential flamers will "take the bait." This term is similar to troll, which is an effort to get a reaction from readers but not necessarily for the purpose of eliciting flames.

flaming On the Internet, flaming is giving someone a verbal lashing in public. Often this is on a Usenet newsgroup but it could be on a Web forum or perhaps even as E-mail with copies to a distribution list. Unless in response to some rather obvious flamebait, flaming is poor netiquette. Certain issues tend to provoke emphatically stated responses, but flaming is often directed at a self-appointed expert rather than at the issues or information itself and is sometimes directed at unwitting but opinionated newbies who appear in a newsgroup.

FTP FTP (File Transfer Protocol) is the usual way you send files to your server if you have a Web site or receive (download) larger files from someone else's Web site. Using FTP, you can also update (delete, rename, move, and copy) files at a server. FTP is an application protocol that runs top of the TCP/IP protocols, the basic protocols of the Internet that every client and server computer uses. FTP has a user command interface for establishing contact with a server, logging in, and sending, receiving, or otherwise changing files. Or you may install a utility that offers a graphical interface. Many access providers include an FTP utility as part of the set-up.

fuzzy logic   Fuzzy logic is an approach to computing based on "degrees of truth" rather than the usual "true or false" (1 or 0) boolean logic on which the modern computer is based.

GIF   GIF (Graphics Interchange Format) is one of the two most common file formats for graphic images on the World Wide Web. The other is the JPEG.

hacker   (1) According to *The New Hacker's Dictionary*, a widely used reference, a hacker is simply a very capable programmer. The book's compiler, Eric Raymond, lists five connotations for this term as applied to programming. A hacker is a person who enjoys learning details of a programming language or system, enjoys actually doing the programming rather than just theorizing about it, capable of appreciating someone else's hacking, who picks up programming quickly or is an expert at a particular programming language or system. (2) Although Raymond deprecates the use of this term for someone who attempts to crack someone else's system or otherwise uses programming or expert knowledge to act maliciously, hacker is nevertheless widely used in newspaper writing as a synonym for cracker.

HTML   HTML (Hypertext Markup Language) is the set of "markup" symbols or codes inserted in a file intended for display on a World Wide Web browser. The markup tells the Web browser how to display a Web page's words and images for the user.

HTTP   The Hypertext Transfer Protocol (HTTP) is the set of rules for exchanging files (text, graphic images, sound, video, and other multimedia files) on the World Wide Web. Relative to the TCP/IP suite of protocols (which are the basis for information exchange on the Internet), HTTP is an application protocol.

intelligent agent   On the Internet, an intelligent agent (or simply an agent) is a program that gathers information or performs some other service without your immediate presence and on some regular schedule. Typically, an agent program, using parameters you have provided, searches all or some part of the Internet, gathers information you're interested in, and presents it to you on a daily or other periodic basis. A intelligent agent is a form of bot.

InterNIC   InterNIC (Internet Network Information Center) is the organization responsible for registering and maintaining the com, edu, gov, net, and org domain names on the World Wide Web. (Currently, the actual registration is performed by a company called Network Solutions, Inc.) If you are creating or already have a Web site for which you would like to have your own domain name, you must register the domain name with InterNIC.

intranet   An intranet is a network that is contained within an enterprise. It may consist of many interlinked local area networks and also use leased-lines in the wide-area network. It may or may not include connections through one or more gateways to the outside Internet. The main purpose of an intranet is usually to share company information and computing resources among employees. An intranet can also be used to facilitate working in groups and for teleconferences. An intranet uses TCP/IP, HTTP, and other Internet protocols and in general looks like a private version of the Internet. With tunneling, companies can send private messages through the public network, using the public network with special encryption/decryption and other security safeguards to connect one part of their intranet to another. Typically, larger enterprises allow connection outside of the intranet to the Internet through firewall servers that have the ability to screen messages in both directions so that company security is maintained.

ISDN (Integrated Services Digital Network)   Integrated Services Digital Network (ISDN) is a set of CCITT/ITU standards for digital transmission over ordinary telephone copper wire as well as over other media. Home and business users who install ISDN adapters (in place of their modems) can see highly graphic Web pages arriving very quickly (up to 128 Kbps).

handheld computer   A handheld computer is a computer that can conveniently be stored in a pocket (of sufficient size) and used while you're holding it. Today's handheld computers, which are also called personal digital assistants (PDAs), can be divided into those that accept handwriting as input and those with small keyboards. The best-known handheld computer is the PalmPilot from 3Com.

hyperlink   On the Web or other hypertext systems, hyperlink is a synonym for both link and hypertext link. Possibly, the term originated because "link" was not felt to be specific enough. And it's shorter than "hypertext link."

Internet Society   The Internet Society is an international nonprofit organization that acts as a guide and conscience for the workings of the Internet. It was founded in 1992 and is based on Reston, Virginia. The Internet Society supports the Internet Architecture Board (IAB), which supervises technical and other issues. Among the IAB's activities is the Internet Engineering Task Force (IETF), which oversees the evolution of TCP/IP. Other IAB activities include the Internet Research Task Force (IRTF), which works on network technology; the Internet Assigned Numbers Authority, which assigns IP addresses; and the Internet Registry, which manages the Domain Name System.

ISP   An ISP (Internet service provider) is a company that provides individuals and other companies access to the Internet and other related services such as Web site building and hosting. An ISP has the equipment and the telecommunication line access required to have points-of-presence on the Internet for the geographic area served. The larger ISPs have their own high-speed leased lines so that they are less dependent on the telecommunication providers and can provide better service to their customers. Among the largest national and regional ISPs are AT&T WorldNet, IBM Global Network, MCI, Netcom, UUNet, and PSINet.

Java   Java is a programming language expressly designed for use in the distributed environment of the Internet. It was designed to have the "look and feel" of the C++ language, but it is simpler to use than C++ and enforces a completely object-oriented view of programming. Java can be used to create complete applications that may run on a single computer or be distributed among servers and clients in a network. It can also be used to build small application modules or applets for use as part of a Web page. Applets make it possible for a Web page user to interact with the page.

JPEG   Along with the Graphic Interchange Format (GIF) file, the JPEG (Joint Photographic Experts Group) is a file type supported by the World Wide Web protocol, usually with the ".jpg" suffix. You can create a progressive JPEG that is similar to an interlaced GIF.

JavaScript   JavaScript is an interpreted programming or script language from Netscape. In general, script languages are easier and faster to code in than the more structured and compiled languages (i.e., C and C++). JavaScript code can be embedded in HTML pages and interpreted by the Web browser (or client). JavaScript is used in Web site development to do such things as automatically change a formatted date on a Web page, cause a linked-to page to appear in a pop-up window, and cause text or a graphic image to change during a mouse rollover.

killer app   "Killer app" is jargon in the computer industry for an application program that intentionally or unintentionally gets you to make the decision to buy the system the application runs on. A classic example of a killer app was Lotus 1-2-3, the first popular spreadsheet program that helped introduce the personal computer into the department level of large and small businesses. A killer app can refer to a generic type of application that hasn't existed before, a particular product that first introduces a new application type, or any application with wide appeal.

link checker   A link checker is a program that tests and reports on the validity of the hypertext links on the pages in a Web site. More advanced link checkers test links to other Web sites as well as links between pages on the same site. A link checker may be a separate program that specializes in this service or part of a larger program that provides a range of Web site publishing services.

listserv   Listserv, like Majordomo, is a small program that automatically redistributes E-mail to names on a mailing list. Users can subscribe to a mailing list by sending an E-mail note to a mailing list they learn about; listserv will automatically add the name and distribute future E-mail postings to every subscriber. (Requests to subscribe and unsubscribe are sent to a special address so that all subscribers do not see these requests.) These programs are also known as list servers.

mail bomb   A mail bomb is the sending of a massive amount of electronic mail to a specific person or system. A huge amount of mail may simply fill up the recipient's disk space on the server or, in some cases, may be too much for a server to handle and cause the server to stop functioning. In the past, mail bombs have been used to "punish" Internet users who have been egregious violators of netiquette (e.g., people using E-mail for undesired advertising, or spamming).

mailing list A mailing list is a list of people who subscribe to a periodic mailing distribution on a particular topic. On the Internet, mailing lists include each person's E-mail address rather than a postal address. Mailing lists have become a popular way for Internet users to keep up with topics they're interested in. Many software producers and other vendors are now using them as a way to keep in touch with customers.

Majordomo Like listserv, Majordomo (from Latin, meaning "master of the house") is a small program that automatically redistributes E-mail to names on a mailing list. Users can subscribe to a mailing list by sending an E-mail note to a mailing list they learn about; Majordomo will automatically add the name and distribute future E-mail postings to every subscriber. (Requests to subscribe and unsubscribe are sent to a special address so that other subscribers do not see these requests.)

markup Markup refers to the sequence of characters or other symbols that you insert at certain places in a text or word processing file to indicate how the file should look when it is printed or displayed, or to describe the document's logical structure. The markup indicators are often called "tags."

mirror site A mirror site is a Web site or set of files on a computer server that has been copied to another computer server in order to reduce network traffic, ensure better availability of the Web site or files, or make the site or downloaded files arrive more quickly for users close to the mirror site. A mirror site is an exact replica of the original site and is usually updated frequently to ensure that it reflects the content of the original site. Mirror sites are used to make access faster when the original site may be geographically distant (e.g., a much-used Web site in Germany may arrange to have a mirror site in the United States).

mouseover In creating pages for a Web site, a mouseover (some people call it a "rollover") is a technique using JavaScript that lets you change a page element (usually a graphic image) when the user rolls the mouse over something on the page (like a line of text or a graphic image).

Mozilla Mozilla is Netscape Communication's nickname for Navigator, its Web browser product. It originated as a name used by Navigator's developers before the product had a commercial name and in varying degrees has continued to be nurtured by the company's founders (of which the chief was Marc Andreessen, who designed Mosaic, the first Web browser with a graphical user interface). Netscape now uses Mozilla as the name of a kind of mascot or cartoon alter ego created by illustrator Dave Titus. There is an unofficial Mozilla Museum with links to various arcana about Mozilla.

netiquette   Netiquette is etiquette on the Internet. Since the Internet changes rapidly, its netiquette does too, but it's still usually based on the golden rule. The need for a sense of netiquette arises mostly when sending or distributing E-mail, posting on Usenet groups, or chatting. To some extent, the practice of netiquette depends on understanding how E-mail, the Usenet, chatting, or other aspects of the Internet actually work or are practiced.

netizen   The word netizen seems to have two similar meanings: 1) a citizen who uses the Internet as a way of participating in political society (e.g., exchanging views, providing information, and voting); and 2) an Internet user who is trying to contribute to the Internet's use and growth. As a powerful communications medium, the Internet seems to offer great possibilities for social change. It also creates a new culture and its own special issues, such as who shall have access to it. The implication is that the Internet's users, who use and know most about it, have a responsibility to ensure that is used constructively while also fostering free speech and open access.

newbie   A newbie (pronounced NU-bee) is any new user of a technology. The term is commonly applied to new users of personal computers and to new users of the Internet. According to *The New Hacker's Dictionary*, the term is a variant of the English public school term new boy, someone in the first year or period of school. The term predates the Web and has been used for some time in Usenet newsgroups.

newsgroup   A newsgroup is a posted discussion group on Usenet, a worldwide network of newsgroups. Newsgroups are organized into subject hierarchies, with the first few letters of the newsgroup name indicating the major subject category and sub-categories represented by a subtopic name. Many subjects have multiple levels of subtopics. Some major subject categories are: news, rec (recreation), soc (society), sci (science), comp (computers), and so forth (there are many more). Users can post to existing newsgroups, respond to previous posts, and create new newsgroups.

OSP   1) An OSP (online service provider) is a term sometimes used to distinguish the very largest Internet service providers (ISPs) such as America Online (AOL), Compuserve, and Prodigy, from all the other ISPs. In general, the companies sometimes identified as OSPs offer their own extensive online array of services apart from the rest of the Internet and sometimes their own version of a Web browser. Connecting to the Internet through an OSP is an alternative to connecting through one of the national Internet service providers, such as AT&T or MCI, or a regional or local ISP. As of May 1998, the service distinctions between OSPs and other ISPs were becoming less clear; the so-called OSPs themselves did not seem to use the term, and the term itself seemed not to be used much. 2) Some companies use OSP in describing themselves as office service providers.

PDA   A PDA (personal digital assistant) is a class of a handheld device that provides mobile computing and information storage and retrieval capabilities at low cost while in a conveniently small format. Some PDAs have the ability to understand handwriting. Typical uses include schedule and address book storage and retrieval and note-entering. The palm-top computer is similar to the PDA, except that it has a keyboard and may have additional capabilities.

PGP PGP (Pretty Good Privacy) is a popular program used to encrypt and decrypt E-mail over the Internet. It can also be used to send an encrypted digital signature so the receiver can verify the sender's identity and determine if message was changed en route.

plug-in Plug-in applications are programs that can easily be installed and used as part of your Web browser. Initially, the Netscape browser allowed you to download, install, and define helper applications or supplementary programs that played sound or that motion video or performed other functions. However, these applications require that a second window be opened. A plug-in application is recognized automatically by the browser and its function is integrated into the main HTML file that is being presented.

Point-of-Presence A point-of-presence (POP) is the location of an access point to the Internet and a has a unique Internet (IP) address. Your independent service provider (ISP) or online service provider (OSP) has a point-of-presence on the Internet. POPs are sometimes used as one measure of the size and growth of an ISP or OSP. A POP may actually reside in rented space owned by a telecommunications carrier, such as Sprint. A POP usually includes routers, digital/analog call aggregators, servers, and frequently frame relay or ATM switches.

POP3 POP3 (Post Office Protocol 3) is the most recent version of a standard protocol for receiving E-mail.

portal and portal space Portal is a new term, generally synonymous with gateway, for a World Wide Web site that is or proposes to be a major starting site for users when they get connected to the Web or that users tend to visit as an anchor site. The term portal space is used to mean the total number of major sites competing to be one of the portals. Leading portals include Yahoo!, Excite, Netscape, Lycos, c/net, and Microsoft Network. With its own private array of sites when you dial in, America Online (AOL) can also be viewed as a portal to its own Web portal at AOL.com. A number of large access providers offer portals to the Web for their own users.

protocol In information technology, a protocol is the special set of rules for communicating that the end points in a telecommunication connection use when they send signals back and forth. Protocols exist at several levels in a telecommunication connection. There are hardware telephone protocols, and there are protocols between the end points in communicating programs within the same computer or at different locations. Both end points must recognize and observe the protocol. Protocols are often described in an industry or national standard.

push technology   Push technology or Webcasting is the prearranged updating of news, weather, or other selected information on a computer user's desktop interface through periodic and generally unobtrusive transmission over the World Wide Web (including the use of the Web protocol on intranets).

RealAudio   RealAudio is a continuous or streaming sound technology from Progressive Networks' RealAudio. A RealAudio player or client program may come included with a Web browser or can be downloaded from the RealAudio or other Web sites. To deliver RealAudio sound from your own Web site, you (or your space provider) need to have a RealAudio server.

search engine   As the term is generally used, a search engine has three parts. The first component is a "robot" or "crawler" that goes to every page or representative pages on the Web. The second part of a search engine creates a huge index. The third part interacts with users, searches the index, and sends back the results.

server   In the client/server approach to distributed computing-in-network (such as the Internet), the server program receives requests from the client program and performs a requested service. On the Web, the server is the program that returns Web pages to the user, whose computer contains the client program. The Web browser in your computer is a client that requests HTML files from Web servers.

SET   Mastercard and Visa have agreed on a common security standard: SET (Secure Electronic Transactions). This standard, which will continue to evolve, makes use of technology from Netscape (SSL, or Secure Sockets Layer), Microsoft (STT, or Secure Transaction Technology), and Terisa System's S-HTTP (Secure Hypertext Transfer Protocol).

signature file   A signature file is a short text file you create for use as a standard appendage at the end of your E-mail notes or Usenet messages. e.g., you might include your full name, occupation or position, phone number, fax number, E-mail address, and the address of your Web site, if you have one. Many people also include a favorite quote, company motto, or short personal statement.

smurfing   "Smurf" is the name of an automated program that attacks a network by exploiting Internet Protocol (IP) broadcast addressing and certain other aspects of Internet operation. Smurf and similar programs can cause a network to become inoperable.

spam   Spam is unsolicited E-mail on the Internet. From the sender's point-of-view, it's a form of bulk mail, often to a list culled from subscribers to a Usenet discussion group or obtained by companies that specialize in creating E-mail distribution lists. To the receiver, it is oftentimes junk E-mail. In general, it's not considered good netiquette to send spam. It's generally equivalent to unsolicited marketing phone calls, except that the user pays for part of the message since everyone shares the cost of maintaining the Internet. A first-hand report indicates that the term was derived from a famous Monty Python sketch ("Well, we have Spam, tomato and Spam, egg and Spam, egg, bacon and Spam . . .") when spam first began arriving on the Internet. (Spam is a trademarked Hormel meat product that was widely used as food for soldiers during World War II.)

spamdexing Coined from spam and index, spamdexing is the practice of including information in a Web page that causes search engines to index it in some way that produces results that satisfy the spamdexer but usually dissatisfy the search engine providers and users. An example of spamdexing is including a key word dozens or even hundreds of times at the end of a Web page so that a search engine will rank it more more heavily than pages on other Web sites.

SSI An SSI (server-side include) is a variable value (e.g., a file "Last modified" date) that a server can include in an HTML file before it sends it to the requestor. The server administrator can make these environment variables usable when the system is set up.

SSL SSL (Secure Sockets Layer) is a program layer created by Netscape for managing the security of message transmissions in a network. The "sockets" part of the term refers to the sockets method of passing data back and forth between a client and a server program in a network or between program layers in the same computer.

streaming sound Streaming sound is sound that is played as it arrives. The alternative is a sound recording (such as a WAV file) that doesn't start playing until the entire file has arrived. Support for streaming sound may require a plug-in player or may come with the browser. Leading providers of streaming sound include Progressive Networks' RealAudio and Macromedia's Shockwave for Director (which also includes an animation player).

surf To surf the Internet is to explore cyberspace without a predefined agenda. Note that many Web users find themselves surfing after starting out with a specific Web site to visit.

tag A tag is a language element descriptor. The set of tags for a document or other unit of information is sometimes referred to as markup, a term that dates to pre-computer days when writers and copy editors marked up document elements with copy editing symbols or shorthand.

TCP/IP Transmission Control Protocol/Internet Protocol is the basic communication language or protocol of the Internet. It can also be used as a communications protocol in the private networks called intranets and in extranets. When you are set up with direct access to the Internet, your computer is provided with a copy of the TCP/IP program.

uploading Uploading is the transmission of a file from one computer system to another. From a network user's point-of-view, to upload a file is to send it to another computer that is set up to receive it.

URL A URL (Uniform Resource Locator) (pronounced YU-AHR-EHL or, in some quarters, UHRL) is the address of a file (resource) accessible on the Internet. The URL contains the name of the protocol required to access the resource, a domain name that identifies a specific computer on the Internet, and a hierarchical description of a file location on the computer. One example of a URL is: http://whatis.com.

URL-minder URL-minder is an agent or robot that notifies you when a particular Web page has changed. At the URL-minder site (http://www.netmind.com/URL-minder/URL-minder.html), you specify the Uniform Resource Locator (URL) for the Web page and the URL-minder periodically checks the page, notices whether it has been updated, and then sends you an E-mail message when it has. URL-minder requires you to specify each page you want minded. You also need to consider whether the page may frequently be updated for trivial reasons. Not all pages are probably suitable for this kind of minding.

Usenet Usenet is a worldwide network of posted discussion groups known as newsgroups with a set of rules for accessing and posting to them. There are thousands of newsgroups. A newsgroup can be hosted on servers that are outside the Internet, and many are.

vaporware Vaporware is software or hardware that is either (1) announced or mentioned publicly in order to influence customers to defer buying competitors' products, or (2) late being delivered, for whatever reason.

vCard A vCard is an electronic business (or personal) card. It is also the name of an industry specification for the kind of communication exchange that is done on business or personal cards.

Veronica Veronica is a program that allows you to search the files of the Internet's Gopher servers for a particular search string. Like Archie, Veronica's equivalent program for FTP servers, Veronica is an indexing spider that visits the Gopher sites, reads all the directory and file names, and then indexes them in one large index.

virtual hosting On the Internet, virtual hosting is the provision of Web server and other services so that a company or individual doesn't have to purchase and maintain its own Web server host with a line to the Internet. A virtual hosting provider is sometimes called a Web or Internet "space provider." Some companies providing this service simply call it "hosting."

virus A virus is a piece of programming code inserted into an application to cause some unexpected and usually undesirable event. Viruses can be transmitted by downloading programming from other sites or be present on a diskette. The recipient is often unaware of the virus. The virus lies dormant until circumstances cause its code to be executed. Some viruses are playful in intent and effect ("Happy Birthday, Ludwig!") and some can be quite harmful, erasing data or causing your hard disk to require reformatting.

virtual private network   A virtual private network (VPN) is a private data network that makes use of the public telecommunication infrastructure, maintaining privacy through the use of a tunneling protocol and security procedures. A virtual private network can be contrasted with a system of owned or leased lines that can only be used by one company. The idea of the VPN is to give the company the same capabilities at much lower cost by sharing the public infrastructure. Companies today use a private virtual network for both extranets and wide-area intranets.

W3C   The World Wide Web Consortium (W3C) is the organization that manages and evolves the standard technologies used on the World Wide Web, including HTTP, HTML, and XML (Extensible Markup Language). Although the W3C is funded by industrial members, it is vendor-neutral, and its products are freely available to all.

Webcasting   The term "Webcasting" is used to describe the ability to use the Web to deliver live or delayed versions of sound or video broadcasts. NetTalk Live! is an example of the former, which uses an Internet site to deliver a RealAudio sound version of a live radio and television program weekly. (They call this a triplecast.)

Webmaster   A Webmaster is a person who either creates and manages the information content (words and pictures) and organization of a Web site, manages the computer server and technical programming aspects of a Web site, or does both.

Webring   A Webring (or Web ring) is a way of interlinking related Web sites so that you can visit each site one after the other, eventually (if you keep going) returning to the first Web site. Typically, users can also elect to go backwards through the ring of sites, skip a certain number at a time, visit sites randomly, or see a list of all the sites on the ring. A ring is managed from one site which includes a CGI application that can select random sites and bypass sites that have dropped out or aren't reachable.

Web site   A Web site (presence, site, or Web site) is a related collection of Web files that includes a beginning file called a home page. e.g., the Web site for IBM has the home page address of http://www.ibm.com. A company or an individual tells you how to get to their Web site by giving you the address of their home page. From the home page, you can get to all the other pages on their site. IBM's home page address leads to many other Web site pages. Since site implies a geographic place, a Web site can be confused with a Web server. A server is a computer that holds the files for one or more sites. A very large Web site may be spread over a number of servers in different geographic locations.

World Wide Web   The World Wide Web is the millions of host computers and their users that exchange information using the Hypertext Transfer Protocol (HTTP).

Year 2000, or "Y2K"   The Year 2000 (also known as "Y2K") raises problems for anyone who depends on a program in which the year is represented by a two-digit number, such as "97" for 1997. Many programs written ten or fifteen years ago when storage limitations encouraged such information economies are still running in many companies. The problem is that when the two-digit space allocated for "99" rolls over to 2000, the next number will be "00." Frequently, program logic assumes that the year number gets larger, not smaller, so "00" may wreak havoc in a program that hasn't been modified to account for the millenium.

WEB SITE INDEX—BY CHAPTER

Chapter 1

History of Accounting • http://www.acaus.org/history/

Net Hype's History of the Internet • http://jrowse.mtx.net/net/hype.html

Hobbes' Internet History • http://info.isoc.org/guest/zakon/Internet/History/HIT.html

Internet Timeline • http://www.pbs.org/internet/timeline/

The Internet Society • http://www.isoc.org/

UUNet • http://www.uunet.net/

PSINet • http://www.psinet.com/

Netcom • http://www.netcom.com/

WhatIs • http://www.whatis.com

Atlas of Cyberspaces • http://www.cybergeography.org/

How the Internet Works • http://www.whatis.com/tour.htm

Chapter 3

A Guide to Getting Started on the Internet • http://www.imagescape.com/helpweb/

Guide to the Internet—Electronic Frontier Foundation • http://www.eff.org/papers/eegtti/eeg_toc.html

Internet Help Desk • http://w3.one.net/~alward/

Acronyms and emoticons • http://www.netpath.net/~gwicker/email.htm

Usenet History • http://www.vrx.net/usenet/history/

List of mailing lists • http://www.kentis.com/alllist.html

InfoBeat • http://www.infobeat.com

FinanceNet • http://www.financenet.gov/financenet/start/news.htm

IRC • http://www.irchelp.org/

"The Net: User Guidelines and Netiquette" • http://www.fau.edu/rinaldi/net/elec.html

WS_FTP • http://www.ipswitch.com

CuteFTP • http://www.cuteftp.com

FTP Explorer • http://www.winsite.com

WAIS Search • http://town.hall.org/util/wais_help.html

Public access WAIS client • telnet://wais@quake.think.com/

ArchiePlex • http://cuiwww.unige.ch/archieplexform.html

Veronica • gopher://gopher.cc.utah.edu/.

CookieCrusher • http://www.thelimitsoft.com/cookie.html

ZDNet Software Download • http://www.hotfiles.com/

Cookie Central • http://www.cookiecentral.com/

Cookies Guide • http://shrike.depaul.edu/~ngreely/cookie.htm

Andy's Cookie Notes • http://www.illuminatus.com/cookie.fcgi

EDI—Electronic Data Interchange • http://www.eia.org/eig/eidx/

EDI—Electronic Data Interchange • http://www.disa.org/

OBI—Open Buying on the Internet • http://www.openbuy.org/

OTP—Open Trading Protocol • http://www.otp.org/

OPS—Open Profiling Standard • http://developer.netscape.com/ops/proposal.html

SSL—Secure Sockets Layer • http://www.w3.org/Security/

SET—Secure Electronic Transactions • http://www.visa.com/cgi-bin/vee/nt/ecomm/main.html?2+0

Truste • http://www.etrust.org/

Tripod • http://www.tripod.com

GeoCities • http://www.geocities.com

JavaScript for Beginners Guide • http://builder.cnet.com/Programming/Javacript/

Chapter 4

PointCast • http://www.pointcast.com/

BackWeb Headliner • http://www.headliner.com/

Intermind Communicator • http://www.intermind.com/

Downtown • http://www.incommon.com/

WebSprite • http://www.dvorak.com/

MSNBC News Alert • http://www.msnbc.com/

Infobeat—E-mail Newsletters • http://www.infobeat.com/

Reference.com • http://www.reference.com/

After Dark Online • http://www.afterdark.com/

Hotmail • http://www.hotmail.com

PushUser • http://www.zdnet.com/products/pushuser.html

RealNetworks RealPlayer • http://www.real.com/

Adobe Acrobat Reader • http://www.adobe.com/prodindex/acrobat/readstep.html

Windows Media Player • http://www.microsoft.com/windows/mediaplayer/

Power Point—Animation Player • http://officeupdate.microsoft.com/welcome/powerpoint.htm

Cornell Video Conference (Cu-SeeMe) • ftp://gated.cornell.edu/pub/video/html/Welcome.html

VDOLive Player • http://www.vdo.net/

Mirabilis—I Seek You (ICQ) • http://www.icq.com/

Macromedia Shockwave • http://www.macromedia.com/

Yahoo! Buddy Pager • http://pager.yahoo.com/

Chapter 5

InterNet Assigned Numbers Authority (IANA) • http://www.iana.org/

Network Solutions Inc. (InterNIC) • http://www.internic.net

The List • http://www.thelist.com

"A Framework for Global Electronic Commerce" • http://www.iitf.nist.gov/eleccomm/ecomm.htm

AICPA's WebTrust site • http://www.aicpa.org/WebTrust/index.htm

Internet Tax Freedom Bill • http://www.house.gov/chriscox/

Online Privacy Alliance • http://www.privacyalliance.org/

Center for Democracy and Technology • http://www.cdt.org/

Federal Trade Commission • http://www.ftc.gov/

U.S. Department of Commerce • http://www.doc.gov/

Better Business Bureau • http://www.bbb.org/

TRUSTe • http://www.truste.org

WebTrust • http://www.aicpa.org/

Kent Information • http://www.kentis.com/

Faxaway • http://www.faxaway.com

NetCentric • htpp://www.netcentric.com

The Phone Company • http://www.tpc.int

National Software Testing Laboratories • http://www.nstl.com/

U.S. Department of Labor • http://it.jobsearch.org/

Chapter 6

America Online • http://www.aol.com/

AT&T WorldNet • http://www.att.net/

Concentric Network • http://www.concentric.com/

Earthlink Network • http://www.earthlink.net/

MindSpring Enterprises • http://www.mindspring.com/

Netcom • http://www.netcom.com/

AGIS—Apex Global Internet Services • http://www.agis.net/

ANS Communications • http://www.ans.net/

America Online • http://www.aol.com/

AT&T WorldNet • http://www.att.com

CompuServe Network Services • http://www.compuserve.com/

Concentric Network • http://www.concentric.net/

DIGEX • http://www.digex.net/

Earthlink Network • http://www.earthlink.net/

Epoch Internet • http://www.eni.net/

Genuity • http://www.genuity.net/

GridNet International • http://www.gridnet.com/

GTE Intelligent Networks/BBN • http://www.bbn.com/

IBM Internet Connection • http://www.ibm.com/

MCI Internet • http://www.mci.com/

MindSpring Enterprises • http://www.mindspring.com/

MSN Premier • http://www.msn.com/

NETCOM • http://www.netcom.com/

PSINet • http://www.psi.com/

SAVVIS Communications • http://www.savvis.com

Sprint Business   •   http://www.sprintbiz.com
TCG CERFnet   •   http://www.cerfnet.com
UUNET Technologies   •   http://www.uu.net/
Juno   •   http://www.juno.com/
Hotmail   •   http://www.hotmail.com/
Yahoo!   •   http://www.yahoo.com/
Excite   •   http://www.excite.com/

Chapter 7

MetaCrawler   •   http://www.metacrawler.com
Inference Find   •   http://www.inference.com/infind/
Exes   •   http://www.exes.com/
FinanceWise   •   http://www.financewise.com/
Northern Light Technology   •   http://www.northernlight.com/
Alexa   •   http://www.alexa.com/
Developer's Search Engine   •   http://www.devsearch.com/
Search Engine Watch   •   http://www.searchenginewatch.com/
Seek Help   •   http://www.seekhelp.com/
The Spider's Apprentice   •   http://www.monash.com/spidap.html

Chapter 8

Netscape Netcenter   •   http://www.netcenter.com/
Browsers.com   •   http:// www.browsers.com/
BrowserWatch   •   http://www.browserwatch.com/
Opera   •   http://www.operasoftware.com/
Arachne   •   http://www.naf.cz/arachne/xch/
Softerm Plus+   •   http://www.softronics.com/
Mosaic   •   http://www.ncsa.uiuc.edu/

Chapter 9

Support Help   •   http://www.supporthelp.com/
Career Mosaic   •   http://www.career.mosaic.com
Monster Board   •   http://www.monsterboard.com
Robert Half   •   http://www.roberthalf.com
Accountemps   •   http://www.accoun-temps.com
Accountants on Call   •   http://www.aocnet.com
Greentree Software, Inc.   •   http://www.greentreesoftware.com/
Coalition Against Unsolicited Commercial E-mail—CAUCE   •   http://www.cauce.org
Sam Spade   •   http://www.blighty.com/spam/spade.html
Spam Abuse Net   •   http://www.junkemail.org/

Spam Scam Page • http://www.junkemail.org/spamscam/
ADP—e-XPENSE • http://www.adp.com/
Databasics—TimeSite • http://www.data-basics.com/
Extensity—Extensity Expense Reports • http://www.extensity.com/
Necho—NavigatER • http://www.necho.com/
Sage—TimeSheet Professional • http://www.timetracking.com/

Chapter 10

Accounting

AICPA

AICPA Online • http://www.aicpa.org/

Directories

Kent Information Service • http://www.kentis.com/
CPAnet • http://www.cpanet.com/
AccountingNet • http://www.accountingnet.com/
RAW—Rutgers Accounting Web • http://www.rutgers.edu/Accounting/raw.htm
LAW—Legal/Accounting Web • http://www.users.cloud9.net/~kvivian/html/legal_accounting_web.html
Will Yancey's Home Page • http://www.willyancey.com/
Accountant's Home Page • http://www.computercpa.com/
B.W. Hutton, CGA • http://icewall.vianet.on.ca/pages/hutton/account.html
WebNet CPA • http://www.webnetcpa.com/

General

Microsoft's Industry Page—Accounting • http://microsoft.com/industry/acc/
AFTF—Accounting for the Future • http://members.aol.com/heinichen1/AFTFweb.html
Author's Guide to Accounting Publications • http://www.lodinet.com/authguid/
The Seamless Website—Law & Legal Resources • http://www.seamless.com/
The Spreadsheet Page • http://www.j-walk.com/ss/

Resources from Big 5 and Large Firms

Arthur Andersen • http://www.arthurandersen.com/
Deloitte & Touche, LLP • http://www.dttus.com/
Ernst & Young, LLP • http://www.ey.com/
KPMG • http://www.kpmg.com/
PricewaterhouseCoopers • http://www.pwcglobal.com/

Topic Specific Resources—Year 2000

AICPA Year 2000 Resource Page • http://www.aicpa.org/members/y2000/index.htm
Year 2000 Computer Crisis Information Center • http://www.year2000.com/
Small Business Administration: Help for the Year 2000 • http://www.sba.gov/y2k/

Federal Reserve Board Y2K Page • http://www.bog.frb.fed.us/y2k/

Tick, Tick, Tick Newsletter • http://www.tickticktick.com/

The SEC and the Year 2000 • http://www.sec.gov/news/home2000.htm

Fried Frank Y2K Page • http://www.ffhsj.com/y2k/y2kmain.htm

Ymark 2000 • http://www.nstl.com/html/ymark_2000.html

Topic Specific Resources—Other

Forensic Accounting Demystified • http://www.forensicaccounting.com/

LIFO Systems • http://www.lifosystems.com/

Yield Management • http://www.geocities.com/WallStreet/Floor/4921/

Periodicals, Publications & News

Electronic Accountant • http://www.electronicaccountant.com/

AICPA News Flash & Publications • http://www.aicpa.org/news/index.htm
     • http://www.aicpa.org/pubs/index.htm

The CPA Journal • http://www.luca.com/cpaj.htm • http://www.cpaj.com/

CPA Wire • http://www.calcpa.org/

Authoritative Organizations

FASB—Financial Accounting Standards Board • http://www.fasb.org/

FASB—Financial Accounting Standards Board • http://www.rutgers.edu/Accounting/raw/fasb/home2.html

AcSEC—Accounting Standards Executive Committee, AICPA
     • http://www.aicpa.org/members/div/acctstd/index.htm

ARSC—Accounting and Review Services Committee
ASB—Auditing Standards Board, AICPA
     • http://aicpa.org/members/div/auditstd/index.htm

SEC—Securities and Exchange Commission • http://www.sec.gov/

State CPA Societies—Top Picks

California • http://www.calcpa.org/

Florida • http://www.ficpa.org/

Idaho • http://www.idcpa.org/

Kentucky • http://www.kycpa.org/

Massachusetts • http://www.mscpaonline.org/

New Hampshire • http://www.nhscpa.org/

New Jersey • http://www.njscpa.org/

State CPA Societies—Web Site List

Alabama • http://www.ascpa.org/

Arizona • http://www.ascpa.com/

Arkansas • http://www.arcpa.org/

California • http://www.calcpa.org/

Colorado • http://www.cocpa.org/

Connecticut • http://www.cs-cpa.org/

Delaware • http://www.dscpa.org/

District of Columbia • http://www.gwscpa.org/

Florida • http://www.ficpa.org/

Georgia • http://www.gscpa.org/

Idaho • http://www.idcpa.org/

Illinois • http://www.icpas.org/

Indiana • http://www.incpas.org/

Iowa • http://www.iacpa.org/

Kansas • http://www.kscpa.org/

Kentucky • http://www.kycpa.org/

Louisiana • http://www.lcpa.org/

Maine • http://www.mecpa.org/

Maryland • http://www.macpa.org/

Massachusetts • http://www.mscpaonline.org/

Michigan • http://www.michcpa.org/

Minnesota • http://www.accountingnet.com/society/mn/

Mississippi • http://www.ms-cpa.org/

Missouri • http://www.mocpa.org/

Montana • http://www.mscpa.org/

Nevada • http://www.nevadacpa.org/

New Hampshire • http://www.nhscpa.org/

New Jersey • http://www.njscpa.org/

New Mexico • http://www.nmcpa.org/

New York • http://www.nysscpa.org/

North Carolina • http://www.ncacpa.org/

North Dakota • http://www.ndscpa.org/

Ohio • http://www.ohioscpa.com/

Oklahoma • http://www.oscpa.com/

Oregon • http://www.orcpa.org/

Pennsylvania • http://www.picpa.com/

Puerto Rico • http://www.prccpa.org/

Rhode Island • http://www.riscpa.org/

South Carolina • http://www.scacpa.org/

Tennessee • http://www.business1.com/cpa/tn/

Texas • http://www.tscpa.org/

Utah • http://www.uacpa.org/

Virginia • http://www.vscpa.com/

Washington • http://www.wscpa.org/

West Virginia • http://www.wvscpa.org/

Wisconsin • http://www.wicpa.org/

Wyoming • http://www.wyocpa.org/

Other Organizations

NAFA—National Association of Forensic Accountants • http://www.nafanet.com/

ACFE—Association of Certified Fraud Examiners • http://www.acfe.org/

API—Accountants for the Public Interest • http://www.accountingnet.com/asso/api/

CVAS—Clearinghouse For Volunteer Accountants • http://www.cpateam.com/cvas.htm

A.A.A.—Association for Accounting Administration • http://www.cpaadmin.org/
Academy of Accounting Historians • http://weatherhead.cwru.edu/Accounting/
The Accounting Hall of Fame • http://www.cob.ohio-state.edu/dept/acctmis/hof/

Assurance and Consulting

Assurance Resources

AICPA Assurance Services • http://www.aicpa.org/assurance/index.htm
WebTrust—AICPA • http://www.aicpa.org/webtrust/index.htm
WebTrust—Commercial Site • http://www.cpawebtrust.org/

Business Valuation Resources

The Institute of Business Appraisers • http://www.instbusapp.org/
American Society of Appraisers • http://www.appraisers.org/asa/default.asp
Zweifler Financial Research • http://www.zweifler.inter.net/

Consulting Resources

Management Consulting Online • http://207.240.64.186:8080/anon/z15/cover.dhtml
Ernie • http://ernie.ey.com/
PA&A Online • http://www.bizbasics.com/
Center for Business Innovation • http://www.businessinnovation.ey.com/
Virtual Consulting • http://www.virtualconsulting.com/
The Expertise Center • http://www.expertcenter.com/

Periodicals & Publications

Strategy & Business • http://www.strategy-business.com/
Harvard Business School Publishing • http://www.hbsp.harvard.edu/
Sloan Management Review • http://web.mit.edu/smr-online/

Research Resources

A Business Researcher's Interests • http://www.brint.com/interest.html

Consulting Organizations

IMC—Institute of Management Consultants • http://www.imcusa.org/
APQC—American Productivity & Quality Center • http://www.apqc.org/
PATCA—Professional & Technical Consultants Association • http://www.patca.org/

Audit

Financial Accounting Audit Resources

PPC's Disclosure Checklist Update • http://www.ppcinfo.com/disclo.htm
ITAudit.org • http://www.itaudit.org/
Jim Kaplan's AuditNet • http://www.auditnet.org/
AuditWatch • http://www.auditwatch.com/

Activity Based Risk Evaluation • http://www.efs.mq.edu.au/accg/resources/abrema/
Audit Serve • http://www.auditserve.com/

Government

GARP—Government Auditor's Resource Page • http://www.trib.infi.net/~zsudiak/
The Yellow Book • http://www.gao.gov/govaud/ybk01.htm
Single Audit Act • http://www.financenet.gov/financenet/state/sinaudit/sinaudit.htm
OMB Circular A-133 • http://www.whitehouse.gov/WH/EOP/OMB/html/circulars/a133/a133.html
Federal Program Compliance and Audits • http://www.thompson.com/audit/

Internal Audit

Internal Audit Online • http://www.columbia.edu/cu/ia/
Institute of Internal Auditors • http://www.theiia.org/
The Information Systems Audit and Control Association & Foundation • http://www.isaca.org/
Control Self Assessment Resource Center • http://www.teleport.com/~jhw/csa/
Internal Control Primer • http://home1.gte.net/tateatty/ic.htm

Government

Government Accounting Organizations

GASB—Government Accounting Standards Board • http://www.rutgers.edu/Accounting/raw/gasb/
FASAB—Federal Accounting Standards Advisory Board • http://www.financenet.gov/fasab.htm
GAO • http://www.gao.gov/
AGA—Association of Government Accountants • http://raw.rutgers.edu/raw/aga/
U.S. Chief Financial Officer Council • http://www.financenet.gov/cfo.htm
NASACT—State Auditors, Comptrollers and Treasurers • http://www.sso.org/nasact/
National Association of State Budget Officers • http://www.nasbo.org/
Government Finance Officers Association • http://www.gfoa.org/
NASBA—National Association of State Boards of Accountancy • http://www.nasba.org/

Government Web Sites of Particular Interest

The White House • http://www.whitehouse.gov
THOMAS • http://thomas.loc.gov/
The United Nations • http://www.un.org/
Government Information Xchange • http://www.info.gov/
Explore the Internet • http://lcweb.loc.gov/global/
U.S. Business Advisor • http://www.business.gov/
Better Business Bureau • http://www.bbb.org/
Census Bureau • http://www.census.gov/
Smithsonian Institution • http://www.si.edu
U.S. Federal Government Agencies • http://www.lib.lsu.edu/gov/fedgov.html
Board of Governors of the Federal Reserve • http://www.bog.frb.fed.us/
Bureau of Labor Statistics • http://stats.bls.gov/
Government Printing Office • http://www.access.gpo.gov/
FedWorld • http://www.fedworld.gov/

Government Nets

FinanceNet • http://www.financenet.gov/
IGNet-Inspector General • http://www.ignet.gov/
BudgetNet • http://www.financenet.gov/budget.htm

Government Web Site Directory

Executive Branch

Office of Management and Budget • http://www.whitehouse.gov/WH/EOP/omb
White House Office • http://www.whitehouse.gov

Executive Agencies

Department of Agriculture • http://www.usda.gov/
Department of Commerce • http://www.doc.gov/
Department of Defense • http://www.defenselink.mil/
Department of Education • http://www.ed.gov/
Department of Energy • http://www.doe.gov
Department of Health and Human Services • http://www.os.dhhs.gov
Department of Housing and Urban Development (HUD) • http://www.hud.gov/
Department of the Interior • http://www.doi.gov/
Department of Justice (DOJ) • http://www.usdoj.gov/
Department of Labor(DOL) • http://www.dol.gov/
Department of State • http://www.state.gov/
Department of Transportation • http://www.dot.gov/
Department of Veterans Affairs • http://www.va.gov
Department of the Treasury • http://www.ustreas.gov/

Department of Treasury Bureaus

Internal Revenue Service • http://www.irs.ustreas.gov/
United States Customs Service • http://www.customs.treas.gov/
Bureau of Alcohol, Tobacco and Firearms • http://www.atf.treas.gov/
Financial Management Service • http://www.fms.treas.gov/
United States Secret Service • http://www.ustreas.gov/usss/
Office of Thrift Supervision • http://www.ots.treas.gov/
United States Mint • http://www.usmint.gov/
Office of the Comptroller of the Currency • http://www.occ.treas.gov/
Federal Law Enforcement Training Center • http://www.ustreas.gov/fletc/
Bureau of Public Debt • http://www.publicdebt.treas.gov/
Bureau of Engraving and Printing • http://www.bep.treas.gov/
Financial Crimes Enforcement Network • http://www.ustreas.gov/fincen/

Judicial Branch

U.S. Federal Courts Finder • http://www.law.emory.edu/FEDCTS/
Federal Judicial Center • http://www.fjc.gov/
Federal Judiciary • http://www.uscourts.gov/

Supreme Court Decisions • http://www.law.cornell.edu:80/supct/supct.table.html

U.S. Sentencing Commission • http://www.ussc.gov/

Legislative Branch

U.S. House of Representatives • http://www.house.gov

U.S. Senate • http://www.senate.gov/

Library of Congress (LOC) • http://lcweb.loc.gov/

GAO-Government Accounting Office • http://www.gao.gov/

Government Printing Office (GPO) • http://www.access.gpo.gov/

Office of Technology Assessment • http://www.wws.princeton.edu/~ota/

Stennis Center for Public Service • http://www.stennis.gov

Independent Agencies

Central Intelligence Agency (CIA) • http://www.odci.gov/cia/

Commission on Civil Rights • http://www.usccr.gov/

Commodity Futures Trading Commission (CFTC) • http://www.cftc.gov/cftc/

Consumer Product Safety Commission (CPSC) • gopher://cpsc.gov/

Defense Nuclear Facilities Safety Board (DNFSB) • http://www.dnfsb.gov

Environmental Protection Agency (EPA) • http://www.epa.gov/

Equal Employment Opportunity Commission (EEOC) • http://www.eeoc.gov/

Export-Import Bank of the United States • http://www.exim.gov

Farm Credit Administration • http://www.fca.gov/

Federal Communications Commission (FCC) • http://www.fcc.gov/

Federal Deposit Insurance Corporation (FDIC) • http://www.fdic.gov

Federal Election Commission (FEC) • http://www.fec.gov/

Federal Emergency Management Agency (FEMA) • http://www.fema.gov/

Federal Housing Finance Board • http://www.fhfb.gov/

Federal Maritime Commission • http://www.fmc.gov/

Federal Reserve Bank of Atlanta • http://www.frbatlanta.org

Federal Reserve Bank of Boston • gopher://ftp.shsu.edu/11/Economics/FRB-Boston

Federal Reserve Bank of Chicago • http://www.frbchi.org

Federal Reserve Bank of Cleveland • http://www.clev.frb.org

Federal Reserve Bank of Dallas • http://www.dallasfed.org

Federal Reserve Bank of Kansas City • http://www.frbkc.org/contents.htm

Federal Reserve Bank of Minneapolis • http://woodrow.mpls.frb.fed.us/

Federal Reserve Bank of New York • http://www.ny.frb.org

Federal Reserve Bank of Philadelphia • http://www.libertynet.org/fedresrv/

Federal Reserve Bank of San Francisco • http://www.frbsf.org/index.html

Federal Reserve Bank of St. Louis • http://www.stls.frb.org/

Federal Retirement Thrift Investment Board • http://www.frtib.gov/

Federal Trade Commission (FTC) • http://www.ftc.gov/

General Services Administration (GSA) • http://www.gsa.gov/

Inter-American Foundation • http://www.iaf.gov/

Merit Systems Protection Board • http://www.fpmi.com/MSPB/MSPBhomepage.html

National Aeronautics and Space Administration (NASA) • http://www.nasa.gov/

National Archives and Records Administration (NARA) • http://www.nara.gov/

National Capital Planning Commission • http://www.ncpc.gov/

National Credit Union Administration (NCUA) • http://www.ncua.gov/

National Endowment for the Humanities (NEH) • http://www.neh.fed.us/

National Labor Relations Board (NLRB) • http://www.doc.gov/nlrb/homepg.html

National Mediation Board • http://www.nmb.gov/

National Railroad Passenger Corporation (Amtrak) • http://www.amtrak.com

National Performance Review (NPR) • http://www.npr.gov/

FinanceNet • http://www.financenet.gov/

National Science Foundation (NSF) • http://www.nsf.gov

National Transportation Safety Board • http://www.ntsb.gov/

Nuclear Regulatory Commission (NRC) • http://www.nrc.gov/

Office of Government Ethics • http://www.usoge.gov/

Office of Personnel Management • http://www.opm.gov/

Office of Special Counsel • http://www.access.gpo.gov/osc/

Panama Canal Commission • http://www.pancanal.com/

Peace Corps • http://www.peacecorps.gov/

Pension Benefit Guaranty Corporation • http://www.pbgc.gov/

Postal Rate Commission • http://www.prc.gov/

Railroad Retirement Board • http://www.rrb.gov/

Securities and Exchange Commission (SEC) • http://www.sec.gov/

EDGAR • http://www.sec.gov/edgarhp.htm

Selective Service System • http://www.sss.gov/

Small Business Administration (SBA) • http://www.sbaonline.sba.gov/

Social Security Administration (SSA) • http://www.ssa.gov/

Tennessee Valley Authority • http://www.tva.gov/

Trade and Development Agency • http://www.tda.gov/

United States Arms Control and Disarmament Agency • http://www.acda.gov/

United States Information Agency (USIA) • http://www.usia.gov/

United States International Trade Commission (USITC) • http://www.usitc.gov

United States Postal Service (USPS) • http://www.usps.gov/

State Government

Alabama • http://alaweb.asc.edu

Alaska • http://www.state.ak.us

Arizona • http://www.state.az.us

Arkansas • http://www.state.ar.us/

California • http://www.ca.gov

Colorado • http://www.state.co.us/

Connecticut • http://www.state.ct.us/

Delaware • http://www.state.de.us/

Florida • http://www.state.fl.us/

Georgia • http://www.state.ga.us/

Hawaii • http://www.state.hi.us/

Idaho • http://www.state.id.us/

Illinois • http://www.state.il.us

Indiana • http://www.state.in.us

Iowa • http://www.state.ia.us

Kansas • http://www.ink.org

Kentucky • http://www.state.ky.us
Louisiana • http://www.state.la.us
Maine • http://www.state.me.us
Maryland • http://www.mec.state.md.us/
Massachusetts • http://www.state.ma.us
Michigan • http://www.state.mi.us/
Minnesota • http://www.state.mn.us/
Mississippi • http://www.state.ms.us
Missouri • http://www.state.mo.us
Montana • http://www.mt.gov
Nebraska • http://www.state.ne.us
Nevada • http://www.state.nv.us/
New Hampshire • http://www.state.nh.us
New Jersey • http://www.state.nj.us/
New Mexico • http://www.state.nm.us
New York • http://unix2.nysed.gov/ils
North Carolina • http://www.sips.state.nc.us
North Dakota • http://www.state.nd.us
Ohio • http://www.ohio.gov
Oklahoma • http://www.oklaosf.state.ok.us
Oregon • http://www.state.or.us
Pennsylvania • http://www.state.pa.us
Rhode Island • http://www.state.ri.us/
South Carolina • http://www.state.sc.us
South Dakota • http://www.state.sd.us
Tennessee • http://www.state.tn.us
Texas • http://www.texas.gov
Utah • http://www.state.ut.us
Vermont • http://www.cit.state.vt.us
Virginia • http://www.state.va.us
Washington • http://www.state.wa.us/
West Virginia • http://www.state.wv.us/
Wisconsin • http://badger.state.wi.us

Personal Financial Planning

Directories & Guides

InvestorGuide • http://www.investorguide.com/
Mining Company—Personal Finance • http://pfinance.miningco.com/
D&T Online—Personal Finance • http://www.dtonline.com/
Financenter • http://www.financenter.com/
The Financial Center • http://www.tfc.com/
Money Club • http://www.moneyclub.com/

Resources

Financial Planning Process • http://www.e-analytics.com/fpdir1.htm
Quicken Mortgage • http://www.quicken.com/mortgage/

Fund Alarm • http://www.fundalarm.com/
Mutual Fund Connection • http://www.ici.org/
Finance Tools • http://www.finplan.com/finance/finmain.htm
College for Financial Planning • http://www.fp.edu/
The American College • http://www.amercoll.edu/

Financial Planning Periodicals

Financial Planning Interactive • http://www.fponline.com/
Money Magazine • http://www.money.com
Smart Money Interactive • http://www.smartmoney.com/
Kiplinger's Personal Finance • http://www.kiplinger.com/magazine/maghome.html
Mutual Funds Magazine • http://www.mfmag.com/
Pensions & Investments Magazine • http://www.pionline.com/

Organizations

Institute of Certified Financial Planners • http://www.icfp.org/
International Association for Financial Planning • http://www.iafp.org/
National Association of Personal Financial Advisors • http://www.napfa.org/
AICPA—PFS • http://www.aicpa.org/members/div/pfp/index.htm
AICPA—PFS—Commercial Site • http://www.cpapfs.org/
International Society for Retirement Planning • http://www.isrplan.org/
American Express Financial Advisors • http://www.americanexpress.com/advisors/

Investment Adviser Resources

Investment Adviser • http://www.proformware.com/invest.html
INVESTools for Independent Investors • http://www.investools.com/
The Securities Law Home Page • http://www.seclaw.com/

Private Industry

Resources

Business Researcher's Jumpstation • http://www.brint.com/Sites.htm
Business Finance Web • http://www.ppcbusiness.com/
Treasury Management Pages • http://www.mcs.com/~tryhardz/tmpaa.html
CEO Express • http://www.ceoexpress.com/
Family Business • http://www.fambiz.com/

Periodicals

CFO Net • http://www.cfonet.com/
Business Finance Magazine • http://www.businessfinancemag.com/
CEO Refresher • http://www.refresher.com/
CIO • http://www.cio.com/
Knowledge Management Magazine • http://www.kmmag.com/
Mobile Computing Online • http://www.mobilecomputing.com/
Sales & Field Force Automation Online • http://www.sffaonline.com/

Organizations

Institute of Management Accountants • http://www.imanet.org/
Financial Management Association • http://www.fma.org/
Institute of Management & Administration • http://www.ioma.com/
National Association of Purchasing Management • http://www.napm.org/
Treasury Management Association • http://www.tma-net.org/
Society for Human Resource Management • http://www.shrm.org/
Corporate Governance Network • http://www.corpgov.net/
The Conference Board • http://www.conference-board.org/
American Society of Corporate Secretaries • http://www.ascs.org/
Insurance Information Institute • http://www.iii.org/

Tax

Directories

Schmidt's Tax Sites • http://www.taxsites.com
Barry Rubin's Home Page • http://home1.gte.net/brcpa/
Frank McNeil's Tax Sites • http://www.taxresources.com/
Danny C. Santucci, JD—Tax Attorney • http://members.aol.com/sdcpa/santucci/
Tax-Related Internet Sources • http://www.bus.utexas.edu/~josephr/384/itaxsrcs.htm
1040.com • http://www.1040.com/strev.htm

General Tax Resources

Tax Analysts • http://www.tax.org/
Tax Prophet • http://www.taxprophet.com/
Taxing Times • http://www.scubed.com/tax/
Tax World • http://omer.actg.uic.edu/
TaxWeb • http://www.taxweb.com/
The Tax History Project • http://www.taxhistory.org/
Roth IRA Web Site • http://www.rothira.com/

Tax News & Publications

IRS Home Page • http://www.irs.ustreas.gov/
Deloitte & Touche's Tax News and Views • http://www.dtonline.com/tnv/tnv.htm
E&Y—TaxCast • http://www.taxcast.com/
PwC –Tax News Network • http://www.taxnews.com/tnn_public/
Washington D.C. Highlights • http://www.riatax.com/washdc.html

Law Resources

American Bar Association Tax Section • http://www.abanet.org/tax/
U.S. House of Representatives Internet Law Library • http://law.house.gov/
Nolo Press • http://www.nolo.com/
Law Journal EXTRA! • http://www.ljx.com/

Uniform Commercial Code   •   http://www.law.cornell.edu/ucc/ucc.table.html
The Federal Court Locator (Villanova)   •   http://www.law.vill.edu/Fed-Ct/
Pillsbury Madison & Sutro LLP Tax   •   http://www.pmstax.com/

Foreign / International Tax

Oz Tax Australian Taxation Index   •   http://www.law.flinders.edu.au/tax/
Tax on Australia   •   http://www.csu.edu.au/faculty/commerce/account/tax/tax.htm
Taxation Institute of America   •   http://www.taxia.asn.au/
Deloitte Tax Net Australia   •   http://www.deloitte.com.au/
Revenue Canada   •   http://www.rc.gc.ca/
Hong Kong Government Tax Information   •   http://www.info.gov.hk/info/taxinfo.htm
Indian Tax System   •   http://sunsite.sut.ac.jp/asia/india/jitnet/india/ibeo/tax.htm
Ireland Chartered Accountants Taxation Summary   •   http://www.icai.ie/catsmenu.htm
Ireland Revenue Commissioners   •   http://www.revenue.ie/
Italian Taxation System   •   http://www.icenet.it/cosver/html/primer_uk.html
Inland Revenue—UK   •   http://www.open.gov.uk/inrev/irhome.htm
Treasury Department—UK   •   http://www.hm-treasury.gov.uk/

Tax Topics

The Bankruptcy Lawfinder   •   http://www.agin.com/lawfind/
Per Diem Travel Allowances   •   http://www.gsa.gov/travel.htm
Social Security Privatization   •   http://www.socialsecurity.org/
1031Exchanges   •   http://www.exchangecpas.com/
Valuation Kelley Blue Book   •   http://www.kbb.com/
California Estate Planning and Trust Law   •   http://www.ca-probate.com/
Estate Planning Links   •   http://users.aol.com/dmk58/eplinks.html
Layne Rushforth's Estate Planning Pages   •   http://www.rushforth.org/planning.html
Robert Clofine's Estate Planning Page   •   http://www.estateattorney.com/

Organizations Web Site List

ABA Tax Section   •   http://www.abanet.org/tax/
Americans for Tax Reform   •   http://www.atr.org/
CATO Institute   •   http://www.cato.org/
Concord Coalition   •   http://www.concordcoalition.org/
Flat Tax Home Page   •   http://flattax.house.gov/
Citizens for Tax Justice   •   http://www.ctj.org/
Center for Budget and Policy Priorities   •   http://www.cbpp.org/
Citizens for Sound Economy   •   http://www.cse.org/cse/
Heritage Foundation   •   http://www.heritage.org/
Joint Economic Committee   •   http://www.senate.gov/~jec/
National Bureau of Economic Research   •   http://www.nber.org/
National Center for Policy Analysis   •   http://www.public-policy.org/~ncpa/
National Taxpayers Union   •   http://www.ntu.org/
Natl. Commission on Economic Growth & Tax Reform   •   http://www.townhall.com/taxcom/
Tax Foundation   •   http://www.taxfoundation.org/

Chapter 11

Business

Practice Development Resources

Accountants Marketing Secrets • http://www.mostad.com/

Parli.com • http://www.parli.com/

Coach University • http://www.coachu.com/

Malcolm Baldridge National Quality Program • http://www.quality.nist.gov/

Outsourcing Interactive • http://www.outsourcing.com/

Personal Development Resources

Mind Tools • http://www.mindtools.com/

The Hall of Business • http://www.achievement.org/autodoc/halls/bus

The Speaker's Companion • http://www.lm.com/~chipp/spkrhome.htm

Speakers Platform • http://www.speaking.com/

Etiquette for Business • http://www.eticon.com/

Resources for Clients

Guides to Understanding Financials • http://www.ibm.com/FinancialGuide/

Online Business Workshop • http://www.sb.gov.bc.ca/smallbus/workshop/workshop.html

Bookkeeping and Accounting from Start to Finish • http://www.onlinewbc.org/docs/finance/

Planning Your Estate • http://ext.msstate.edu/pubs/pub1742.htm

Accounting Over Easy • http://www.ezaccounting.com/

The Credit Process: A Guide for Small Business Owners • http://www.ny.frb.org/pihome/
   addpub/credit.html

Business Periodicals

Business Week • http://www.businessweek.com/

The Economist • http://www.economist.com/

Forbes Digital Tool • http://www.forbes.com/

U.S. News Online • http://www.usnews.com/

Fast Company • http://www.fastcompany.com/

Business UpShot • http://www.ey.com/upshot/

Finance

Directories

E-Analytics Directory • http://www.e-analytics.com/

WWW Virtual Library Finance and Investments • http://www.cob.ohio-state.edu/dept/fin/overview.htm

Mining Company Finance • http://economics.miningco.com/

Mining Company Stocks • http://stocks.miningco.com/

FinanceWise • http://www.financewise.com

Wall Street City • http://www.wallstreetcity.com/

Yahoo! Finance • http://biz.yahoo.com/

General Finance Resources

CNN Financial Network • http://cnnfn.com/

Dow Jones • http://www.dowjones.com

The Motley Fool • http://www.fool.com/

Quicken.com Investments • http://www.quicken.com/investments/

Reuters Moneynet • http://www.moneynet.com/

TheStreet.com • http://www.thestreet.com/

Investor Guide • http://www.investorguide.com/

Silicon Investor • http://www.techstocks.com/

InfoBeat Finance • http://www.infobeat.com/

Financial Data Finder • http://www.cob.ohio-state.edu/dept/fin/osudata.htm

Finance Periodicals

Bloomberg Online • http://www.bloomberg.com/

Fortune • http://www.fortune.com/

Red Herring Online • http://www.herring.com/

Upside Online • http://www.upside.com/

Topic Specific Finance Resources

CorpFiNet —Corporate Finance Network • http://www.corpfinet.com

Hedge Fund Home Page • http://www.hedgefunds.net/

IPO Central • http://www.ipocentral.com/

Initial Public Offering Resource Page • http://linux.agsm.ucla.edu/ipo/

Bondsonline • http://www.bonds-online.com/

Investing in Bonds • http://www.investinginbonds.com/

JP Morgan Risk Metrics • http://www.jpmorgan.com/RiskManagement/RiskMetrics/RiskMetrics.html

Riskview • http://www.riskview.com/html-inf/riskview_splash.html

Company Research

Hoover's Online • http://www.hoovers.com/

Zacks Free Investment Research • http://www.ultra.zacks.com/free.html

Investment Research via the Internet • http://www.ibbotson.com/Research/iafp96.htm

MultexSystems, Inc. • http://www.multexnet.com/

Annual Report Gallery • http://www.reportgallery.com/

National Investor Relations Institute • http://www.niri.org/

The Public Register • http://www.annualreportservice.com/

SEC & EDGAR

SEC—Securities and Exchange Commission • http://www.sec.gov/
SEC—EDGAR • http://www.sec.gov/edgarhp.htm
Who Where? EDGAR • http://www.whowhere.com/Edgar/index.html
EDGAR Online • http://www.edgar-online.com/
FreeEDGAR • http://www.freeedgar.com/

Economics

FINWeb—Financial Economics • http://www.finweb.com/
Resources for Economists • http://www.rfe.org/

Calculators

OANDA Currency Converter • http://www.oanda.com/
Kurt's Currency Rate Comparisons • http://www.dna.lth.se/cgi-bin/kurt/rates

Stock Quotes

Daily Stocks • http://www.dailystocks.com/
Thomson Real Time Quotes • http://www.thomsonrtq.com/index.sht

Stock Exchanges

NYSE • http://www.nyse.com/
NASDAQ • http://www.nasdaq.com/
Chicago Mercantile Exchange • http://www.cme.com/

Organizations

Association for Corporate Growth • http://www.acg.org/
IMAP—International Merger and Acquisition Professionals • http://www.imap.com/

Online Trading List

Accutrade • http://www.accutrade.com/
Ameritrade • http://www.ameritrade.com/
Charles SchwabE-Trade • http://www.etrade.com/
Lombard • http://www.lombard.com/

Investment Banks List

Bankers Trust • http://www.bankerstrust.com/
Bear, Stearns & Co. Inc • http://www.bearstearns.com/
BT Alex. Brown • http://www.alexbrown.com/
Deutsche Morgan Grenfell • http://www.dmg.com/
Donaldson, Lufkin & Jenrette • http://www.dlj.com/
Fidelity • http://www.fidelity.com/
Furman Selz • http://www.furmanselz.com/

Goldman Sachs • http://www.goldman.com/

Hambrecht & Quist • http://www.hamquist.com/

J.P. Morgan • http://www.jpmorgan.com/

Lehman Brothers • http://www.lehman.com/

Merrill Lynch • http://www.ml.com/

Morgan Stanley • http://www.ms.com/

NationsBanc Montgomery Securities • http://www.nationsbancmontgomery.com/

PaineWebber • http://www.painewebber.com/

Robertson Stephens • http://www.rsco.com/

Salomon Smith Barney • http://www.salomonsmithbarney.com/

Warburg Dillon Read • http://www.sbcwarburg.com/

Toronto-Dominion Bank • http://www.tdbank.ca/

Entrepreneur

General Resources

Financing Business Growth • http://www.dtonline.com/finance/bgcover.htm

Building Business Agreements • http://www.jian.com/biz.html

Trademark Information • http://www.naming.com/

The Interactive Business Planner • http://www.cbsc.org:4000/

Sample Business Plans • http://www.bplans.com

Directories

EntreWorld • http://www.entreworld.org/

EntrepreNet • http://www.enterprise.org/enet/index.html

Smart Biz • http://www.smartbiz.com/

Periodicals

Inc. Online • http://www.inc.com/

Entrepreneur Weekly • http://www.eweekly.com/

Entrepreneurial Edge Online • http://edgeonline.com/

The Entrepreneur's Mind • http://www.benlore.com/index2.html

Entrepreneur Magazine • http://www.entrepreneurmag.com/

Venture Capital Resources

PwC Money Tree Report • http://www.pwcmoneytree.com/

NVST Investment Network • http://www.nvst.com/

Organizations

National SBCD Research Network • http://www.smallbiz.suny.edu/

National Business Incubation Association • http://www.nbia.org/

Research Institute for Small & Emerging Business • http://www.riseb.org/

National Venture Capital Association • http://www.nvca.org/
NASBIC—National Association of Small Business Investment Companies • http://www.nasbic.org/

Small Business

Resources

CCH's Small Business Toolkit • http://www.toolkit.cch.com/
American Express Small Business Exchange • http://www.americanexpress.com/smallbusiness/
Forbes Small Business Center • http://www.forbes.com/growing/
Online Women's Business Center • http://www.onlinewbc.org/
Small Business Tax Review • http://www.smbiz.com/
Small Business Administration • http://www.sba.gov/
Microsoft's Focus on Small Business • http://www.microsoft.com/smallbiz/
Consultant's Corner • http://www.pwgroup.com/ccorner/

Banking

Periodicals & Trade Journals

American Banker • http://www.americanbanker.com/
U.S. Banker • http://usbanker.faulknergray.com/
Financial Service Online • http://fso.faulknergray.com/
The Credit Union Journal • http://www.cujournal.com/

Banking Resources

21st Century Banking Alert • http://www.ffhsj.com/bancmail/bancpage.htm
Financial Net • http://www.financial-net.com/
Online Banking and Financial Services • http://www.orcc.com/banking.htm
BankWeb • http://www.bankweb.com/
Bank Rate Monitor • http://www.bankrate.com/
Credit Union Land • http://www.culand.com/

Federal Organizations

FDIC • http://www.fdic.gov/
Federal Reserve Resources • http://www.frbsf.org/system/indx.sys.html
Office of the Comptroller of the Currency • http://www.occ.treas.gov/

Organizations

ABA—American Bankers Association • http://www.aba.com/
Bank Administration Institute • http://www.bai.org/
The World Bank • http://www.worldbank.org/
FMS—Financial Managers Society • http://www.fmsinc.org/

Chapter 12

Information and News

Newswires

The Associated Press • http://www.ap.org/
PR Newswire • http://www.prnewswire.com/
Business Wire • http://www.businesswire.com/
Dow Jones • http://bis.dowjones.com/
Reuters • http://www.reuters.com/
United Press International • http://www.upi.com/

Aggregated News Sources

Andover News Network • http://www.andovernews.com/

Periodical & News Directories

AJR NewsLink • http://www.newslink.org/
Ecola • http://www.ecola.com/
Newspapers Online • http://www.newspapers.com/
American City Business Journals • http://www.amcity.com/
MediaFinder • http://www.mediafinder.com/

RealAudio

Daily Briefing • http://www.dailybriefing.com/
Timecast • http://www.timecast.com/
Broadcast.com—Business • http://www.broadcast.com/business/
PBS—Online Newshour • http://www.pbs.org/newshour/realaudio.html
PBS—Frontline • http://www.pbs.org/wgbh/pages/frontline/
News Radio • http://www.pcworld.com/news/newsradio/index.html
Tech Talk • http://www.ttalk.com/
FlightTalk Interviews • http://www.flighttalk.com/

Popular Newspapers

Wall Street Journal • http://www.wsj.com/
Financial Times Online • http://www.ft.com/
The Washington Post • http://www.washingtonpost.com/
Nando Times • http://www.nando.net/
The New York Times • http://www.nytimes.com/
The Mercury News • http://www.mercurynews.com/

Television Broadcasting

CNN & CNNfn • http://www.cnn.com/ • http://www.cnnfn.com/
ABCNEWS.com • http://www.abcnews.com/

MSNBC & CNBC • http://www.msnbc.com/ • http://www.cnbc.com/
CBS • http://www.cbs.com/

Professional Publishers—Authoritative Literature Sources

CCH Incorporated • http://www.cch.com/
Faulkner & Gray • http://www.faulknergray.com/
Harcourt Brace Professional Publishing • http://www.hbpp.com/
Lexis-Nexis • http://www.lexis-nexis.com/lncc/
Irwin McGraw-Hill • http://www.mhhe.com/business/accounting/
Practitioners Publishing Co. (PPC) • http://www.ppcinfo.com/
Prentice Hall • http://www.prenhall.com/
John Wiley & Sons, Inc • http://www.wiley.com/college/busin/accnt
South Western College Publishing • http://www.swcollege.com/acct/accounting.html

Bookstores

Amazon.com • http://www.amazon.com/
AudioBooks • http://www.audiobooks.com/

Events & Conferences

Microsoft Worldwide Events • http://events.microsoft.com/
Trade Show Central • http://www.tscentral.com/

Industry

Industry Information Sources

Infoseek Industry Watch • http://www.industrywatch.com/
Mining Company Industry Pages • http://home.miningco.com/business/
PR Newswire Market Focus • http://www.prnewswire.com/
NewsPage from Individual • http://www.newspage.com/
How to Learn About an Industry • http://www.virtualpet.com/industry/howto/search.htm
IOMA Industry Resources • http://www.ioma.com/industry/
IRN Industry Research • http://irn.net/industry/industry.idc?

Specific Industries Resources

Aerospace & Aviation

AeroWorldNet • http://www.aeroworldnet.com/
Aerospace.net • http://www.aerospace.net/
Aerospace Resources on the Internet • http://www.cranfield.ac.uk/cils/library/subjects/airmenu.htm

Agriculture

Agriculture Online • http://www.agriculture.com/
Pro Farmer • http://www.profarmer.com/

AgriBiz • http://www.agribiz.com/
Farm Journal Online • http://www.farmjournal.com/

Biotechnology & Pharmaceutical

Biotechnology Industry Organization • http://www.bio.org/
Bio Online • http://www.bio.com/
BioSpace • http://www.biospace.com/

Chemical

Chemical Industry Home Page • http://www.neis.com/
Chemical Online • http://www.chemicalonline.com/

Education

ACUA—Association of College and University Auditors • http://www.acua.org/

Energy and Oil & Gas

Oil & Gas Journal Online • http://www.ogjonline.com/
Power Marketing Association • http://www.powermarketers.com/
OilOnline • http://www.oilonline.com/

Entertainment

Hollywood Reporter • http://www.hollywoodreporter.com/
Paul Kagan Free Features • http://chaplin.pkbaseline.com/features.html

Healthcare

Reuters Health eLine • http://www.reutershealth.com/frame_eline.html
Healthcare Financial Management Association • http://www.hfma.org/

Insurance & Risk

National Association of Insurance Commissioners • http://www.naic.org/
RISKWeb • http://www.riskweb.com/

Manufacturing

Industry Week • http://www.iwgc.com/
ISO Online • http://www.iso.ch/

Nonprofit

The Nonprofit Times • http://www.nptimes.com/
Internet Nonprofit Center • http://www.nonprofits.org/
Philanthropy News Digest • http://fdncenter.org/phil/

Retail

National Retail Federation • http://www.nrf.com/default-java.htm
The Apparel Strategist • http://www.appstrat.com/

Telecommunications

Telecommunications Industry Association • http://www.tiaonline.org/

Telecom Information Resources on the Internet • http://china.si.umich.edu/telecom/

Telecommunications Library • http://www.ntu.edu.sg/library/telecomm.htm

International

Primary International Organizations

IFAC—International Federation of Accountants • http://www.ifac.org/

IASC—International Accounting Standards Committee • http://www.iasc.org.uk/

Africa

South African Institute of Chartered Accountants • http://www.saica.co.za/

Accounting in South Africa • http://mbendi.co.za/werksmns/sabus07.htm#7.3

Asia

Confederation of Asian and Pacific Accountants • http://www.jaring.my/capa/

Accounting News in Japan • http://www2g.biglobe.ne.jp/~ykawamur/

ABN—Asia Business News • http://www.abn.com.sg/

Australia/New Zealand

Institute of Chartered Accountants in Australia • http://www.icaa.org.au/

The Australian Financial Review • http://www.afr.com.au/

New Zealand Press Online • http://www.press.co.nz/

Europe

AccountingWeb • http://www.accountingweb.co.uk/

European Accounting Association • http://www.bham.ac.uk/EAA/

AIA—Association of International Accountants • http://www.a-i-a.org.uk/

Financial Times • http://www.ft.com/

Russia Today • http://www.russiatoday.com/

Middle East

Arab World Online • http://www.awo.net/

MENA.net • http://www.mena.net/

North America

Canadian Institute of Chartered Accountants • http://www.cica.ca/

Morochove's AccountNet • http://www.morochove.com/netguide/

South America

Latin World • http://www.latinworld.com/

Latin American News • http://www.latinnews.com/

E-commerce

Directories & Resources

Mining Company—Electronic Commerce   •   http://ecommerce.miningco.com/
A Framework for Global Electronic Commerce   •   http://www.iitf.nist.gov/eleccomm/ecomm.htm
E-Commerce Glossary of Terms   •   http://www.helpfindit.com/glossa.html
Security Risks Associated with the Internet   •   http://www.fdic.gov/banknews/fils/1997/fil97131.html

Organizations & Standards

Commerce.net   •   http://www.commerce.net/
RosettaNet   •   http://www.rosettanet.org/
OBI Consortium—Open Buying   •   http://www.openbuy.org/
OTP—Open Transaction Protocol   •   http://www.otp.org/
E-commerce Advisory Council   •   http://www.e-commerce.ca.gov/

Articles & Publications

E Business   •   http://www.hp.com/Ebusiness/
ZDNet—E-Commerce User   •   http://www.zdnet.com/products/ecommerceuser.html
eMARKETER   •   http://www.emarketer.com/

Companies Involved in E-Commerce

BizRate Guide   •   http://www.bizrate.com/
iCat   •   http://www.icat.com/
Intershop Communications   •   http://www.intershop.com/
IntraNet Software   •   http://www.paybutton.com/
Pandesic   •   http://www.pandesic.com/
VeriSign   •   http://www.verisign.com/

Community Resources

General Discussion Forums

Deja News   •   http://www.dejanews.com/
Liszt's Usenet Newsgroups Directory   •   http://www.liszt.com/news/
Reference.com   •   http://www.reference.com/
Forum One   •   http://www.forumone.com/
MSNBC Forums   •   http://www.msnbc.com/bbs/default.asp
Pathfinder—Money and Business Forums   •   http://boards.pathfinder.com/cgi-bin/webx?14@@

Specific Discussion Forums

AICPA Forums   •   http://www.aicpa.org/forums/index.htm
Electronic Accountant Forums   •   http://www.electronicaccountant.com/#discuss
WebTrust Alliance Forum   •   http://www.webtrust.net/alliance/
CalCPA Town Hall   •   http://www.calcpa.org/townhall/

Ethnic / Gender Organizations

ASWA—American Society of Women Accountants • http://www.aswa.org/

The Educational Foundation for Women in Accounting • http://www.efwa.org/

AAHCPA—American Association of Hispanic Accountants • http://www.aahcpa.org/

Firm Alliances

AGN—Accountants Global Network—International • http://www.agn.org/

AAFI—Associated Accounting Firms International • http://www.aafi.org/

ACPA—Affiliated Conference of Practicing Accountants • http://www.acpaintl.org/

BDO Seidman Alliance • http://www.bdo.com/

BKR International • http://www.bkrintl.com/

CPAAI—CPA Associates International, Inc. • http://www.cpaai.com/

HLB International • http://www.hlbi.com/

IA—Independent Accountants International • http://www.iai.org/

Inpact Americas • http://www.inpactam.org/

International Association of Practising Accountants • http://www.iapa-accountants.com/

International Group of Accounting Firms • http://www.igaf.org/

JHI—Jeffreys Henry International • http://www.jhi.com/

Kreston International • http://www.kreston.com/

Moore Stephens North America, Inc. • http://www.msnainc.com/

NATP—National Association of Tax Practitioners • http://www.natptax.com/

Nexia International • http://www.nexia.com/

Summit International Associates, Inc. • http://www.siaglobal.com/

AFAI—Accounting Firms Associated, Inc. • http://www.afai.com/

NACPAF- National Associated CPA Firms • http://www.nacpaf.com/

Academia & University

Resources

Accounting Students • http://www.accountingstudents.com/

University Links • http://www-net.com/univ/

OSU AMIS Site • http://www.cob.ohio-state.edu/~acctmis/

IMA Students • http://www.imastudents.org/

ANet Accountancy Network • http://www.csu.edu.au/anet/

The Summa Project • http://www.summa.org.uk/

ARN—Accounting Research Network • http://www.ssrn.com/

World Lecture Hall • http://www.utexas.edu/world/lecture/acc/

Accounting Scholars Directory • http://www.cob.ohio-state.edu/~tomassin/acc_sch/

Financial Analysis Online Project • http://www.cob.ohio-state.edu/~tomassin/fanon.html

Publications

The Scout Report • http://scout.cs.wisc.edu/scout/report/bus-econ/

Journal of Finance • http://www.cob.ohio-state.edu/~fin/journal/

Organizations

BAP—Beta Alpha Psi • http://www.bap.org/

American Accounting Association • http://www.rutgers.edu/Accounting/raw/aaa/

Continuing Professional Education

CPE Top Web Sites

NASBA—National Association of State Boards of Accountancy • http://www.nasba.org/

AICPA • http://www.aicpa.org/cpe/index.htm

CPA Education Foundation • http://www.calcpaed.org/

Bisk CPEasy.com • http://www.cpeasy.com/

CareerTrack • http://www.careertrack.com/

CPEInternet • http://cpe.uophx.edu/

MicroMash • http://www.micromash.com/

Evoke • http://www.evoke.com/

SEC Institute • http://secseminars.com/

McGraw-Hill Online Learning • http://www.mhonlinelearning.com/

ValuED • http://www.valued.com/

Western CPE • http://www.umt.edu/ccesp/wcpe/

Other CPE Companies List

Accounting Professionals • http://www.cpanews.com/courses.asp

ASCE—American Society for CE • http://www.asce.com/

Bureau of National Affairs • http://www.bna.com/

Carswell—Canada • http://www.carswell.com/

CCH—Commerce Clearing House • http://www.cch.com/

Controller Magazine • http://www.controllermag.com/

CPA Associates, Inc. • http://www.cpassoc.com/

CPE Accounting and Tax Institute • http://www.cpecredit.org/

CPENet • http://uu-gna.mit.edu:8001/~compass/

Foundation for Continuing Education • http://fce.org/

Gleim Publications • http://www.gleim.com/

Harcourt Brace—Online Testing • http://www.hbpp.com/cpetest/

K2 Enterprises • http://www.k2e.com/

Kent Information Services, Inc. • http://www.kentis.com/cpe.html

KRL Consultants & Publishers • http://www.poweradz.com/krlcp/cpe.htm

Lexis-Nexis Communication Center • http://www.lexis-nexis.com/

PPC Practitioners Publishing Company • http://www.ppcinfo.com/cpe.htm

RIA—Research Institute of America • http://www.riatax.com/elecsub.html

Surgent & Associates • http://www.surgent.com/

Taft University School of CE • http://www.taftu.edu/ce1.htm

Warren, Gorham & Lamont • http://www.wgl.com/acct/acct.html

Wiseguides • http://www.wiseguides.com/

State Boards of Accountancy

Alaska • http://www.commerce.state.ak.us/occ/pcpa.htm
Arizona • http://www.accountancy.state.az.us/
California • http://www.dca.ca.gov/cba/
Colorado • http://www.dora.state.co.us/Accountants
Connecticut • http://www.state.ct.us/sots/SBOA/bdacc.htm
District of Columbia • http://www.gwscpa.org/dcba/
Florida • http://www.gwscpa.org/dcba/
Idaho • http://www2.state.id.us/boa/
Illinois • http://www.illinois-cpa-exam.com/
Indiana • http://www.ai.org/pla/accountancy/
Iowa • http://www.state.ia.us/government/com/prof/acct/acct.htm
Kentucky • http://www.state.ky.us/agencies/boa/
Maine • http://www.state.mc.us/pfr/lcd/account/
Maryland • http://www.dllr.state.md.us/occprof/account.html
Mississippi • http://www.msbpa.state.ms.us/
Missouri • http://www.ecodev.state.mo.us/pr/account/
Nebraska • http://www.nol.org/home/BPA/
Nevada • http://www.state.nv.us/boards/accountancy/
New Jersey • http://www.state.nj.us/lps/ca/nonmed.htm
New York • http://www.nysed.gov/prof/cpa.htm
North Carolina • http://www.state.nc.us/cpabd/
North Dakota • http://www.state.nd.us/ndsba/default.htm
Ohio • http://www.state.oh.us/acc/
Oregon • http://www.boa.state.or.us/boa.html
South Carolina • http://www.llr.sc.edu/bac.htm
Tennessee • http://www.state.tn.us/commerce/tnsba/
Texas • http://www.tsbpa.state.tx.us/
Utah • http://www.commerce.state.ut.us/web/commerce/dopl/dopl1.htm
Virginia • http://dit1.state.va.us/dpor/acc_main.htm
West Virginia • http://www.state.wv.us/wvboa/
Wyoming • http://www.wyocpa.org/borad.htm

Exams

CPA Exam

Accounting Institute Seminars • http://www.ais-cpa.com/
Becker • http://www.beckercpa.com/
CPAexam.com • http://www.cpaexam.com/
Conviser Duffy • http://www.conviserduffy.com/
CPAexcel • http://www.cpaexcel.com/
Gleim • http://www.gleim.com/
Kaplan • http://www.kaplan.com/accounting/
Lambers • http://www.lamberscpa.com/
MicroMash • http://www.micromash.com/

Tutorial Group • http://www.tutorialgroup.com/
Wiley • http://www.wiley.com/products/subject/accounting/cpa/

Other Exams List

CMA—Certified Management Accountant
CFM—Certificate in Financial Management
     • http://www.rutgers.edu/Accounting/raw/ima/ (profiled in Private Industry section)
CFP—Certified Financial Planner • http://www.cfp-board.org/ (profiled in Financial Planning section)
CFE—Certified Fraud Examiner • http://www.acfe.org/whatis.html (profiled in Accounting section)
CIA—Certified Internal Auditor and CPD • http://www.theiia.org/ (profiled in Audit section)
GMAT • http://www.gmat.org/ (not profiled elsewhere)

Exam Preparation Resources

Test Success Guide • http://www.emc.maricopa.edu/academics/success_guide/
Study Break Stretches • http://www.balancenet.org/workout/stretch/stretch.html

Chapter 13

The CPA Toolbox

Reference

Information Please • http://www.infoplease.com/
Encyclopedia.com • http://encyclopedia.com/
WWWebster Dictionary • http://www.m-w.com/dictionary
Roget's Thesaurus • http://www.thesaurus.com/
My Virtual Reference Desk • http://www.refdesk.com/
iTools • http://www.itools.com/
Library Spot • http://www.libraryspot.com/
Measurement Units Translation • http://www.mplik.ru/~sg/transl/
Acronym Finder • http://www.mtnds.com/af/
Cliché Finder • http://www.westegg.com/cliche/
World Holiday and Time Guide • http://www.worldtime.com/
JP Morgan Holiday Calendar • http://www.jpmorgan.com/cgi-bin/HolidayCalendar

Computer Resources

ZD University • http://www.zdu.com/
PC-Help Online • http://www.pchelponline.com/
BugNet • http://www.bugnet.com/
Virus Central • http://www.drsolomon.com/vircen/
Win Drivers • http://www.windrivers.com
Windows Resources • http://www.winfiles.com/

E-mail Spam Resources

Fight Against Spam • http://www.cauce.org/
Junk E-mail Resource Page • http://www.junkemail.org/

Limiting Unsolicited Bulk E-mail • http://www.imc.org/imc-spam/
Spam Abuse Net • http://spam.abuse.net/

Directories & Search

Directories

Broadcast.com • http://www.broadcast.com/
Northern Light Search • http://www.nlsearch.com/
Mining Company • http://www.miningcompany.com/
Essential Links • http://www.el.com/
eBLAST Encyclopædia Britannica's Internet Guide • http://eblast.com/
Argus Clearinghouse • http://www.clearinghouse.net/

The Top Search Engines & Portals

Yahoo! • http://www.yahoo.com/
HotBot • http://www.hotbot.com/
AltaVista • http://www.altavista.com/
Lycos • http://www.lycos.com/
Excite • http://www.excite.com/
Webcrawler • http://www.webcrawler.com/
Infoseek • http://www.infoseek.com/
Goto.com • http://www.goto.com/
LookSmart • http://www.looksmart.com/
MSN • http://www.msn.com/
Netscape Netcenter • http://www.netcenter.com/

Other Search Engines

100hot.com • http://www.100hot.com/
EuroSeek • http://euroseek.net/
GOD • http://www.god.co.uk/

Top Metacrawlers & Metasearch Engines

MetaCrawler • http://www.metacrawler.com/
Inference Find • http://www.inference.com/ifind/
Dogpile • http://www.dogpile.com/
Internet Slueth • http://www.isleuth.com/
OneSeek • http://www.oneseek.com/

Other Interesting Search Sites

Alexa • http://www.alexa.com/
Ask Jeeves • http://www.askjeeves.com/

Search Resources

Search Language Help • http://www.dejanews.com/help/help_lang.shtml
Search Engine Watch • http://searchenginewatch.com/

Statistical Sources

U.S. Statistical Abstract • http://www.census.gov/prod/www/abs/cc97stab.html
Statistical Resources • http://www.lib.umich.edu/libhome/Documents.center/frames/statsfr.html
FRED — Consumer Price Indexes • http://www.stls.frb.org/fred/data/cpi.html

Job Search

Online Job Search Companies

Accountingjobs.com • http://www.accountingjobs.com/
CareerWeb • http://www.careerweb.com/
Accountants on Call • http://www.aocnet.com/
Accountemps • http://www.accountemps.com/
Accounting.com • http://www.accounting.com/
Accounting Partners • http://www.apartner.com/
AICPA ResuméMatch • http://www.resume-link.com/society/expl.htm
JobOptions • http://www.joboptions.com/
Law Jobs • http://www.lawjobs.com/
Michael Page International • http://www.michaelpage.com/us/
Online Career Center • http://www.occ.com/
Robert Half • http://www.roberthalf.com/

Career Resources

WSJ Careers • http://careers.wsj.com/
Career Magazine • http://www.careermag.com/
Hard@Work • http://www.hardatwork.com/
Vault Reports • http://www.vaultreports.com/
Homefair Relocation Resources • http://www.homefair.com/
Management Consulting Jobs • http://www.cob.ohio-state.edu/~opler/cons/mco.html
Career Shop • http://www.careershop.com/
The Business Job Finder • http://www.cob.ohio-state.edu/~fin/osujobs.htm
Career Center • http://www.ceoexpress.com/hr.htm
Career Strategies • http://www.businessknowhow.com/bkhcareer.htm

Travel Resources

Booking Resources

Expedia • http://expedia.msn.com/
American Express Travel • http://www.americanexpress.com/corporateservices/
Biztravel.com • http://www.biztravel.com/
Travelocity • http://www.travelocity.com/
Internet Travel Network • http://www.itn.net/
Preview Travel • http://www.previewtravel.com/
The Trip • http://www.thetrip.com/
LowestFare.com • http://www.lowestfare.com/

Resources

EmbassyWeb • http://www.embpage.org/

Travel Updates • http://travel.state.gov/travel_warnings.html

Foreign Currency Converter • http://www.oanda.com/

MapQuest • http://www.mapquest.com/

Fodor's Travel Online • http://www.fodors.com/

Business Travel Etiquette • http://www.traveletiquette.com/

HotelView • http://www.hotelview.com/

The Weather Channel • http://www.weather.com/

AltaVista Translator • http://babelfish.altavista.digital.com/

WebFlyer • http://www.webflyer.com/

The Subway Page • http://www.reed.edu/~reyn/transport.html

Microsoft TerraServer • http://terraserver.microsoft.com/

Runzheimer International • http://www.runzheimer.com/

Guides

Foreign Languages for Travelers • http://pathfinder.com/travel/language/

Duty Free Shopping & Tax Free Shopping • http://www.webscope.com/duty_free/

Entertaining

Zagat Dining Guide & Zagat Survey • http://www.zagat.com/

Playbill Online • http://www.playbill.com/

Internet

Resources

How the Internet Works • http://www.whatis.com/tour.htm

The List • http://www.thelist.com/

NetLingo • http://www.netlingo.com/

The Net: User Guidelines and Etiquette • http://www.fau.edu/rinaldi/net/index.htm

Browser Tune • http://www.browsertune.com/

Internet Traffic Report • http://www.internettrafficreport.com/

David J. Farber's Home Page • http://www.cis.upenn.edu/~farber/

Organizations

Electronic Frontier Foundation • http://www.eff.org/

Periodicals

InternetWeek • http://pubs.cmpnet.com/internetwk/

[clip] for the Internet Insider • http://www.compaq.com/clip/

CIO WebBusiness • http://webbusiness.cio.com/

Internet.com • http://www.internet.com/

Web Site Development

Web Site Development Resources

Builder.com • http://www.builder.com/
Developer Zone • http://www.projectcool.com/developer/
HTML Goodies • http://www.htmlgoodies.com/
Site Builder Network • http://www.microsoft.com/sitebuilder/
DevEdge Online • http://developer.netscape.com/
Web Developer • http://www.webdeveloper.com/
WebReference.com • http://www.webreference.com/
Web Developers' Virtual Library • http://www.stars.com/Index.html
Elsop's Webmaster Resource Center • http://www.elsop.com/wrc/refroom.htm
Index Dot HTML • http://www.blooberry.com/html/
JavaScript Source • http://www.javascriptsource.com/
Jasc Paint Shop Pro • http://www.jasc.com/

Resources

InterNIC • http://www.internic.net/
20 Reasons to Get on the Internet • http://www.net101.com/20_1.html
Connecting Online • http://www.connectingonline.com/
FrontPage Intranet Guide • http://www.microsoft.com/frontpage/intranet/
Web Trends • http://www.webtrends.com/

Web Site Marketing & Promotion

Web Marketing Today • http://www.wilsonweb.com/webmarket/
A Webmaster's Guide to Search Engines • http://searchenginewatch.com/webmasters/
Web Site Banner Advertising • http://www.markwelch.com/bannerad/
VirtualPROMOTE • http://www.virtualpromote.com/

Organizations

W3C World Wide Web Consortium • http://www.w3.org/
HTML Writers Guild • http://www.hwg.org/

Java Break

The Art of Napping • http://www.napping.com/
Jet Sales Comparison • http://www.jetsales.com/
The Comic Zone • http://www.unitedmedia.com/comics/
The Bathrooms of Madison County • http://www.nutscape.com/
The Straight Dope • http://www.straightdope.com/
Easter Eggs • http://www.eeggs.com/
Driveways of the Rich & Famous • http://www.driveways.com/
6 Degrees of Kevin Bacon • http://www.wjh.harvard.edu/~minga/sdokb/
Drudge Report • http://www.drudgereport.com/
Hollywood Stock Exchange • http://www.hsx.com/

Blue Mountain Animated Cards   •   http://www.bluemountain.com/
Slate   •   http://www.slate.com/
Eating Well   •   http://www.eatingwell.com/
Reader's Digest World   •   http://www.readersdigest.com/

Software and Hardware

Accounting Software Resources

Accounting.org   •   http://www.accounting.org/
CTS Guides   •   http://www.ctsguides.com/
The CPA Software News   •   http://www.cpasoftwarenews.com/

Software Resources

Benchin Software Review   •   http://www.benchin.com/
SoftSearch   •   http://www.softsearch.com/
ZDNet Software Download Library   •   http://www.hotfiles.com/
Support Help   •   http://www.supporthelp.com/

Hardware

Maven Computer Buying Guide   •   http://www.maven.businessweek.com/index.htm
Computer Discount Warehouse   •   http://www.cdw.com/
PC Mechanic   •   http://pcmech.pair.com/

Chapter 14

InterNIC's   •   http://www.internic.net/
High Five   •   http://www.highfive.com/
Web Page Design for Designers   •   http://www.wpdfd.com/
Web Monkey   •   http://www.hotwired.com/webmonkey/
Yale C/AIM Web Style Guide   •   http://info.med.yale.edu/caim/manual/
Creating Killer Web Sites   •   http://www.killersites.com

Chapter 15

Microsoft FrontPage   •   http://www.microsoft.com/frontpage/
Adobe PageMill   •   http://www.adobe.com/prodindex/pagemill/
Site Technologies QuickSite   •   http://www.sitetech.com/
Clnet's Know the Code: HTML for Beginners   •   http://builder.cnet.com/Authoring/Basics/
Raggett's Ten Minute Guide to HTML   •   http://www.w3.org/MarkUp/Guide/
A Few Design Tips   •   http://builder.cnet.com/Authoring/Htmltips/
WS_FTP32   •   http://www.ipswitch.com/
Archie Services   •   http://www.nexor.com/archie/

W3C • http://www.w3.org/

Web Site Garage • http://www.Web sitegarage.com/

SiteInspector • http://www.siteinspector.com/

SiteHog • http://www.redhog.com/redhog/

Add a Custom News Ticker—TotalNews • http://www.totalnews.com/

Become an Amazon.com Associate • http://www.amazon.com/

Give Your Site Some Flash—Macromedia • http://www.macromedia.com/

Inside DHTML • http://www.insidedhtml.com/

Tripod • http://www.tripod.com/

Inc. Magazine Business Directory • http://www.inc.com/createsite/

GeoCities • http://www.geocities.net/

Builder.com • http://www.builder.com/

Developer Zone • http://www.projectcool.com/developer/

HTML Goodies • http://www.htmlgoodies.com/

Site Builder Network • http://www.microsoft.com/sitebuilder/

DevEdge Online • http://developer.netscape.com/

Web Developer • http://www.webdeveloper.com/

WebReference.com • http://www.webreference.com/

Chapter 16

Top Hosts • http://www.tophosts.com/

The Ultimate Web Host List • http://www.webhostlist.com/

Hiway Technologies • http://www.hway.net/

Dynamic Web • http://www.dynamicweb.net/

CI Host • http://www.cihost.com/

ConcentricHost • http://www.concentric.com/

TABNet • http://www.tabnet.com/

Netcom • http://www.netcomi.com/

Tri Star Web • http://www.tristarweb.com/

WebAxxs • http://www.webaxxs.net/

WEB 2010 • http://www.web2010.com/

Alabanza • http://www.alabanza.net/

Interactive Web Host Chooser • http://builder.cnet.com/Servers/Publish/Personal/ss01a.html

HostSearch • http://www.hostsearch.com/

Yahoo! • http://www.yahoo.com

Chapter 17

AltaVista • http://www.altavista.com/av/content/addurl.htm

Excite • http://www.excite.com/Info/add_url.html

HotBot • http://www.hotbot.com/addurl.html

Infoseek • http://www.infoseek.com/AddUrl?pg=DCaddurl.html

Lycos • http://www.lycos.com/addasite.html

Open Text • http://index.opentext.net/main/submitURL.html
Starting Point • http://www.stpt.com/general/submit.html
WebCrawler • http://www.webcrawler.com/WebCrawler/SubmitURLS.html
Yahoo! • http://add.yahoo.com/fast/add?
PositionAgent • http://www.positionagent.com/
WebPosition • http://www.webposition.com/
ScoreCheck • http://www.scorecheck.com/
Internet Gain • http://www.internetgain.com
Rank This • http://www.rankthis.com/
The Informant • http://informant.dartmouth.edu/
Did-It • http://www.did-it.com/

Chapter 18

Nua Internet Surveys • http://www.nua.net/
GVU Survey • http://www.cc.gatech.edu/gvu/
American Internet User Survey • http://etrg.findsvp.com/
Boston Consulting Group • http://www.bcg.com/
GVU Web User Survey • http://www.cc.gatech.edu/gvu/
MIDS Survey • http://www.mids.org/index.html
Nielsen-CommerceNet Survey • http://www.nielsenmedia.com/demo.htm
FIND/SVP Survey • http://etrg.findsvp.com/
Project 2000 • http://www2000.ogsm.vanderbilt.edu/
CyberAtlas • http://www.cyberatlas.com/

Chapter 19

Inc. Magazine • http://www.inc.com/createsite/
CPA Firms • http://www.cpafirms.com/
AccountingNet • http://www.accountingnet.com/
Peter Gugerell's Medialist • http://www.ping.at/gugerell/media/
MIT Usenet E-mail Addresses • http://usenet-addresses.mit.edu/
Publicity on the Internet • http://www.wiley.com/compbooks

Chapter 20

OneSoft Corporation • http://www.onesoft.com/
Extranet—a reference page • http://www.netg.se/~kerfor/extranet.htm.
Clnet Computers • http://www.computers.com/
Internet Firewalls Frequently Asked Questions • http://www.clark.net/pub/mjr/pubs/fwfaq/
General Firewall White Paper • http://www.ntresearch.com/firewall.htm
Charting the Data VPN Movement • http://www.teledotcom.com/.
ServerWatch • http://serverwatch.internet.com/
KVG —Knight, Vale & Gregory, CPA's • http://207.220.114.50/Intranet/

Chapter 21

AuditNet E-mail Directory • http://www.cowan.edu.au/mra/home.htm

WavePhore • http://www.wavephore.com

Actuate Software Corp. • http://www.actuate.com

Seagate Software Inc. • http://www.seagatesoftware.com

SQRIBE Technologies • http://www.sqribe.com

IBM Host on Demand • http://www.software.ibm.com/enetwork/hostondemand/

Walker Richer and Quinn Reflection InterView • http://www.wrq.com/

3Com's Palm Pilot • http://www.palm.com

The Pilot Zone • http://www.palmpilotzone.com

Angoss • http://www.angoss.com/

Cognos • http://www.cognos.com/

DataMind • http://www.datamindcorp.com/

IBM • http://www.software.ibm.com/

Thinking Machines Corp. • http://www.think.com/

Data Junction Corp. • http://www.datajunction.com/

Datawatch • http://www.datawatch.com/

Spalding Software • http://www.spaldingsoft.com/

Crosswise • http://www.crosswise.com

VocalTec Ltd. • http://www.vocaltec.com

Farallon Communications Inc. • http://www.farallon.com

MicroTouch Systems, Inc. • http://www.microtouch.com

Microsoft Corp. • http://www.microsoft.com

Paradise Software Inc. • http://www.paradise.com

Novell Inc. • http://www.novell.com

Open Text Corp. • http://www.opentext.com

Lotus Development • http://www.lotus.com

INDEX